Work

Occupations &

PROFESSIONALIZATION

Race
gender
class
occupation
culture jobs Merit
opportunity power
prestige Training
JOBS justice
credentials rank
STATUS Occupation
semi-professional market
Professional Consultant ability
Meritocracy expert
inclusion identity
work place
temp part-time
industry
Nurse culture
career
CV sector
vet Skill
Medic
labour credit
respect

Edited by Stephen E. Bosanac

&

Merle A. Jacobs

Stephen's Dedication

Vincent "Vinnie" James Bosanac 1976-2007
and
Gordon Edward Colvin 1943-2010

Merle's Dedication

Doreen Jacobs
and
Malo Pandit

Work
Occupations & Professionalization

Edited by

Stephen E. Bosanac and Merle A. Jacobs

de Sitter Publications
111 Bell Dr.
Whitby, ON
L1N 2T1
CANADA

deSitterPublications.com
289-987-0656
info@desitterpublications.com

Library and Archives Canada Cataloguing in Publication

Work, occupations and professionalism
edited by Stephen E. Bosanac and Merle A. Jacobs.

Includes bibliographical references and index.
ISBN 978-1-897160-40-4

1. Work--Sociological aspects. 2. Occupations--Sociological aspects.
I. Bosanac, Stephen E II. Jacobs, Merle

HD6955.W667 2010   306.3'6   C2010-906140-3

Copyright © 2011 de Sitter Publications

All rights are reserved. No part of this publication may be reproduced, translated, stored in a retrieval system, or transmitted in any form or by any means, electronic, mechanical, photocopying, recording or otherwise, without prior written permission from the publisher.

Authorization to photocopy items for internal or personal use is granted by the publisher provided that the appropriate fees are paid directly to de Sitter Publications. Fees are subject to change.

Cover design and layout by de Sitter Publications.

de Sitter Publications
111 Bell Dr.
Whitby, ON
L1N 2T1
CANADA

deSitterPublications.com
289-987-0656
info@desitterpublications.com

TABLE OF CONTENTS

Acknowledgements vii

About the Authors ix

Foreword
    Work, Occupations and Professionalization:
    Cultures of Coercive Credentialism
    L.A. Visano xiii

Introduction
    Stephen E. Bosanac and Merle A. Jacobs 1

Chapter 1
    The Importance of Considering Race, Gender and Work in
    Context through Intersectionality
    Stephen E. Bosanac 11

Chapter 2
    A Structural Functional Approach to the Study of
    Work and Professions
    Timothy P. McCauley 53

Chapter 3
    The Culture of Professions and the Individual
    L.A. Visano 73

Chapter 4
    Nursing's Journey from Semi-professional to Professional
    Merle A. Jacobs 99

Chapter 5
    The Potential for Transformative Justice in Nursing
    Rebecca Hagey, Lillie Lum, Jane Turrittin,
    and Robert MacKay 117

Chapter 6
    Crossroads in Anthropology's Professionalization:
    The Contrasting Pathways of Horatio Hale and Franz Boas
    David A. Nock 133

Chapter 7
    Obstacles Faced by Women in the Criminal Justice Professions
    Tammy Turner and Stephen E. Bosanac 155

Chapter 8
    Equity and Work
    Merle A. Jacobs 177

Chapter 9
    Credentialism: What is it and Why Should I Care?
    Greg Scott 189

Chapter 10
    The Foreign Credentials Gap: Understanding the
    Dynamics of Racialized Immigration in Canada
    Lorne Foster 215

Chapter 11
    The Community College Con:
    "Change Your Life Through Learning"
    Randle W. Nelsen 259

Chapter 12
    The Future of Sociology as a Profession
    Stephen E. Bosanac 277

Index 297

ACKNOWLEDGEMENTS

Stephen's Acknowledgements

I would like to express my gratitude to many people for their support, both professionally and personally, in this endeavour. First, I will address those who offered me their invaluable professional support. I thank Merle for her support and confidence in me throughout the duration of this project. She shared my vision and trusted my judgment and kept my spirits up during the many tribulations we faced in reaching the goal of publishing this text in a manner that held to our vision. Accordingly, I also extend my gratitude to each of the contributing authors who I had the pleasure of working alongside in the development of this text.

My friend and colleague Greg, one of the invaluable consultants from NTW Consulting & Research Alternatives, served at various times as editor, sounding-board, grammatical consultant, researcher, and data analyst. He also served as a vital source of conversation about the myriad issues I examine in the three pieces I contributed to in this text. These often intellectually stimulating, sometimes mentally exhausting discussions, were vital in my synthesis of the issues at hand.

I must also extend my appreciation to Livy Visano and John O'Neill for their unending support and for more coffees and chats than I can recall. They always leave you feeling positive about yourself at the end of a conversation. That type of support is a rare gift.

Further, I offer my gratitude to David Nock and Randy Nelsen. They each served as mentors to me, and now my dream of working with them on a professional project has finally come to fruition. Randy has a special way of providing understated guidance that is simultaneously supportive and inspirational. David pushed me to my limits in all respects and would not settle for anything less than my best efforts. The work I did with David stands as the basis for much of the work I do now, so saying his influence on me and my work is significant is an understatement.

Finally, I must acknowledge Karen Woychyshyn who keeps David and Randy in line and makes sure our lines of communication are open and effective. She is always there for me, ready to lend a helping hand and an open ear. I appreciate her efforts more than she knows.

Personally, I must extend my appreciation to all of the members of my family, in particular Joseph and Paula for affording me the opportunity to begin my academic/intellectual life anew in 1993. The road was rocky at times, but they allowed me to follow it and helped me to follow it when I was physically unable to do so on my own in 1998-1999. They have always been there for me when I needed them, and had confidence in me when others (and even I) did not. Sometimes people walk in front of you, sometimes people walk beside you, sometimes people walk behind you. The best people are those that do each of these at all the appropriate times. Joseph and Paula are that type of people. Further, I need to acknowledge the support of Tony and Vincent—each who support me in their own way whether they are aware of that fact or not. Chandra has been a guiding light in my life and is the most honest and forthcoming person I know. Watching her intellectual and personal growth is an inspiration to me, and I can only hope to achieve the work ethic standard she has set. I also thank Pam, Rudy, and Sam who are always in my thoughts. Dorothy, the miles between us only stand as a measurement to the vastness of my caring for you.

I also need to thank Gordon and Sharon for helping me to move closer to self-actualization both personally and professionally. I must also acknowledge, Scott, Gidget, and Gerry who have filled an important space in my life. I cannot neglect to mention Tammy—peer, colleague and twin in so many ways. She has played a significant role in the refinement of my theoretical approach to gender and the reasons why this is so vital. She understands me when I do not understand myself. And, I must mention Ashley, who—although she does not know it yet—can do anything she wants in this life. You are an amazing individual.

Finally, I offer my fondest thoughts and respect to Elin. My contributions to this volume are fully rooted in the ceaseless, unwavering, and sincere unconditional support she provides each and every day. I am so proud to know her and know with certainty that my life is fuller, richer, and more meaningful because of her presence.

Merle's Acknowledgements

A number of people have contributed to the completion of this book. First, I would like to thank the authors. This book would not have been possible without the encouragement and support of our publisher Shivu Ishwaran and my co-editor Stephen Bosanac who made us meet our deadlines.

Much gratitude goes to Livy Visano for our endless discussions. His experience and wisdom helped lay the groundwork for this book. He provided considerable academic and intellectual support.

I thank my friend and copy-editor Aloma Lively for helping me with my chapter. Acknowledgements are due to friends and colleagues for putting up with my questions and providing data for this project. As well, I am always grateful to the many students who continually enrich my life.

Finally, I wish to acknowledge my partner FAD for the support and encouragement he provides in motivating me to engage in these projects. I deeply appreciate his time, effort, advice, and debates.

ABOUT THE AUTHORS

Stephen E. Bosanac received his HBA in Sociology and BA in Psychology with Minors in Indigenous Learning and Religious Studies and his MA in Sociology from Lakehead University in Thunder Bay, Ontario. Stephen recently received his Ph.D. in sociology at York University. He is currently focusing on the political economy of cyberspacy, and the intersections of race, gender, and work in contemporary society.

Lorne Foster is an educator, researcher, and community activist who specializes in the areas of ethnic and race relations and anti-racism, social inequality, critical race theory, and diversity issues in a Canadian context. He is author of *Ethnic Marketing in Canada* and *Turnstile Immigration: Multiculturalism, Social Order and Social Justice*. In addition to his academic work, he is active in multicultural community service and development, and has created several award-winning diversity and anti-racism programs that have been delivered across Canada for school districts, law enforcement organizations, and community and professional associations.

Rebecca Hagey is first author on a participatory action research report (2005) funded by the Canadian Race Relations Foundation entitled *Implementing Accountability and Ending Racial Backlash in Nursing*. Her research focus is on resistance to equity and racial conflict in the health sector. She is an associate professor and teaches Primary Health Care at the Faculty of Nursing, University of Toronto. She received the Praxis Award from the Washington Association of Professional Anthropologists for the synthesis of theory, research, and practice in her role as founding member of Anishnawbe Health Toronto, Canada's first urban Aboriginal Community Health Centre. She is a member and past visiting research scholar at the Wellesley Centres for Research on Women and has a certificate of mediation from Harvard Law School's Program on Negotiation.

Merle A. Jacobs is currently Chair, Department of Equity Studies, York University. Dr. Jacobs teaches in the area of Occupations and Professions, Health and Health Care and Families. She has also served on the Board of Toronto's Queen Street Mental Health Centre and is a member of the Registered Nurses Association of Ontario's Mental Health Interest Group, as well as its Policy Committee. She is a practicing nurse psychotherapist and owns The Lawrence Centre. She is a director of the Roots Cultural Foundation and Royal Business Training Centre and Chairs the Friends for the Marcus Garvey Centre. She recently published *The Cappuccino Principle*, a book focusing on health, culture, and social justice in the workplace and in society.

Lillie Lum currently teaches nursing ethics and professional development courses in the collaborative degree program at the Atkinson School of Nursing at York University. She has extensive university teaching experience in Canada and the United States. As a researcher, she is the principal investigator on recent and current nationally funded projects in organizational justice, globalization, health human resources management, and distance education. Specific research interests include health human resources management, organizational justice in healthcare, administrative justice in healthcare, mental health nursing, distance education, and learning communities. Her doctoral research concerning informed consent and breast cancer patients was funded for three years by a scholarship from the National Health Research Development Program. Dr. Lum maintains clinical currency through two order-in-council appointments to Ontario health tribunals. She adjudicates appeals concerning the Ontario Health Insurance Act, the Ontario Mental Health Act and the Criminal Code of Canada.

Timothy P. McCauley is a Lecturer in Sociology at York University in Toronto. He has taught the subject of Sociology for over fifteen years at various Canadian Universities in Alberta and Ontario. His current publications and research focus on the subjects of capitalism, ethnicity, and social inequality. He is interested in how the various sociological paradigms and theoretical models examine the nature of capitalism and the ways in which these ideas are then grounded through empirical sociological investigations into areas such as professions and professionalism. His specific theoretical interests flow from the comparative differences between Weberian concepts such as status groups, social closure, and bureaucracy versus Marxist notions of false consciousness, alienation, and division of labor.

Robert MacKay teaches Disability and Cultural Studies at the University of Toronto. He is a proponent of the social model in his writing and disability activism.

Randle W. Nelsen is Professor of Sociology at Lakehead University where he has taught for the past twenty-nine years. Previously he taught at Trent, McMaster, Laurentian, and Concordia. He was born and raised in Portland, Oregon and has taught in the United States at the University of Hawaii, State University of New York at Albany, and Union College. His major areas of interest are in the sociology of higher education and professionalism, social organization and the study of bureaucracy, social thought, mass media, and popular culture. His two most recent books are *Inside Canadian Universities: Another Day at the Plant* (1997) and *Schooling As Entertainment: Corporate Education Meets Popular Culture* (2002), both published by Cedarcreek. His two most recent articles can be found in *The American Sociologist* 34:3, 2003 ("Remembering Reuel Denney: Sociology as Cultural Studies") and in *The Semiotic Review of Books* 14:2, 2004 ("Replaying Reuel Denney").

David A. Nock teaches sociology at Lakehead University where he has been since 1976. He received his Ph.D. in Sociology from the University of Alberta in 1976 and his M.A. in Canadian Studies from Carleton University in 1973 after completing a B.A. in sociology and history in 1970. Adding to the research that came out of his M.A. thesis, Nock completed a book in 1998 entitled *A Victorian Missionary and Canadian Indian Policy*. This book was a biographical portrait of the Rev. Edward F. Wilson (1844-1915) who worked among Canada's First Nations from 1868-1893 as a missionary, educator, and amateur anthropologist and ethnohistorian. In the course of his research on Wilson, Nock discovered that he had been greatly influenced by Horatio Hale (1817-1896), a scholar of considerable reputation in the nineteenth century but a reputation that has waned since his death. Nock has published three books to date, and over forty peer-reviewed articles in academic journals and scholarly books.

Greg Scott is a teacher, a freelance writer, and a social activist. He graduated from Lakehead University in 1997 with degrees in English and Education. He spent 3 years teaching in Colombia, South America, where he met his wife, Maria Felix. Since returning to Canada in 2000, he has obtained a diploma in E-Commerce. Although he is a teacher by training, his professional experience also includes work in journalism, web development, human resources management, and consulting. He has worked in both the private and public sector and speaks three languages, English, Spanish, and French.

Tammy Turner received an Associate of Science Degree in Computer Technology from Edinboro University of Pennsylvania (1986), a Bachelor of Science in Computer Science from Edinboro University of Pennsylvania (1990), and a Master's degree in Justice Administration from Norwich University, Vermont (2004). She has held the position of Institutional Business Manager at a State Correction Institution in Pennsylvania, since January of 1995. She is active in Pennsylvania Department of Corrections statewide committees, training, leadership symposiums and the development of institutional character profile policy, all intended to standardize procedures in the Department of Corrections.

Jane Turrittin is a social anthropologist. For the past 10 years, she has been involved in research and advocacy work promoting equity in nursing. Jane has also done fieldwork in Mali, West Africa and in Toronto, Canada, focusing on the labour market experiences of immigrant women from the Caribbean island of Montserrat and of African immigrant and refugee women.

L.A. Visano is an Associate Professor of Sociology at York University (Ph.D. University of Toronto) and coordinator of the Sociology program. He has published extensively (dozens of articles, six books, and delivered numerous keynote addresses at international and national conferences. He has also served as Dean at Atkinson Faculty of Liberal and Professional Studies, and Chair of the Department of Sociology. He has supervised dozens of doctoral dissertations in addition to serving as consultant to several federal, provincial, and local governments and agencies. He is currently completing two major studies: Youth and Ideology, and Institutions and Injustice. He has been awarded numerous awards for his outstanding contributions to teaching.

FOREWORD

Work, Occupations and Professionalization: Cultures of Coercive Credentialism

L.A. Visano

The professionalization of work is ideologically grounded in evolving traditions of modernity, capitalism, and liberalism. Modernity, as an ideology with its emphasis on both the "rational" and the division of labour, has impacted on work to such an extent that relations have been reduced to a rational calculation of "social value" (contractual considerations/exchanges) that justifies distorted claims of efficiency by armies of specialized technicians. In addition, professional values and beliefs have exaggerated forms of social solidarity which now woefully displace and replace any vestiges of authentic collective consciousness. Professionalization contributes to the classification and division of occupational concepts, the analysis and synthesis of work rules, the testing of performance indicators—all of which are calibrated according to a "rational" logic of instrumentality. The organization, allocation, and integration of widely dispersed work activities reflect particular social orders, that is, a socialized acceptance of the balance obligations and expectations.

Relying on rationalist methodologies and so called "objective" indicators, professions strive to ensure highly specialized roles and the diversity of functions guided by incorporating (a) a hierarchy of authority; (b) an impersonality of rules that explicitly state duties, responsibilities, standardized procedures and conduct of office holders; (c) rules of conduct that define achievement and trained competencies; (d) a specialized division of labour; and e) efficiency, that is, appointments to these offices are made according to technical superiority. Consequently, work is increasingly fragmented into autonomous spheres of specialized and mechanized knowledges. Fuelled by the "technical as rational," the ethics of integrity in professions relate to self-serving functions of surveillance (control of information) that regulate and incorporate fully the mental and material production processes. Professionalism has also produced a set of disciplinary institutions, practices, and discourses which legitimate relations of ruling. Likewise, the "professionalization of work" refers to an organized and recognized constellation of values replete with norms, roles, and attitudes that are specific to technical activities.

Professionalism, the normative conceptualization of the cultural impact on work, is a historically transmitted pattern of symbolic meanings that communicate, perpetuate, and develop "forms of knowledge." This inscription of dominant ideologies (narratives) frames opportunity structures that support self serving professional occupational cultures which in turn impact on the text of identities, social representation, and the sense of belongingness that stresses shared attributes around which group members coalesce. This collective wisdom guides and validates perspectives and activities. The emerging collective identity normalizes attributes and images that confer essentialized master identities based on credentials, and the appropriation of technical knowledge and experiences. These values further reproduce a symbolic framework for the development and maintenance of particular notions of collective and individual self esteem as well as offer a collective solution to actual and perceived occupational strains. Professionalism enhances group standards, behaviours, and values that establish hierarchies, membership requirements, informal rules, and coping strategies (accommodation and resistance) vis-á-vis the "outsider." Symbols, rituals, mythologies, rhetorical devices weigh considerably in recruitment, retention, and promotion of various role incumbents.

Herein lies the problem to which *Work, Occupations and Professionalization* turns its attention in a timely, critical, and bold manner. This edited volume inquires into the social organization of professions especially in terms of cultural manipulations, legitimation performances, and frames of reference that justify professional practices and protect privilege. In addition, this book challenges marketplace conditions, professional standing, "de-politicizing" strategies and the role of financial compensation. For Bosanac and Jacobs the culture of professional interests and complicity have diverted attention away from the more enlightened voices and action of members and their respective client groups. Economic as well as bureaucratic convenience often shapes the delivery of "knowledge." Despite the gaze of professionalism with its mimetic gestures of benevolence, there are inherent problems associated with accountability, independence, and credentialism that conceal as much as reveal how professionalization has become fluid, loose, and continually emerging webs of interaction characterized by shifting membership, limited involvements, role discrepancies, norm ambiguities, incomplete rules, and change.

Keeping this in mind, Bosanac and Jacobs, ask readers to recognize the tensions and contradictions that underpin conventional notions of professionalism and urge readers to explore the more transcendent possibilities of critical pedagogies. Transcendence, the movement beyond established practices, roles and expectations of the profession, situates professions in the struggle for social justice. Specifically, this book introduces the reader to the critical issues, important trends, theories, and various interdisciplines in the current manifestation of professions. Contributors to this volume examine critically the emerging theoretical issues, the transformation of professions and the problematic issue of credentialism. Imbricated within these fruitful analyses are themes of hegemonized market mentalities, mainstream or "commonsensical" concerns, as well as meaningful comparative perspectives on this diverse body of scholarship. This project interrogates accommodative and challenging discourses that discipline the constitution and contributions of extant practices and policies that inform professionalization. This much needed study challenges liberal tinkering, extant thinking that serves as resources for maintaining the "margins" for the "other," for creating contagious mythologies and for ensuring compliance with social injustices.

This anthology is a skillful, well-informed, balanced, and compelling presentation of traditional and contemporary theoretical concerns that confronts critically the professionalization of work. This highly accessible book approaches eloquently competing and complementary approaches that guide the ideological and institutional constitutions of professions by journeying beyond the academic issues to implicate praxis and policy concerns, emphases which will provide some fascinating classroom discussions. Briefly, this book is a powerful engagement that finally moves research on professions well beyond its ethnocentric borders towards a more inclusionary framework of comparative and interdisciplinary thought. Further, this text moves beyond prevailing normative claims by investigating conceptually the reproduction of the professional "self." The inquiries into professional socialization implicate social, political, and economic struggles that reflect fundamental issues of inequality. That is, institutional forms of socialization are examined in terms of their respective relationship(s) with the state, political economy, law, and culture. The acting subjects and subjected actors, within the cultural calculus, are linked to hegemonic practices. Individually and collectively the chapters herein enrich our conceptual appreciation of the dynamics of conflict and contribute to an understanding of generic processes that extend beyond the specific context of professionalism. The studies comprising this volume demonstrates vividly how creativity pushes the field forward by interrogating privilege, deference to authority, and the arrogant imputations of dangerous defiance in the workplace.

The thought provoking and stimulating chapters, provide a solid contribution to critical thought and research by addressing pervasive mediations of commodity exchanges and market conditions. Professionalism as a mediated communication of mass society, administered politically and founded culturally, forms and informs identities in relation to commoditized work. Prevailing ideologies are unravelled within significant interactions, social organizations, and social structures. In an effort to address and enlighten these issues the editors have constructed a specific set of readings and arguments, involving an engagement with the themes of intersectionality. There is also clear evidence throughout the anthology of an attempt to hold on to a broad theoretical epistemology in order to elucidate as well as resolve a number of thorny issues which to date have obfuscated theoretical integration. The editors present a compelling and innovative approach to the use of professions as a resource for the production of consensus, professions as contested terrains, and professions as ideological processes. The arguments are articulated within a plethora of themes based on social location, hybridity, cross-cultural communication, narratives of ideological climates and the mediations of culture and professional organizations which together create a system of meanings or moral/control narratives. Professions defined by dominant discourses determine thought, affect, enjoyment, meaning, and identity and various exigencies. The sensitivity to details of interpretations is a refined one, and it enables readers to yield some very significant insights and to open up a key of contemporary theorization in a potentially far-reaching way. Professions as a constituted complex set of mediations that interconnects consciousness and society, as well as culture and economy, is a view with which I fully concur. I thus welcome this anthology as a novel attempt to demonstrate the character of a hitherto neglected subject by illuminating the enduring and complex influences on decision-making practices of professionals.

This book should be required reading since it challenges the congested closures of conventional canons characteristic of so many mainstream edited volumes. I congratulate the efforts of the editors and contributors who complement each other in defying the defining gaze of professional authority and for overcoming the debilitating ethnocentrism that ignores universal inequalities of class, sexual orientation, race, and gender.

INTRODUCTION

Stephen E. Bosanac
and
Merle A. Jacobs

Why Write this Text?

After directing undergraduate sociology courses on professions, occupations and work for over five years, we were still having little luck finding a fully applicable, comprehensive text on the subjects of professions, professionalization and the related processes to offer our learners as an aid in their respective learning processes. Several texts on work exist, and some of these are excellent, but many serve to marginalize or negate the points of interaction we feel are most pertinent and meaningful in the study of professions and occupations at this point in history. Most available texts that do focus specifically on professions and the related processes tend to situate these concepts as genderless, raceless, classless generalizations. We find this approach to the material to be inappropriate and seriously lacking in meaning. This ineffectuality of the body of knowledge developed through this myopic approach is a result of the relentlessly universalizing character of this technique and the reductionistic, and consequently deterministic, nature of the associated incremental methodology. We hope to improve upon that situation herein.

Further, the focus on work per se, while certainly important in its own right, tends to diminish ideas surrounding professionalization processes, the evolution and/or devolution of professions and credentialism. It also minimizes the dynamic and fluid 'line' that lies between what were once easily recognized as white collar and blue collar professions, and the historically novel conception of pink collar professions.

However, the most problematic element we encountered in our on-going literature search is the common presentation of work/professions/occupations as a universal, monolithic phenomenon that creates a generalized body of ideal knowledge that applies to everything and nothing simultaneously. While the problems with this style of knowledge building are myriad, our belief is that the greatest difficulty found in this style of presentation is the manner in which the most vital social elements are homogenized, thus negated, in favour of an ineffective, inapplicable template. This results in the negation of an equitable, inclusive body of knowledge that appropriately and easily provides for considerations of culture, gender, race and class-based differences in global and local experiences of professionalization and professional work.

What this means for the reader is that our text provides a conceptual model of professionalism that features an approach that is simultaneously intellectual, academic, inclusive, and based on society's need for social equity and social justice. Historical consciousness and on-going processes of globalization support our contention that the amalgamation of this assortment of views is necessary in order to provide a cohesive, applicable and meaningful presentation of any material.

We have found several excellent texts outside of our specialization that provide powerful addresses of race OR gender, but only a few that attempt to bridge the artificial divide between these concepts, especially in considerations of professions, occupations and/or work. Those texts that do achieve this end are cited in the forthcoming pages and we are thankful for these entry points into the material we are presenting herein.

Additionally, terms including "work," "professions" and "occupations" are often used interchangeably. This serves to diminish the vital points of separation between these concepts and eliminates considerations of the points wherein these concepts intersect and diverge. The reader will see each of these terms used throughout this book, but should note that each time one of these key terms occurs in the text, its use is intentional and not simply born of a desire to liven up the text through word choice or an overzealous utilization of the thesaurus.

One might ask, given our view that most texts focus on work at the expense of professionalization and its processes, why we discuss work herein. Congruent to the problematic nature of negating ideas of race, gender and class, the negation of ideas of work in considerations of professions is equally inappropriate. Yes, our primary focus is on professions and professionalization, but this must be done in a comprehensive, relational and reflexive manner in order to be of value to the reader and the field. Consequently, we will discuss work and occupations as appropriate.

In the twelve original pieces written specifically for this text, we feel the previously mentioned oversights have been rectified. The reader needs to understand that justice or injustice is not mere moral reasoning but the experiences of social relations and the power of the state. The United Nations, in article 23 of the Universal Declaration of Human Rights Article 23 (1948 http://www.un.org/en/documents/udhr/) states:

(1) Everyone has the right to work, to free choice of employment, to just and favourable conditions of work and to protection against unemployment.
(2) Everyone, without any discrimination, has the right to equal pay for equal work.
(3) Everyone who works has the right to just and favourable remuneration

ensuring for himself and his family an existence worthy of human dignity, and supplemented, if necessary, by other means of social protection.
(4) Everyone has the right to form and to join trade unions for the protection of his interests.

With this in mind the area of gender and race and their overall status in the workforce must be judged within a human rights' framework.

Gender is a crucial component of our overall analysis. Race is a pivotal intersection and provides a valuable point of interaction with the material. The intersection of these two points with work and professionalization provides a rich presentation on the subject that we feel will make a valuable addition to the body of knowledge in each of these areas. However, we do not inundate the reader with this material. Each chapter has its own focus and style and offers a unique approach to the material. Some chapters focus and rely heavily on the discourse of race and gender, others focus primarily on race, still others focus predominantly on gender, while yet others take a "neutral" approach to the specific subject matter. This allows the reader to apply the tools given them in the theoretical chapters of Part One in the development of their own analyses and ideas. There is no better learning tool. Further, some of the chapters offer divergent views on a single phenomenon and it is left to the reader to critically analyze these presentations and develop their own perspective on the material.

To meet these ends, we offer a dynamic presentation of the three keys to the study of the professionalization of work in a contemporary context. These are theory, practice and problems. Theory is specifically addressed in Part One. Practice and problematic elements are specifically considered in Parts Two and Three respectively, as well as interwoven throughout the text.

We are obliged to mention that the model of professionalism and professionalization visible throughout this text has been anticipated in the works of Eliot Freidson (1986; 1994; 2001). His model has certainly informed our understanding of professionalization at its basic level. Freidson anthropomorphizes professions and the related processes in a vital and compelling manner that brings out the significant and powerful nature of the effect professions and work have on our lives and our development of self. We exercise and extend Freidson's model through ideas of race, gender, culture and class.

Further, Freidson provides a unique critique of the critique of professionalism. Through this discourse, he offers important insight into the professionalization/monopolization conundrum. The challenge of equitable professionalization is maintaining an effective balance between limiting the potential for monopolization that is inherent to most forms of credentialism, and the prudent and utilitarian nurturing and regulation of specialized bodies of knowledge that require control mechanisms for safe, useful and fair public practice.

Freidson's focus on specialization, formal training, autonomy, credentials and monopolization is lucid and practical. He reveals how sheltered labour markets where professionals interact are based on reciprocal relationships and ideas of meritocracy. In these relationships, professionals and their governing organizations/associations have formal, codified standards and practices. Deviation from these standards and/or practices is subject to sanctions that vary in degree from informal to legally actionable. This power to organize and control work and workers represents a labour market shelter that provides workers with the ability to negotiate rewards and/or exclusive jurisdiction of a given specialization.

Professionalism: The Third Logic on the Practice of Knowledge (2001), one of Freidson's latest works, views professions as receptive to the rationalizing forces of bureaucracy. Why? Because within contemporary, capitalistic bureaucracies, the regulation of professional labour, and measurements of the quality of professional labour have remained within the purview of professionals. However, one of the components of bureaucracy is control, which competes with the technical autonomy of the professional. Eventually, bureaucracy's "tendency to control" might impose a form of social interaction that is incompatible with ideal-typical professionalism wherein professionals, with the support of the state, find ways to safeguard their position of power.

It is the specialized knowledge within professions and the use of this knowledge that controls the agenda in both external and internal labour markets. It is the battle for this control that serves as one of the primary influences on the shape of professionalization processes today. This text further develops the applicability of these ideas across nations, cultures, races and genders.

About this Book

Part One sets forth a strong theoretical grounding in professions, occupations and work with a specific focus on how the experience of these cultural artifacts differs and is affected by one's worldview. This takes into account race, gender, class and education level and opportunities.

Chapter one, "The Importance of Considering Race, Gender and Work in Context through Intersectionality," by Stephen E. Bosanac, summarizes and outlines the key conceptual, theoretical, ontological and methodological underpinnings of theory surrounding professions, occupations and work with an emphasis on the social construction of gender, race and the meaning of work. Through a discursive consideration of the meaning of professions and occupations, this chapter examines the impact of these core themes on conceptions of the meaning of professionalization, professionalism and work in contemporary society. It also considers the impact of the meaning society affords to work on social norms, values and these core themes while pulling out the deeper significance of work as a social agent affecting and affected by the normalizing processes of the social construction of race and gender.

Timothy P. McCauley's Chapter two, "A Structural Functional Approach to the Study of Work and Professions," further aims to explore the theoretical foundations for research into professions, occupations and work. This reading provides a solid theoretical understanding of how social theorists develop ideas and concepts directing empirical research into how professional life and work is organized in contemporary capitalistic culture. Fundamental paradigms including structural functionalist, Neo-Weberian, Marxist, Post-Modernist and Feminist are explored, and it is demonstrated how these concepts are operationalized in empirical research dealing with work generally, and in the study of professions specifically.

The final chapter of Part One, Chapter three, "The Culture of Professions and the Individual," by Livy Visano, acknowledges the influence of situational and structural aspects of professions. This chapter provides a long overdue method for appreciating how forms and functions influence situational and structural aspects of careers. Specifically, in light of the differential impact of ideologies and institutions on professions, it considers how actors organize themselves as meaningful role occupants within their work. Culture, ideology, and the political economy of work are noted as vital to the shaping of a person's role within society. Therefore, professions are constructions that exist within wider interpretive schemes. Visano stresses that the concept of career embodies wider social and cultural influences than are often noted. Consequently, the concept of "career" can tell us much about the structure of professions. A career, therefore, is a way of being, a state of knowing and a form of sociation which imposes meaning in an actor's occupational world. Using the concept of career, Visano is able to focus on the processes of occupational choice, development and transformation.

Part Two of this text provides practical, "real-life" considerations of the transformation of professions in practice. Accordingly, it offers insight into the internal mechanisms of the professionalization of work and how this process unfolds within a field, discipline and/or work environment.

Chapter four, "Nursing's Journey From Semi-professional to Professional," by Merle Jacobs considers how the occupational culture of nursing, rooted in ideas of patriarchy and sexism, guides and interprets the tasks and social relations of nursing as a profession. Specifically, this chapter considers how nursing in Ontario, Canada, became a profession through lobbying efforts and the development and promotion of a specialized body of knowledge through the College of Nurses of Ontario (CNO). Jacobs reveals nursing as a complex, multi-dimensional profession that is often misunderstood by those outside AND inside the field. Further, after stripping it of the religious elements of loving care and self-sacrificing duty, Jacobs reveals the origins of nursing as a feminized ghetto of cheap labour. More generally, this chapter also considers the idea that professionalism is a masculine institution that contributes to the oppression of women by women, regardless of the demographics of a profession or occupation.

Chapter five, "The Potential for Transformative Justice in Nursing," by Rebecca Hagey, Lillie Lum, Jane Turrittin and Robert MacKay introduces a model based on transformative justice, procedural justice and Aboriginal Theory including restitution ethics to address problems of ongoing racial discrimination and ensuing conflict in the profession of nursing. Hagey et al. demonstrate how administrative interventions of equilibration can build ethnoracial safety and lead to equal access, participation and leadership development within nursing. These ideas can be extended to other fields to a certain extent through critical thought and reflective analyses. The model presented herein favours a proactive dispute process, seeing formal legal proceedings as a last resort. The transformative model proposed seeks to sustain ethnoracial safety in everyday work relationships by balancing privilege and power through critical self-reflection and responsibility that is rewarded instead of discouraged within organizational hierarchies. Transparency, accountability and restitution are requirements in this model that has to be owned by the entire employer/employee community. Finally, this chapter points toward the formal and informal policy changes necessary to support implementation of this model of anti-racism throughout the nursing profession in Canada.

Next, Chapter six by David A. Nock, "Crossroads in Anthropology's Professionalization: The Contrasting Pathways of Horatio Hale and Franz Boas," moves the reader into a consideration of the development of anthropology as an academic profession. It notes how the profession of anthropology in North America is generally written as a transition from the era of amateurs to a professionalized discipline characterized by socialization and employment in a university setting. The move to professionalization within anthropology is generally seen as progressive and incremental in nature, with serious and committed scholars replacing dilettantes and hobbyists. This transition is generally associated with Franz Boas who pioneered the removal of amateurs from the field, but this presentist narrative neglects the powerful influence of the work of Horatio Hale. Hale was a senior figure in the pre-professional period of anthropology who directed Boas' early research. Nock effectively demonstrates that Boas' "innovations" in anthropological thought, including espousing cultural relativism and rejecting evolutionary social Darwinism, were greatly influenced by the work of Hale. Boas acknowledged this in obituaries published in 1896-97 and then never referred to Hale again. Nock attributes this rejection to Boas' desire to professionalize the field at the expense of amateurs including Hale. Consequently, Nock asks if anthropology may have lost something by espousing an in-house, inbred style of discourse as represented by Boas and his heirs as opposed to the more expansive multi-tasking of the "amateur" Hale.

Tammy Turner and Stephen E. Bosanac's Chapter seven, "Obstacles Faced by Women in the Criminal Justice Professions," examines criminal justice professions and how female criminal justice professionals contend with a multitude of challenges including societal stereotypes, the pressure to assume normative gender roles, limited familial, societal and administrative support, and professional/occupational segregation. They note that each of these issues serves to create ideological obstacles for the female criminal justice professional before she ever sets foot inside a work site. These challenges are compounded by more "mundane" and often discussed impediments including, but not limited to, sex/gender discrimination, sexual harassment, tokenism, and ideological resistance to a gender/sex balanced work environment. This chapter examines how these ideologically entrenched concepts are reinforced and maintained by organizational structures and cultures within criminal justice professions.

Chapter eight, "Equity and Work," by Merle Jacobs, introduces the fact that the ideology of our neoliberal capitalist society is based on inequality from the very beginning. This chapter locates inequality in order that we can come to an understanding of Equity in the workplace. We usually know what we do not like and it is this routine interaction within the self that can lead us to an understanding of Equity. Like ethnicity, inequality is a broad and over employed term. However, when we view this term in relationship to access to resources it provides a road map to understanding the relationships that take place in our work lives.

Part Three of this text problematizes a key component in the professionalization of work–credentialism. We begin in Chapter nine, "Credentialism: What is it and Why Should I Care?," by Greg Scott, with an introduction to the unwieldy nature and evolution of credentialism. This brief survey will enable readers to further explore some of the particular social issues and concerns arising from the practice of credentialism, by providing them with the tools necessary for critically examining the issues raised in the chapters that follow. Scott considers the history and development of credentialism as it relates to professionalism and labour market participation, with a special emphasis on the impact being felt by today's increasingly skilled, increasingly marginalized professionals. Accordingly, it is noted that credentialism has, in some cases, become an element of socioeconomic, gender and race-based discrimination. Traditionally subjected to problematic hiring practices, visible minorities, women and persons with disabilities have been disproportionately represented among those negatively affected by increasing credentialism. In the new knowledge economy, credentialism has, ironically enough, become the means by which the knowledge worker finds it increasingly difficult to enter the labour market.

Chapter ten, "The Foreign Credentials Gap: Understanding the Dynamics of Racialized Immigration in Canada," by Lorne Foster, examines the especially relevant and topical issue of accreditation barriers faced by immigrants, with a special focus on visible minority immigrants. This reading argues that credential barriers are one of the key obstacles to equity in the labour market for immigrants of colour, and this is one of the primary sources of newcomers' dissatisfaction with living in

Canada. Foster notes that finding ways to improve access to trades and professions is the place where economic productivity and social progress converge. While over half of Canada's 200,000 immigrants enter as 'skilled' immigrants each year, many find their university degrees and trade diplomas of little value. Further, these immigrants often encounter a variety of systemic barriers that lead to under-employment or unemployment. This includes exorbitantly expensive credential assessments and qualifying exams, obtuse, culturally-insensitive rules and standards maintained by federal, provincial and professional regulatory bodies, unclear requirements/prerequisites of educational institutions, unreasonable hiring and promotion practices, and the tautological demand for "unobtainable" Canadian experience. The result is a Canadian workplace environment where untapped talent-pools lay dormant and ineffective, leading to a decline in social capital as well as national economic well-being.

Randle W. Nelsen's piece, "The Community College Con: 'Change Your Life Through Learning,'" constitutes chapter eleven. This work addresses, in a very practical and rigorous manner, the dictates of professional training and bureaucracy, and the way in which these phenomena are brought together in post-secondary education. Through observations and interviews conducted over a twenty-five year period, Nelsen analyzes common practices at a community college. Education in this circumstance is described as a process of attitude adjustment for both student and teacher. This process is described as indicative of a professional academic culture that is shaped by and reproduces prevailing socioeconomic arrangements. The chapter argues that promoting "education that works" is part of a confidence or con job characterizing the bureaucratized training that is found throughout many post-secondary institutions. Finally, an important focus of this chapter is upon what happens to those students who are unable to present "normal" cases to the professionally-oriented schooling bureaucracy. In other words, cases that the bureaucracy is incapable of understanding and serving without changing its terms of reference. Special attention, then, is paid to how contemporary schooling treats "deviant" students, attempting to "break" them to the bureaucratic mould.

Finally, Chapter twelve, "The Future of Sociology as a Profession," by Stephen E. Bosanac asks what is the tenor of sociological praxis today, and how does this affect sociologists' ability to communicate sociological knowledge with those outside the field? To these ends, this chapter considers issues of professionalization and credentialism with an emphasis on academia, education and the ideological climate that shape sociological works and the professionalization of sociologists. Two elements are interwoven into the examination of these questions: 1) an analysis of the abuse, overuse and reproduction of sociology's jargon, and 2) a consideration of "pop-sociology." Bosanac asks if pop-sociology has the potential to redress the problematic effects of the professionalization and hegemonic ideological underpinnings of sociology. Similar to the work of Nelsen, this chapter asserts that students are being deprived on some levels of an appropriate education and the tools necessary to the development of an accessible body of knowledge, all in the name of professionalization. Bosanac concludes that this is due to the fact that while sociologists are learning more effective methods of data collection based in the relatively recent qualitative tradition to varying extents at most universities, they are not learning how to make this invaluable sociological knowledge accessible. A substantial portion of the education, and the education dollar of the sociology student, is directed toward ingraining an obscure and inaccessible linguistic and conceptual tradition and a methodological approach that is not always effective. In conclusion, Bosanac asks if this problematic tautology can be overcome.

What is the professionalization of work? How does this process occur? Why does this matter? These are the issues we hope to expand upon and illuminate throughout the broad-based and diverse approach of this collection. Further, we will achieve this goal in a vital and meaningful manner through our purposeful inclusion of the interaction points of gender and race in our analyses. Professionalization simply means recognizing the special skills, experience and education required to gain entry into a specific field of work either paid or unpaid. Professionalization involves bestowing professional status on those who have a long-term commitment to a field or discipline. Professionalization also means setting qualifying standards for new entrants. Professional bodies are officially recognized in laws, regulations and policies, and are working towards these ends.

Why is professionalization important? In any form of work or employment, recognition of professional status gives an individual a sense of pride, achievement and security. Also, effective and fair professionalization practices ensure adequate services while preserving the integrity and viability of a field of specialized knowledge. Some guiding principles for the professionalization of work include the following. First, professionalization must be led and controlled by legitimate organizations that work for the benefit of both practitioners and clients. Second, professionalization must be developed on a reflexive, relational basis to reflect the needs and beliefs of differing cultures, races, genders, classes, religions, organizational structures, priorities and timetables. Third, the knowledge, experience and expertise of laypersons must be recognized by professionalization and certification systems.

In the coming years, the issues surrounding professionalization covered in this text will continue to evolve. The course of this development is not predetermined, and there is nothing that requires us to pursue any one path over another in this process, even though hegemonic, ideological structures would sway our choices. Nevertheless, there are many possible futures. We will invariably make choices, either actively or by default. Understanding and *participating* in these choices starts with an appreciation of the societal and human dimensions of employment and professions generally. It continues with considerations of how these elements work within and among different constituent groups and points of social interaction that

MUST include considerations of gender and race. It is our hope that this text contributes to both understanding and participating in these processes.

Each chapter, and this collection as a whole, invites readers to take up the debates surrounding the politics of professionalization. As these readings suggest, both individually and collectively, the relationships between professions, professionalization, credentialism, work, gender, race and class are complex, important and encompass a significant part of our lives. The political ramifications and social stakes of these processes are high, and it is only through careful and reflexive analyses of the issues at hand that one can effectively negotiate these processes in a personally and socially productive manner.

References

Universal Declaration of Human Rights Article 23. 1948. http://www.un.org/en/documents/udhr/.

Chapter 1

The Importance of Considering Race, Gender and Work in Context through Intersectionality

Stephen E. Bosanac

Learning Objectives:

1. Consider key components of theory surrounding professions and occupations.

2. Understand how ideological conceptions of gender and race affect the meaning of work.

3. Develop a basic knowledge and understanding of the foundational theorists who contributed to contemporary understandings of the intersections of professions/occupations, gender and race.

4. Learn to question assumptions surrounding the social construction of race, gender, professions and work.

5. Examine the normalizing processes of the social construction of race and gender and the effect of these on professions and occupations.

> Where *is* the system of sexual power that we have called patriarchy? All the institutions and practices we know of are already ascribed: to the mode of production and its class relations. Is the sex/gender system somewhere else, then, in the interstices of capitalist society, somewhere where capitalist relations are *not*? In answer to this question we used to say 'it's in the family', where men and women relate most intimately. But now that we understand that the family too can serve capitalism and be structured by it, we do not even feel confident of this.
>
> ~Cockburn 1983: 195

Introduction

This discussion will summarize and outline the key conceptual, theoretical, ontological and methodological underpinnings of a strong pedagogical and intellectual approach to the theory surrounding professions and occupations. It is important to note that each of these elements will be significantly marked by an emphasis on the themes of the social construction of gender, race, and the meaning of work in contemporary society. These vital elements will be interwoven throughout this discourse.

Why have race and gender not historically been part of the sociology of professions? After examining this question, I will discuss why these elements are essential to discourses on this subject and pedagogical challenges this creates. In this chapter, some important gaps are identified in the classical literature regarding the negation of considerations of race and gender with reference to theorists including Braverman, Marx, and Weber. This omission is questioned and I ask why it is important that these considerations stand as a regular component of analyses of professions and occupations.

Further, I will present some of the emerging and crucial questions posed regarding the intersections of race, gender, and work. I will also survey, with a critical eye, some of the classical literature on the sociology of professions and occupations. This includes considerations of texts by authors such as Braverman, Edwards, Marx, Rinehart, and Weber. It also contains a discussion of feminist contributions from Cockburn, Armstrong, Pupo, Vosko, and Reiter. Finally, the discussion incorporates an inspection of some anti-racist contributions by theorists including Westwood, Hill Collins, Das Gupta, Frankenberg, and Arat-Koç and Giles.

Through a discursive consideration of the meaning of professions and occupations, it is revealed how these core themes impact our conception of the meaning of professionalization, professionalism, and work in contemporary society. Consideration is also given to the impact of the meaning we afford to work on social norms, values, and these core themes. This binary is necessitated by the fact that these forces simultaneously influence and are influenced by one another as our conceptions of professions and occupations and their meaning evolve and devolve over time. The meaning of work has a profound effect on our identity formation and our self image (Mills 1951; Lowe 2000).

This critical review teases out the deeper significance of work as a social agent affecting and affected by the normalizing processes of the social construction of race and gender. This review is facilitated by humanizing the elements of professions and occupations that are often left in a faceless, isolated state by a preferred, but sometimes reductionist, Marxist approach. As the Marxist approach diverges from the more dynamic ideals of its originator, it inadvertently provides for a monolithic, or universal, approach to knowledge on work and workers. This form of Marxism claims to provide a generalized, multi-purpose body of knowledge. But, in attempting to provide knowledge that is applicable to all, it provides a body of knowledge that is, in actuality, applicable to none.

I will also touch upon conceptions of race and gender and the social construction of the meaning of each of these elements individually and in concert. This requires a multi-variate, anti-racist and feminist approach to the material that is both dynamic and fluid. This is required in order to facilitate the sensitive and potentially inflammatory nature of these themes in a manner that is both culturally sensitive and inclusive, but also intellectually comprehensive.

Why race and gender? Within the contemporary intellectual and academic environment there is a growing preponderance of female practitioners, and cultural diversity has become the norm. This is particularly true when considering many humanities programs offered in universities and colleges. Consequently, it is now more important than ever to tailor the learning experience to the educational needs of these previously neglected cohorts who are most directly affected by issues of gender and race in their daily lives. This is the primary motivation behind my choice to shape this discussion on the theory of professions and occupations in this fashion and to utilize these elements as points of entry into the material. Of course, this initial reasoning is both superficial and analytical and I will expand upon this reasoning throughout this dialogue. This is not to vitiate the importance of tailoring a learning experience to the audience, but to emphasize that I am aware that there are both practical and intellectual motivations behind my choice to emphasize these themes. I will unravel some of the elements behind both of these motivations as this work progresses.

Social Location and Ideological Underpinnings

In order to understand my approach to this material it is important for the reader to know about my social location and ideological underpinnings. I am an advocate of the political economy approach put forth by Karl Marx in his seminal works, which have withstood the test of time despite some important shortcomings. I believe most things in our world have been commodified. This commodification has been carried out by the people or groups who control the production/extraction of these commodities and the means to obtain them at the expense of those who do not hold similar power or resources.

As a relationist, I do not believe that I can introduce anything during the course of this discussion that will be of absolute/universal value to others either within, or apart from, the discipline. That does not equate to a statement of surrender on my part. Rather, it is my goal and hope, to present as many things as possible.

I realize that the epistemologies responsible for the value I place on a reflexive address of social location, for instance, feminist and race studies, are historically speaking, in their infancy. This is true even though each of these discourses are often clearly rooted in a political economy approach, and are also based to a certain extent in the works of Karl Mannheim (1936) and his development of the concept of relationism in the early part of the twentieth century. Nevertheless, we must remember that neither discourse—feminist or race studies—is thoroughly established within white, "malestream" sociology. As a consequence, both of these factors are often negated in works that would clearly benefit from their inclusion.

While this type of reflection and analysis is on the rise within academia, it is still fair to say that issues of gender and race have been ignored in the works of many social scientists, especially the classical theorists. The lack of a consistent and effective address of these topics often leaves the reader in a peripheral position within knowledge building. Consequently, race and gender are frequently left aside rather than presented as the primary subjects of a reflexive history.

Recently, this negation has lessened to a certain extent. But, this process can hardly be described as unproblematic:

> Increasingly, women become a more prominent category, integrated in the text…however, publications devoted to examining women all too often merely insert…women in place of men, without transforming the concepts to make them sex-conscious. (Armstrong and Armstrong 1990:130)

To conduct research in this manner is neither adequate nor realistic. Within the academic tradition, gender and/or race are regularly described as one of many interchangeable universal variables with little or no consideration of the unique traits inherent to these concepts that make them worthy of focused attention.

As a thirty-nine year old white male, I am a member of the "privileged" white male demographic. However, I do not feel privileged. I do realize nonetheless, that I am a member of this demographic group. It is difficult, if not impossible, to live the life of one who benefits from the "invisible" perks of "white maleness" and to simultaneously envision with accuracy and clarity the lives of those who do not. My reality does not allow me to escape these binds, but by recognizing them, I might allow an audience to better understand my position, while concurrently allowing myself to better understand theirs.

Race and Gender in Theoretical Considerations of the Sociology of Professions and Occupations

Two of the most dynamic variables in the development of the theory around professions and occupations are race and gender. Each of these elements carries highly divergent historical and cultural connotations. "Recent scholarship on African American, Latina, Asian American, and Native American women reveals the complex interaction of race and gender oppression in their lives" (Nakano Glenn 1996:115). Nevertheless, the vast majority of classical and contemporary theorists have tended to ignore or dismiss the value of these considerations within broad-based analyses of professions and occupations.

These elements are often considered within the boundaries of additive models or incremental styles of knowledge building. These models have proven to be inadequate because they generally consider race and gender as independent variables that function in isolation (Nakano Glenn 1996). In other words, notions of gender and/or race are simply layered on top of existent knowledge bases or subsumed within generalizing models. These models tend to provide an idealized template of the "meaning of work" that applies to no one. In fact, these templates are even further removed from the gendered or racialized worker as these models most appropriately mirror the life experiences and perspectives of non-racialized men (Nakano Glenn 1996).

Why this negation? Perhaps the most important reason for this exclusion is that much of the work performed by these equity-seeking groups is performed outside or on the periphery of the capitalist market. First, let us consider women. Much of the work done by women, both inside and outside the home, can be fairly described as socially reproductive labour. This type of labour can be defined as:

> the array of activities and relationships involved in maintaining people both on a daily basis and intergenerationally. Reproductive labor includes activities such as purchasing household goods, preparing and serving food, laundering and repairing clothing, maintaining furnishings and appliances, socializing children, providing care and emotional support for adults, and maintaining kin and community ties. (Nakano Glenn 1996:115)

This reproductive labour is often in addition to her labour in the market, which is generally marked by its "domestic" character (McDermott 1994).

Hochschild (1989) describes the commitment, effort, and time required to carry out this additional labour as the second shift. She shows how the second shift occurs not only after but during the "first shift." Hochschild (1989) also reveals how men very rarely perform an equal share of this labour. This is a product of gender ideologies and the resultant gender strategies. People, "seem to have developed their gender ideology by unconsciously synthesizing certain cultural ideas with feelings about their past" (p.16). Opportunity, social location, and life chances are also factors. The combination of these factors results in a "common sense" image of what it means to hold a particular gender status. Thus far, this ideologically constructed image provides a fairly clear sexual division of labour. This image reinforces notions of women as primarily responsible for the completion of socially reproductive labour whether this type of work is done in the home or the market. Pupo (1997:144) notes, for instance,

> [w]hile distinct separations between mothers' and fathers' participation in domestic labour *may* no longer reflect the reality of modern family life, there *may* be a tendency to overproject the degree to which couples are equitably dividing domestic work. (Emphasis added)

The marginalization of socially reproductive labour is not only carried out on the "practical" level. It can also be evidenced theoretically.

Braverman (1998) considers feminist theorists as best suited to address the gendered elements of work and work life both within and outside of the market when he states that his own work omitted this element for practical reasons.

> Beyond the fact that a consideration of household work would have fallen far outside the bounds of my subject (not to mention my competence), there is also this to consider; that household work, although it has been the special domain of women, is not thereby necessarily so central to the issues of women's liberation as might appear from this fact. On the contrary, it is the breakdown of the traditional household economy which has produced the present-day feminist movement. (Braverman 1998: 311-312).

It might be fair for Braverman to avoid delving into issues that extend beyond his skills. However, it is a weakness in his analysis. The above passage is oddly out of place in an otherwise powerful work. It seems that he is "splitting hairs" in order to make a distinction between household work and its breakdown in order to present to his critics a dyad that was beyond his analytical capabilities. He used this dyad to substantiate his decision to negate the importance of reproductive labour in his analysis. This is unacceptable. The breakdown of an element requires the existence of that element, and if the breakdown of socially reproductive labour is so pivotal to the evolution of women's labour, then by default that element requires more attention than Braverman afforded it in a treatise that was supposed to embody a comprehensive analysis of labour.

This is not to belittle the overall importance or quality of the Braverman text. It is both pivotal and foundational to the sociology of work and studies of work generally. In Braverman, unpaid domestic labour is shown as an affront to the production of desire that is inherent to capitalism. Why? Because it results in no "tangible" profit, or capital, other than well-raised children, a well-managed home, and social and familial cohesion. So even though his consideration of the gendered division of labour is minimal at best, it does nudge open the door to analyses of women in the work place. In doing so, it provides the impetus from which many gendered considerations of work might take root.

Since the "capital" of reproductive labour belongs predominantly to women, women are in turn devalued and degraded by conceptions of domestic labour that fail to account for the "real" value of this work. This phenomenon tends to diminish the importance of the intersections of gender and work. "Work and family emerge as separate, discrete spheres, with paid work done outside the household deemed more valuable than unpaid work performed for families" (Hill Collins 1990:46).

Socially reproductive labour, and accordingly women, are subjected to technological developments that are overtly designed to ease the burden of "less valuable" domestic labour while latently commodifying this type of labour and redistributing it in a manner that allows it to generate profit. "To some extent, new household technologies intensify household labour while diminishing the physical strength involved in some tasks" (Pupo 1997:146). The associated growth and development of the service sector economy has resulted from, and contributed to, the commodification of domestic labour as it is brought into the "profitable" market sphere. Technological subjugation of the labour process and the worker for the sake of profit is not only evident in domestic labour; it is visible within most types of work (Milkman 1987).

Domestic work, and consequently professions that are associated with domestic work, is still primarily described and defined as woman's work. It is not the worker that has changed in this sector. Rather, the location and distribution of the work has changed significantly and domestic work has evolved into an occupation that diverts the labour of the woman from the home and her own family. In other words, regardless of this change of venue, this evolution has done little to change the form of domestic labour or the associated patriarchal nature and expectations of the work and those who perform it (Luxton, Rosenberg, and Arat-Koç 1990; Armstrong and Armstrong 1978).

However, as this type of work has moved into the public sphere, it has not brought about many considerations of the gendered nature of this work. Rather, it has informed analyses of WORK, a faceless, genderless, monolithic element that is to be subjected to sterile, intellectual considerations that provide tidy conclusions that meet the needs and requirements of industrial applications of knowledge building.

This process is both marginalizing and precarious. More often than not it is women who fill the temporary and part-time positions in the labour market brought about by technological and industrial "advancements." These numbers have increased as the labour force participation rate for women has risen. Temporary and part-time workers consistently receive lower levels of pay, benefits, training, and opportunities for advancement in various occupations (Vosko 2000). "Another indication that temporary…work is a form of precarious employment is the sizeable percentage of temporary help workers who hold more than one job" (p.172). More than twice as many temporary and part-time workers hold multiple jobs than do their permanent and full-time counterparts. The lack of respect and esteem associated with less than full-time, permanent work acts as a marginalizing agent for those equity-seeking groups that are most directly associated with these emerging alternative employment arrangements.

It is arguable whether child-rearing and house cleaning are forms of capital. However, it is not arguable that within the capitalist system, such cultural capital is not considered as viable or valuable regardless of its necessity to the overall functionality of society. Accordingly, those who primarily possess or produce domestic capital are limited in their ability to succeed in capitalist society. "Whoever does not adapt his manner of life to the conditions of capitalistic success must go under, or at least cannot rise" (Weber 1958:72). These tasks are of obvious importance to the functioning of society, but they are devalued in a system where the exchange of goods and services for legal tender, or "coin of the realm" is of paramount importance. Only the accumulation of legal tender can contribute to the accumulation of wealth in the capitalist sense.

In a capitalist economic system, legal tender takes on a superincumbent value that is beyond the intrinsic value of socially reproductive labour. These tasks carry no more value when carried out by a male which necessitates a consideration of what forces are actually at work in the devaluation of socially reproductive" labour. Is it that domestic labour is generally carried out by women? Or is it that such labour, when done in the home of the worker, creates no surplus value and/or fails to lead to the development or exchange of capital? The key to this process in either scenario is the development of the family unit as a consuming unit and, "this socialization of the domestic sphere has occurred primarily in the interests of maximizing profit" (Reiter 1991:15).

I believe it is fair to assert that it is a combination of both elements at work. A male who takes on the uncommon role of running the family home is judged by his association with a female master status and his "choice" not to contribute to the capitalist process. It is more likely that a man might choose to do domestic work and work in the external labour market. In this circumstance, his "choice' to do domestic work is often related to his position as head of the household and may or may not be entirely equitable. For instance, Pupo (1997:162) argues,

> [a]ttitudes toward men engaging in housework and being openly involved in their children's lives have softened, but the level of their participation in do-

mestic work and the types of work around the home they do are largely related to their identity as breadwinners.

Conversely, a woman in a similar position is judged by her association with a domestic position and also her *"inability"* to produce surplus value. Choice is rarely an option for a woman in this situation.

Is this accurate? Does the surplus value created by a person who maintains a household and prepares their offspring for a role within capitalist society actually contribute to that system through alternative means by preparing future members of the capitalist work force? Regardless, long-standing power structures linked to the patriarchal nature of most societies have relegated women to the lower status forms of labour. It is a tautological model wherein the lower status of women negatively impacts the image of the work they do, and the lower status of the work they do negatively influences how society views women. "[T]he occupational prestige of the jobs performed by housewives is generally very low" (Armstrong and Armstrong 1978:66). When a "housewife" performs a job within the home that is generally held in high esteem when performed in the market, the prestige of that job is diminished. Armstrong and Armstrong (1978:68) wrote:

> Since selection for work in the home is more often based on physical and social attraction than on skill levels, even the jobs which do command respect outside the home are unlikely to make the same impression when performed by the housewife.

Consequently, women suffer the disadvantage of being associated by default with lower-status work whether they are CEO's or entry-level employees of a house cleaning service. This clearly points to the significant relationship between work and gender. Males escape this labeling based solely on their maleness and regardless of whether they are associated with a "female" occupation. Paid labour has different meanings for women and men (Parr 1990). Males do not have to live under the filters of womanhood. A man's work is often described as his purpose in life. Conversely, a woman's work is often noted as a place for her to pass the time and "remain under the protection of male kin while [waiting] for their life's work, in marriage and outside the market, to begin" (p.186).

We must also consider the element of race. As earlier stated, much of the work performed by equity-seeking groups is service sector labour or socially reproductive labour that is performed outside or on the periphery of the capitalist market. Socially reproductive labour has been studied, but usually gender is described as the predominant factor in the division and valuation of domestic work. Most authors choose to recognize "gender as the sole basis for assigning reproductive labor, however, they imply that all women have the same relationship to it and that it is therefore a universal female experience" (Nakano Glenn 1996:116). That is to say, most of the existing literature has established the worker within socially reproductive labour as once again, a nameless, faceless entity—one without gender and race.

This praxis serves to "white"-wash considerations of labour in two ways. First, it caucasianizes the worker into the traditional norm of whiteness which is, in fact, becoming less easily evidenced in North American society (Yancy 2004). Second, it "white"-washes the overall experience of work as it covers over, in effect dismissing, the life experiences, perspectives and worldviews of diverse workers while privileging Caucasian experiences (Das Gupta 1996; Nakano Glenn 1996). In other words, work is seen through the eyes of an idealized Caucasian norm and other social locations are neglected:

> This conception does not explain the different and contradictory experiences and responses of workers on the basis of such socially-defined features as gender and race. Their location within class relations as well as their experiences within similar positions are fundamentally conditioned by such features. (Das Gupta 1996:4)

There are theories that demonstrate how Caucasian workers might benefit from the racial division of labour. "However, they either take for granted or ignore women's unpaid household labor and fail to consider whether this work might also be 'racially divided'" (Nakano Glenn 1996:116). Consequently, racialized experiences of work are dismissed.

As a result of this, three very important intersections of discourse are overlooked. The intersection of race and work is dismissed in lieu of an all (none)-encompassing model. The intersection of gender and work is dismissed as unimportant. And finally, the intersection of race, gender, and work is ignored as a "malestream," "white"-washed template is tacitly accepted as adequate for all levels and cohorts of analysis:

> In short, the racial division of reproductive labor has been a missing piece of the picture…This piece, I would contend, is key to the distinct exploitation of women of color and is a source of both hierarchy and interdependence among white women and women of color. It is thus essential to the development of an integrated model of race and gender, one that treats them as interlocking, rather than additive, systems. (Nakano Glenn 1996:116)

This applies not only to analyses of reproductive labour, but also to considerations of market labour and professionalization. Labour in general features both racial and gender divisions that have evolved along with the "advancement" of the capitalist, industrial market. The primary difference is that socially reproductive labour that used to be carried out almost exclusively within the home has been commodified and professionalized and is being carried out both in the home and in the market. Nevertheless, this work is still predominantly carried out by equity-seeking groups, primarily female, in precarious employment situations (Vosko 2000).

Again we refer to the seminal work of Braverman, who certainly acknowledged his marginalization of the gendered aspects of labour. But, he never acknowledged that he omitted race in his discussion of labour. He is not alone in these weaknesses, and it would be an error to lay sole responsibility for these limitations in studies of professions and occupations at his feet. What was originally a highly differentiated labour force has been homogenized to a certain extent over time by both capitalism/ industrialization and the body of work that stands as the discourse surrounding professions and occupations. The works of Braverman, Marx, Weber, and Durkheim all contributed to this phenomenon:

> Both exogenous divisions (especially racial and sexual ones) and new distinctions of capitalism's own making have become embedded in the economic structure of society. And the divisions within the working class have distorted and blunted the class opposition to capitalism, making for a weak socialist movement and a long period of relative stability within the regime of monopoly capitalism. (Edwards 1979:163)

Monopoly capitalism is an ideology that does not account for race and gender in the classical texts discussed thus far.

As forms of gender and racial discrimination have become entrenched in contemporary ideologies and institutionalized within prevailing social structures, they have become "common sense," "natural" practices (Edwards 1979; Preston and Man 1999). This is equally true in most labour markets featuring socially reproductive labour and in academic circles. In most of the classical literature, labour and labourers are tacitly put forth as nameless, faceless, bodyless, sexless, genderless, white or raceless entities whose primary function is to sell their labour power to the highest bidder on the open market.

Accordingly, the relationships between race, gender, and work have been ignored, negated, and devalued in a climate that has for too long failed to emphasize the impact of differing perspectives on experiences of work and work life. This trend has begun to change in the last two decades. Nevertheless, much of the work of women has been stigmatized as "valueless" in the capitalist market. Further, the differences in the experiences of racialized workers have been dismissed as unimportant or non-existent in favour of additive and incremental models of knowledge building that simply apply universalized templates of "professionalization" to any cohort under analysis. Additive and incremental modes of knowledge building merely layer new knowledge upon old knowledge and assume that this accumulation of "facts" is fairly applied to all elements of concern within this knowledge collective. Consequently, these two vital elements have not historically been a significant part of the discourses that have developed around labour, labour studies, considerations of work and analyses of professionalization that are ideologically dependent upon male whiteness as the primary object of analysis.

Gender and Race and Analyses of Professions and Occupations: Pedagogical Challenges

It is essential that gender and race be rigorously introduced and advanced in discourses in these areas of analysis. Why? Because the negation of these elements, as established earlier in this chapter, does violence to both the body of knowledge related to work and professions and occupations, and more importantly—to the work and work life experiences of marginalized groups. In other words, excluding specific demographic factors from analyses of professionalization and work leaves us with an incomplete body of knowledge.

But we must substantiate calls for more inclusive approaches to research on the professionalization of work with facts. First, domestic labour, which is carried out predominantly by women, is worth billions of dollars to the Canadian economy and could be valued at more that 50 percent of the Canadian gross domestic product (GDP) (Pupo 1997). This enormous contribution by women to the GDP alone is enough to justify considering the importance of gender in the context of studies of the professionalization of work (Anderson 2000).

Second, men and women experience paid and unpaid labour differently (Pupo 1997). Women work considerably more hours of unpaid labour than their male counterparts, despite a relatively recent trend that shows a slight increase in the amount of time men spend doing unpaid labour in the home (Hochschild 1989). The sexual division of socially reproductive labour coupled with the stigmatization of "women's work" situates women in a unique context. And this context is notably different than that experienced by their male counterparts when seeking employment outside of the home. "The lopsided division of domestic labour suggests that women must create the conditions that allow them to enter the labour force" (Pupo 1997:151). In other words, women must ensure that unpaid domestic tasks associated with their households are taken care of and/or streamlined before they seek a paid profession.

Third, a woman's opportunity for advancement and positive experiences within paid labour are affected by several elements. Her availability for overtime and extra work is often limited by her domestic responsibilities. Also, her "second shift" interferes with her participation in important networking opportunities and her ability to engage in projects that present time management problems. The organizational culture that can be found in most professions contextualizes women employees as less committed to their positions, less interested in career advancement, unavailable for networking opportunities, and physically incapable of withstanding the rigors of jobs that require "higher" levels of output and/or performance (Pupo 1997; Cockburn 1983).

Finally, there exist clear divisions between men and women within paid labour as most professions have niches based on gender. These divisions can be found within and between certain occupations and professions. The patriarchal ideology that surrounds this subordination and maintains patriarchal bases of authority serves to situate women as a distinct group within the work force. "[A]uthority relations located in the social division of labour…specifically promote the subordination of women as gendered subjects in the workplace" (Westwood 1984:24). Moreover, as a clearly distinct element of the labour force with divergent experiences and perspectives on work and work life, women are easily described as a worthy element for intellectual/academic consideration in studies of professions and occupations. Within the capitalist system, feminized domesticity is consistently subordinated to masculinized wage labour and authority (Hill Collins 1990).

Race is also a neglected feature in work-related research. Race and gender contribute significantly to the discourse on professions and occupations. We examine race and gender separately in order to avoid glossing over the differences that can be found when comparing and contrasting the work experiences, for instance, of Caucasian and visible minority women. Nevertheless, these variables are intrinsically related, thus we consider how race, and also how race and gender together shape professions and the experiences of workers.

> Racially segmented labor markets, gender ideologies in both segmented labor markets and family units, and the overarching capitalist class structure in which Black women's specific race, gender, and social class positions are embedded all structure Black women's work. And yet traditional social science research assesses African-American women's experiences in families using the normative yardstick developed from the experiences of middle-class American and European nuclear families. (Hill Collins 1990:47)

As Hill Collins astutely points out, most of the existing literature has established the worker as an entity without directly considering gender and race, and as a consequence of this, these issues come to be viewed through the overarching ideologies of whiteness that dominate capitalist economic systems.

The difficulties caused by the construction of work, professionalization and workers as "white" are numerous. Since the preponderance of unpaid work and domestic labour is completed by women, particularly racialized women, and much research overlooks these elements, paid, public labour is privileged over unpaid, domestic, private labour and accounts for what has tacitly come to "qualify" as "work" (Giles and Arat-Koç 1994; Pupo 1997; Nakano Glenn 1996).

The result of this is research that cannot account for, forgets, or significantly undervalues the experiences of persons performing work within realms that fall outside of generally understood boundaries. That is to say, a "disconnect" between idealized and actual labour is reinforced through the adherence to flawed definitions that fail to recognize a sizable portion of the population. Consequently, socially reproductive labour is rendered apolitical and non-economic because it is effectively removed from analyses of the professionalization of work. Unfortunately, on those occasions when race and gender are considered, these elements are segregated into independent categories and the vital intersection of these elements is abrogated.

The division of labour by gender allows for the "common sense" acceptance of a male-oriented public sphere and a female-oriented private sphere. "Gender roles are tied to the dichotomous constructions of these two basic societal institutions: men work and women take care of families" (Hill Collins 1990:46). Visible minority women's experiences of work and home life have never been summed this neatly and succinctly, and this is at least partly due to cultural differences and the associated ideas of familial responsibility and structure. "[C]lass and race conspire with gender to create different conditions" (Barndt 2002:220). Analyses of these conditions are almost completely absent from the classical literature on professions and occupations.

In order to provide comprehensive theoretical coverage of professions and occupations, one must go beyond the traditional body of work in this area. Feminist and anti-racist theorists do focus on such issues. "[G]ender, race and ethnicity are representations that challenge particular socially reproduced and historically rooted social orders" (Neugebauer 2002:271).

The negation of these considerations is about power and the social construction of difference. "The use of gender as a category constructs differences, which show that gender is not neutral but contributes to power relations" (Jacobs 2002:4). It can also be said that, "[l]ike gender, race and ethnicity as well as class are categories in our society that construct differences" (p.4). These differences are rooted in prevailing patriarchal, paternalistic, ideological power structures, and those who study professions and occupations are not immune from their influence.

Das Gupta outlines thirteen manifestations of managerial racism at the workplace. Some of these tenets can be slightly reworked and easily applied to studies of work and work life and the deliberation of gender and/or race. As such, they can be demonstrated as a vital part of the "differences" alluded to by Jacobs that serves to marginalize considerations of race and gender.

Targeting. "Targeting occurs when one worker is singled out for differential treatment" (Das Gupta 1996:35). By targeting the Caucasian male as the focal point of inquiry for considerations of labour, classical theorists including Marx, Weber, and Durkheim, by default, ignore racialized and gendered components of labour. Targeting in the literature serves to silence and segregate the worker.

Marginalization. In isolating race and gender elements from considerations of professions and occupations, classical theorists have eroded and devalued the experiences of the majority of people who are part of the labour force. Highly esteemed modern theorists have continued this tradition, for example, Braverman. This does a disservice not only to equity-seeking groups, but also to those who are trying to learn about the 'reality' of labour and its practice.

Infantalization. The patriarchal nature of most classical texts serves to infantilize women and visible minorities. It does this under the umbrella of a male-dominated and oriented hierarchical system that is in place to serve them by offering a body of knowledge that "knows better" than they do about their own work experiences. This privileges the experiences of the dominant cohort at the expense of all others. This treatment implies implicitly and explicitly that other cohorts are unworthy of consideration or analysis.

Tokenism. Often times, when issues of gender and race are mentioned in classic texts on work, these elements are quickly "glossed over" and/or dismissed as anomalies within the system. For example, in Braverman (1998), he makes brief mention of gender in his initial work. In following editions, he responds to this criticism in a dialogue that is considerably longer than was his fleeting "discussion" of gender issues and labour. Braverman (1998) also does not account for race in any edition of his text. Rinehart (2001) can be critiqued similarly in regard to his very brief "discussion" of race.

And finally, *Lack of accommodation.* The general failure of traditional works on professions and occupations to accommodate the experiences of women and visible minorities implies a level of disbelief regarding the existence and value of these experiences. Again, this privileges the experiences of the Caucasian male. Some contemporary work in feminist and anti-racist theory seeks to balance this by advocating for the equal consideration of all perspectives and contexts of experience:

> Written by men, sociology involved the study of men and NOT humankind, much less women: sociology examined only half of social reality. Clearly, the first task of feminist sociology was to add the missing half…These early-1970's arguments by feminist sociologists transcended the criticism that sociology was incomplete without a consideration of women and their typical experiences, however: more important, feminists declared sociologists understanding of society to be systemically distorted because it was informed by men's experiences alone. (Fox 1989:121; emphasis added)

While this passage is aimed specifically at sociology, it is easily applied to most other traditions that have provided examinations of professions and occupations. Fox shows us that traditional theorists overlook a significant body of data, which is often fundamentally flawed due to the limited coverage of race and gender.

The pedagogical challenges to this approach are intertwined throughout my analysis. The lack of classical texts that account for race, gender, and work is certainly an issue. However, there is a growing body of literature that does examine the links between gender, race, and work. The primary pedagogical challenge of our approach to professions and occupations is teaching an audience that is ideologically entrenched in traditional beliefs surrounding the appropriateness of a patriarchal system. If they have tacitly accepted the normative appropriateness of the Caucasian experience as a generalizing agent, the introduction of this material will be difficult.

A Consideration of Gender and Race in Classical Texts

Marx, Braverman, and Edwards

Karl Marx

While Marx's original concepts from 1867 are consistently utilized in the studies of work (Braverman 1998; Edwards 1979; Krahn and Lowe 2002; Rinehart 2001). His research is a fundamental point of entry into these more specialized and unique issues because of the revolutionary and groundbreaking nature of his work (Honderich 1995). To this day, Marx's descriptions of alienation, the development of capitalism, and the future (or current state) of labour in all its forms are unparalleled (Honderich 1995:524).

It was not Marx's intent to exclude any specific variable in his analysis. Rather, his focus was on the capitalist system, its shortcomings and the path of its development and inevitable disintegration in a social context, and as such, it was rather inclusive. "In the earlier epochs of history, we find almost everywhere a complicated arrangement of society into various orders, a manifold gradation of social rank" (Marx and Engels 1872:80). These hierarchical social structures predominantly determine and are determined by the dominant means of production within a society. "To be a capitalist is to have not only a purely personal but a social *status* in production" (p.97). Marx clearly intended to include in his work all of the elements that determine social position and contribute to alienation, thus, it could include race, gender, class and the relationship between these variables.

Commodity is central to Marx's conceptualization of capitalist society.

> The commodity is, first of all, an external object, a *thing* which through its qualities satisfies human needs of whatever kind. The nature of these needs, whether they arise, for example, from the stomach, or the imagination, makes no difference. Nor does it matter here how the *thing* satisfies man's need, whether directly as a means of subsistence, i.e. an object of consumption, or indirectly as a means of production. (Marx 1867:125; emphasis added)

The determination of what these "things" are is open to interpretation. They might easily include race and gender, although he did not explicitly mention these elements.

According to Marx (1867), history determines what is useful, redundant, and of social significance. This includes concrete items as well as abstract conceptions of our world. This idea of use-value clearly opens the doors of analysis for race and gender (Marx 1867). The value of a thing is determined by its usefulness in a social context. Gender and race are used within the capitalist system to ensure a cheap pool of labour and an even cheaper pool of reserve labour (Vosko 2000; Das Gupta 1996). Thus, these concepts have a use-value and may be considered in a social context and accordingly in studies of professions and occupations.

Marx and Engels (1872:119) wrote: "The Communists fight for the attainment of the immediate aims, for the enforcement of the momentary interests of the working class; but in the movement of the present, they also represent and take care of the future of that movement." In this declaration, who determines the "immediate aims" and the "momentary interests"? Who judges the appropriate "care" for and direction of the future of the worker's movement? These unanswered questions provide an easy point of criticism for those who disagree with the ideas of Marx and Engels as well as "opening the door" for our considerations of race and gender.

Capital, Volume One establishes his many theories surrounding capitalism, labour, money, commodity fetishism, and surplus value. The establishment of these abstractions is crucial to carrying over his ideas to some of the more specific issues surrounding work that we now consider in studies of professions and occupations, including gender and race.

There are many specific issues that Marx did not directly point out in his writings. Why did he not mention the importance of race and gender in this theorizing? First, it is clear that the theories he devised were intended to be widely and liberally applied. His models were macro-oriented as was the style of the day. Even his contemporaries, including Hegel, attempted to develop the "ultimate" model for describing and examining the functions and patterns of the human world (Taylor 1967).

Second, when Marx was writing his volumes, men dominated the labour force. The participation of women in the labour force was minimal. Second, visible minorities were few in his geographic location. Where they were present, they were often relegated to "invisible" tasks that were seen as beneath Caucasian workers and carried out far from view (Edwards 1979). Furthermore, when women were employed, largely as care-givers, their work was done behind the scenes.

Apart from generalizing beyond specific issues such as race and gender, Marx's approach to the structure and nature of the worker and the labour process under capitalism is static and lacks a humanizing element.

> The problem with much of the Marxist discussions of labour processes and of paid work is that the working class is seen as a faceless, monolithic ab-

straction. This conception does not explain the different and contradictory experiences and responses of workers on the basis of such socially-defined features as gender and race. (Das Gupta 1996:4)

Harry Braverman

Braverman's analysis of Marxism is an important reminder of the exploitative nature the capitalist system. He argues that the success of a market economy lies in its ability to create and maintain a market which has no particular connection to "actual" human needs in the utilitarian sense. He also provides a classic explanation of scientific management and its primary purpose:

> [I]n order to ensure management control and to cheapen the worker, conception and execution must be rendered separate spheres of work, and for this purpose the study of work processes must be reserved to management and kept from the workers, to whom its results are communicated only in the form of simplified job tasks governed by simplified instructions which it is thenceforth their duty to follow unthinkingly and without comprehension of the underlying technical reasoning or data. (Braverman 1998:81)

Thus, the main objective of scientific management is gaining complete control of all aspects of production. This includes control over the means of production and the development of markets. This process culminates in the mastery of the end product of human labour. It is for these reasons that Braverman is useful in considerations of professions and occupations.

While Braverman (1998) did call for micro analyses of work, he left it up to feminist discourse to address issues of women and work that were beyond his examination. Why did Braverman gloss over race and gender? We cannot know why he failed to consider race, but he stated that he did not consider gender because it was out of his arena of expertise (pp. 311-315). Perhaps race was too? In 1974, race and gender were beginning to be considered and recognized to varying extents. Interestingly, shortly after the release of his book *Labour and Monopoly Capital*, he was sharply criticized for overlooking components of gender and race:

> Precisely because the working class is a class, and not merely a collection of individuals, its culture and experience must be understood as simultaneously diverse and united...Socialist strategies that do not take into consideration the totality of this experience run the risk not only of leaving out women, blacks, and other groups who have not historically been identified as the proletarian archetype, but equally run the risk of failing to address the actual experience of even white male workers. (Baxandall et al. 1976:7)

Richard Edwards

Richard Edwards (1979) in his text, *Contested Terrain: The Transformation of the Workplace in the Twentieth Century,* sometimes moves away from Braverman's temperance and becomes overly dependent on the idea of the "seeming invincibility" of capitalism and the capitalist enterprise. Edward's work is solid and fairly recognized as one of the better critiques of Braverman. But, even among the best works in this genre there is a notable tendency to become too deterministic in anthropomorphizing capitalism and positioning it as an unruly, universal force of nature (Baxandall et al. 1976).

Braverman's work was published in the United States at the upswing of the feminist movement and the Equal Rights Amendment (ERA). Given that the movement peaked in popularity between 1972 and 1982, it is unlikely that Braverman was unaware of it. Only five years later, Edwards picked up on this gap. Edwards' inclusion of women's issues and work was by no means comprehensive. Nevertheless, he did briefly discuss various types of discrimination women faced at work including the wage gap and the differential assignment of types of work which occurs along gender lines. He also considered the sexualization of the employee/employer relationship that many women experience in work sites featuring a patriarchal, paternalistic hierarchy.

Edwards also developed an important, but brief, dialogue around ideas of the institutionalization of racism and the "replacement" of overt racism with insidious forms of latent, less obvious racism. A considerable weakness in Edwards's writing is the additive or incremental manner in which he considers race and gender. Such an approach tends to nullify the value of the experiences of these equity-seeking groups. But, this is still an improvement on Braverman's superficial discussion of women and general disregard of race.

Weber, Durkheim, and Rinehart

Max Weber

Weber was interested in historical processes and their impact on ideology. For Weber, all social processes had to be considered in light of the historical development of culture and ideology. Weber also believed in the division between studies of nature and studies of people. Processes in nature could be examined causally, but human behaviours and patterns had to be interpreted in order to reveal the full depth of meaning that defined human experience. Nature was not prone to such a level of "meaningfulness." Humans were noted as special and unique and required more rigorous methodologies in order to develop an understanding of them (Weber 1958). "Understanding" is pivotal to the illumination of human behaviour.

Weber was one of the first to draw on Marx's body of work and to try to develop specific areas of Marxist thought. He was especially interested in Marx's idea that the development of capitalism and the future of the world economy could be best viewed from a relational perspective in the Mannheimian sense of the concept. In other words, effective, meaningful analyses of economic systems should generally be contextualized within the social locations of the audience to whom they are being presented (Giddens 1972). In rudimentary terms, he linked the development of capitalism to the spread of Calvinism and the resultant Protestant ethic which moved beyond asceticism and allowed for the personal pursuit of prosperity and financial success because these could be seen as evidence of a person's participation in steady, rigorous work:

> Here asceticism seems to have turned much more sharply against the acquisition of earthly goods than it did in Calvin, who saw no hindrance to the effectiveness of the clergy in their wealth, but rather a thoroughly desirable enhancement to their prestige. (Weber 1958:157)

In other words, Weber linked psychological conditions brought about by cultural development to social processes generally, and the acceptance of certain economic goals and conditions specifically. The problem with the acquisition of wealth could be found only when it resulted in laziness and diverted one from living a moral and virtuous life. "Not leisure and enjoyment, but only activity serves to increase the glory of God, according to the definite manifestations of His will" (p.157).

He did not adopt Marx's revolutionary position nor did he accept Marx's prophetic assertions about the coming revolution. In fact, he was often critical of contemporaries who adhered too closely to Marx's literal presentation. Where Marx saw struggle, Weber saw rationalization, and he viewed this process as practical. Weber viewed rationalization as the inevitable result of the evolution of economic ideology towards the efficiency that he felt could only occur as a result of the bureaucratization of the economic system. Rationalization started within religious denominations as they worked to develop a straightforward path to salvation. These tenets were carried over into the work lives of the members of the congregation:

> The Baptist denominations along with the predestinationists, especially the strict Calvinists, carried out the most radical devaluation of all sacraments as means to salvation, and thus accomplished the religious rationalization of the world in its most extreme form. (Weber 1958:147)

Work was envisioned as a vital manner in which to bring glory to God and to pave one's way to a life of righteousness. The development of a rationalized economic system is contingent upon a society that is capable of developing, and willing to adopt, a legal and technical system wherein the bureaucracy necessary for such an economic structure can function.

Durkheim, who we will discuss next, also had a deeply rooted interest in religion and its effects on the lives of people, the social processes they engaged in, and their patterns of interaction. And like Weber, he made little or no mention of gender and race issues and the relationship of these elements with experiences of work, work life or professions. The reasons for this omission are similar to why Marx did not mention them: the dominant sexism and racism of their day, and the invisible nature of the work done by equity-seeking groups. This is once again problematic, but in this context, the "oversight" can be fundamentally understood.

It would have been preferable for each of these classical theorists to provide a more effective examination of these issues. Nevertheless, we must include the work of these foundational theorists in any discussion of professions and occupations because they, especially Marx, establish the basis of this discourse, and are fundamental to the development of feminist and anti-racist works that eventually followed.

Emile Durkheim

Whereas Weber framed his work as a pragmatic consideration of the effects of religious phenomena on the development of capitalism, Durkheim (1933) took a moralistic position on the subject and framed most of his questions accordingly. Nevertheless, Durkheim (1933:1-2) insists that his coverage of the topic is amoral: "We repeatedly insist in the course of this book upon the state of juridical and moral anomy in which economic life actually is found." But, this is not the case as many of his questions are framed around the idea of the moral nature of a specific issue. The text is overtly replete with moral and ethical implications and analyses.

Durkheim (1933) observed that the division of labour was increasingly becoming specialized. He argued, "[s]uch a fact evidently cannot be produced without profoundly affecting our moral constitution." He asks, "…is the division of labor, at the same time that it is a law of nature, also a moral rule of human conduct…" (p.41)? That fact that much of his discussion on this topic is woven into a consideration of the application, meaning, and significance of criminal justice over time is in itself a moral tool for the excavation of the material under consideration.

This is not to diminish the overall quality or importance of Durkheim's work, but rather to contextualize it appropriately. Durkheim explained professions and occupations through the implications these social facts have for the functioning of society and the ability of these social facts to foster or diminish levels of social solidarity. He saw industrialization and capitalism as leading to the evolution of society from mechanical to organic solidarity. As organic solidarity came to be, people would become steadily more dependent upon one another. This would result in an internally dependant society and a vertically and horizontally integrated social structure. This is not to say that power would be equitably distributed, but rather to emphasize the necessity of interlocking social cohesion. Mechanical solidarity is based on commonality while organic solidarity is based on difference:

> The totality of beliefs and sentiments common to average citizens of the same society forms a determinate system which has its own life; one may call it the *collective* or *common conscience*. (Durkheim 1933:79)

This type of social relationship is prevalent in societies prior to industrialization and is based on the commonality of life in general and the lack of an industrial division of labour. It is about social cohesion that results from the choice of members of a society to share such a bond.

Organic solidarity came with industrialization and was based on the division of labour and a potentially dangerous level of interdependence. This was rooted in a technical division of labour that made it nearly impossible for one person to function and obtain the basic necessities of life without the aid of others. This type of solidarity

> directly links things to persons, but not persons among themselves. In a strict sense, one can exercise a real right by thinking one is alone in the world, without reference to other men. Consequently, since it is only through the medium of persons that things are integrated in society, the solidarity resulting from this integration is wholly negative. It does not lead wills to move toward common ends, but merely makes things gravitate around wills in orderly fashion. (Durkheim 1933:116)

In other words, organic solidarity is not freeing, but rather confining as it subjugates human action and behaviour to the will and intentions of those who control the means of production and work. In this sense, the increasingly specialized division of labour is seen by Durkheim as problematic.

James Rinehart

Rinehart follows Marx's approach and directly contextualizes work as a social problem. He locates the nexus of this problem in what he describes as an industrial capitalist labour process that has fostered an increasingly alienated labour force:

> In roughly 150 years, developments in the ownership of the means of production, the division of labour, and markets have combined to transform the nature and organization of work in Canadian society. From a rural society of small, independent producers and shopkeepers in the middle of the nine-

teenth century, Canada has become a nation dominated by giant corporate and government bureaucracies. (Rinehart 2001:58)

Unlike Marx, Rinehart openly expressed an emphasis on the importance of history in considering the development of work in the capitalist context.

His extension and explanation of Marx's concept of alienation is one of the most accessible and lucid available. Rinehart, while generally adhering to Marx's doctrines, primarily builds on his concept of alienation.

Most significantly, Rinehart provides one of the first commonly used, highly regarded books that offers insight into the gendered division of labour and describes the experiences of women and work. Again, this coverage is by no means elaborate, but it is clearly better than the other classic texts that I have described. It genuinely affords the female experience a place of value. For instance, he outlined the ideological nature of the gendered division of labour in the following manner:

> Underlying the gendered division of labour (in and out of the workplace) was a constellation of entrenched beliefs: Women's primary responsibilities were in the home (cult of domesticity, women as secondary wage earners); the ideal of a "family wage" (men should be paid enough to be the sole support of their families); women were naturally unsuited to a broad range of "men's" jobs, including most types of skilled manual labour. (Rinehart 2001:32)

This ideology of patriarchy reinforced discriminatory practices and trends in employment and the division of labour. The introduction of this feminist critique of labour in a mainstream text is quite significant. The work of Rinehart stands as one of the earliest attempts to present this type of analysis to a mainstream audience. He also considers, to varying levels of effectiveness and depth, women's unpaid work, women's work in the service sector, and the part-time, temporary nature of much of women's paid work (Rinehart 2001).

Feminist Contributions to the Analysis of the Professionalization of Work

The feminist approach builds upon Marxist theory in a manner that values the experiences of women and elevates them to a subject in their own right (Cockburn 1991:22). Feminist theory values women's ways of knowing and knowledge building while simultaneously staking a claim for the intrinsic value of existing as a woman (Hill Collins 1990).

Perhaps the greatest achievement of feminist theorists is "in identifying not only woman but womanhood as a source of strength, it clearly *embodied* women" (Cockburn 1991:27). The act and process of embodiment provides for the consideration of women as "real" subjects in the "real" world. Consequently, embodiment implies and extends the idea of tangibility and value to women and their worldviews. In providing for the "presence" of women, feminism irreversibly opened the door to considerations of women as the legitimate, primary subjects of academic research.

Marxism locates all work-related social and individual problems within a universal entity known as the "worker." Cockburn expands upon this idea to include the different positions men and women hold in the world:

> Marxism tends to explain the disadvantaged position of women at work as the result of a simple desire by capital to exploit cheap labour, and of men to protect themselves against capital. Such a theory overlooks the economic, social and political benefits accruing to men of all classes from women's long subordination. (Cockburn 1983:6)

Feminist thought focuses on the ideological bases of hierarchies of power, the structure of social relations, the development of gender ideologies, and the corresponding interaction patterns and life experiences (Cockburn 1983). "The gender we live socially, ('I am a man', 'She is a woman'), is not a natural phenomenon like the sex features we are born with" (Cockburn 1983:6). Consequently, the social construction of gender is open to analyses and we can ask "why" and "how" this system came into being. The construction of gender ideologies is not a naturally occurring, random event. Rather, social constructs such as these are developed and reinforced over time (Williams 1987).

One of the most interesting points Cockburn (1983) addresses is whether we should consider social systems of capitalism and patriarchy as working parallel to one another or in concert. The parallel, or dual systems approach, seems to me the most appropriate manner in which to consider capitalism and patriarchy. For example:

> This of course is the point at which, having confronted the patriarchal nature of capitalism, we come face to face with the capitalist nature of patriarchy-as-we-know-it. For the uses to which women's labour is put worldwide are not only or merely the uses of individual men or even men as a sex, but the uses of capital. (Cockburn 1991:74)

As feminist theory tries to privilege the experiences of women in context, a dual systems approach allows the capitalist system a privileged position in the social order, and equally affords the patriarchal system a position of social importance. Combining these elements in a universalizing praxis would likely lead to the subjugation of one to the other and consequently marginalize the consideration of that element. It is vital to maintain a discourse on professions and occupations wherein each of these elements is viewed as having a profound level of influence on the other.

The level of interaction is invaluable, but only under conditions which afford each of these conditions equivalent levels of importance within the predominant social system (Cockburn 1991).

According to Armstrong and Armstrong (1978), women and their work, paid and unpaid, have been ghettoized within *each* of these systems. "Work which falls outside the official definition of the 'labour force' has been ignored or treated as a separate aspect of women's role, not as work" (Armstrong and Armstrong 1978:13). Consequently, women's work in the home has been devalued. Simultaneously, their work in the market has been segregated, undervalued, and stigmatized as somehow "less than" men's contributions to market labour. "Within the industrial unit, women are still concentrated in the low-skilled, low-paid, unattractive jobs where productivity tends to be low" (Armstrong and Armstrong 1978:179). That is to say, both glass walls and glass ceilings have limited the potential and participation of women in the labour market, regardless of media images to the contrary (Armstrong and Armstrong 1978). A common belief is that women's experiences with work have improved significantly in recent history:

> However, the increasing visibility of women outside the home and the emphasis on female attainment of jobs at the top of the ladder have camouflaged the lack of basic change in women's work. In actual fact the division of labour by sex has changed little…In Canada today, there is men's work and women's work. Women are segregated into the domestic unit where they perform the household chores. Within the industrial unit, women are concentrated into a limited number of occupations, into sex-typed jobs. (Armstrong and Armstrong 1978:14)

Although it must be recognized that this situation has improved since the 1970s, we must also recognize the limitations to this improvement. It has been argued this recognition has contributed to an increase in women's levels of alienation and lower levels of job satisfaction in the current environment (Vosko 2000).

The differentiation described by Armstrong and Armstrong can be seen in the preponderance of women working in the rapidly growing service industry. This sector is known for its prevalence of low-quality and/or temporary jobs, and the relatively small number of men working in this area. "Not only were women concentrated in a limited number of occupations, they also tended to dominate these occupations, that is, to outnumber the men in them" (Armstrong and Armstrong 1978:34). This cannot be attributed merely to ideas of biology (sex) or socialization (gender role) alone. "Segregated employment encourages the development of sex-specific characteristics" (Armstrong and Armstrong 1990:22). In other words, while some sex-based differences may exist, these are likely influenced to some extent by ideological structures and the corresponding agents of reinforcement. Additionally, "biological differences take on a particular significance under the capitalist mode of production" (Armstrong and Armstrong 1978:27). Consequently, these purported "common sense" biological differences often serve as the primary cause of the sexual division of labour.

Armstrong and Armstrong (1990, 1978) provide a solid consideration of the sexual division of labour and the manner in which sex and/or gender differences influence, and are influenced by this process. They advocate that women's work, and thus work generally, cannot be theorized without a gendered consideration of paid and unpaid work, the ideological conditions of capitalism, prevailing patriarchal conceptions of sex/gender, and ideas and means of resistance.

In considering the gendered division of labour, Pupo (1997) does an effective job of reviving Hochschild's (1989) idea of the second shift and the "supermom" in a contemporary context. Pupo (1997) also sheds light on the realities of commonly held beliefs regarding the division of domestic labour in a contemporary context:

> While distinct separations between mothers' and fathers' participation in domestic labour may no longer reflect the reality of modern family life, there may be a tendency to overproject the degree to which couples are equitably dividing domestic work. Popular images of and discourses on sharing the load may misconstrue the difficulty of balancing paid work with family responsibilities. (Pupo 1997:144)

It is politically correct for people to state that they are cooperative members of a home and family wherein domestic labour is equitably distributed among all members. Men feel obliged to claim that they are contributing to the household, and women feel equally obligated to display that they have successfully negotiated a fair balance regarding domestic work in their lives. This represents a tautological process wherein men and women reinforce each other's claims to equity regardless of the accuracy of these portrayals. This is a process wracked with guilt and expectations (Hochschild 1989).

This is not to say that the respondents do not genuinely believe in the reality of the portrayals they share. Rather, as Pupo (1997:144-145) so clearly states:

> Couples may negotiate their own standards of fairness in dividing the household work, but they do so within the context of cultural assumptions and expectations regarding men's and women's roles and a social structure that may not easily accommodate their desire for change.

The gendered division of labour, especially domestic/reproductive labour, is a long-standing societal norm that has been consistently reinforced through ideologically-rooted ideals of femininity, masculinity, the nuclear family, and customary patterns of socialization. Women often feel compelled to provide for their male partner's "need/requirement" to perform in the external labour market, and men sometimes feel that their masculinity is threatened by engaging in what is known as "women's work" (Pupo 1997; Hochschild 1989).

Importantly, Pupo (1997) argues that an inequitable division of domestic labour coupled with the *belief* that the division *is* equal impacts women's experiences in the external labour market. With these beliefs intact, assumptions are drawn and expectations are set in place based on notions of "equity." These assumptions have had a profound impact on the nature of reproductive labour, household technologies and novel, alternate forms of employment that are predominantly filled by women (Pupo 1997). Expectations and opportunities are generally viewed as egalitarian, but this is often out of context.

The division of household labour still appears to adhere to traditional patterns wherein women do the "inside" chores including food preparation, cleaning, and laundry, and men do "outside" chores including home maintenance, shopping, and "chauffeur" duties:

> In arranging their household work, family members tend to carve out for themselves the most reasonable course given the circumstances and alternatives. Since husbands usually out earn wives, for example, the most reasonable arrangement is for the husband to maximize his hours on the job. (Pupo 1997:146)

This has the consequence of leaving the wife in a position where she has to "sacrifice" her external labour market potential in order for the husband to realize his maximum potential. The motivation behind this is generally that the family might enjoy the greatest possible benefit from the earning power of the husband and wife as an economic unit. Additionally, it must be said that given the cultural expectations placed on women regarding the importance of a clean home and "appropriate" meal preparation, one of the "alternatives," at least for men, is to do as little domestic work as possible based on the duties the wife will take on "by default."

Household work is dramatically different than it once was. But, this is not to be mistaken for a decrease in the overall volume of the task (Pupo 1997; Baxandall et al. 1976). Due to the "Martha Stewart" influence, most technological "advances" in household work have increased expectations regarding the quality of the task they are designed to "ease," and thus increased the overall time and effort required to complete the task (Pupo 1997:158). For example, where a pot of coffee was once adequate, now a freshly made cappuccino is the norm. Or, where a simple, but nutritious dinner was acceptable, now a beautifully-plated gourmet entrée is required.

According to Pupo, each of these factors has contributed to a variety of novel forms of employment, and these may often be accurately described as gendered and exploitative to varying degrees:

> Interestingly, even women who jump the hurdles to gain entry to some of the so-called nontraditional occupations for women are less likely than their male counterparts to work full year, full time. (Pupo 1997:154)

This is in part because of what Pupo (1997) describes as the unequal share of domestic work women are generally responsible for. We must also consider the effect this has on their availability for external market work and the image this affords them in the eyes of their employer or potential employer. "Many women report working part time in order to accommodate paid work, family, and child care responsibilities" (p.153).

How can we effect noticeable change and shift towards greater levels of equity in the division of domestic labour and women's external work opportunities and experiences? The development of non-patriarchal policies coupled with an effective implementation plan is needed on all levels of government and within the workplace (Pupo 1997).

Vosko (2000) draws on Pupo's idea that gendered, problematic forms of employment have risen in response to the conditions created by capitalist ideology, which is steeped in notions of patriarchy and paternalism. Vosko adds to the vital idea that the feminization of work has the potential to negatively impact *all* members of the external labour market. The feminization of employment features several dimensions:

> [F]eminization not only connoted rising female labour force participation rates but three other central dimensions as well: namely, persisting sex segregation; continuing income and occupational polarization between women and men, and among women and men themselves; and growing casualization or the "gendering of jobs". (Vosko 2000: 252)

Each of these elements lends to the commodification of work. For marginalized workers, this often equates to a relationship with work that is marked by low-quality professions and occupations. Jobs of low-quality are generally marked by a lack of benefits, no unionization, low pay, few safety standards, and little if any opportunity for either vertical or horizontal movement within the company. An important phenomenon that grew from and contributed to this and expedited the proliferation of gendered, low-quality jobs is the temporary help industry (Vosko 2000).

This kind of employment relationship is becoming the norm for many cohorts as the amount of full-time, full-year jobs decline. But, women and racialized persons are particularly effected (Vosko 2000; Nakano Glenn 1996). The lack of permanence and job quality has created what Vosko (2000:260) terms a "precarious employment relationship":

> Moreover, when the persistently precarious character of the [temporary employment relationship] is examined in light of macro-level trends associated with the feminization of employment, the larger significance of its spread signals more than simply the extension of feminized employment relationships to a growing diversity of working people: if developments in the [temporary help industry] are indicative of broader changes in the labour market, then the spread of the [temporary employment relationship] signifies the feminization of employment *norms.*

Thus, Vosko effectively situates gendered considerations of work into a new context. Herein, these precarious conditions are clearly applicable to a much more universal consideration of work and experiences of work which includes most, if not all, cohorts. In other words, this is no longer "only a woman's problem." The quality of work is gradually devolving to a state wherein the generally low-quality of jobs associated with women is spreading to include more and more professions and occupations each year. As a consequence of this, so-called high-quality "good/male" jobs are also being degraded.

Reiter (1991) examines the impact of the public sphere on the private sphere of the family. "This book begins in the home as a reminder that 'real' life and 'real' work encompasses both private life and paid work" (p.5). While focusing primarily on gender issues, Reiter's book includes an important, albeit brief, acknowledgement of race-related issues surrounding the "reality" of choice and opportunity for equity-seeking groups in the workplace.

Reiter (1991) shows how the quick rise and high profits of the fast food industry are based on the encouragement of a part-time, highly gendered and racialized labour force that leaves the preponderance of power in the hands of the corporate managers:

> The need to maximize profit propels capitalists both to expand the market by growing larger, and to employ less skilled labour, that is at once cheaper and more easily controlled. It is not "human nature," but a particular organization of industry that explains the desire for more profitability, at the expense of the worker, the consumer, or both. Individual businessmen have only two choices—to compete, to grow and to increase their profits, or to fold. (P.48)

This need for perpetual growth as originally described by Weber is a characteristic of a capitalist system and necessitates the marginalization of an exploitable, expendable labour force. In most businesses, the human element is the most costly part of doing business. Thus, by continually minimizing the investment in this resource, business can nearly ensure steadily rising profit margins, and thus ensure shareholder satisfaction.

To encourage this growth, the fast food industry, as well as most other commodity producing industries, has moved into the family sphere in order to expand its market base and labour pool (Reiter 1991). In other words, through the proliferation of the family sphere, business has created both consumers and workers—the key to success in a capitalist economy. Reiter (1991) argues, "The restaurant industry in Canada provides an example of how an activity that used to take place at home for household consumption became a business undertaking" (p.21).

Creating a market is perhaps more difficult than creating a commodity for that market. But, mass production and the generally associated lowering of costs has fostered "common sense" notions that it simply makes more sense (or cents) to purchase services and products outside the home. It is often considerably more costly to produce within the home, and a person's earning and productive capacity could be put to more effective use in the external labour market (Reiter 1991).

In this sense, both product and consumer are subjugated to the tenets of scientific management. Production in both the home and at work is segmented into its smallest elements and simplified. Meanwhile, to provide workers and consumers with a sense of "belonging," and in hopes of avoiding the development of both an alienated labour pool and alienated consumers, employees are given "humanizing" name tags and consumers are assured that the chicken they just purchased for tonight's family dinner is "just like mom used to make." The cake they might bake this weekend is of course "fresh," because they "added the egg" themselves.

This process is pivotal in "freeing up" women's labour because it is primarily women who have been socialized to take responsibility if their families are not eating properly or receiving an adequate amount of domestic support. Once women are assured that their family responsibilities are adequately taken care of, they are better able to enter the external labour market. Here, the devaluation of domestic/reproductive labour that women are generally associated with contributes to the marginalization of women workers as a group. This marginalization lends to the provision of the low cost work force necessary for high levels of profitability, particularly in the service sector. "For decades, retailing corporations have paid rock-bottom wages for this female-dominated service work which historically has been at the heart of often huge profits" (McDermott 1994:113).

Anti-Racist Contributions

Analyses related to the intersections of race, gender, and professions and occupations as individual factors influencing professionalization and work have increased in recent history, but the intersections of these phenomena require more attention in contemporary research (Vosko 2000; Das Gupta 1996; Frankenberg 1993, 1997; Giles and Arat-Koç 1994; Hill Collins 1990; Westwood 1984). While the focus of this section is on anti-racist contributions, the authors considered in the forthcoming pages also try to incorporate gender issues in their analyses (keeping in mind the difficulty in separating these concerns).

Giles and Arat-Koç's (1994) volume focuses on paid domestic work that is performed in a commercial setting and emphasizes the importance of both race and gender. They consider service industry-based occupations that feature jobs that are typically associated with socially reproductive labour, and the association of these jobs with marginalized groups of workers. This includes housekeeping, child care, restaurant work and retail work. Unfortunately, most considerations of domestic work are predicated on the idea of the universal experience of being a woman:

> While sharing the criticisms of the domestic labour debate that it has not provided *feminist* answers to questions on women's oppression, we do not believe it would be adequate to provide *feminist* answers if that implies *solely* a concern with issues of gender expressed in universal terms. (Giles and Arat-Koç 1994:5)

The lack of a multivariate approach to the study of work that includes issues of race, gender, class, capitalism and patriarchy stands as a serious oversight in the field.

Through an inclusive and relational approach, Giles and Arat-Koç outline how socially reproductive labour is undervalued in the external labour market and how this intersects with ideas of race and gender. "[T]he dilemma of capitalism is that while the reproduction of labour power is necessary, the capitalist goal is to create profit and thus keep the costs of reproduction low" (Giles and Arat-Koç 1994:7). Capitalism has successfully kept the costs of social reproduction low in an economic environment wherein ideals of patriarchy and race have served to marginalize the associated cohorts and the types of work they do which are primarily domestic/service-based. They argue that this is a tautological process wherein marginalized people are directed towards marginalized types of labour and the association of these things, each with the other, serves to further reinforce the marginalization of each.

This marginalization is entrenched systemically through both policy and practice. "The laws and policies of labour-importing states such as Canada provide a critical point of articulation for the global migration patterns of domestic workers" (Macklin 1994:13). Many of these policies demarcate in law the boundaries of marginalization. It is through an analysis of Canadian policy that we can locate the inclusion/exclusion paradox that marks the life and work experiences of immigrants in Canada and institutionalizes the marginalization of these peoples. Immigrants are allowed into Canadian homes, but not into the House of Commons; they are "granted" employment, but not employment rights. These barriers dramatically influence the social construction of people and their work (Macklin 1994).

Another important theme in Giles and Arat-Koç's text is resistance. The authors in this volume generally adhere to the Marxist ideal of the development of a class consciousness, among racialized women in particular, that results in resistance of varying forms:

> Contrary to some popular opinions about women as unionists, even immigrant women, whether divided or not by cultural and class origins, whether socially distanced and isolated from each other as well as other workers, demonstrated that they will take part in militant strikes when required and when conditions make it possible…[T]hey have also found ways of challenging the hierarchical social relations of their workplace, including strikes, leaving their jobs, and working collectively rather than in isolation. (Neal 1994:77, 87)

The stereotype of docile woman continues to flourish despite women actively controlling their work and its organization (Romero 1994).

Westwood (1984) provides a powerful analysis of the dual layers of oppression women face at home and in the external labour market, and the nature of racialized women's oppression in each of these spheres. Westwood (1984:230) stresses the importance of racialized and non-racialized women in analyses of professions and occupations:

> I have emphasized throughout this book that, in looking at the texture of women's lives across racial and cultural boundaries, it is important to hold both similarity and difference in one's mind's eye. Only in this way can we hope to grasp the contradictions which mark women's lives, giving rise to strength and sisterhood alongside weakness and division.

She considers commonalities and differences between and within divergent groups of women and their work as opposed to universalizing their experiences.

Westwood (1984) wove together ideas of patriarchy, capitalist economic systems, and resistance in both the home and the external workplace. She also considers the relationship between the variables to provide various levels of meaning to the experience of work. Moreover, she detailed how processes of reinforcement and marginalization function in her presentation of how women attempt to domesticate their workplace through the wearing of slippers, the production of personal aprons, and the decorating of their workspaces:

> The problem with the insertion of the culture of femininity was that it was collusive. It reinforced a definition of woman that was securely tied to do-

mesticity and, more than that, to domestic labour in the home. (Westwood 1984:22)

According to Westwood (1984), this process serves to reinforce the marginalization of women's work in the workplace. It also diminishes the value of women's work in the home through its association with marginalized socially reproductive labour and the related devalued skill set. It also substantiates a gendered division of labour both inside and outside of the home. It perpetuates the gendered social construction of a culture of women as mothers and nurturers without any "real" interest in working outside the home or entering into traditional professions and occupations that are considered to be "men's work." "Cultures in this sense are bound to a common-sense understanding of the world through what we now call practical ideologies" (Westwood 1984:89). Much of the gendered and/or racialized division of labour can be traced to such tacit types of knowing.

In spite of the many problems inherent to differentiating the experiences of racialiized and non-racialized women, Westwood focuses throughout the text on the idea of struggle and the potential for social change:

> Despite the ideological and economic climate which seeks to marginalize black struggles, women's issues and socialist alternatives, there are indeed powerful contradictory forces at work…[W]hat is clear is that both the black struggle and feminism have given a new impetus to politics…which has meant that now at least race and gender issues are on the agenda—for some of us. (Westwood 1984:241)

The organization of this struggle is increasingly complex given the evolution of globalization and changing patterns of immigration, and evident in the lives and experiences of divergent groups of professionals (Westwood 1984).

In her text, *Racism and Paid Work*, Das Gupta examines racism in the external labour force through a Marxist perspective tempered with an anti-racist, feminist approach:

> As industrial capitalism developed, the drive to increase profits and thus future investments led entrepreneurs and managers to seek out "cheaper" forms of labour. As mentioned, the ideology of racism has, in post-slavery and post-colonial days, still resulted in the over-representation of Black workers and workers of colour in the least desirable, least secure, poorest paid segments of the workforce. Simultaneously, they have been excluded from better paid, secure, more desirable jobs through systemic practices in the labour market and in other related institutions, such as the educational system. (Das Gupta 1996:14-15)

Much of the segregation that can be found in the racial division of labour, professions, occupations, and education is rooted in what this discussion repeatedly refers to as "common-sense" notions of difference that are underpinned by the dominant ideological climate.

These forms of racist praxis have become institutionalized and are supported by those same structures they have put into place (Das Gupta 1996). The effect of this on labour is clear. "The labour of people of colour and of Black people is assumed to be 'natural', 'unskilled', and therefore inferior similar to the evaluation of women's labour" (Das Gupta 1996:15). This means that racialized women's work is exponentially more devalued and negated through the interaction of race and gender. It is not my intention to imply an additive model here. Rather, I allude to a model that is considerably more complex than one that considers only race or gender.

Another important facet of Das Gupta's (1996) work is her assertion that we should be wary of making the mistake of "collapsing race into class" (p.15). In other words, we cannot universally assume that all equity-seeking groups belong to a lower class simply because of their minority status. "Even though there is a close connection between the two sets of relations, there are anomalies and they each have autonomous dynamics" (p.15). But this is not to say that members of equity-seeking groups who are members of "higher" classes do not suffer from social and employment inequities (Das Gupta 1996). Accordingly, Das Gupta discusses ideas of tokenism, scapegoating, targeting, excessive monitoring, bias in work allocation, infantalization, lack of accommodation, and underemployment.

Ruth Frankenberg (1993, 1997) offers a unique perspective by considering Caucasian as a race. Regardless of the privileged position of whiteness, it is a race and must be contextualized accordingly. This combination of privilege and classification means that whiteness must be positioned as both racializing and racialized.

But, this vital point of interaction is often left out of analyses of women and their work in favour of a universal vision of "woman as worker" as I have mentioned many times previously. However, it is not only theorists who make this error. Frankenberg (1993) perceptively points out that often, white women simply think *through* race, thus negating the issue. That is to say, they generally do not directly, or at all, engage in a significant level of analysis of race-related issues, and instead remain "oblivious" to the problematic nature of the concept (1993, 1997):

> For many white people in the United States, including a good number of the women I interviewed, "color-blindness"—a mode of thinking about race organized around an effort to not "see," or at any rate not to acknowledge, race differences—continues to be the "polite" language of race. (Frankenberg 1997:142)

This selective, and more importantly evasive, process of colour-blindness appears benign on the surface. In fact, it ignores the underlying power structures and the ideologically rooted hierarchies that reinforce and perpetuate norms and expectations surrounding race. Frankenberg's work here is relational in the Mannheimian sense in that it emphasizes the necessity of contextualizing knowledge.

Race has a social geography. This implies both a physical and a social context which fosters our conception of race as a social construction:

> Moreover, racism emerges not only as an ideology or political orientation chosen or rejected at will but also as a system of material relationships with a set of ideas linked to and embedded in those material relations. (Frankenberg 1997:70)

Race and racism are dynamic and fluid concepts that are in a constant state of flux in a socially constructed set of circumstances that must be included in any effective analysis of women in any context. Further, these experiences cannot be universalized and presented in a reductionist manner.

Frankenberg (1993) describes a socialization process for white women that involves the development of a "common sense" conceptual framework surrounding race that occurs as a result of the interaction of experience and interpretation. The perceived "naturalness" of this process leads many women, racialized and non-racialized, to rethink their past experiences and to reconcile them with the predominant belief system/ideology of their society. "[W]omen frequently reinterpreted their material landscapes over time, in effect remaking their experiences and seeing them, as it were, through new eyes" (p.137). As the norms associated with whiteness have been so broadly applied and normalized, whiteness has become a vague and ill-defined cultural space. The obtuse nature of whiteness and the scope of the ideological umbrella that supports and shelters it has left the idea of whiteness an unwieldy element for investigation and positioned it as a sometimes insidious cultural phenomenon (Frankenberg 1997).

Hill Collins (1990) discusses how this process works to shape the consciousness of Black women in dual ways. It shapes the image of self that Black women share with the outside world as it also influences the development of their internalized self-image.

Hill Collins is theoretically rooted in the political economy tradition that emphasizes the struggles and conflicts Blacks have faced in developing and disseminating their perspectives and worldviews. To this end, she provides an historical analysis of Black women's literary contributions. This is utilized to construct a history of the development of Black feminist thought which is described on both the macro and micro levels as oppressed. "While essential to the survival of African-Americans, the knowledge produced in Black communities was hidden from and suppressed by the dominant group and thus remained extant but subjugated" (Collins 1990:10). This subjugation of the life experiences of racialized persons must be redressed in order to facilitate fully applicable and reliable considerations of professions and occupations.

How do these conflicts play out? Black women observe Caucasian ideologies and master them while simultaneously developing their own sense of self that is often obscured from the view of dominant white culture:

> Black women intellectuals have long explored this private, hidden space of Black women's consciousness, the "inside" ideas that allow Black women to cope with and, in most cases, transcend the confines of race, class, and gender oppression. (Collins 1990:92-93)

This process includes elements of assimilation and antagonism. "Behind the mask of behavioral conformity imposed on African-American women, acts of resistance, both organized and anonymous, have long existed" (p.91). This mastery of Caucasian ideologies coupled with the simultaneous development of a clearly defined Black women's worldview has been "essential to Black women's survival" (p.93). The complex and conflicting nature of this dialectical process is self-evident as the external cultural identity of Black women is greatly determined by being female and a visible minority.

Hill Collins states that Black women are well-aware of their marginalized position in a culture that is dominated by Caucasian-based ideology. This awareness allows them to work within and outside of the system to develop and maintain a strong sense of self-worth. The resistance that accompanies this awareness can be located on a continuum of social action which ranges from "apparently" inactive silence to overt political acts (Hill Collins 1990; Giles and Arat-Koç 1994).

However, Hill Collins might overstate this level of awareness. Her approach here is clearly Marxist and consequently somewhat deterministic. Some parts of her work fall prey to the universalizing elements that are visible in the work of Marx. She describes Black women as sharing a collective consciousness and *relentlessly* working towards a more equitable social hierarchy. While Black women are most likely aware of their social location, and many are working for a more inclusive society, it is probably not quite as clearly defined and directly motivated as Hill Collins describes it.

Nevertheless, her presentation is lucid, inclusive, and most of all compelling. Of particular importance is her powerful consideration of Black women's experiences with work inside and outside of the home. Hill Collins discuses how several elements intersect in a pivotal confluence of events that serves to dramatically influence Black women's experiences of work. The metaphor she employs to describe this experience is dramatic and insightful:

> One core theme in Black feminist thought consists of analyzing Black women's work, especially Black women's labor market victimization as "mules". As dehumanized objects, mules are living machines and can be treated as part of the scenery. Fully human women are less easily exploited. (Hill Collins 1990:43)

Her analogy of the Black woman as "mule" applies to the labour market outside and inside the home. Conceptions of race, class, gender, and work all intersect with conceptions and expectations of family and contribute to an "overarching political economy of domination" that surrounds the life experiences of Black women and the social construction of visible minority status (Hill Collins 1990:45).

Conclusion

> *Work may be a mere source of livelihood, or the most significant part of one's inner life; it may be experienced as expiation, or as exuberant expression of self; as bounden duty, or as the development of man's universal nature. Neither love nor hatred of work is inherent in man, or inherent in any given line of work. For work has no intrinsic meaning (sic).* (Mills 1951:215)

Despite the sex/gender-biased language, Mills clearly indicates that the meaning of work is a socially constructed phenomenon, and that this meaning can vary widely based on myriad factors. Throughout this chapter, we have alluded to these ideas and to how the intersections of gender and race might result in different experiences with, and perspectives on, professions and occupations and work both in the home and in the external labour market. This opens the door to many emerging and crucial questions:

- The research shows that there is a significant disparity between what people describe as a substantial increase in the equitable division of socially reproductive labour in their lives and households and the *actuality* of the division of this type of labour (Pupo 1997; Hochschild 1989). How does this affect experiences of work? What impact does this have on opportunities in the labour market? In particular, what does this perception of equity do to "real" versus "perceived" opportunities for the equity-seeking groups who carry most of the burden of socially reproductive labour? Why has this idea of equity been so widely reinforced and accepted despite the plethora of evidence to the contrary? For example, in the external labour market earn approximately two-thirds of what men in Canada earn when all wage earners are considered (Statscan 2004).

- Why do clearly demarcated divisions of race and gender in professions and occupations persist despite people recognizing the existence of segregation and the inappropriateness of these phenomena? How can we encourage society to "see race," instead of "seeing through it" (Frankenberg 1993, 1997)? Would this consideration be enough to help rectify the problematic nature of accommodating race? What policy measures can be taken both provincially and federally to ensure work and pay equity while also ensuring minimal negative repercussions on equity-seeking groups and dominant groups? Should these policy measures include a novel approach to child and elder care? What other concerns might be effectively addressed through policy implementation? When these policies do include measures that address the inequities inherent to our division of socially reproductive labour, why are they so often defeated or amended until they lose most or all of their potency and effectiveness and have minimal positive impact on professions and occupations, if any?

- As many good jobs deteriorate into bad jobs and many other jobs are eliminated, reduced to part-time, or contracted out to individuals or temporary employment agencies through down-sizing, corporate migration, and the various incarnations of scientific management, what must be done to overcome the further marginalization of equity-seeking groups into professions and occupations featuring the lowest levels of job quality (Duffy 1997; Duffy et al. 1997; Vosko 2000)? What can be done to ensure the financial maintenance of the family in a globalized economy that reduces health, safety, educational, and environmental standards to the lowest common denominator?
- What are the functions of racism and sexism in the capitalist system? These divisions have persisted for so long, that they must be described as functional on some level to someone regardless of their problematic nature and the lack of foundation for these practices. Is it merely to ensure the availability of a cheap and convenient pool of reserve labour and to perpetuate the powerlessness necessary to keeping the labour force submissive and docile? This system of repression is based in ideas and conceptions of what is "normal," "natural," "obvious," and "important" in white "malestream" society. Differences between races and genders are assumed to be "normal" and they become (dys)functional in that respect. How can this be overcome? Who sets these definitions, norms and boundaries? What is their motivation?

An inter-disciplinary approach has been utilized in this discussion in order to address these questions and also to avoid the problem of developing or contributing to an impractical body of idealized and universal knowledge. Alone, a Marxist, anti-racist or feminist approach would be inadequate. These three perspectives work in concert with one another in order to provide a more accurate picture of work life and professions and occupations in Canada. We can work across and within these disciplinary confines and boundaries in order to challenge the weaknesses and exploit the strengths of each approach. I hope that this discussion shows that this is not only acceptable, but necessary to the development of valid and reliable research on professions and occupations.

References

Anderson, Bridget. 2000. *Doing the Dirty Work?: The Global Politics of Domestic Labour.* London: Zed Books.

Armstrong, Pat and Hugh Armstrong. 1978. *The Double Ghetto: Canadian Women and Their Segregated Work.* Canada: McClelland and Stewart Limited.

_____. 1990. *Theorizing Women's Work.* Toronto: Garamond Press.

Barndt, Deborah. 2002. *Tangled Routes: Women, Work, and Globalization on the Tomato Trail.* Aurora: Garamond Press.

Baxandall, Rosalyn, Elizabeth Ewen, and Linda Gordon. 1976. "The Working Class has Two Sexes." *Monthly Review: Technology, the Labor Process, and the Working Class* 28(3):1-9.

Braverman, Harry. 1998. *Labor and Monopoly Capital: The Degradation of Work in the Twentieth Century.* New York: Monthly Review Press.

Cockburn, Cynthia. 1983. *Brothers: Male Dominance and Technological Change.* London: Pluto Press.

_____. 1991. *In the Way of Women: Men's Resistance to Sex Equality in Organizations.* Basingstoke: Macmillan.

Das Gupta, Tania. 1996. *Racism and Paid Work.* Toronto: Garamond Press.

Duffy, Ann. 1997. "The Part-Time Solution: Toward Entrapment or Empowerment?" Pp. 166-188 in *Good Jobs, Bad Jobs, No Jobs: The Transformation of Work in the 21st Century,* edited by Ann Duffy, Daniel Glenday, and Norene Pupo. Toronto: Harcourt Canada.

Duffy, Ann, Daniel Glenday, and Norene Pupo, eds. 1997. *Good Jobs, Bad Jobs, No Jobs: The Transformation of Work in the 21st Century.* Toronto: Harcourt Canada.

Durkheim, Emile. 1933. *The Division of Labor in Society.* Translated by George Simpson. New York: The Free Press.

Edwards, Richard. 1979. *Contested Terrain: The Transformation of the Workplace in the Twentieth Century.* New York: Basic Books.

Fox, Bonnie J. 1989. "The Feminist Challenge: A Reconsideration of Social Inequality and Economic Development." Pp. 120-167 in *From Culture to Power: The Sociology of English Canada,* edited by Robert J. Brym and Bonnie J. Fox. Toronto: Oxford University Press.

Frankenberg, Ruth. 1993. *White Women, Race Matters: The Social Construction of Whiteness.* Minneapolis: University of Minnesota Press.

_____. 1997. *Displacing Whiteness: Essays in Social and Cultural Criticism.* Durham: Duke University Press.

Giddens, Anthony. 1972. *Politics and Sociology in the Thought of Max Weber.* London: Macmillan.

Giles, Wenona and Sedef Arat-Koç. 1994. *Maid in the Market: Women's Paid Domestic Labour.* Halifax: Fernwood Publishing.

Hill Collins, Patricia. 1990. *Black Feminist Thought: Knowledge, Consciousness, and the Politics of Empowerment.* New York: Routledge.

Hochschild, Arlie Russell. 1989. *The Second Shift.* New York: HarperCollins Publishers.

Honderich, Ted, ed. 1995. *The Oxford Companion to Philosophy.* Oxford: Oxford University Press.

Jacobs, Merle, ed. 2002. *Is Anyone Listening?: Women, Work, and Society.* Toronto: Women's Press.

Krahn, Harvey J. and Graham S. Lowe. 2002. *Work, Industry & Canadian Society.* Canada: Thomson Nelson.

Lowe, Graham S. 2000. *The Quality of Work: A People-Centered Agenda.* Don Mills: Oxford University Press.

Luxton, Meg, Harriet Rosenberg, and Sedef Arat-Koç. 1990. *Through the Kitchen Window: The Politics of Home and Family.* Toronto: Garamond Press.

McDermott, Patricia C. 1994. "Domestic Labour in the Retail Sector: Department Store Work." Pp. 113-128 in *Maid in the Market: Women's Paid Domestic Labour,* edited by Wenona Giles and Sedef Arat-Koç. Halifax: Fernwood Publishing.

Macklin, Audrey. 1994. "On the Inside Looking In: Foreign Domestic Workers in Canada." Pp. 13-39 in *Maid in the Market: Women's Paid Domestic Labour,* edited by Wenona Giles and Sedef Arat-Koç. Halifax: Fernwood Publishing.

Mannheim, Karl. 1936. *Ideology and Utopia: An Introduction to the Sociology of Knowledge.* San Diego: Harcourt, Inc.

Marx, Karl. [1867] 1990. *Capital: Volume 1.* Translated by Ben Fowkes. London: Penguin Books, Ltd.

Marx, Karl and Friedrich Engels. [1872] 1985. *The Communist Manifesto.* London: Penguin Books Ltd.

Milkman, Ruth. 1987. *Gender at Work: The Dynamics of Job Segregation by Sex During World War II.* Urbana: University of Illinois Press.

Mills, C. Wright. 1951. *White Collar: The American Middle Classes.* New York: Oxford University Press.

Nakano Glenn, Evelyn. 1996. "From Servitude to Service Work: Historical Continuities in the Racial Division of Paid Reproductive Labor." Pp. 115-156 in

Working in the Service Society, edited by Cameron Lynne MacDonald and Carmen Sirianni. Philadelphia: Temple University Press.

Neal, Rusty. 1994. "Public Homes: Subcontracting and the Experience of Cleaning." Pp. 65-79 in *Maid in the Market: Women's Paid Domestic Labour*, edited by Wenona Giles and Sedef Arat-Koç. Halifax: Fernwood Publishing.

Neugebauer, Robynne. 2002. "Marginal Women: Examining the Barriers of Age, Race and Ethnicity." Pp. 271-291 in *Is Anyone Listening?: Women, Work, and Society*, edited by Merle Jacobs. Toronto: Women's Press.

Parr, Joy. 1990. *The Gender of Breadwinners: Women, Men, and Change in Two Industrial Towns, 1880-1950*. Toronto: University of Toronto Press.

Preston, Valerie and Guida Man. 1999. "Employment Experiences of Chinese Immigrant Women: An Exploration of Diversity." *Canadian Woman Studies* 19(3):115-122.

Pupo, Norene. 1997. "Always Working, Never Done: The Expansion of the Double Day." Pp. 144-165 in *Good Jobs, Bad Jobs, No Jobs: The Transformation of Work in the 21st Century*, edited by Ann Duffy, Daniel Glenday, and Norene Pupo. Toronto: Harcourt Canada.

Reiter, Ester. 1991. *Making Fast Food: From the Frying Pan into the Fryer*. Montréal: McGill-Queen's University Press.

Rinehart, James W. 2001. *The Tyranny of Work: Alienation and the Labour Process*. Toronto: Harcourt Canada.

Romero, Mary. 1994. "Chicanas and the Changing Work Experience in Domestic Service." Pp. 40-55 in *Maid in the Market: Women's Paid Domestic Labour*, edited by Wenona Giles and Sedef Arat-Koç. Halifax: Fernwood Publishing.

Statscan. 2004. Retrieved May 3, 2004 (http://www.statcan.ca/english/Pgdb/labor01a.htm).

Taylor, A.J.P. [1967]1985. "Introduction." Pp. 7-47 in *The Communist Manifesto*, written by Karl Marx and Friedrich Engels. London: Penguin Books Ltd.

Vosko, Leah F. 2000. *Temporary Work: The Gendered Rise of a Precarious Employment Relationship*. Toronto: University of Toronto Press.

Weber, Max. 1958. *The Protestant Ethic and the Spirit of Capitalism*. Translated by Talcott Parsons. New York: Charles Scribner's Sons.

Westwood, Sallie. 1984. *All Day, Every Day: Factory and Family in the Making of Women's Lives*. Urbana: University of Illinois Press.

Williams, Raymond. 1987. *Culture and Society: Coleridge to Orwell*. London: Hogarth.

Yancy, George, ed. 2004. *What White Looks Like: African-American Philosophers on the Whiteness Question*. New York: Routledge.

Chapter 2

A Structural Functional Approach to the Study of Work and Professions

Timothy P. McCauley

Learning Objectives:

1. Learn about the evolution of the structural functionalist approach to the study of professions.

2. Describe the symbolic interactionist perspective on work and professions, and how it differs from the functionalist approach.

3. Consider the Marxist approach to professions and work, and describe where professionals fit into this perspective.

4. Note the importance of feminist theory in considerations of work and professions, and describe the primary objective of feminist theorists.

The theoretical foundations for researching the sociology of professions and work have undergone major shifts over the last sixty years. While structural functional orthodoxy dominated in the mid-twentieth century, a new focus emerged towards the end of the century, which was more inclusive, dynamic, and action-oriented. Radical social change through the late 1960s and early 1970s produced a more critical emphasis developed through the use of neo-Weberian concepts such as "iron-cage," "social closure," Marxist notions of social control, and postmodernist terms including "discourse" and "diversity." These approaches tended to be more inclusive, dynamic, and action-oriented and they enabled sociologists to go beyond the view that occupations and professions were merely "embodiments of the central values of the society" (Macdonald 1995:xi). Consequently, contemporary theories view work and professions as "emergent phenomena" comprised of "action-oriented groups" involved in a "bid for monopoly will" (p.xii). This chapter will illustrate and critique the various paradigms in the study of work and professions.

Structural Functionalism

Based on the ideas of Emile Durkheim, structural functionalists provided one of the earliest models in the analysis of work and professions. In *The Division of Labour in Society*, Durkheim showed that modern society produces a functional division of labour where workers are integrated into an overall system characterized by organic solidarity. It was from his model of a functional economy and society that Durkheim developed his analysis of the professions and raised concerns about unhealthy solidarity and anomie produced by complex divisions of labour (Durkheim [1893]1957). He maintained that anomie and increased individualism threatened social solidarity and led to an unhealthy social order. According to Watson (2003), "the particular form of anomie Durkheim worried about was one in which the 'organic integration' of society would be threatened by unrestricted individual aspirations and hence a lack of social discipline, principles or guiding norms" (p.28). Thus, Durkheim's analysis of anomie and his concerns about social solidarity and integration provided a key theoretical foundation for viewing work and professions as integral elements of the social organism.

Expanding on Durkheim's notion, functionalist scholars of the mid-twentieth century, including Elton Mayo (1949), utilized the anomie concept to show that the managerial elite of any industrial enterprise must serve as functional agents of expanding industries. Mayo (1949) believed that a modern and progressive industrial order operates more efficiently when it guards itself against anomie. Mayo thus proposed that industries should establish moral communities within all economic enterprises, and that among all occupational and professional groups, a healthy individualism must be balanced against collective interests. As such, professionals and managerial elites are vital social groupings that must work together with other occupations in the social hierarchy to ensure a functional economic order.

Although Durkheim's sympathies were not with elites, the ideas of Mayo expanded upon Durkheim's basic premise to show that professionals and elites must cooperate with other workers to achieve a harmonious, functional, and balanced economic industrial enterprise (Watson 2003:51). In addition, to achieve this balance, elite and professional groups must use managerial skills and communications to promote group affiliations with lesser occupations as they strive for worker satisfaction. Thus, consistent with Durkheim, Mayo's functionalist view aimed to show that integrated work and professional activity was required in order to avoid social breakdown and industrial conflict.

Moreover, within his famous work entitled, "Professional Ethics and Civic Morals" Durkheim showed that the professions are functional social forces which provide professionals a role as "intermediaries between individuals and the state" (Macdonald 1995:2). In other words, professionals possess the capacity to promote relationships between individual entrepreneurs and nation states throughout the world because they are unbound to national economies. Consequently, for Durkheim, the professions operate as "morally inspired reaction to the disintegrating effects of the egoism and self interest" (Watson 2003:51).

Clearly then, Durkheim's framework focused upon institutions and the role of professions in contributing to the moral health of the social order. Within this framework, professions are viewed as providing regulatory functions for modern society. Professions are viewed as upper-level occupations that are sufficiently inclusive so as to ensure their functioning, while at the same time contributing to an interconnectedness of the larger society. He argued that within and among professions, "a body of rules is…assumed by spontaneously established relations…sufficient in contact and sufficiently extensive" (Johnson 1972:184). Durkheim believed that the professions contribute to society's collective health and serve to integrate structurally differentiated societies (Lynn 1963). Consequently, it was from the Durkheimian model that numerous functional analyses arose in the mid-twentieth century. For example, Carr-Saunders and Wilson (1933) claimed in 1933, "the great professions stand like rocks against waves against…crude forces which threaten steady and peaceful evolution" (Johnson 1972:2).

Despite the limited, but descriptive, critical analyses provided by mid-twentieth century functionalists, they did provide useful analyses of the roles, structures, and statuses of professions in complex societies. Parsons (1939), for example, used Durkheim's notions to generate his concept of the social system, and from this foundation he sought to show how members of various professions provided a "collective orientation" in which their overall interconnectedness with the social structure generated a common set of beliefs and values in support of the existing social order.

Moreover, Marshall (1963) supplemented Parsons' assertion, by illustrating how professions emphasize socially functional traits such as altruism.

Marshall (1963) believed that professions contribute to a functional society through their concern for others in the culture. From Marshall's foundation, Goode (1957), Etzioni (1969), and Hickson and Thomas (1969) generated a continuum of status categories to classify and identify the professions in relation to other occupational groups of the social hierarchy. Etzioni (1969), for example, classified occupational groups in terms of "professional," "nonprofessional," and "semi-professional." Hickson and Thomas (1969) utilized a Guttman (1950) scale of professionalism on a continuum of "postulated dimensions of professionalism among a variety of occupational categories" (Thomas 1969:46). Thus, research into patterns and processes of professions from the functionalist paradigm is essentially an exploration into the ways in which professionals solidify a structurally differentiated society.

To further illustrate the functionalist foundation to the study of professions, it is helpful to generate critical analysis of Parsons' model that illustrates how professions are integral elements of highly differentiated capitalistic societies. In the Parsonsian model there is an acceptance of an earlier view by Marshal that professions can be distinguished from other occupations by their "altruistic concern for the common good and for service" (Johnson 1972:13). For Parsons, professions are instrumental in modern industrial societies in that they serve through their "collective orientation rather than self orientation" (Johnson 1972:13). But, in essence, the ideas of Parsons, which predominated academic sociology from the 1930s to the 1970s, deflected theoretical attention away from issues of class, power, and domination through "taking American liberalism at face value" (Johnson 1972:79). Parsons' functionalism was highly in favour of the industrial system emerging through the mid-twentieth century.

The Parsonsian optimism about the professional notions of achievement over ascription, egalitarianism over tradition, and occupation over property painted a naïve picture of the promises of the modern world. Parsons' analysis of professions generated an essentially white middle-class view of society under the guise of science and research. Accordingly, Parsons emphasized the integrative functions of society, and the importance of all social institutions for socialization. He ignored the role of the State in maintaining bourgeois hegemony. He essentially adopted the view of American elites similar to that espoused by former U.S. presidents Jefferson and Madison, and he purposely ignored more critical analyses of the social system (Rossides 1998). Parsons essentially maintained a misplaced faith in the non-political aspects of society and he favoured the notions of harmony, equilibrium, and adaptation. Like the American forefathers Jefferson and Madison, he denied the political role of the State as an oppressive one which served to disguise awareness of how the State was used extensively by elites to maintain hegemonic status. Thus,

Parsons' functional view of professions illustrates that even the most scientific and apparently objective analysis provided by a "detached" social scientist, can indirectly serve to legitimate the status quo opposition to dialectical thought and open discourse.

Moving beyond Parsons' classical structural functional approach to professions, contemporaries such as Goode (1957) adopted a more dynamic emphasis and explored the extent to which professions are a community within a community. Goode (1957) maintained that, "a profession is a community without physical locus and, like other communities with heavy in-migration, one whose founding fathers are linked only rarely by blood with the present generation" (p.194). Some of the ways in which professions resembled communities for Goode included "a sense of identity; continuing status; definite roles understood only by internal members; boundaries not physical or geographical but social; and socialization for new members" (p.195). Socialization, for example, was a key method utilized by the professional community for social control of its members. Goode (1957) contended that:

> Socialization and social control in the professions are made important by the peculiarly exploitative opportunities the professions enjoy. The problems brought to the professional are usually those the client cannot solve, and only the professional can solve. The client does not choose the professional by a measurable criterion of competence, and after the work is done, the client is not competent to judge if the work is done properly. (P.196)

Thus, for Goode a profession was like a community. Professional members were socialized into a professional community, fully conscious of symbols, power structures, and the elements of social control within and beyond the community itself. The professional community sought to maintain its integrity vis-à-vis the client, by utilizing working codes of ethics that were internally enforced, but subject to the scrutiny of the larger social order. It was through this internal policing of the professions that they achieved a community which was understood and recognized by the professionals, their clients, and by members of the larger society.

The Symbolic Interactionist Perspective

Symbolic interactionism, as a general paradigm in sociology, moves beyond descriptive categories and is concerned with the social construction of reality on the day to day micro-sociological level of understanding. Interactionists who examine work and professions begin from the point of view of "individual workers, the small group and on meanings" (Watson 2003:34). The foundation of the approach derives from the work of famous Chicago School Sociologists Cooley (1902), Mead (1934), and

Park and Burgess (1921) who believe that behaviour and communication derives from words, gestures, clothing, and other symbols that provide individuals with shared understanding of the roles and expectations of the culture (Watson 2003:21).

Moreover, in the context of work and professions, interactionists suggest that it is important to observe members' activities through the codes they utilize for acting out the social drama of work. For example, sociologists of the Chicago School were famous for looking not only at functional occupations, but also at the "nuts and sluts" of the occupational hierarchy (Watson 2003:35). Prostitutes, slum-dwellers, and drug-dealers were all occupations or professions of interest to the group of scholars most associated with the symbolic interactionist paradigm. Within this model, every occupation or profession contains patterned processes "whereby different groups make use of rules, procedures and information in the day to day negotiations that occur between them about what is to happen in any given situation at any particular time" (p.34).

The study by Abbott (1988) is a good example of an interactionist approach in the way it illuminates how professions are interactive communities' working towards professionalism. Abbott's work is clearly a product of the Chicago School in the way it attempts to understand professions as a system with both formal and informal social structures. He argues that professions are corporate groupings with mobility projects aimed at the control of work. Abbott's findings indicate that the overriding dynamic of professions is an obsession with competition and misguided monopolization. Thus, Abbott (1963) essentially observed what Hughes labeled the "professional project" from a symbolic interactionist stance. Essentially, one must ask the question, "what are the circumstances in which people in an occupation attempt to turn it into a profession and themselves into professional people?" The answer to the question can only be interpreted through the symbolic interactionist framework.

Throughout the 1970s, the functionalist and interactionist approaches to the study of professions were each called into question by sociologists who sought an even more open-ended, critical and constructionist approach to research. As a result, unique forms of theoretical discussion began to emerge from critical neo-Weberians, Marxists, post-modernists, and feminists. These scholars sought to explore the dynamics of professions in terms of unique patterns and processes from the micro-level perspectives of individuals, groups, classes, and genders. For instance, by 1970, even functionalists such as Merton (1957) pointed out the limitations of his own approach taken in 1947, when by 1957, he noted that it was not enough to show how certain professions function and interact within themselves for the stabilization of the over-arching social order. It is also important to be aware of how certain professions "come to be indoctrinated with an ethical sense of limited responsibility" (p.80). As a result of Merton's self-criticism, many other sociologists began to generate a more critical view of both work and professions, including those theorists who work within the neo-Weberian tradition.

The Neo-Weberian Approach

The neo-Weberian approach to work and professions shares many similarities to the interactionist view, but with the inclusion of larger concerns for "historic change and economic and political conflicts" (Watson 2003:37). In essence, Weber defined sociology as "the study of social action," whereby individuals orient themselves to meaningful behaviour based upon ideas and values of the "legitimate" social order (p.38). Consequently, the neo-Weberian perspective takes into account the meaningful action of the individual and larger historical, social processes.

Within various occupations and professions in modern capitalistic economies, individuals are motivated increasingly to the "rational pursuit of profit coordinated through bureaucratic means" (p.46). For example, Goldthorpe et al. (1969), utilizing Weber's model, showed how factory workers develop an "orientation to work…which links actions in the workplace and the external community and cultural life of employees" (p.87). Goldthorpe et al. essentially re-worked Weber's model made famous in *The Protestant Ethic and the Spirit of Capitalism*, that showed how the unintended consequence of the ideas of Calvin and Luther fostered a "spirit of capitalism" and an increasingly rationalistic view of the world. Goldthorpe et al.'s notion of an orientation to work derived from Weber was used to show that individuals in either occupations or professions generate meanings which they take into their workplaces and situations. Moreover, it is through this orientation that individuals develop the ability to function in an increasingly rationalized workplace setting in meaningful ways.

Unlike a Marxist approach, Goldthorpe et al. place less emphasis upon class conflict between workers in the system, and focus more directly upon how individual workers form status groupings and utilize social closure against other status groups in the workplace. In other words, for the neo-Weberian scholar of occupations and professions, it is the ideas and values of individuals and groups at all levels of the economic order that are the ethos for meaningful economic activity for individuals at every level of the occupational hierarchy.

C.W. Mills (1953), for example, drew upon Weber's concepts of closure and bureaucracy to show that in highly complex cultures, individuals who were afforded/earned professional status created closure around themselves within bureaucratic agencies. He showed that as professions become increasingly absorbed by administrative details, standardization and routine, they essentially produce closure around themselves and other status categories within an economic structure. He states that:

> As the old professions and the new skills have become involved in new middle class conditions, professional men and women have become dependent upon the new technical machinery and upon the great institutions within whose routines the machines are located. (P.114)

In other words, Mills argued that the internal "ethos" of the professions was increasingly enclosed and bureaucratic. The professionals were merely elements of the "iron cage of rationality" imprisoning all status groups.

In addition, like Weber, Mills raised concerns about the limitations of knowledge produced by specific professional categories. Mills was one of the first scholars to note that the knowledge produced by professional communities is suspect "because it is generated by selectivity" (Rossides 1998:20). The IQ test, for example, is a perfect illustration of how the psychological and educational communities are able to both create closure and exert power over groups and individuals. Despite claims of standardization and objectivity in determining IQ, the test is clearly linked to social activities including educational streaming and social power (Burrage and Torenstahl 1990:38). Thus, Mills' framework falls within the neo-Weberian tradition by its exploration of the processes by which professional status groups create closure around their knowledge systems. Ultimately, Mills argued that to avoid the iron cage of rationality each profession must grow more open to the scrutiny of the larger social community.

Neo-Weberian scholars who focus upon work and professions can be distinguished by two levels of analysis. The first level of analysis identifies the characteristics of a profession versus a non-profession. The second level of consideration isolates variables and processes associated with professions as a status category (Weber 1978). At both levels, Weberian concepts associated with his theory of social closure are often utilized to evaluate how occupations and professions define themselves as status groupings within the occupational hierarchy. Barber (1963), for example, utilizes the terms "style of life," "corporate solidarity" and "socialization processes" to show that professions are both unique and similar to other occupational groups. In this view, professionals are *not* "the differentia specifica," (special categories in themselves) and a consensus among sociologists as to what constitutes a profession is achieved (Jackson 1970:24).

Barber (1963) suggests that this is particularly the case "if one extracts from the most commonly cited definitions all the items which characterize a profession… a commendable unanimity is disclosed: there are no contradictions and the only differences are those of omission" (p.25). Barber has worked along with others within this paradigm to firmly construct the meaning of a professional as opposed to other occupational categories. For example, he isolates four attributes of a profession including, "a high degree of generalized and systematic knowledge; primary orientation to the community interest rather than to individual self-interest; a high degree of self control of behaviour through codes of ethics internalized in the process of work socialization; and a system of reward" (Esland and Salaman 1980:341).

Generally, the approaches of structural functionalists, interactionists, and neo-Weberians found in the works of Durkheim, Parsons, Goode, Weber, Mills, and Barber are politically liberal as opposed to radical in their outlook. The main issues for these scholars centers on the problem of classifying occupations and professions in relation to non-professions and in identifying labour processes of capitalistic societies. Work and professionalism are monetary and honorary processes, primarily characterized by a set of symbols centered upon achievement and a means to some individual self-interest. This type of theorization would be viewed as limited in comparision to Marxist theorists who call for more radical changes.

For Marxist scholars, bourgeois ideologies such as egoism and the self-pursuit of goals are elements of the professional's false consciousness and they exist at the expense of the collective class-consciousness. Thus, a more liberal view of occupations and professions is an attempt to establish and disclose the nature of the status categories, occupations and professions and to locate their functioning within the larger social system. And while it is the case that some liberal scholars did produce a certain degree of critical analyses of work and professions, their analyses fall significantly short of any Marxist theorizing which includes the important action-oriented concepts of "class consciousness," "praxis," and "social transformation."

The Marxist Approach

The Marxist approach is founded upon Karl Marx's (1976) basic premise that human beings are fundamentally producers, and this characteristic carries vital, multi-layered levels of meaning for both the labourer and the owner of the means of production wherein the labourer exchanges their efforts for a wage. To the Marxist, it is through labour that the social world is created. However, through various historically notable modes of production including ancient communal, feudal, and capitalistic, the control of labour/production has fallen increasingly under the control of the ruling/elite classes. Although Marx does not directly examine professions in his writings, he did produce a theory of class conflict that in some instances, situated professions with other occupations as either with or against the bourgeoisie. Burrage and Torstendahl (1990:1) contend that:

> Some of [Marx's] remarks suggest that he thought they would be aligned with the bourgeoisie, at other times [Marx] seemed to think [professionals] should be placed with the proletariat and at still others they were *dritte Peronen*, third parties or by-standers who might side either way.

For Marxists, whichever direction the professionals assume, in the last instance their wage labour contributes to the demise of capitalism.

Marxists maintain that the bringing together of increasingly larger numbers of workers he believed, would create the very contradictions necessary for workers to become aware of their own class-consciousness and to create a classless society that would be known as communism or socialism. A contradiction for the professional might include his notions of powerlessness against the multinational corporations, media, and culture that drives professionals to the endless pursuit of profit from other individuals whom he/she hopes to serve with a sense of selflessness. Thus, ultimately in the works of Marx, even the professional will realize that it is in his/her best interests to transform the system into a more humane, classless reality.

The critical neo-Marxist theory of professions emerged during the 1970s, and utilizes a critical historical approach to professions and professionalism. The key element of this perspective is that it explores the historical development of professions "in the dialectical synthesis of class relations" (Macdonald 1995:23). For example, Johnson (1994) demonstrated that professionalism must be understood in terms of its relationship to the State insofar as the professions were crucially dependent upon State sponsorship for their livelihood. For Johnson, a dialectical relationship exists between the state and the professions whereby professional groups articulate the objectives of the ruling class, which, by virtue of its plurality in modern society, lacks coherence. Johnson then shows that both capitalistic societies and other more totalitarian regimes are characterized by a State apparatus that functions to control professional knowledge. The professions, he argued, are bound up in processes that support existing bourgeois ideology and further entrench existing systems of stratification and domination. For Johnson, the professions function within "the logic of exploitative relations of production" (Macdonald 1995:24). Professionals, in other words, legitimate the hegemonic status of the bourgeoisie through their belief in ideologies such as meritocracy, achievement, and the natural inequalities between individuals in society.

Another theory in the Marxist framework is provided by Haug who generates an interesting account of professionals in relation to capitalistic forces of production. In his analysis, Haug (1973) expresses concern for the social and political events of the late 1960s and 1970s. He suggests that the professionalization of modern capitalistic economies should in fact be viewed as a de-professionalization, and part of a larger socio-historical process known as proletarianization. Further, he contends that the proletarianization of professionalism refers to the notion that as the capitalistic marketplace grows increasingly competitive and monopolistic, the trend among professionals is "away from self employment both for individual professionals and for professions as a whole" (Freidson 1994:135). Haug finds that increasingly, professions are merely functional elements of a bureaucratized workplace which "virtually reduces the status of all workers to the status of proletariat, i.e., dependent on selling their labour in order to survive and stripped of all control over the substance and process of their work" (Haug 1973:213). In other words, the elite status of professions/ professionals is diminishing over time.

At the foundation of Haug's thesis are the positions of Braverman (1974) and Oppenheimer (1973) that suggest the formal definition of working class is a group of individuals who possess nothing but their labour power "to sell to capital in return for subsistence" (Braverman 1974:378). This thesis has been instrumental in illuminating the degree to which professions, despite owning informal methods to influence peers and holding authority over others, are essentially instruments of broader economic and social processes of ruling class domination. In other words, professionals are victims or by-products of Marx's central theory of history. Professionals are simply wage labourers, and their employment, rather than self-employment, is evidence that the forces of production under capitalism have intensified.

Another important element of Johnson's classical Marxist approach to the study of the professions is often referred to as international Marxism. The concern of the international Marxist is to promote research that goes beyond attempts "toward explaining the emergence of professions in a global perspective—which has recently been called the move from naturalism to history" (Jones 1991:vii). It is an approach that often explores the relationship between the professions and global systems of dependency between the "first" and "third" worlds. In contrast to functionalist scholars who focus upon the contribution of professions to global economies, international Marxist analyses attempt to show how professions are able to control their position in economic structures throughout the first and third worlds. Jones (1991) finds that although functional approaches have been useful in the development of practical bourgeois research, functionalism reveals little of how professions operate in particular contexts, subject to the rules and regulations of various State systems.

Ultimately, international Marxists are concerned with how governments in historical Socialist societies including the Soviet Union, China, and Cuba were able to maintain control over professions that pose a danger to party control of these societies. The international Marxist approach can be classified as "cross-national political sociology of profession-state relations in historical perspective" (1991:3). International Marxists call into question traditional studies of professions that focus upon the functions of professions, such as the professional—client relationships, or professions as corporate group actors vis-à-vis the marketplace. This international approach draws attention to the historical relationship between the professions and the State, and other State relationships. The aim of this approach is to evaluate the balances of power between States, markets, and professional groups in various political economies.

In recent studies of professions, Marxist sociologists have become highly critical of modern developments in knowledge building. As part of this concern, there is a growing trend to focus upon how professions are entrenched within larger systems of capitalism and neo-liberalism (Rossides 1998:47). Two notable scholars who work within this paradigm include Freidson and Abbott who argue that the rise of professions and professionalism is not a trans-historical, meritocratic process leading to facts, functions, and progress. Rather, professions are part of a political process of institutionalizing knowledge within state-enforced standards. This critical perspective, labeled the socio-political radical conflict view, combines the concepts of Marx and Foucault. This line of argumentation defines the development of all knowledge as "an arbitrary process…defining their subject matter in narrow artificial terms assuming that other factors are constant and inconsequential" (Rossides 1998:49).

A good illustration of the arbitrary nature of knowledge is evident in the way natural scientists pursue what they assume are frontiers of knowledge, unaware that their priorities are set for them by the corporations and government agencies who supply the funding for their research. Liberal professions, in other words, maintain and work within the status quo and symbolize "the structured nature of ignorance and ineffectiveness of the entire spectrum of disciplines" (Rossides 1998:49). Radical Marxist theories of professions seek to illustrate the fact that professions are not value-free and are perpetuators of bourgeois false consciousness.

Finally, a theory that combines elements of Marxism with Weberian concepts of social closure is evident in the work of Larson. Larson's (1977) conceptualization of the professions is grounded in her notion of the great transformation which saw the coming together of dual processes of modernity, namely, scientific knowledge and the free market. The two processes she argues, illustrate the importance of qualifications and expertise as well as property, in the process of capitalization and income potential. Professionalization is thus a process that attempts to translate scarce resources—special and economic skills—into other social and economic rewards" (Macdonald 1995:9). She believes professions gain their hegemonic status through their association with elites of an earlier period. For example, the elites who contributed to the development of the educational system and ensured that their children were directed to the best schools. This legitimized the professionalization of education (Polanyi 1957).

In her Marxist/Weberian analysis of professions, Larson develops her notion of the professional project (Macdonald 1995). Professions, she maintains, overstate and idealize their scarcity in the social system in an effort to use their occupational role in "the conquest of social status" (Larson 1977:66). Professions, she argues, emphasize a coherent and consistent course of action, control a body of relatively abstract knowledge, and standardize and restrict access to their knowledge as a means to "reinforce the ideological persistence of stratification structures" (p.66). Consequently, Larson generates a unique critical analysis of professions utilizing concepts derived from Marxist notions of stratification combined with Weberian notions of closure and meaningful action. She demonstrates that the politics of professions and the professional are essentially the politics of exclusion, stratification, and status. Each profession develops ideologies and codes of conduct that act as boundaries restricting access to the rewards and privileges associated with the profession.

Post-Modernism and Post-Structuralism

Post-modernism is a unique theoretical position rejecting Western ideas of the enlightenment. It questions the existence of an objective reality and systematic explanations of historical development, progress, and modernization. The post-modernist approach to work and professions places emphasis on human language and the post-structural contention that there is no over-arching, pre-existing reality beyond the text or particular discourse (Watson 2003:47). To the post-modernist, notions of human progress embedded in structural and conflict theories should be abandoned as "the incredulity towards meta-narratives" (p.48).

Consequently, post-modernists believe that when looking at an empirical topic such as work and professions, the individual worker's or professional's reality cannot be understood beyond their own contextual subjectivity. Each occupational/professional subject makes decisions "in the context of social constraints…directed narrowly and in self-disciplined fashion towards actions that give people a 'sense of security and belonging'" (p.49). The average employees' subjectivity, for example, would be constrained by disciplinary mechanisms, surveillance, and knowledge of authority within the workplace.

The post-modernist view emphasizes the fragmented nature of reality, rejecting romanticist beliefs that there are "essentials of the universe" (p.49). In other words, social reality, to the post-modern thinker, is fluid. Reality is in constant motion and subject to interpretation at any given moment. Post-modernists essentially hold that society has moved into a new epoch called post-modernity in which multiple realities exert power over people. As such, there has been a de-centering in which realities must be understood from the context that surrounds individuals.

The post-modernist perspective has been challenged by criticism about its ability to raise important questions about changing societies. Some have called post-modernism, a "fatal distraction," while others argue that the approach is valid, but leads to phenomenological and ethnomethodological forms of research. From the post-modern perspective, emphasis must be placed upon subjectivity and how individuals continually construct social reality as they seek to fit into the constantly evolving social world. The recent emphasis on post-modernism in the study of professions has produced new forms of dynamic, inclusive, and action-oriented research calling into question modernist notions embedded in traditional Weberian and Marxist thinking.

The new forms of research in the areas of linguistics, literary theory, feminism, and critical legal studies have drawn from the ideas of Foucault as opposed to

Marx or Weber. Foucault's post-modern view holds that "knowledge comes from discourse and that there is no method, scientific or otherwise, that yields truth" (Watson 2003:47). In other words, Foucault is in support of the phenomenological notion that traditional epistemology is misguided through its notions of objective truth. Truth is only relative to particular power structures and communities which enforce consensus (Foucault 1980). Foucault's concepts have enabled scholars to view different occupations and professional communities in ways that depart from both structural and power-based conceptions of professions.

Leitch (1991), for example, looks at post-organizational workplaces and sees them as "de-bureaucratized and neo-entrepreneurial, where people rely on social networks across long distances to secure and maintain professional contacts and employment" (p.219). Bureaucracies, Leitch argues, are in many contexts, reconstructed and deconstructed to produce social relationships that are more egalitarian in nature. Further, older bureaucracies produced and perpetuated gender and racial inequalities through their protection and reproduction of elite employees, pension plans, and regular promotions. However, newer post-modern institutions rely upon the recognition of personal competence, or credentialism, which frees people from traditional hierarchies and stereotypes. Newer institutions draw upon what Leitch (1991: 220) terms internal labour markets:

> The growing use of networks and the decline of bureaucracy as an organizing principle in the elite division of labour is the process of eliminating a regular feature of many managerial workplaces; the internal labour markets are orderly job progressions that are accompanied by a progressive development of skill and knowledge.

In this view, workers in the post-modern workplace, both professional and non-professional, must discard modernist notions of bureaucracy, hierarchy, and inequality in order to develop awareness of how different forms of employment are unique discourses which are fluid and socially constructed at every given instance. In the post-modern context, older chains of command and clear systems of accountability are replaced by more fluid and ever-changing entrepreneurial realities. Additionally, for Leitch, while these neo-entrepreneurial workplaces will increase the status of some occupations and professions, they will certainly decrease the positioning of others. Thus, one key theme in the post-modernist approach to the study of work and professions is the examination of the very structures that make differing types and levels of employment possible.

One interesting study that evaluates professions and professionalism from a post-modern perspective is by Roth who combines post-modernist thought with phenomenology and ethnomethodology (Roth 1974). For the ethnomethodologist interested in the post-modern world, organizations of all types are an accomplishment and a negotiated order. Roth uses this approach in his analysis of professions and professional emulators. He argues that those who seek to gain success and emulate professions are dupes. The emulator is a dupe in that they follow systems that are by their nature unfair. Emulators are dupes, as are those scholars who "undertake critical evaluations of others' definitions and analyses" (p.22). They are all dupes, both of managerial programs of deskilling and proletarianizing professional work, and of "working class movements aimed at reducing pay differentials and barriers to entry into professional jobs" (p.27).

Freidson (1983) notes that the term "profession" is in fact a folk concept wherein we must observe the category not as a thing in itself, but as a method through which people establish professions through their attitudes, perceptions and activities. He suggests that rather than sociologists defining professions "by fiat," they would do better to "devote themselves to the study and explication of the way ordinary members 'accomplish' profession independent of sociological definitions" (Freidson 1983:29). Thus, this view critically examines what a profession is phenomenologically. Professionalism is not determined solely by the members of other occupational groups that lead others to respond to them as professional. Rather, there are different perspectives and performances that equally accomplish the status category currently known as "profession." Clearly then, the work of Roth and Freidson illustrates the post-modern notion of a fragmented world of multiple discourses and realities wherein considerations of the social construction of reality on a case-by-case basis is necessary (Dingwall 1982).

The Feminist Approach

Feminist theorizing has a great historical tradition in sociology. There are various branches of feminism including radical, liberal, post-modernist, and anti-racist. All of the various branches, however, are primarily concerned with how human society is patriarchal and gendered, and seek an equal space and commensurate validity for female ways of knowing and knowledge production. Feminists often utilize the various sociological paradigms including structural functional, interactionist, neo-Weberian, Marxist, and post-modernist to develop their analyses of a gendered society.

For instance, Ann Witz (1992) uses Weber's closure theory to develop a feminist critique of professions. She conceptualizes all occupational politics of professions as closure strategies, constructed upon gendered systems of meaning. She argues that not only are working men and women embroiled in a struggle between capital and labour in which men have the advantage, but in addition, men "have access to the resources of class as well as gender privilege" (p.37). She suggests that a theory is needed that "can cope with the fact that 'women' as well as men are engaged in professional projects" (p.37). She further argues that professions are clearly marked by gender exclusion and that "the credentializing process is overlaid by gender exclusion" (p.43).

Professional projects are pursued by legalistic and credentialist tactics and mobilized within the institutional terrain of civil society through the endorsement of the state. The state, in turn, grounds the professional project within the structural parameters of patriarchal capitalism. Furthermore, Witz (1992) grounds this argument through an examination of women who sought a medical education in the modern universities of the late nineteenth century. She asks:

> How were women to mobilise the means of credentialism when the modern university was an exclusive male preserve that admitted only men, was governed by men and used its powers to exclude women? How were women to lobby the state when it was a patriarchal capitalist state to which women had no access, save by proxy male power? (P.67)

In other words, for Witz, the dynamics of professions both in the nineteenth century and today, are filled with competition and misguided monopolization in favour of men.

Moreover, the feminist approach to the analysis of professions has alerted scholars to the fact that professions are gendered social constructions. The social constructionist view adopted by feminists including Merchant (1996), illustrates how natural science, capitalism, and masculinity go together to create a "violation of the natural" (Rossides 1998:16). She contends that the Western commitment to empiricism not only led to a questioning of natural hierarchies, but it also gave rise to a vast growth in intelligence gathering within realms of authority. She suggests that empiricism gave rise to "the police, government bureaus, and the emerging social sciences, and a proliferation of professions to deal directly with social problems" (p.17). Thus, like all symbolic activity, empirical research and professional activity is related to structural power. In other words, the knowledge that sets some people free results in non-freedom for others. For example, women's oppression became entrenched within professional communities rooted in an historical symbolic culture of capitalism and patriarchy. More specifically, it was the symbolic nature of the discipline of mathematics, its teachers and its culture, that rooted the field in masculine social constructs. She maintains that these patterns explain why feminists since the 1980s have been concerned with gendered education in the areas of mathematics and science (Mandell and Duffy 1995:63).

Future Trends

The preceding chapter has sought to generate an understanding of the theoretical foundations for research into the area of work and professions. It has argued that over time, these theoretical works have become more dynamic, inclusive, and action-oriented. A succinct synopsis of the developmental process in theoretical accounts, for example, is evident in the work of Burrage and Torstendahl (1990) who identify three main approaches to professions. They note that theories of work and professions begin from one of two sides. Either they begin to identify the basic characteristics of professions, or they denote the forms of collective action taken by professions. The first approach was primarily adopted by structural functional scholars, and the latter by both neo-Weberians and Marxists.

Burrage and Torstandahl (1990) argue that the Marxist framework has become predominant in the 1990s and beyond as professionals are "receding under the strain of something called de-professionalization (a line of thought especially used by Marxist authors), which is most often thought of as a new tendency in social development in the West" (p.45). The professions have undergone what has been termed a process of proletarianization. He notes that while the three approaches do not exclude one another, the first focuses on how groups *identify professions*, the second on how they *act professionally*, and the third on how *professional groups change* in relation to changes within the capitalist system.

Kocka (1986) adds that both the functionalist and the neo-Weberian social closure models contain "a latent idealism" insofar as their theoretical models are simply representative of a professional managerial class of scholars who serve as "specific functionaries of the system" (Burrage and Torstendahl 1990:80). Thus, he contends that only Marxists seek a new vocabulary and research focusing on class analysis on the structural level, in contrast to the level of organization. He argues that theories of professions demand analysis of political action and social structure in "a wider social context" (Burrage and Torstendahl 1990:81). In essence, Burrage and Torrendahl seek to expand theoretical understanding of professions to move research beyond conventional approaches in a more action-oriented Marxist direction.

Another trend in the overall theoretical analysis of professions has been towards post-modern analysis of the language of professions including the language of political policies, informed and advised by professional people. Historically, it was the case that policy-making emerged from the excesses of nineteenth century liberal democracies. Policy-making was an attempt to apply rational-choice models to the decision-making processes of those in the political realm (Blau 1964). Policy was viewed as a technical approach to society for "updating and running it more efficiently" (Rossides 1998:251). In contrast, post-modern deconstruction of policy language shows that both the manifest and latent functions of policy science, wittingly and unwittingly supports the interests of the powerful.

Post-modernists contend that powerful groups create different symbolic worlds to support and further their interests. Despite their well-motivated desire to confront reality, powerful groups consistently create false and contradictory images of reality. The post-modernist contends that our social indicators and other forms of professional language must be deconstructed so that an awareness of multiple realities can emerge (Burrage and Torstendahl 1990:38). In this perspective, the use of language is found to be a particular discourse promoting fragmentation among communities and social classes.

The importance of the post-modernist stance, and other models that point to language and other socially constructed aspects of professions, is found in the manner in which these approaches illuminate the fluidity of professions in a rapidly changing, multi-cultural and multi-faceted world. They draw attention to the relative power of occupational and professional groups in which substitution is replacing traditional forms of worker and professional competition. They demonstrate that we live in an age wherein the social contracts between groups and social classes can no longer be taken for granted. The professions, for example, must consider the changing managerial project insofar as processes of capital flight and global capital flow occur concurrently. In other words, the post-modern understanding of language and reality construction is important for understanding how work and professions are entrenched in a new world order that must be de-constructed. Post-modernism is a more inclusive, dynamic, and action-oriented means to interpret older social formations in the context of multidimensional possibilities (Rossides 1998:252).

Conclusion

This chapter has sought to examine some of the theoretical foundations into the analysis of work and professions. It began by looking at the functionalist paradigm and the work of Durkheim, Parsons, and Goode and it showed how the functionalists of the mid-twentieth century generally identified and classified the role and status of work and particularly, professions for the industrial order of the time. These scholars sought to show that professions filled a key role in maintaining a functional society despite its increasing complexity and rising individualism. Next, the chapter moved on to discuss some of the other paradigms in sociology that have produced increasingly dynamic, inclusive, and action-oriented analyses of work and professions. The chapter showed how Marxist and post-modern theorizing have enabled scholars to see professionals as both monopolizers and monopolized by increasingly fragmented and pluralistic class structures. Lastly, it has attempted to illustrate that future trends in the analysis of work and professions are increasingly dynamic, inclusive, and action-oriented in order to accommodate the increasing fluidity of post-modern social institutions. Thus, we may conclude by suggesting that theoretical analyses of work and professions are an integral element to developing sociological understanding of the changing patterns of human societies and social structures.

References

Abbott A. 1988. *The System of Professions.* London: University of Chicago Press.

Barber, B. 1963. "Some Problems in the Sociology of Professions." *Daedalus* 12:29-50.

Braverman, Harry. 1974. *Labor and Monopoly Capital: The Degradation of Work in the Twentieth Century.* New York: Monthly Review Press.

Burrage, Michael and Rolf Torstendahl. 1990. *Professions in Theory and History.* London: Sage Publications.

Blau, Peter M. 1964. *Exchange and Power in Social Life.* New York: Wiley.

Carr-Saunders, A.M. and P.A. Wilson. 1933. *The Professions.* London: Frank Cass.

Dingwall Robert. 1982. *Sociology of Professions.* New York: Saint Martin's Press.

Dingwall Robert and P. Lewis, eds. 1983. *The Sociology of Professions.* London: MacMillan.

Durkheim, Emile. 1984. *The Division of Labour in Society.* Translated by W.D. Halls. London: MacMillan.

Durkheim, Emile. [1893]1957. *Professional Ethics and Civic Morals.* New York: The Free Press.

Esland, Geoff and Graham Soloman, eds. 1980. *The Politics of Work and Occupations.* Toronto: University of Toronto Press.

Etzioni, A. 1969. *The Semi-Professions and their Organizations: Teachers, Nurses and Social Workers.* New York: Free Press.

Foucault M. 1980. *Power/Knowledge.* Brighton: The Harvester Press.

Freidson, Eliot. 1994. *Professionalism Reborn: Theory, Prophecy, and Policy.* Chicago: University of Chicago Press.

Freidson, Eliot. 1983. "The Theory of Professions: State of the Art." In *The Sociology of Professions*, edited by R Lewis and P. Dingwall. London: The MacMillan Press.

Goode, W. 1957. "Community within a Community: The Professions." *American Sociological Review* 22:194-200.

Goldthorpe J. H., D. Lockwood, F. Bechofer, and J. Platt. 1968. *The Affluent Worker: Industrial Attitudes and Behaviour.* Cambridge: Cambridge University Press.

Haug, M.R. 1973. "Deprofessionalization: An Alternative Hypothesis for the Future." *Sociological Review Monograph* 20:195-211.

Hickson. D.J. and M.W. Thomas 1969. "Professionalism in Britain: A Preliminary Measure." *Sociology* 3(1):37-53.

Hughes, E. C. 1963. "Professions." *Daedalus* 92:655-68.

Jackson J.A., ed. 1970. *Professions and Professionalization.* Cambridge: The University Press.

Johnson, T. 1972. *Professions and Power.* London: MacMillan.

_____. 1994. "Expertise and the State." Pp. 139-153 in *Foucault's New Domains*, edited by M. Game and T. Johnson. London: Routledge.

Jones, Anthony. 1991. *Professions and the State.* Philadelphia: Temple University Press.

Larson, M.S. 1977. *The Rise of Professionalism: A Sociological Analysis.* London: University of California Press.

Leitch, S. July 1991. "Reconstructing the Public Sector: A Case Study of New Zealand" *Political Science* 43:220.

Lynn, K. 1963. "Introduction to Professions." *Daedalus* Fall:IX-XIV.

Macdonald, Keith. 1995. *The Sociology of Professions.* London: Sage Publications.

Mandell Nancy and Ann Duffy. 1995. *Canadian Families: Diversity, Conflict and Change.* Toronto: Harcourt Brace.

Marshall, T.H. [1939] 1963. "The Recent History of Professionalism in Relation to Social Structure and Social Policy." *Canadian Journal of Economics and Political Science* 5:325-340.

Marx, K. 1976. *Capital.* Harmondsworth: Penguin.

Mayo, E. 1949. *The Social Problems of an Industrial Civilization.* London: Routledge and Keagan Paul.

Mead, G.H. 1934. *Mind, Self and Society.* Chicago: The University of Chicago Press.

Merchant, Carolyn. 1996. *Earthcare: Women and the Environment.* New York: Routledge.

Merton, R.K. 1957. *Social Theory and Social Structure.* Glencoe: The Free Press.

Mills, C.W. 1953. *White Collar.* New York: Oxford University Press.

Parsons, Talcott 1939. "The Professions and Social Structure." *Social Forces* 17.

Pavalko, Ronald, ed. 1972. *Sociological Perspectives on Occupations.* Illinois: F.E. Peacock Publishers.

Polyani, K. 1957. *The Great Transformation.* Boston: Beacon Press.

Rossides, Daniel W. 1998. *Professions and Disciplines: Functional and Conflict Perspectives.* New Jersey: Prentice Hall.

Roth, J. 1974. "Professionalism: The Sociologists Decoy." *Sociology of Work and Occupations* 1:6-23.

Watson, Tony J. 2003. *Sociology, Work and Industry.* London: Routledge.

Weber, Max. 2002. *The Protestant Ethic and the Spirit of Capitalism.* Translated by Stephen Kalberg. Los Angeles: Roxbury Pub. Co.

_____. 1978. *Economy and Society.* London: University of California Press.

Witz, Anne. 1992. *Professions and Patriarchy.* New York: Routledge.

CHAPTER 3

The Culture of Professions and the Individual

L. A. Visano*

Learning Objectives:

1. Critically discuss the utility of the concept of career for understanding work and professions.
2. Discuss how contingencies shape the nature of career stages.
3. Discuss critically the ideology—institutions—identity nexus.

---

*The author gratefully acknowledges the assistance and support provided by Dr Brenda Spotton Visano.

Introduction: The Concept of Career

Work occupies a central place in the lives of people. Sociologists analyze work as an important clue in determining the perceptions people have of themselves, the world vision through which people construct their version of social reality and the specific social relationships in which they are involved (Bejian and Salomone 1995; Bruner 1990; Hall 1975: 2; Hughes 1958:7, 43; Lore 1998; Oplatka, Bargal, and Inbar 2001; Slocum 1974:2; Woollacott 1980:192). The concept of career has been developed as a fruitful device for investigating the professional transformation of work. Clearly, the concept of career refers to the progression of related experiences and identity changes through which actors move during their working lives. A career is a socially recognized process involving a relatively orderly "sequence of movements" (Becker 1963:24). This constellation of activities and values serves as a framework for interpreting action (Hughes 1937) and for charting identities (Rock 1979:140). A career, therefore, is a way of being, a state of knowing and a form of association which impose some intelligibility in the actor's occupational world. Using the concept of career, we are able to focus on the processes of occupational choice, development, and transformation. This chapter provides a long overdue method for appreciating how forms and functions influence situational and structural aspects of careers. Specifically, in light of the differential impact of ideologies and institutions on professions, how do actors organize themselves as meaningful role occupants? Central to this purpose is an examination of the acquisition of a general framework of work within the wider landscape of alienating images and reified semblances.

In general, all individuals in any occupation follow career patterns. If one looks back over one's career, one can chart the sequence of upward, downward, lateral, linear and cyclical moves, as well as points of transition. Careers are usually characterized by identifiable and discrete stages through which actors pass as they experience a life's work in a given occupation. But, as Hughes (1958:127-8) suggests, these career stages are not necessarily noticed, nor even admitted. Actors construct knowledge of their occupational worlds by assessing situations and by assigning meanings to activities in the form of classificatory schemes. The classification of stages is used by all actors to indicate routine rules for interaction. Through each stage they acquire cumulative knowledge about the world of work. Members of an occupational group are able to provide accounts of career sequences by means of acquired perspectives, that is, actors define social reality on the basis of a belief in the "objective facticity" of various sets of rules contextualized in time and space. When subjective views become patterned, one may speak of the emerging "rules of the game" towards which actors differentially orient themselves (Silverman 1978:213). In general, this degree of institutionalization, as well as the nature of compliance to rules, remain problematic.

In particular, a number of contingencies shape movement through career stages. As a sensitizing concept (Becker 1963; Prus 1984), a career contingency involves the integration of objective and subjective elements. The former factors include aspects of social structure, affiliations, resources, and skills. The latter contingencies reflect ideology, general orientations or perspectives, motivations and rationales, and self-concept. Consequently, this chapter examines structural and experiential factors which contribute to relatively patterned occupational activities.

In pursuing their occupational activities, workers usually define and legitimate their careers in reference to a body of organizationally given norms. These norms include clear-cut hierarchies, fixed rules, limited goals, discipline, and reward structures. But, there are many occupational pursuits in which actors construct the organization of their work without alluding to this rigid conceptual scheme. Nevertheless, the social organization of all careers consists of socially constructed stages that *link biographies and relationships*. All careers entail various features of the initial *"getting connected"* or "becoming" stage, which involves aspects of exposure, exploration, entry (recruitment or induction), trial, and initiation, or training and apprenticeship; the *"staying connected"* or "being" established stage, which pertains to the maintenance of identity, achievement, stability as well as advancement, promotion or specialization; and the "disconnecting" or "reconnecting" stage of a career pursuit, which is characterized by graduation, expulsion, termination, or retirement as well as transformation, conversion, or greater induction into another occupation. In other words, work consists of a wide spectrum of differentially constituted activities of getting connected, staying connected and disconnecting which represent empirically related but analytically distinct levels of accomplishments. Each career stage of this social enterprise represents an interplay of identity formations, social interactions, and temporal-spatial contexts.

Typically, careers are depicted as orderly progressions up the ladder of statuses within a profession (Dubin 1958:276-78). But, as Campanis (1970:318) notes in his analysis of bureaucratic settings:

> Careers today are more ill defined, hazardous mazes than ladders. Managers run the course with no hint of what the next turn will reveal, while they try to cope with moral dilemmas, conflicting interpersonal relationships and general uncertainty.

In addition, there is considerable overlap among the various stages of one's career (Sonnenfeld and Kotter 1982:27). An actor may enter at any stage only to move forward, backward, or out of the process completely. Moreover, passing through these career stages is not a smooth process but a tensive interplay of ideologies, institutions, and identities.

Participation in a career stage depends upon a number of specific contingencies that condition the constitution of identities and interactions. According to Becker (1963) and Krause (1971:41), contingencies are those factors that either characterize the individual or are relevant to him or her in ways that influence the development of a career. Contingencies do not necessarily operate "simultaneously" (Becker 1963:24). They are often relevant to the actor during different stages of career commitments. At each stage, a number of tightly interwoven contingencies operate and assume different meanings. For Lemert (1972:79), an analysis of recurrent or typical contingencies awaiting someone who continues a course of action is a productive focus of inquiry. This approach requires the specification of patterns of interactions which enable the development of appropriate responses to "turning points" that are integral to one's becoming, being, and changing orientations. These career shifts inevitably signal new evaluations of self and others, of events and objects.

According to Strauss (1969:92), however, the transformation of self is irreversible—once having changed, there is no turning back. Actors can look back, but they can only evaluate the past from their new status. Three related contingencies are fundamental in building and maintaining symbolic worlds of careers: constituting *skills* of actors, *reactions* of others, and *self identity*. Firstly, movement within any career is conditioned by the acquisition of interpersonal skills. Rewards are maximized by the ongoing development and application of knowledge. An aspirant's interest alone is not sufficient to qualify him or her for mobility; she or he must learn a stock of beliefs, values and ways of acting that will ensure continued participation. An actor is expected to interpret the rewards offered and the chances of realizing them. That is, choice as defined by the institutional norms (administrative or organizational rules and the values of the occupational culture) requires information which an actor presumably channels within different stages (Becker, Geer, Hughes, and Strauss 1961). This acquisition of skills is influenced by an actor's interpretation of a number of pressing conditions: abilities or qualifications, specific occupational information, and orientation to the specific work relations.

Secondly, the perspectives of other acting units are important contingencies of career movement (Blumer 1969). This reference to "previous significant others" is instrumental in securing access to skills, services, and information (Gerth and Mills 1953:93). Occupational contacts for example, enable actors to gain and maintain a wider reach of information (Krause 1971:43). More significantly, associations with similarly circumstanced others "validate" and sustain a convenient self concept (Lemert 1972:81). It is this "audience" to which an actor addresses claims of self-worth (Hughes 1958:43). By attending to the reactions of others, the actor learns favourable definitions of experience and of self which, in turn, guide new strategies of interaction. The actor acquires his role by interpreting the roles and reactions of others. As Blumer (1979:ix) describes:

> The acts of others constitute the social setting for one's own act, serving to incite, to inhibit, to temper, and to guide one's own line of actions as one takes note of what others are doing or are likely to do.

As the responses of significant others are extrapolated for the self, this frame of reference aids in organizing perceptions and experiences (Rock 1979:137). The increasing appropriation of occupational roles brings one into contact with, and under pressure to accept certain perspectives, "incorporating values, attitudes, and views" (Salaman 1974:15).

Thirdly, the construction of appropriate self-concepts influences an actor's career. An actor establishes and situates meaningful identities for the self and for others at different stages (Goffman 1961:127-169). Career movements depend upon the ways in which identity is established and sustained, the strategies used to ensure recognition and acceptance of self, and the ways in which the actor seeks out relationships that are conducive to his or her occupational expectations. The influence of an individual's self-concept has received considerable attention primarily within the vocational choice tradition (Holland 1973; Keon et al. 1982; Sonnenfeld and Kotter 1982; Bruner 1990). Accordingly, vocational development is defined as the process of implementing one's self-concept in career choices wherein personality orientation becomes the overriding factor in selecting a career congruent with one's self image (Holland 1973). On the other hand, an interpretive framework provides more promising directions by stressing the notion of the developmental perspective of the emerging and knowing self. An actor's social character and his or her relationship to roles are continually evolving and not normatively fixated in the course of interaction. Socialization facilitates the learning and maintenance of an appropriate self-concept by specifying the necessary world-view, skills, and knowledge. That is, these products are based upon the actor's image as reflected in interaction with others (Lemert 1972:78). The premise of this model suggests that there are a number of *situational* and *subjective* contingencies which an actor interprets, selects, and even resists at various stages. These contingencies are not objectively given and necessarily accepted. That is, a career study is not limited solely to "affinities" which pre-ordain, nor to "affiliations" which convert the actor (Matza 1969:119-21). Rather, shifting relations assist actors in coping with these affinities and affiliations in deference or in defiance. At each stage, actors accomplish the necessary skills and identities in order to respond strategically and at times spontaneously to various career challenges. The nature of these contingencies is significant in affecting the next stage actors will pursue in advancing, maintaining, subverting or abandoning their careers.

According to a social action perspective, the process by which meanings are assigned is a focal point of inquiry (Weber 1969:88; Blumer 1969; Silverman 1978). This perspective highlights the need to consider the negotiations of meanings behind the formation of career stages and their contingencies. The action of individuals stems from a complex set of definitions, derived from a shared stock of knowledge, which defines social reality (Silverman 1978:127). Actors assign meanings to the situations of their occupational roles and to the career expectations of others and, in turn, react according to the interpretations suggested by these meanings. Careers, as social accomplishments, are staged and skillfully played out in terms of occupational roles; enacted and re-enacted with a degree of certainty determined by prior and ongoing negotiations between the symbolic order of work and the nature of joint action. This action frame, according to Silverman, pays close attention to the orientation of actors who might be differentially attached, and who themselves create, sustain and change "the rules of the game" (1978:216).

A career, as experienced, unfolds and cannot be known ahead of time (Krause 1971:44). Careers consist of situated interactions among significant others, occupational role enactments, and ongoing monitoring of one's audiences. Within this perspective, the concept of career reflects the quotidian properties of work, interaction and social identity. Since as Salaman (1974:14) explains, a career refers to progress through identity-bestowing situations, it can be legitimately used in analyzing the process of becoming a madam as of becoming a psychiatrist, or becoming a criminal as of becoming a policeman.

A career is a running perspective articulated against a backdrop of significant meanings. This perspective is not fixed as to points of view, direction or destination (Hughes 1958:63). The social organization of careers—stages and contingencies, enters into action only to the extent that it shapes both the situations in which people act or react, and the symbols which people use in interpreting these situations (Blumer 1969). A career, as a meaningful concept, is ordered reflexively by social actors into a human enterprise and presented as the outcomes of the actors' consciously applied skills. Far too frequently, however, emphasis is placed on the problem solving aspects of interaction (Becker 1963; Hughes 1971; Lemert 1972; Matza 1969). Given the social nature of a career, an actor's identity cannot be solely defined according to narrow institutionally imposed criteria that measure the performance of tasks. Likewise, the facile attribution of a master status with identifiable characteristics can vary in desirability, direction, and duration. To minimize "status contradictions," actors are compelled to keep their occupational relationships formal and specific by developing specialized talents and catering to a specific audience. Irrespective of whether this assigned status is presented in a positive or negative manner, the actor develops strategies for responding to the new status and to the ratifiers of this master status. These strategies become more evident in situations where the actor, playing many roles, seeks to balance all the identities that this role playing supplies.

The centrality of this *master status* can be studied by examining "status passage" (Glaser and Strauss 1971:3). As Glaser and Strauss (1971) note, status passage reflects changes in the social structure and its functioning. This notion of status passage enables us to investigate social reactions to, and configurations of objective status in the form of financial rewards, deference, prestige, and privilege (Blankenship 1977:210). As Willis (1980) notes, individuals are active appropriators who reproduce existing structures "through struggle, contestation, and a partial penetration of these structures" (p.175). Furthermore, this "passage" highlights internal dimensions of the subjective career—the moral career. A moral career is based on the reactions of the status holder to himself or herself within a specific situation, leading to ongoing revisions and shifts in the conception of self (Willis 1980). Moral careers involve movement, that is, "regular sequences of changes that career entails in the person himself and his framework of imagery for judging himself and others" (Goffman 1961:128). In conjunction with status, the concept of commitment is pursued in discussions of careers. Commitment usually refers to the perceived level of satisfaction in the present or expected status. According to Silverman (1978:186), an actor's acceptance of prevailing social expectations influences commitment. Specifically, commitment is a point in the history of a career where more goods and rewards are lost by leaving the career (Becker 1960:32). But for Becker, a person is committed to a career not necessarily because of what he or she has chosen but because of what has happened to him or her. The latter includes prior actions of the person, recognition of this involvement, and the consistency of the activity pursued.

In general, the study of occupational careers involves two sociological orientations—*social structure* and *process*. Each approach addresses significant issues and neglects others. While the structural approach is criticized for overlooking the subjective meanings of relations (Blau and Scott 1962; Silverman 1978), the process perspective is equally attacked for "failing to do justice to the influence on human behaviour of wider structures of power and ongoing historical processes" (Saks 1983:5). Nevertheless, there are a number of stimulating classical studies which move beyond determining which approach is more adequate (Ditton 1979; Giddens 1976; Willis 1980). Rather, a more prudent inquiry requires a sensitive assessment of the relevant influences of both structure and interaction. The former approach situates work in larger social, economic, and political contexts. Admittedly, modernization, neoliberalism, and bureaucratization perniciously affect the quality of career opportunities. The latter processual perspective stresses the process of socialization, subjective experiences, and dilemmas.

To elucidate, the political economy and its class structure determine career opportunities and aspirations as explained by the contributions of many early scholars who explained the emergence of modern industrial society in terms of the transformation of the structure of social relations. The immediate processes of work, careers, and roles reflect larger structural changes. As Marx noted, actors do not perform as individuals, but as personifications of economic categories laid down by definite class relations (Fleischer 1973:32). The dehumanizing and alienating effects of the worker's loss of control over both the products and process of labour constrain any career potential. Likewise, Weber's (1969) concern with the negative effects of increasing bureaucratization on workers are expressed in terms of alienation. In brief, work has also been presented as a forced form of cohesion based primarily on exchange relationships (Durkheim 1933 [1893], 1964[1895]). Alienation occurs when individuals have little or no control over the purposes and products of the labour process, the overall organization of the workplace, and the immediate work process itself. Within this structural orientation, social class is advanced as a determinant of career attainment (Blau et al. 1956; Clement 1975; McFarlane 1968:299-302; Mills 1951; Porter 1965). Social class influences careers by shaping the process of socialization and the occupational opportunities available to actors (Blau et al. 1956). Careers, as responses to available occupational opportunities, link the structural features of the labour market and the socioeconomic aspirations of workers.

Likewise, a bureaucratic model has dominated the study of careers. Career patterns are defined rigidly as a succession of related jobs, arranged in a hierarchy of prestige, through which workers move in ordered sequences. That is, career stages are organized so that one enters at a low level and, under given conditions, progresses upwardly within an organization. According to this perspective, careers entail the development of a more progressive performance of occupational skills over a number of years (Slocum 1974:6). This conventional view holds that the bureaucratic design of work is created as a result of scientific, industrial, and organizational demands placed upon efficiency (Fox 1980:180). But, workers' expectations and orientations are also very important in understanding bureaucratic opportunities, rewards, or deprivations (Salaman 1980:26). But, how far can people make informed choices that will fulfill their ambitions and self-concepts within the boundaries of occupational structures? To further complement this structural approach, the human relations model examines the role of workers in their occupational setting (Hamilton 1980:45). This model identifies the conditions under which workers are more productive and more cohesive. It is discovered that the range of options available to workers is limited (Blau et al. 1956:535).

In many organizations, choice is restricted because knowledge about existing opportunities is unevenly distributed. Such attributes as race, gender, class, sexuality, and age are also factors in structuring mobility. For instance, competition between older role occupants and younger role aspirants often results in the formers' withdrawal from occupational pursuits (Rosenfeld 1980:584). In addition to investigating the alienating effects that are structured in large-scale organizations, considerable attention is given to exploring employees' modes of accommodation. Presthus (1962) details three ideal types of manipulations: upward-mobiles, indifferents, and ambivalents. The "upward-mobiles," usually executives, adapt by displaying high morale, strong identification with the organization and acceptance of the legitimacy of organizational demands. The "indifferents," the wage-earners, are usually interested in off-the-job pursuits and pay lip-service to organizational demands. Lastly, the "ambivalents" are described as introverted employees with limited skills and interests. Therefore, career mobility depends on the level of positive identification with organizational goals, negotiations, and conviviality (1962:195, 23). Likewise, in his study of undergraduate careers, Davis (1965) outlines four types of adaptations: loyalists, defectors, recruits, and residuals. For Davis, mobility is influenced by differential exposure to, and familiarity with organizational values.

In brief, analyses of careers explain the behaviour of employees by alluding to stable, impersonal, and structural characteristics of formal organizations (Etzioni 1974; Stinchcombe 1973; Whyte 1956). There is a growing body of research which recognizes the informal as well as the formal features of organizations (Blau and Scott 1962; Silverman 1978). The performance of organizational roles can arise from extra-organizational statuses (Silverman 1978:217). An informal structure of rules and relationships emerges in all organizations. This informality is an integral part of all organizations. Specifically, it affects routine work activities in functional as well as dysfunctional ways. Informal work behaviour is an outcome of conflict between the expressive needs of actors and the impersonality of the formal structure (p.194). This informal structure emerges when workers face persistent problems that are not solved by the formal system. Formal work becomes supplemented and modified by informal relationships. Since formal structures are inadequate for getting the job done, workers often bend, break, or redefine the rules of their workplace (Blau and Scott 1962; Slocum 1974). Informal relationships function to create unofficial goals and new channels of mobility. In his study of managerial roles in modern bureaucratic structures, Dalton (1966) explores the coexistence of formal and informal systems of work. Dalton highlights the importance managers attach to the human process of compromise, the unofficial requirements for mobility, and informal rewards for achieving desired ends (p.178). Similarly, Blankenship's (1977:215) study of organizational careers in collegial settings demonstrates the functional priority of negotiations in career enactments. According to Blankenship, the formal rules of an organization are often exaggerated; careers can be better understood by addressing the nature of situated interactions between peers and significant others (p.214).

Similarly, blue collar workers develop informal strategies which make their work a more meaningful experience. Workers elect to humanize their work by extending an element of control over it, or by escaping from work by doing as little as possible (Rinehart 1975). Others reduce tension and assert control over their work by "conscious action or inaction directed towards mutilation or destruction of the work environment" (Taylor and Walton 1971:219). Workers are accustomed to obtaining part of their wages "in kind," or "perks" to supplement their objective material earnings (Ditton 1977). These supplements help to make work more meaningful. Moreover, the meanings workers attach to their labour also arise in the non-work roles that they play with fellow workers off the job (Salaman 1974). Workers often pursue their "central life interests" outside their workplace altogether.

In contrast to the above structural approaches, occupational life has been analyzed in terms of ongoing processes of stage development. That is, careers reflect successive experiences which shape and re-shape work orientations. Within this tradition, the pioneering efforts of the Chicago School provide a thorough examination of a wide variety of life histories and occupational pursuits. The writings of Everett Hughes (1958) remain pivotal in the study of occupational sociology. Unlike the traditional approaches which consider occupations as fixed roles played by actors, Hughes is fundamentally concerned with the ongoing construction of occupations. For Hughes, it is necessary to determine how careers are shaped by the nature of work, and how work is shaped by the careers of its members. In other words, "an occupation in essence is not some particular set of activities: it is part of an individual in an ongoing set of activities" (Hughes 1965:445). In highlighting the social relationships surrounding an occupation, the financial or even alienating aspects of work are considered to be elements of a more inclusive set of social relationships. Thus, Hughes and his students are interested in the interactional strategies and the social meaning of work as interpreted by the workers (Becker, Geer, Hughes, and Strauss 1961). According to Hughes (1971:342):

> Our aim is to penetrate more deeply into the personal and social drama of work, to understand the social and social psychological arrangements and devices by which men make their work tolerable, or even make it glorious to themselves and others. Specifically, we need to rid ourselves of any concepts which keep us from seeing that the essential problems of men at work are the same whether they do their work in the laboratories of some famous institution or in the messiest vat room of a pickle factory (sic).

Clearly, Hughes (1971:301) advances a conceptual perspective for the comparative analysis of careers.

He is equally interested in legitimate and illegitimate careers. "Bastard institutions" are compared with more respectable occupations according to preparation, education, occupational roles, and routine problems (pp.98-105). For Hughes (1958:50), "dirty work" is found in all occupations, and its form may range from just being physically disgusting to being a symbol of degradation that wounds one's dignity. In general, traditional models of career mobility are not appropriate for dirty work. Many low status occupations are not tied to complex institutional contexts within which actors can move (Salaman 1974:16). Moreover, knowledge acquired in these occupations is seldom transferable to other occupations. Accordingly, there are few career alternatives and opportunities for upward mobility.

The ordering of work varies. According to Hughes (1958), work routines can be "open, intentional and institutionalized" (p.12). But, work in non-institutional settings has received limited attention. Instead, comparative studies of occupations present the typology of work within a rigid dichotomy of formal-complex organizations on the one hand, and loose social organizations on the other (Silverman 1978:12). A more appropriate framework, according to Silverman is a *continuum*, with formal and social organizations on opposite sides. Within his occupational typology, Ritzer (1972:5) also distinguishes occupational categories in terms of professions, managers, middle-level occupations, low status, and deviant occupations, according to the degree of formal organizational linkages. Moreover, Glaser (1968:1) defines work according to organizational and occupational careers. In discerning these career types, he presents the former as a specific resource offered within an organizational context. The latter career-type is simply a general category that refers to a patterned path of geographic, organizational, and social mobility in any line of work.

Getting Connected

The above career taxonomy provides a framework within which an organized account of careers can proceed. This section clarifies the process by which individuals enter professions and/or occupations. By exploring the unfolding drama of how neophyte actors get connected, we unravel the circumstances under which these actors set themselves both "apart" from existing norms, and perceive themselves as "part" of work culture. We follow an approach to becoming a worker that focuses on two general contexts: pre-occupational experiences of dislocation and exposure, and the development of work relations. Getting connected requires a collective effort wherein the interests and involvements of "significant others" are central. A starting point of inquiry focuses on early work experiences and contingencies influencing choice of roles.

Before one can assume a particular work habitus, a number of contingencies need to exist which enable actors to assess their immediate situations. Newcomers arrive on the work scene from a variety of social backgrounds. They immediately learn to depict work in terms of a hierarchy of positions of least prestige. In order to provide a clearer insight into pre-occupational experiences, we need to consider historical reconstructions, that is, an appreciation of prior work which frames prior experiences from two different, though obviously related points of view. Accounts are framed within dual forces of dislocation and exposure. In reconstructing and co-ordinating their biographical maps, actors rely exclusively on factors that "push" them out of previous work/engagement, and factors that "pull" them towards the seemingly more attractive alternatives of the new work. The logic of accounts hangs together and is contingent upon the available stock of information and the relevant socialization immediately preceding early work involvements.

Admittedly, background factors, as Heyl (1979) explains, are static in the sense that they alone do not deal with ongoing adjustments, turning points, or entry processes. Nonetheless, antecedent conditions are instructive precisely because they serve to legitimize work selection. To ignore what these seekers consider as crucial factors invites banal interpretations that often border on crude reductionism. It is argued that these accounts, however distorted, are assigned an actuality, or "objective facticity," of the interpretive framework (Holzner 1968). What actors say, imagine, or believe is very much an integral part of their real life as newcomers.

Linguistic devices that newcomers employ to evaluate their previous work life often take the form of excuses. Excuses, as Lyman and Scott (1970:112-14) note, are accounts expressed in socially approved vocabularies in which one admits the act in question is bad, wrong or inappropriate, but denies full responsibility. Newcomers, for example, attribute the problem of looking for a job to deterministic causal factors with specific reference to faulty personal relationships that allegedly propel them to move "outside" their familiar environments. Such a biography becomes incorporated into a perspective that can be manipulated (Willis 1980).

The status of marginality is central to seeking supportive relations in the workplace. The paradox of being "at" work and not "of" that work does not solely determine directions to pursue. But, it is against these background accounts that newcomers justify the development of collegial work relations. Early difficulties, especially in reference to securing information about benefits, promotion, and salaries, contribute to a lowering of defenses and a greater susceptibility to involvements with more seasoned employees, who are willing to offer even a modicum of support. Just as the new work is perceived as a solution, work relations are also held to be a solution to immediate problems of survival for the solitary newcomer. By focusing on these interactions, we explore the process of admission into the world of work.

Becoming a worker requires a collective accomplishment. Work emerges out of the various social relations that newcomers develop. As a form of secondary socialization, the process of "becoming" consists of both self-induction or enlistment and recruitment by others. The workplace, therefore, becomes a social setting facilitating "seekership" and encouragement (Prus 1984). The circumstances of being "at work" is a starting point for our analysis primarily because this early exposure is a significant prerequisite for initiating collegial connections, which eventually introduce newcomers to work as an attractive alternative. This early stage involves the learning of a newcomer's role, especially with its emphasis on naiveté and subservience. Recent arrivals organize their responses around the preliminary reactions of strangers with whom they form loose, fleeting, and casual groupings or "clusters." An important contingency involves the experience of being publicly accepted. In the course of their interactions, newcomers pick up the requisite jargon and listen attentively to the legends, successes, and conflicts that seasoned colleagues communicate to them. As a result of their common situation, previously unacquainted colleagues develop bonds with each other. These relationships function to provide general assistance and provisions of support for newcomers. The latter become informed about the norms, occupational culture, rules, and roles associated with the work environment. The process of introducing oneself to an existing reference group is not without difficulties. Not only are newcomers expected to defer to more seasoned colleagues, but acceptance is also based on the performance of certain tasks. In many of these occupational groupings, newcomers are regarded with caution and suspicion wherein loyalties need to be "tested." The process of affiliation is purposive and rational.

A second, related issue concerns the social construction of choice. Choices are made according to the evidence available and the attractiveness of various options. Newcomers drift into a reference group for whom their limited occupational experience makes them eligible candidates. Fortuitous encounters are undoubtedly responsible for many initial introductions. Nevertheless, the process of enlistment, or what Matza (1969) refers to as the "ordaining of self" is an active human accomplishment. More significantly, it is in the context of loose and fleeting peer acquaintances that newcomers begin to discover inviting associations. Older seasoned workers typically go out of their way to help newcomers. In addition, newcomers are invited to participate in various non-occupational pursuits. Established links with unacquainted newcomers are also established only after collectively sharing their experiences, community, and family experiences.

The relationship between private and public worlds, therefore, continues to be a focus of sociological investigation. Many studies indicate the significance of the private world as basic to an understanding of public involvements. These links remain conceptually threadbare and are reduced to assumptions derived from prevailing cultural values about work as public. Work is often decontextualized and too readily extricated from other social relations. Conventional approaches to becoming a worker often understate complex interactions of a variety of blended relationships. These limitations result from a failure to direct inquiry into multiple work and nonwork involvements, associations which facilitate and inhibit decisions regarding identity.

In brief, this section identified a number of factors that are associated with the process of becoming a worker. Factors which facilitate the likelihood of becoming a worker include both subjective and situational contingencies: identity, relationships, perspectives, and activities. Subjective evaluations vary according to interactions that serve to define and organize the appropriateness of action. Interactions with significant others provide a framework for interpreting the substance and structure of this learning process. Interpretations are influenced by the social organization of information, relations, and emerging cultural values of work.

Newcomers avail themselves of opportunities for attaching themselves to others. From the outset, the newcomer typically makes interpersonal contacts with others in the same situation who help the transition. Collegial and acquaintance-based associations provide many benefits; information is shared concerning the accessibility of assistance. Less experienced newcomers, therefore, seek the attention of many inviting groupings. This recruitment enhances an "embeddedness." Experienced workers orient neophytes to various techniques of survival. These ties are essential for "learning the ropes" and for developing a repertoire of manipulative skills. The accessibility to various contacts carries serious implications for the social organization of getting connected. Thus, the nature of relations influences plans of action. Having access to a number of associations increases the newcomer's exposure to work knowledge. Relationships generally vary in kind and intensity. There are a number of different and continually intersecting associations. At one extreme, there are interpersonal relations based on friendship. At the other extreme, there are the typical work relations based on the acquisition of resources. Although more prevalent than the former, the latter associations tend to be central to an extension of social orientations.

Since survival is a central concern for newcomers, these early relationships at work are fundamentally instrumental. Initially, newcomers invest considerable effort in trying to secure resources that range from tangible benefits like information, to more intangible elements such as companionship and emotional support. For women, however, many of these processes are challenging since many women are deprived of and denied supportive relations to which male newcomers are usually exposed. Depending on the actual representation of women at all levels in the workplace, women tend to establish relations that are spatially and socially concentrated whereas men seek a greater diversity of acquaintances which provides a far reaching range of information, opportunities, and experiences. Much of this is attributable to exclusionary practices concomitant with the chilly climate and a dominant misogynist culture. The content of these interactions is shaped by the immediate issues at hand. Women newcomers, for example, move beyond these limited networks when support is not forthcoming.

Conceptually what is suggested herein is a perspective on social order which depicts newcomers as attending to certain features of their respective affiliations. Upon closer scrutiny, it is evident that participation in different associations influences this process of getting connected. It is argued that the broader the base from which newcomers operate, the greater the likelihood that work will be pursued as a long-term investment. As work becomes less controlled by the assessments of "loose peer clusterings," newcomers are more able to secure continuity in and commitment to the workplace. To reiterate, the structure of relations affects the nature of social control. Newcomers, who are more isolated from formal and informal associations are less susceptible to the norms of the occupation. In loose peer group associations, social control is fragmented, less consistent, and less effective. The imposition of social control is facilitated in dependency relations. The nature of associations, combinations of colleagues and friends, and intensity of interpersonal relationships shape the information actors use in interpreting the initial encounters at work. This perspective cements disparate accommodations to the workplace by legitimating the acquisition of information. Pragmatism unfolds as a "generic feature" of interactions (Prus 1984). Newcomers develop attitudes towards immediate issues of survival by alluding to this all encompassing framework of seekership.

Table 3.1 describes situational and subjective contingencies which influence the process of getting connected to work.

Staying Connected

Occupational sociology seeks to analyze the social organization of work, the social conditions and consequences of work, and the patterns of work behaviour within wider social, cultural, political, and economic contexts. In general, work consists of

Table 3.1
The Construction of Occupational Identities

	Situational Contexts	Subjective Features
Identity	(push/ pull pressures) circumstances of dislocation	work as a solution paradoxes of marginality
Relations	(recruitment and traiing) exposure and affiliation	relations as a solution and the skills development identity paradoxes
Activities	involvement (in/outside the workplace)	perspective (rules, ongoing assessment of associations, client/colleagues)

a set of differentially constituted tasks that "results in the provision of goods and services" (Rinehart 1975:6) in return for direct or indirect social and financial consequences (Hall 1975). This basic social activity is located in an economy wherein a worker is responsible for the production and/or distribution of goods or services (West 1978). By analyzing how workers accomplish their tasks according to values articulated within an occupational framework, we are able to determine how actors stay connected to a career.

The selection of occupational tasks arises from repeated and meaningful interactions. All work is subject to routine performance. Reciprocal recognition and expectations of duties emerge in such a manner that actors learn to anticipate and incorporate the responses of their significant interactants. Workers repeatedly engage in acts of productivity to develop attitudes that frame favourably the context of their experiences. Their ongoing on-the-job socialization reinforces the collective knowledge and wisdom of their significant others. A working ideology emerges and revolves around the major functions of the services they provide. This occupational culture is comprised of experiences and values that direct, in a real and symbolic manner, the appropriateness of choices. Although there exists a considerable degree of cultural relativism, a set of well-articulated meanings is shared and consistently invoked to describe one's relationship to work, colleagues, and clients. An occupational perspective, therefore, enables actors to transcend the immediately situated features of encounters by relating them to a broader social context of work. For these actors, an occupational perspective is particularly well-suited and integrally related to the process of making sense of their accomplishments.

This occupational frame of reference departs from the generalized getting connected stage described earlier. Admittedly, symbolic typifications of work are generally elusive objects of inquiry. While they cannot be addressed directly, inferences certainly can be drawn from accounts and observations of workers. Inferences about work values range from broad and axiomatic pronouncements of administrative or managerial (disciplinary) rules to sets of ideas that sustain and pattern adjustments and relationships as well as societal mores that define the significance of work (a way of securing a livelihood). A common identification emerges in the course of effective and routine interactions with fellow workers. Staying connected goes beyond apprenticeship and the acquisition of an occupational perspective. This process requires the performance of a number of interrelated activities. These include the development of relationships and the management of contingencies. Together, these techniques buttress a coherent and meaningful image of work. These techniques vary according to the context of encounters. In exchanges that occur in public work settings, actors "take charge" immediately and assert their authority by clearly indicating their sense of belongingness, maintaining control, and securing a degree of cooperation and agreement with expected rules of conduct. But, they also operate within an organizational structure that demands accommodative techniques.

Actors learn to establish occupational perspectives and skills as methods of securing some stability in their lives. In general, work becomes defined in terms of rules of conduct, emotional attachment and the importance of service. This process consists of a range of activities that include: securing a comfort zone, promoting an investment by attending to competencies, appearances and preparation, managing routines, establishing proficiencies, enforcing authority and controlling information about themselves. This list is not exhaustive, rather it is a beginning to understanding the role of careers in people's lives.

Disconnecting and Reconnecting

The concept of a career incorporates past work experiences, current involvements, and expectations about the future. Sociological studies of careers have paid scant attention to the disconnecting processes. That is, acts of disengagement from particular pursuits are frequently overlooked. Disconnecting from an activity—whether in the manner of dropping out, graduating, or retiring—is a career stage that is experienced by all actors. In general, disconnecting occurs when actors subjectively abandon their involvements for some significant period of time (Meisenhelder 1977:319). Disengagement is seldom an abrupt act. Rather, it is a complex process that requires a series of ongoing evaluations and adjustments. Mainstream sociology, with its notion of socialization and its implications of passive transmission, misses the tension and uncertainty inherent in disengagement (Willis 1980).

A more comprehensive analysis of disconnecting warrants an examination of both continuities and discontinuities, as well as changes in style and content of work. An interactionist perspective highlights the need to consider not only the general process of transition but also the conditions under which changes occur. Actors stage their careers by responding to the contingencies of self-typifications, experiences, and the reactions of significant others. In general, two contingencies are central to the disengagement process: occupationally-related factors and social relations. Accordingly, these general influences determine the responses of actors to structures that enhance and/or exacerbate a commitment to work. The transformation of occupational identities in reference to levels of commitment to particular pursuits and to personal associations clarifies empirically and theoretically, the links between the specific world of work and the wider social environment. This framework, as Blachford (1981: 184) notes, suggests an intersection between the dominant social order that generates problems, and specific cultures that mediate problems.

As noted earlier, a frame of reference for studying careers is also the framework for studying identities (Strauss and Becker 1975:95). Identities are never fully developed nor sustained indefinitely. Instead, identity formations are ongoing accomplishments. An interactionist perspective stresses the interpretive processes of taking stock of feelings and experiences. Actors orient their retrospective accounts by attending to the responses of those they regard as their significant others. Identities vary as actors acknowledge to themselves and signify to others the meaning of these interpretations. Irrespective of the inconsistency of these identities, interpretations warrant analysis because they indicate how actors define various situations. Assessments are fundamental features of self-concepts. Subjective accounts enable us to ascertain stability and change. As Plummer (1981:54) indicates, doing and experiencing can become consolidated into "being" through the actor's own categoric labeling. Although there is no absolute congruency between doing, thinking or feeling, identities are anchored in time and space. Basic to any discussion of becoming, being, or abandoning one's role as a worker is the linkage between identity and social position. Rather than limit identity to a single normative conception, it is essential to integrate identity with occupational and general social affiliations. As Holzner (1968:44) suggests, an actor's identity is found to be dynamically related to his understanding of the world in which he or she participates. Identity, as an amalgam of evaluations, is shaped by audiences before whom an actor performs a number of roles. Occupational roles are significant social anchors.

An occupation is a social context in which actors recognize and bestow identities according to specific roles. Actors become increasingly identified with a version of themselves as workers or professionals by enacting a series of occupational roles that pattern social contacts. The level of significance that the role of professional represents depends on the degree to which actors orients their lives to work. A crucial determinant of the predominance of this role is the meaningfulness of this activity for the actor. The more internalized one's self definition in both public and private interactions, the greater the likelihood that a master identity of worker or professional exists. In essence, identities are integral aspects of the social structure of work (Strauss 1975:245). The social order of work, however, is not static. There are different stages of involvement that reflect temporal and interpersonal contingencies. Occupational identities change as a result of both slow and painstaking processes, and factors that contribute to their discontent. Older workers, in particular, become increasingly disgruntled with the following working conditions: many years invested with little or no assurances of successful promotions, reduced financial compensation, boredom, lack of respect, and acceptance. A block in mobility also influences an appraisal of continued involvements.

For instance, just as the dominant culture celebrates and commoditizes youth, the integration of age and work is pervasive in the workplace with stigma attached to the old. Age stratification is a critical contingency, especially when youth is equated with a greater ability to attract business. The related occupational emphasis on the ethos of individualism (survival of the fittest/slickest) exacerbates anxieties. Work that was once considered exhilarating and adventurous is defined as limited, monotonous, and laden with illusions of status, money or challenges. Even though seasoned workers have mastered interpersonal skills and techniques, they experience considerable insecurity about their work. This discontent is more fully appreciated when placed within a theoretical framework of alienation (Rinehart 1975:13).

Alienation is a multi-dimensional concept that is subject to a plethora of meanings. On one hand, alienation exists when actors have little or no control over the purpose and products of their labour, the immediate work processes, and the overall organization of the workplace (Rinehart 1975: 17). It is built into the structured relationships of the workplace and exists independently of the consciousness of workers. On the other hand, alienation is attributable to actors in specific social situations and becomes lodged in social action. In his study of industrial technology, Blauner (1967) provides a social psychological approach to alienation that focuses upon workers' attitudes and relates them to wider aspects of the social organization of productive enterprises. Blauner's operational definition of alienation is comprised of four components: powerlessness, meaninglessness, isolation, and self-estrangement. These elements are instructive in appreciating the phenomenon of disengagement. Exiting from work is not simply an automatic stimulus-response behaviour. Disengagement is a learned accomplishment that is contingent upon the actor's sense of conditions that contribute to alienation. Workers seldom single out any one factor that would cause them to abandon a pursuit. Instead, they provide a cluster of impressions relating to alienation. Interestingly, the previously celebrated features of security, money, and autonomy are increasingly minimized at this stage. As older workers find themselves unable to influence their work conditions and events, they are more likely to explore alternatives or even attach themselves to other roles.

Throughout the disconnecting stage, actors occupy several simultaneous roles. Role conflict often emerges as a result of incompatible expectations of various roles. For example, as workers experience inter-role conflicts, incongruous demands of their role, disagreements among colleagues and superiors, corruption, mediocrity, cowardice, hypocrisy, and contradictions—they become disenchanted with their current career. Disengagement is the most favourable solution to this career crisis. A career crisis is a critical turning point that prompts readjustments (Sheehy 1981:19). As Plummer (1981:72) notes, "a drastic restructuring of self-conceptions at critical turning points" occurs. But, an identity transformation is more manageable if support from significant others is forthcoming. Consequently, actors interested in disengagement must be able to enlist the support of those who can both ratify their new self-concept and facilitate their adjustments. In addition to occupationally-related contingencies, disengagement is influenced by the social relations which actors develop. Exiting occurs within situations that involve other actors with whom they acquire meaningful bonds.

Relationships are basic to career transformations primarily because they serve to mediate objective conditions of work. In general, friendship groupings facilitate disengagement by providing emotional support, certification of new identities, protection from stigma, alternative life-styles, and material resources. Clearly, work is abandoned more easily in supportive social contexts. The acceptance of others is central to the decision to disengage. This "reference to others," however, does not foreclose social action (Hughes 1971). Rather, disengagement is constructed on the basis of a social dialogue in which actors interrogate, compare and judge the perspectives and experiences of audiences accessible to them. Disengagement is related to the nature of social relations actors develop. The suggestions of "others" regarding disengagement assume greater significance when accompanied by the actor's growing disenchantment. Specifically, the quality of relationships either sustains further involvements in the workplace or opens up new prospects in a wider community.

The social construction of disengagement consists of multiple involvements of actors. A discussion of this process is conceptually more comprehensive when we focus on the content and context of these associations. The premise that disengagement is an expression of interactions located within supportive affiliations is intellectually promising. The links between identity transformations and significant others have been treated in a cursory manner in the literature. Implicit in this undertaking is the intent to stimulate a critical evaluation of what Baldwin and Bottoms (1976:1) refer to as, the underlying dimensions of social processes that are related to a wider social order of relations. Close and relatively stable friendship relations at work make it difficult for actors to disengage. The stronger the identification of members with one another, the greater the bonds that unite them. Consequently, anxieties about remaining at work are often alleviated by conceding to certain attitudes held by those whom they have learned to trust.

These sentiments do not disappear quickly given the emotional dependency that characterizes these relations. Workers, however, who are more isolated from informal associations disengage sooner. The *structure* of the network of personal ties (single-stranded or multiple strands; loose-knit or tight networks) affects access to resources. In addition to the morphological elements of these networks, the *content* of social relations is also viewed as significant. Content refers to the meanings actors attribute to their relationships. In other words, content, as the focus of interactions, includes an actors' investments in social relations. Relations are activated to secure the flow of resources, ranging from tangible elements like materials, loans, information, assistance—to those more intangible, such as sociability or emotional support. These relationships are utilized for various problem-solving purposes—coping with manifest difficulties of daily living and resolving more complicated identity issues. These associations are important sources of personal identification, support, and information. The nature of relations influences the acquisition and application of skills, self-concept, and social reactions of others which in turn are central to the exiting process.

The premise of this section is that two sets of factors contribute to the disengagement process: occupationally related contingencies and the effects of social relations. The former features include a sense of alienation that results from a perceived inability to sustain an identification as worker. Secondly, social relations are significant in introducing actors to new opportunities in different fellowships and involvements in the work community. These contingencies influence the relationship between self-concept and occupational commitments. Furthermore, these factors account for identity differences during inter-career and intra-career stages. Again, occupations exist in the context of a wider environment from which they draw values. Formal systems of support and control also impinge on the world of careers.

Conclusion

This chapter acknowledges the influence of *situational* and *structural* aspects of work. Social structures are depicted as contexts that shape rather than determine human action. Culture, ideology, and the political economy of work shape behaviour insofar as they influence the setting and provide symbols that could be used to interpret situations. Social structure is realized in the actions of individuals. Work, therefore, is a construction that exists within wider interpretive schemes. As an orienting tool, the concept of a career facilitates an analysis of both interactional and structural influences. Actors interpret their existential experiences within this perspective. Additionally, this concept embodies wider social and cultural influences. Analyses of careers seek to uncover the structures that underlie complex and often incoherent surface appearances of work interactions. Careers can tell us much about the structure of professions—the sets of mental and physical activities related to work. Structural aspects of careers include: career lines, status, culture, linkages with other social systems, rules, and roles.

Alternatively, the concept of career reveals the interactive stages of becoming and of being, distinctions previously often overlooked in occupational studies. Career stages consist of options that actors use to make sense of their occupational involvements. They involve specific perspectives, conditions, and patterns of interaction associated with processes of becoming connected with, continuing in, and discontinuing from occupational pursuits. Movement through stages depends on contingencies which make problematic the notion of career movements as unilinear, sequential or fixed. Contingencies are factors that account for the likelihood of pursuing career stages, ranging from isolated features of individual stages to the generic processes of work. This management of contingencies is highly consequential for the development, maintenance, and disengagement from work.

Unlike role theory, network analysis assigns actors a greater role in the construction of strategies. This approach moves beyond the specific aspects of a social actor's work and draws upon the actor's repertoire of multiple realities. This full range of participation in both professional and non-professional realms is extremely relevant to appreciating the nature of work primarily because it considers the complex of social worlds within which actors are embedded. What has been advanced is a perspective which depicts actors as attending to the configuration of relations during the course of their career pursuits. It was argued that work must be viewed in the context of all meaningfully constructed affiliations. Networks of relations affect careers because they forge possibilities and set limitations to social action. This emphasis on inside and outside relations, that is, the environmental milieu of relations within the workplace, influences occupational orientations and investments.

References

Baldwin, J. and A. Bottoms. 1976. *The Urban Criminal.* London: Tavistock.

Barley, S. 1989. "Careers, Identities, and Institutions: The legacy of the Chicago School of Sociology." Pp. 41-65 in *Handbook of Career Theory*, edited by M. Arthur, D. Hall, and B. Lawrence. New York: Cambridge University Press.

Becker, H. 1963. *Outsiders: Studies in the Sociology of Deviance.* NY: Free Press.

Becker, H., Geer, B. E. Hughes, and A. Strauss. 1961. *Boys in White.* Chicago: University of Chicago.

Bejian, D. V. and P. R. Salomone. 1995. "Understanding Midlife Career Renewal: Implications for Counseling." *The Career Development Quarterly* 44(1):52-63.

Blachford G. 1981. "Male Dominance and the Gay World." In *The Making of the Modern Homosexual*, edited by K. Plummer. London: Hutchinson.

Blankenship, R. 1977. "Organizational Careers: An Interactionist Perspective." In *Colleagues in Organizations: The Social Construction of Professional Work*, edited by R. Blankenship. New York: J. Wiley and Sons.

Blau, P. and R. Scott. 1962. *Formal Organizations.* San Francisco: Chandler.

Blau, P. et al. 1956. "Occupational Choice: A Conceptual Framework." *Industrial and Labor Relations Review* 9:531-543.

Blauner, R. 1967. *Alienation and Freedom* Chicago: University of Chicago Press.

Blumer, H. 1969. *Symbolic Interactionism.* Englewood Cliffs: Prentice-Hall.

_____. 1979. "Introduction." In *Stations of the Lost*, edited by J. Wiseman. Chicago: University of Chicago Press.

Bruner, J. 1990. *Acts of Meaning.* Cambridge, MA.: Harvard University Press.

Campanis, P. 1970. "Normlessness in Management." In *Deviance and Respectability*, edited by J. Douglas. New York: Basic.

Clement, W. 1975. *The Canadian Corporate Elite.* Toronto: McClelland and Stewart.

Collin, A. and Watts, A.G. 1996. "The Death and Transfiguration of Career and of Career Guidance?" *British Journal of Guidance and Counseling* 24(3):385-398.

Dalton, M. 1966. *Men Who Manage.* New York: John Wiley and Sons.
Davis, J. 1965. *Undergraduate Career Decisions.* Chicago: Aldine.
Ditton, J. 1979. *Controlology—Beyond the New Criminology.* London: Macmillan.
Dubin, R. 1958. *The World of Work.* Englewood Cliffs: Prentice-Hall.
Durkheim, E. [1893]1933. *Division of Labour in Society* New York: Free Press.
_____. [1895]1964. *The Rules of the Sociological Method.* New York: Free Press.
Etzioni, A. 1974. "Organizational Control." In *Modern Sociology*, edited by P. Worsley. Markham: Penguin.
Fleischer, H. 1973. *Marxism and History.* Frankfurt: Suhrkamp.
Fox, A. 1980. "The Meaning of Work." In *The Politics of Work and Occupations*, edited by G. Esland and G. Salaman. Toronto: University of Toronto Press.
Gerth, H. and C. W. Mills. 1953. *Character and Social Structure.* New York: Harcourt, Brace and World.
Giddens, A. 1976. *New Rules of Sociological Methods.* New York: Basic.
Glaser, B. 1968. *Organizational Careers.* Chicago: Aldine.
Glaser, B. and A. Strauss. 1971. *Status Passage.* Chicago: Aldine.
Goffman, E. 1961. *Asylums.* New York: Doubleday.
Gray, D. 1994. "Turning Out: A Study of Teenage Prostitution." *Urban Life and Culture* 1(4):401-426.
Hall, R. 1975. *Occupations and the Social Structure.* Englewood Cliffs: Prentice Hall.
Hamilton, P. 1980. "Social Theory and the Problematic Concept of Work." In *The Politics of Work and Occupations*, edited by G. Esland and G. Salaman. Toronto: University of Toronto Press.
Heyl, B. 1979. *The Madam As Entrepreneur.* New Brunswick: Transaction.
Holland, J. L. 1973. *Making Vocational Choices: A Theory of Careers.* Englewood Cliffs: Prentice Hall.
Holnzer, B. 1968. *Reality Construction in Society.* Cambridge: Schenknan.
Hughes, E. 1937. "Institutional Office and the Person." *American Journal of Sociology* 43 (November):409-410.
_____. 1958. *Men and Their Work.* Glencoe: Free Press.
_____. E. 1971. *The Sociological Eye.* Chicago: Aldine.
Keon, T., Latack, J. and Wanons J. 1982. "Image Congruence and the Treatment of Different Scores in Organizational Choice Research." *Human Relations* 35(2):155-166.
Krause, E. 1971. *The Sociology of Occupations.* Boston: Little, Brown and Co.
Lankard, B. 1996. "Acquiring Self-Knowledge for Career Development." ED399414. ERIC Digest No.175. ERIC Clearinghouse on Adult, Career, and Vocational Education, Columbus, Ohio.
Lemert, E. 1972. *Human Deviance, Social Problems and Social Control.* Englewood

Cliffs: Prentice-Hall.
Lore, Nicholas. 1998. *The Pathfinder.* New York: Simon and Schuster.
Lyman M. and M. Scott 1970. *The Sociology of the Absurd.* New York: Appleton-Century-Crofts.
Matza, D. 1969. *Becoming Deviant.* Englewood Cliffs: Prentice-Hall.
McFarlane, B. 1968. "Retirement to Dentistry." In *Canadian Society,* edited by B. Blishen et al. Toronto: Macmillan.
Meisenhelder, T. 1977. "An Exploratory Study of Exiting From Criminal Careers." *Criminology* 15(3):319-334.
Mills, C. W. 1951. *White Collar.* New York: Oxford U. Press.
Oplatka, I., D. Bargal, and D. Inbar. 2001. "The Process of Self-Renewal Among Women Headteachers in Mid-Career." *Journal of Educational Administration* 39(1):77-94.
Plummer, K. 1981. *The Making of the Modern Homosexual.* London: Hutchinson.
_____. 1995. "Life Story Research." Pp. 50-63 in *Rethinking Methods in Psychology,* edited by J. N. Smith, R. Harre, and L. V. Langenhove. London: Sage.
Porter, J. 1965. *The Vertical Mosaic.* Toronto: U of T Press.
Presthus, R. 1962. *Organizational Society.* New York: Vintage.
Prus, R. 1984. "Anthropological and Sociological Approaches to Deviance: An Ethnographic Prospect." Unpublished paper presented at Deviance in a Cross-Cultural Context Conference, University of Waterloo.
Rinehart, J. 1975. *The Tyranny of Work.* Don Mills: Academic.
Ritzer, G. 1972. *Man and His Work: Conflict and Change.* Englewood Cliffs: Prentice Hall.
Rock, P. 1979. *The Making of Symbolic Interactionism.* London: Macmillan.
Rosenfeld, R. 1980. "Race and Sex in career Dynamics." *American Sociological Review* 45:583-609.
Saks, M. 1983. "Removing The Blinders? A Critique of Recent Contributions to the Sociology of Professions." *Sociological Review* 31(1):233-254.
Salaman, G. 1974. *Community and Occupation.* London: Cambridge University Press.
Sheehy, G. 1981. *Passages.* New York: Bantom.
Slocum, W. 1974. *Occupational Careers: A Sociological Perspective* Chicago: Aldine.
Silverman, D. 1978. *The Theory of Organizations.* London: Heinemann.
Sonnenfeld, J. and J. Kotter. 1982. "The Maturation of Career Theory." *Human Relations* 35(1):19-46.
Stinchcombe, A. 1973. "Formal Organizations." In *Sociology,* edited by N. Smelser. New York: J. Wiley and Sons.
Strauss, A. 1969. *Mirrors and Masks.* San Francisco: Sociology Press.
_____. 1975. *Professions, Work and Careers.* New Brunswick: Transaction.

Strauss, A. and H. Becker. 1975. "Careers, Personality and Adult Socialization." In *Professions, Work and Careers*, edited by A. Strauss. New Brunswick: Transaction.

Taylor, L. and O. Walton. 1971. "Industrial Sabotage: Motives and Meanings." In *Images of Deviance*, edited by S. Cohen. Harmondsworth: Penguin.

Weber, M. [1947]1969. *The Theory of Social and Economic Organization*. New York: Free Press.

West, W. G. 1978. "The Short-Term Careers of Serious Thieves." *Canadian Journal of Criminology* 20(2):169-190.

Whyte, W. H. 1956. *The Organization Man*. New York: Simon and Schuster.

Willis, P. 1980. *Learning to Labour*. Farnborough: Gower.

Woollacott, J. 1980. "Dirty and Deviant Work." In *The Politics of Work and Occupations*, edited by G. Esland and G. Salaman. Toronto: University of Toronto Press.

Zunker, V. G. 1990. *Career Counseling: Applied Concepts of Life Planning*. Pacific Grove, CA: Brooks-Cole.

Chapter 4

Nursing's Journey from Semi-professional to Professional

Merle A. Jacobs

Learning Objectives:

1. Understand the professionalization of nursing.

2. Consider how the labour participation of women is managed.

3. Note the organization of power in pink collar professions.

4. Describe professional practice.

Introduction

The study of occupations and professions has a lengthy and prominent tradition in the social sciences. Research shows that women predominantly occupy the "subordinate" positions in the field. Originally, the term profession (Freidson 1986, 1990, 2001) was reserved for occupations based on expert knowledge, autonomy, self regulation, monopoly, and a service orientation for the good of the public. This chapter will look at the process of how nurses went from being a semi-professional occupation to a profession and the issues that still remain within this pink profession. It is not at all historically accurate to refer to the care of the sick as being a female task, or somehow outside the physical capabilities of men.

Men in nursing comprise a small percentage of professional nurses in North America (Squires 1995). Male nurses fare as well if not better that their female colleagues and are over represented in administrative positions (Williams 1995). There is little difference between men and women working in the same position regarding wages and seniority. However, men are more likely to advance into highly visible areas such as the emergency departments, intensive care units or managers (Williams 1995). Several assumptions exist around men in nursing. The two most common inferences about men in nursing are the linkages to homosexuality and that they chose nursing because they failed to become physicians. These issues certainly fuel gender discrimination in nursing services.

Eliot Freidson (1990) stated that medicine, nursing, and other health-care occupations are part of a coordinated division of labour, and these disciplines function together around patients within the hospital system. What was noted in his discussion is that the position of nursing in the health-care system is not autonomous. Nurses struggle to claim a set of tasks with clearly defined boundaries that are stable from one circumstance to another and performed exclusively by those with special training.

Although hospitals are no longer assigned the task of educating and training nurses, they do maintain a voice in nursing practice when it comes to nurses working in acute care. Hospitals are still the major employer of registered nurses and thus educate them regarding health policies and procedures. Professional practice is tied to professional autonomy. Nurses working within the hospital have little autonomy and must work according to the mandate set by the employer. Staff nurses who practice at the bedside have informed the State of their desire to have a baccalaureate in order for them to practice at a higher level. Perhaps the motive is to move nursing towards professionalizing? In order to professionalize, nurses had to establish a specialized knowledge base and university education. This led to the creation of a Ph.D. programme in Canada in the 1990s. In the following chapter we will look at intergroup dynamics and caring work and how professionalism is achieved.

Pink Collar Work

Occupation culture guides and interprets the tasks and social relations of work. Occupation culture becomes the master determinant of social identity, self-conception, and social status of people working (Hughes 1971). Women's work has long been discussed by feminist scholars (Eichler 1980; Smith 1987) along with strategies for change. More women work outside the home in the labour force. While this has undermined traditional patriarchy, it has burdened women with double the work load and exposed them to unjust circumstances in the work place.

When women entered into the occupation of nursing, it was hospital bureaucracy, not nursing that controlled nursing positions. Nurses did not have autonomy or a body of knowledge and depended on hospitals for their training. They worked under the direction of physicians and the relationship between nurse and physician has been one in which the doctor gives orders to the nurse. Nurses do not give orders to doctors.

The history of nursing is well documented (Bingham 1979) as being little more than domestic work and caring for the sick. The fact that most nurses are women is relevant. In their seminal work on women, children and poverty in America, Stallard, Ehrenreich and Sklar (1983) coined the phrase "pink collar ghetto" (p.18). The axiom has been used to describe fields traditionally dominated by women—teaching, nursing, early childhood education, day care, and secretarial work. All have derogatory implications and poor employment conditions. The excuse in the past for putting women in these wearisome or low-paid positions is that they are allegedly better at care giving, intuitive or communicative jobs. These jobs were seen as pick collar work and therefore nonprofessional, at best they were delegated to semi-professional status.

In *Sexism in the Hospital Family*, Ashley (1976) concluded that nursing, perhaps more than any other profession, has been influenced by social conceptions regarding the nature of women. Ashley states that sexist and paternalistic attitudes toward nurses persist in the training nurses receive, which in turn causes deep resentment. Staff nurses still resent being subordinate to physicians and to nurses in the upper levels of the professional hierarchy. Del Bueno (1986) saw power as an important variable in any workplace and stated power must be accepted, understood, and used by nurses. This power has been used by nurse leaders to transform nursing from a semi-professional occupation to one which can be labelled professional. Although nursing researchers view nursing as a profession, the work environment does not allow for those at the bedside to behave within the criteria as described by Hughes et al. (1958).

Like most women's paid or unpaid-work, nursing is grossly under valued (Grow 1991). Valentine (1992) asserts that nurses have not been encouraged to become involved in the women's movement. Interestingly, feminists devalue nursing as a viable career choice for women (p. 21). Since nurses can now practice as Clinical Nurse Specialist, society allows nurses to provide treatment and care in hospitals and in the community. However, they are not given the same autonomy as other health care professionals when it comes to patient care. Social workers do not have to rely on physicians to take care for patients, but nurses (other than a narrow area of practice) must follow orders from physicians. Yet, nursing is the only profession within the hospital that is needed twenty four hours a day and seven days a week.

The Florence Nightingale Pledge: A Foundation of Semi-Professionalism

Nursing is a complex process and much of nursing practice is poorly understood by those outside the profession, as well as some within the profession. Present day nursing developed out of the tradition of Nightingale. The Florence Nightingale Pledge for Nurses maintains the following:

> I solemnly pledge myself before God and in the presence of this assembly to pass my life in purity and to practice my profession faithfully. I will abstain from whatever is deleterious and mischievous, and will not take or knowingly administer any harmful drug I will do all in my power to elevate the standard of my profession, and will hold in confidence all personal matters committed to my keeping, and all family affairs coming to my knowledge in the practice of my calling. With loyalty will I endeavour to aid the physician in his work, and devote myself to the welfare of those committed to my care. (Harper Hospital 1893)

Understanding the above pledge highlights the values that the leaders in nursing from the time of Nightingale provided their members in terms of ethical behaviour, which is still part of the value system in nursing. This oath also shows a service oriented occupation with strong religious ties, and allows the reader to understand the devotion or care that nurses must have toward the physician and their patients. During this period, female nurses were subordinated to male dominance both by virtue of being female in a patriarchal society and by being seen as assistants to the male-dominated medical profession. Stripped of its religious elements of loving care and self-sacrificing duty, nursing is still revealed to be a female ghetto of cheap labour compared to medicine. Nowadays, nursing finds itself in a scientific profession, the rapid proliferation of biomedical technology and the changes in communication systems, yet this occupation is still highly labour intensive providing emotional, physical, and spiritual care. We can say that nursing is no longer a place where women have to work but a place where some women choose to work. However, we need to be familiar with how nursing is viewed within the profession and in society in order to comprehend why so many leave the profession and why this profession is still pink.

Nurses are in constant contact with patients in homes, hospitals, and clinics. When lay people are asked to evaluate the role of staff nurses in health care, they usually rely on information acquired from mass media. The public at large still perceives nurses as doing what physicians tell them to do when they are admitted to hospitals. Therefore, maintaining stereotypes and public misinformation about nurses reinforces the notion that physicians are superior in both knowledge and skill and that nurses are the physician's handmaidens. The public in general does not understand the specialized knowledge that nurses have or nursing autonomy.

The view that nursing was a subordinate part of medical practice, existing solely to meet the needs of physicians, led early researchers to view their actions as a service and labelled nursing as semi-professional by scholars in the area of professions and occupations (Hughes et. al. 1958; Ross 1961; Suryamani 1989; Freidson 1990). Discussion centered on issues around the ideal profession, authority, and the role of the nurse. During this period nurses were aspiring to professional status. However, the state, the public, their employers, and researchers in the area of professions did not view nursing and nurses in the same way. We can contend that in part nursing was seen as women's work, and the term "profession" was reserved for male-dominated professions.

The role of nursing has been conceptualized in terms of bureaucratic, professional, and service orientations (Hughes et al. 1958; Ross 1961; Corwin 1961). The bureaucratic conception emphasizes rules and regulations within the organization; the professional role conception is associated with principles and standards of the profession. According to Suryamani (1989), the ideal role of a nurse as expressed by doctors (physicians) is to provide physical care to patients and to follow the instructions of physicians. Her study shows that there are discrepancies between the ideal role and the performance of nurses as expressed by doctors. Nurses were not working according to how physicians expected them to behave as handmaidens and subservient to the medical profession. Kinney (1985) discussed the service role orientation and associated it with values such as humanity, compassion, and dedication to the patient. Grow (1991) focussed on the duties of staff nurses and control over nursing care and their role within the health care system. Grow viewed the role as one of caring which is emotional and has been relegated to women by society (p.120).

It is clear that the role of nursing is complex. It has been idealized in terms of legal, ritual, moral, and mothering characterizations.

How Nurses Perceive their Occupation

Corwin (1961) found that baccalaureate graduates held high professional role conceptions more frequently than did diploma graduates. When nursing leaders responded to meet the criteria of professionalism, they recognized that nursing had to establish a scientific knowledge base. Thus, academically prepared nurses were further divided from those practicing at the bedside with diplomas. This divisiveness is characteristic of the horizontal violence of oppressed groups (Corwin 1961:361).

Nurses in institutional settings do exhibit oppressed group behaviour and have internalized patriarchal values to such an extent that nursing values are marginalized. Fear of being destroyed by the oppressor and fear of change prevents revolt by the oppressed and perpetuates submissive behaviour. Female traits such as caring, tenderness, compassion, and supportiveness are viewed as less desirable, unnecessary and even inferior to objective "rational" male traits (Corwin 1961:21). Given the traditional hierarchies in staff nursing and nursing administration, it is not surprising that staff nurses feel like they are at the bottom of the ladder. "If nurses look down upon each other, what can we expect from the public and the interdisciplinary team?" (Dalton 1990:17).

Subdividing the professional group into subordinate and superordinate interaction provides a level of understanding of the nursing professionalism. For example, the oppression of women in a male-dominated work environment. In addition, we see that the professionalization of nursing adds a horizontal layer of subjugation whereby oppressed women oppress other women (Jacobs 2002).

In summary, inside hospitals, staff nurses who feel oppressed will continue to feel the pressure of heavy workloads, the change in government policies and funding, the lack of real input into hospital policies that influences their work and the issues of gender, race, class, albeism, heterosexualism, and entrenched hierarchies of hospital life.

More Credentials: A Way to Professionalism

Initially, nurses were trained within hospital schools of nursing where students worked as unpaid labour for room, board, training and a small stipend. Training then shifted to universities and colleges. Students no longer entered into an Internship at a hospital. Instead, as part of their academic studies they would gain experience at a hospital through Field Education. In this form of education student paid university fees as well as out of pocket expenses for their field experience. This move occurred in Ontario in the 1970s which allowed for full autonomy, a body of knowledge, and self governance. Within nursing, a value is placed on professionalism as a way to shift the focus of being called "handmaiden," "battle-axe" or semi-professional to have society view nursing as an occupation that could be part of the elite group of occupations—a profession.

The move to universities for nursing education was to provide a new context for learning that would ground nursing as a science and an art distinct from medicine. In this environment, the curricula could be controlled by a College of Nurses

(CNO) that would provide standard accreditation exams and nurses would be taught non-medical theories and more holistic concepts of health care. The Dubin report (1983) recommended that hiring preference be given to those with nursing degrees, a suggestion supported by the Registered Nursing Association of Ontario (RNAO). Rank and file nurses saw the proposal for a degree requirement as elitist. There is an absence of research that supports the contention that a nurse with a degree actually does a better or worse job than a nurse graduating with a diploma. In Canada, nursing care is provided in many institutions by practical nurses who are regulated by their college, but supervised by registered nurses (RN). Along with the Registered Practical Nurses (RPN), many institutions use unregulated workers to provide care to patients. For those receiving care, how do they discern who is a professional nurse?

In working toward the goal of baccalaureate training, the Canadian Nursing Association (CAN 1982) had to contend with the following three major developments: (1) changes in the health of Canadians; (1) the nature of nursing practice; and, (3) changes in the health-care delivery system. The specializations and diversity within hospitals demand professional competence. The combination of the push for higher education for nurses by the RNAO, Justice Dubin's report, and the CAN contributed to changing how nurses were trained and also increased the cost for those entering this pink profession. Nurse leaders lobbied the government, promoted their theories and through the CNO went from semi-professional to professional status. In her early research, Travelbee (1966: 44) describes a nurse as

> [a]n individual who has been irrevocably and profoundly changes as a result of her specialized knowledge and education. She has learned a body of scientific knowledge and has the ability to use it, has developed new skills; but more important, she has been confronted with the vulnerability of the human being in a way that an adolescent of young adult entering another occupational field has not. The most profound changes are brought about by exposure to illness, suffering and death, in that these experiences are irrevocably removed from the status of comfortable abstractions, becoming instead profound realities.

She recognized what scholars were considering as the ideal type within professions and set out the objectives of what nursing should look like. For this to occur, nurses had to be educated in a university just like other professionals. One of the significant results of these educational requirements is the demoralizing effect that it has had on some young recruits. The new recruits spend time and money for nursing education, and yet they compete for similar employment alongside Registered Practical Nurses who did not make the same financial sacrifice.

The Baccalaureate Model: The Professional Nurse

Based on a historical analysis of nursing education in Canada, Baumgart and Larsen (1988) noted several reasons why professional nursing moved towards a baccalaureate program. For instance, the competition within the hospital for power and control over patient care with other professionals who are university trained played a part in the nursing profession establishing their own degree program. As well, at a CNO annual meeting (CNO 1998), Margretta Styles stated: "the level of nursing education has contributed to the way in which the profession is viewed and to the way in which nurses are able to handle themselves in dealing with other disciplines" (p.7). Dealing with physicians, the attainment of autonomy for nursing has been an implied goal within the nursing profession since the days of Florence Nightingale (Bingham 1979). However, formal university training is described by the nursing profession as a profession changing roles to keep pace with changes in society rather than any other reason discussed earlier (Chitty 1997). We can argue that this change is not about interpersonal relations but more about obtaining status as a profession within the health care team.

Introspection of nursing education led to the belief that schools of nursing should be placed under the jurisdiction of institutions where both professional and cultural instruction is provided. The professional organizations, both at the national and provincial levels, support the view that a baccalaureate degree in nursing is the only logical entry level for nurses in the twenty-first century (CNA 1986). Discussion in this area is directed toward the skills and education that will serve the nurse as a professional. The issue of educational preparation for nurses was addressed by the Royal Commission on Health Services (Government of Canada 1964) to universities and linked the emerging profession of nursing to other more established professions in the university (King 1970). The CNA, which is the organization for the nursing professional in Canada, has supported the baccalaureate program through various reports (CNA 1982). The CNA's adoption of this position on entry to practice has been incorporated within the mandate of the RNAO and implemented by the CNO in 2005. Nursing now controlled the training credentials for entry and career mobility. Baccalaureate and graduate programs established an intellectual base from which collegial interaction could and should take place. However, these graduates quickly become enmeshed in a bureaucratic system as a labour force rather than as professionals who control their own nursing practice.

As stated earlier, this view is perceived by staff nurses to be that of the elites within the profession. The experience of staff nurses was devalued, universities wanted them to learn what they already knew and practiced. They were expected to upgrade their education and training while working full time and fulfill family obligations. Immigrant nurses who were once welcomed due to a shortage of nurses were now facing a hostile environment where nurse leaders were less accommodating and credentials were used to disenfranchise them. Even with the current shortage in nursing, immigrant nurses face many hurdles. Our system is Eurocentric in training in spite of the diversity of the population. The orientation of newcomers is more about how the dominant groups view health rather than the accumulative knowledge and cultural competencies that they bring with them to Canada. The testing that occurs is not familiar as it is very North American. There are other ways of evaluating skills and knowledge. Nurses with the same substantive knowledge can differ in their skill at solving abstract problems. Immigrant nurses may not have the Canadian classroom jargon but have experience which has been learned by working in hospitals prior to coming to Canada. Rather than blaming the foreign trained nurse for not passing exams or understanding the orientation process, the host country needs to understand how they test for competence or proficiency. It may be beneficial to have foreign trained nurses who work in the system orientate new comers. They could use their experience and formal knowledge to explain the essential characteristic of nursing in Canada and address their questions. This discussion represents a relationship between working knowledge, formal knowledge, and Eurocentric ways of educating "the other."

Occupational classrooms are concerned about the future employers. Little and Brian (1982) found that additional education affected most nurses, but not in the same way. They investigated changes in role conceptions as nurses advanced from an initial two year or three-year nursing programs through a baccalaureate degree. State of readiness and receptivity were suggested as influencing variables. This demonstrates that programs differ in readiness. Therefore, some universities who have two-year programs may not be providing their students with the same skills and knowledge as those with a full four-year program. According to Kramer (1974), nurse educators are creating greater expectations of professional autonomy in new graduates and that these expectations are not met in practice when employed by hospitals or in the community. In a Canadian study, Cairns and Cragg (1987) found more dissatisfaction expressed by baccalaureate nurses employed as staff nurses in hospitals and that major issues for all staff nurses included pay, shift work, and lack of autonomy. It is difficult to assess how changes in the educational experience of nurses has been able to keep pace with changes in society. Women no longer need to work in this pink ghetto. The price of nursing education may motivate women to seek other areas of employment such as engineering.

Specialized Knowledge

Specialized knowledge is the creation of credential and boundaries. The abundance of certificates and specializations in nursing safeguards the domination of those in power. The CNA Certification Program was initiated by a membership request in June 1980 through a biennial resolution directing CNA to study the feasibility of developing examinations for certification in major nursing specialties. Nurses in leadership positions within hospitals and universities are expected to have extra clinical skills and education. These credentials provide them with expert knowledge and intellectual specialization. Experts also depend on the compliance of the less calculating and overworked staff nurse group to keep their role and status as expert nurses. Occupationally controlled division of labour is a necessary component of professionalism. Nursing has achieved this.

Nursing educators working at universities play an important part by formulating theoretical constructs for nursing practice (Johnson 1959; King 1981; Roy 1983; Orem 1985). These theorists provide structure and understanding to the actions of nursing through their theories. Nurse leaders points to the role of nursing theory and research as the body of knowledge that makes nursing a profession. The first nursing theorist, Johnson (1959) was influenced by sociologists. Her theory draws directly from general systems theory. Nursing theories such as Roy's (1983) theory of adaptation are regarded by nurse managers and nursing leaders as a basis for nursing practice in many hospitals. Nurse administrators use nursing theories as the culture of practice. It is a culture that is expected to promote certain values within the nursing department or division of that institution. Nurses higher in the professional hierarchy can appropriate ideas and theories and promote these ideas as the ideal for nursing care. They become experts in translating the rules and regulations for the larger group of staff nurses. Within this cultural sphere, there is considerable deference expected by the expert nurse. Their credentials allow them to create a labour market shelter that is an exclusive right to perform certain types of work such as interpreting the norms, values, and theoretical constructs.

In my observation, nursing theory has not been widely accepted by the staff nurse as a process in providing patient care, although all nurses are aware of nursing theory because of the college and university curriculum. Therefore, through educational processes, specialized knowledge is promoted. Through their training period, nursing theories help student nurses practice nursing care. Hospitals may not use nursing theory as a model of care. Instead they may use a business or medical model instead. This makes nursing knowledge subservient to other knowledge within the institution.

Staff nurses have specialized knowledge and work in units such as emergency departments, psychiatry, and intensive care units. These nurses have more control and power than their counterparts who work on medical or general surgical units. Hospitals hire nurse educators, case managers, and clinical nurse specialist who work at a higher level than these nurses and are seen to have extra knowledge within the department. Nurses speak about having layers of nurses working on one patient due to specialized knowledge. Like other "older" professions such as medicine, nursing represents occupational rather than patient interest.

Other types of specialized knowledge within nursing are budget information, staff-patient care models, and business skills leading to the formation of business degrees in nursing at the graduate level. They use business knowledge to control the nursing agenda within their departments, hospitals, and even at the societal level. Given the growth of knowledge, nursing as a profession has adopted other forms of knowledge in order to maintain their numbers in administration. Today with programme management, other health professionals have taken on unit management roles.

Nursing leaders can take the lead in hospitals and in society without the support of the staff nurse group and many times in conflict with this group. Ideas are sometimes appropriated from the staff nurse level by the leadership, used either in new policies or in academic papers without the credit accorded to those who generated the idea. Decision making is assigned to the management level with several levels of power and prestige that advocates a system where staff nurses have been aliens in the rule making process. Decisions are made from the top-down. Power is used to shape perception and also to prevent opposition from occurring. It is a dimension in the determination of authority-subject relationships within the nursing profession. The degree that the individual controls power within the group will affect the individual's relationship with the group. The staff nurse is at the low level of the pyramid as is the nursing management compared to the administrators and the medical profession.

Nursing management has views of what they expect clinical practice to be within the hospital. Research-based practice within many hospitals is also advanced from the top-down. Although this affects the staff nurse on an organizational level, it is not a top priority for the staff nurse who feels over worked and lacks the time to give adequate patient care. These nursing concepts which come from scholarly studies help build the structure of professionalism through specialized knowledge. It can be argued that the major portions of nursing accomplishment have been built on the backs of the staff nurses who have to practice nursing care and who do not get the benefits of professional autonomy.

Licensing and Professional Organizations

Professional organizations or associations have their formal culture codified to a certain extent. This code is called the descriptive culture of the association. It allows individuals to follow a code of interaction with clear expectations and boundaries. The code of the CNO is equipped with sanctions that are enforced when deviations occur. The CNO provides the exams for registration and it is the place for the public to lay complaints when concerned about nursing practice.

The CNO and the RNAO have rules surrounding professionalism and collegial behaviour. These groups promote the self-interest of experts within the nursing profession. Rules and regulations are often created at the professional or organization level and are invoked as part of a power play providing for a bureaucratic decision-making process. It is also the level where experts exert power over the group. Nursing theories which started developing in the early 1960s (Bullough and Bullough 1994) are ideologies that prevail within the culture of the nursing profession. The RNAO provides workshops and other educational seminars and presentations given by elites within the profession. Staff nurses who also have specialized knowledge based on everyday work experience may not have the same opportunities to express their knowledge. This division of power and status is not much different than when physicians taught nurses in hospitals.

Wuest (1994) documents that professionalism has failed to bring the power and prestige anticipated by the early leaders of the professionalization movement in nursing. Wuest views professionalism as a patriarchal invention and by its very nature is alienating to women. Nurses seeking professionalization upgraded their educational preparation. Research became an issue for nurses as they attempted to establish a scientific knowledge base. However, they did not take into account the staff nurse in this model. Benner (1982, 1984) developed a frame of reference for nursing that went form novice to expert. Benner became a foundation for nurses to identify where they fit on the professional ladder and for nursing managers to evaluate their nursing staff. Benner argues that a competent nurse and a proficient nurse will not approach or solve a clinical situation in the same way. For Benner, a competent nurse typifies a nurse who has been on the job in the same or similar situations for two to three years. The competent nurse lacks the experience, speed, and flexibility of the proficient nurse. Experience plays a part in the professional role. Intuitive judgment is an essential part of clinical judgment. The value of experience in making decisions rather than merely understanding theoretical knowledge needs to be addressed by the profession. Competency is tied to experience in nursing, making clinical practice complex, and does not provide a smooth framework for researchers.

Professional Practice and Autonomy

Professional practice is tied to professional autonomy. The staff nurse who practices at the bedside needs to have a baccalaureate model in order to be viewed as a professional nurse. Questions will be raised if the staff nurse has the same status as the nurse who has more control over his or her practice. In the quest for professionalism, the hazards inherent in the masculine institution of professionalism have resulted in the oppression of women by women.

Building on the comments of Cantor and Mischel (1979), a number of investigations have been focused on the behaviours and qualities associated with professional practice. Professional autonomy in nursing has been defined by Mass and Jacox (1977) as "members of an occupation governing and controlling their own activities" (p.17). Singleton and Nail (1984) contend that nurses fail to exercise much of the autonomy they already have. Part of the problem of professional autonomy as stated by Mundinger (1980) is that all members need to exercise autonomy. Ashley (1976) in her historical study identified paternalism as a major force that restricts the professional autonomy of nurses. Muff (1982) states that the nurse-physician relationship reinforces the idea that nurses should not be autonomous in that nursing work has been greatly influenced by medical dominance (Armstrong, Choiniere, and Day 1993). Nursing research on professional practice shows that the concern for autonomy relates more to nursing leadership than with the staff nurse. Dennis and Prescott (1985) addressed specific qualities and behaviours associated with Nightingale which included patients (care), maturity, commitment, and intelligence. Autonomy was not addressed by these researchers, although Nightingale wanted nursing to be autonomous from medicine (Bingham 1979). The lack of career commitment among nurses is another force that affects professional autonomy (Mundinger 1980). Nurses are leaving the profession due to dissatisfaction with the role, the work environment, and other occupational opportunities.

Professional practice is discussed in terms of nursing ethics, autonomy, and patient care issues. Viens (1989) notes that in the constant evolution of nursing, the code of ethics has both guided and mirrored its journey toward professionalism as defined earlier in this chapter. Professional practice is centered on patient-nurse relationships and the management of the balance between knowing when to help and when to refrain from helping. The anxieties, wishes, needs, and demands distort the nurse's ability to perceive the wants and needs of those one is helping. A nurse who is not aware of her or his own needs will not be able to discern the needs of the patient (pp. 40-42). This research provides the issues, debates, and struggles that nursing has faced over the years. The nurse participates in the profession's efforts to establish and maintain conditions of employment conducive to high quality care. Veins states that the code of ethics has provided guidance for the profession and has helped determine the position nursing as a profession in society (p.49). In order to provide a patient with a safe and therapeutic environment geared toward health, it is essential that the nurse remain focused on the patient's needs (Pilette, Berck, and Achber 1995). Pilette et al. defined and set boundaries which the authors saw as the cornerstone of the nurse-patient relationship. Professional practice for the nurse is about patient care issues as well as autonomy and behaviour related to decision-making.

Conclusion

The profession of nursing when viewed as a structure is made up of several parts such as professional education and training (colleges and universities), professional associations (RNAO), professional colleges (CNO), and professional bargaining units and unions (Ontario Nurses Association ONA 1993). Together they form the structure, where nurses communicate at an organizational level with each other and are engaged in managing the system. As a structure, the profession of nursing is a formal system. When we only look at organizations involved in nursing, the Ontario Hospital Association (OHA) would not be an organization that comes first on the list. However, the OHA represents hospitals and therefore has a major influence in what occurs within the profession of nursing. The OHA interacts with the Ministry of Health and together with nursing unions and associations discuss the role of the nurse and the compensation that goes along with the job. Nursing organizations are also involved in advocating nursing excellence and professional standards even though each plays a different role and provide different viewpoints when interacting within the structure. The views they share with the public impacts on how the public places the importance of nursing within society. Together, all these organizations have helped move nursing from a semi-professional to a professional occupation.

Nursing is a sheltered profession even though it may not have real autonomy due to the state and the Ontario Hospital Association. However, nursing meets the criteria established by Hughes, Freidson, and other scholars in the fried of professionalism. As Freidson (2001) states it "is a set of institutions which permit the members of an occupation to make a living while controlling their own work (p.17).

Wuest (1994) in discussing feminism, professionalism, and nursing states that "the evolution of nursing knowledge and nursing as a practice discipline has been stunted by the quest for professionalism. Liberal and socialist feminist theory clarifies the hazards inherent in the masculine institution of professionalism for a predominately female discipline" (p.357). However, female nurse leaders—Old Girls network—like Old Boys network, a select group of individuals, overwhelmingly male, who are in a position to wield power and influence in the corporate sector; have the same influence within the nursing profession and in the health care system. These elite women view professionalism as a positive goal for their occupation. For professionalization to happen the work must have certain characteristics and the profession must be able to make certain ideological claims about serving the public interest. In terms of serving the public interest, since Nightingale this occupation has always served the public interest.

The key ingredient to professionalization is state support for a labour market shelter, which is a monopoly providing a certain type of service. This monopoly is the cornerstone of the classic professions such as medicine. Although, nursing as a professional status and has moved from a semi-profession, women in this profession serving the public do not control their worklife. Governmental restraint on finances cause nurses to loose jobs and lack confidence in their government. Hospitals have to be made accountable for how they acquire nursing care hours and spend government funding. Nursing possess the basic qualities of a profession. However, for nurses to gain greater autonomy over their work, according to Freidson (2001), women in this profession who serve the public do not control their worklife. As a society we can transform nursing when we understand the social relations, the advancements made, and the limitations that exist.

References

Armstrong, P., J. Choiniere, and E. Day. 1993. *Vital Signs: Nursing in Transition.* Toronto: Garamond.

Armstrng, P., J. Choiniere, G. Fieldberg, and H. Rosenberg. 1994. "Voices From The Ward: A pilot Study of the Impact of Cutbacks on Hospital Care in ONA 1994." 1-38. Toronto: ONA.

Ashley, J.A. 1976. *Hospitals, Paternalism, and the Role of the Nurse.* New York: Teachers College Press. Columbia University.

Baumgart, A., and J. Larsen. 1988. "Overview: Nursing practice in Canada." In *Canadian nursing faces the future: Development and Change*, edited by A. Baumgart and J. Larson. Toronto: C.V. Mosby.

Benner, P. 1982. "From Novice to Expert." *American Journal of Nursing* March: 402-407.

_____. 1984. *From Novice to Expert.* Addison: Wesley Publishing Company Inc.

Bingham, S. 1979. *Ministering Angles.* New Jersey: Medical Economics Co. Book Division.

Bullough, B., and V. Bullough. 1994. *Nursing Issues: for the Nineties and Beyond.* New York: Spring Publishing Company.

Canadian Nursing Association Website. 1982. "The Origins of Nursing Specialty Certification in Canada." Available at (http://cna-aiic.ca/CNA/nursing/certification/about/history/default_e.aspx).

Cantor, N., and W. Mischel. 1979. "Prototypes in Person Perception." *Advances in Experimental Social Psychology* 12:3-52.

Chitty, K.K. 1997. *Professional: Concepts and Challenges.* Philadelphia: W. B. Saunders Co.

College of Nurses of Ontario. 1998. "Nursing with Styles: Forces of Change Move the Profession Forward." *Communiqué* 23(3):6-7.

Corwin, R.G. 1961. The professional employee: A study of conflict in nursing roles. *The American Journal of Sociology* 66:604-615.

Cairns, B.J.S. and C.E. Cragg. 1987. "Sources of Job Satisfaction and Dissatisfaction among Baccalaureate Staff Nurses in Hospitals." *Nursing Papers* 19(1):15-29.

Dalton, C. 1990. "The Sleeping Giant Awakes." *The Canadian Nurse* 86(9):17-20.

Del Bueno, D.J. 1986. "Power and Politics in Organizations." *Nursing Outlook* 34(3):124-128.

Dennis, K. E. and P. A. Prescott. 1985. "Florence Nightingale: Yesterday, Today, and Tomorrow." *Advances in Nursing Sciences* 7:66-81.

Dubin on Health Care .1983. Available at (http://www.ontla.on.ca/hansard/ committee_debates/36_parl/session1/estimates/e033.htm).

Eichler, Margit. 1980. *The Double Standard: A Feminist Critique of Feminist Social Science.* London: Croon Helm

Freidson, Eliot, 1988a. *Profession of Medicine.* Chicago: University of Chicago Press.

_____.1988b. *Professional Powers.* Chicago, University of Chicago Press.

_____. 1989. *Medical Work in America.* New Haven: Yale University Press.

_____. 1990. "Professionalism, Caring, And Nursing." Paper prepared for The Park Ridge Center, Park Ridge, Illinois.

_____. 2001. *Professionalism: The Third Logic.* Chicago, University of Chicago Press.

Government of Canada. 1964. *Royal Commission on Health Services.* Vol. 1. Queen's Printer. Ottawa.

Grow, S. J. 1991. *Who Cares?: The Crisis in Canadian Nursing.* Toronto: McClelland and Stewart Inc.

Harper Hospital. 1893. *Florence Nightingale Pledge for Nurses.* Prepared by a special committee. Adopted by the Grand Council of the International Council of Nurses, Sao Paulo, Brazil, July 10, 1953.

Hughes, E.C., H. Hughes, and I. Deutscher. 1958. *Twenty Thousand Nurses Tell Their Story.* Montreal: J. B. Lippincott Company.

_____.1958. *Men and their Work.* New York: The Free Press.

_____. 1971. *The Sociological Eye.* New Brunswick, NJ: Transaction Press.

Jacobs, M. 2002. *Is Anyone Listening? Women, Work, and Society.* Toronto: Women's Press.

Johnson, D. 1959. "A Philosophy of Nursing." *Nursing Outlook* 7:198-200.

Kelefian, S. 1985. "Professional and Bureaucratic Role Conceptions and Moral Behaviour among Nurses." *Nursing Research* 34:248-253.

King, I. 1981. *A Theroty for Nursing: Systems, Concepts, Process.* New York: Wiley.

Kinney, C.K.D. 1985. "A Re-Examination of Nursing Role Conceptions." *Nursing Research* 34:170-176.

Kramer, M. 1974. *Reality Shock: Why Nurses Leave Nursing.* St. Louis: C. V. Mosby.

Mass, M. and A.K. Jacox. 1977. *Guidelines for Nurse Autonomy/Patient Welfare.* New York: Appleton-Century-Crofts.

Neuman, P. 1982. *The Neuman Systems Model.* Norwalk, CT: Appleton-Lange.

Ontario Nurses Association (ONA). 1993. *Rethinking Health Care: Report on the State of Helath Care in Ontario.* Toronto: ONA.

Orem, D.M. 1985. *Nursing Concepts of Practice.* 3d ed. Englewood Cliffs: Prentice Hall.

Pilette, P.C., C.B. Berck, and L.C. Achber. 1995. "Therapeutic Management of Helping Boundaries." *Journal of Psychosocial Nursing* 33(1):40-47.

Muff, J. 1982. *Socialization, Sexism and Stereotyping*. St. Lousi: The C.V. Mobsy Company.

Mundinger, M.O. 1980. *Autonomy in Nursing*. Germantown, MD: Aspen.

Ross, A.D. 1961. *Becoming a Nurse*. Toronto: The Macmillian Co. of Canada.

Roy, C. 1983. *Introduction to Nursing: An Adaptation Model*. 2d ed. Englewood Cliffs: Prentice Hall.

RNAO. *Action Alert: RNAO Advocacy Campaign*. RNAO.

Smith, Dorothy E., 1987. *The Everyday World as Problematic: A Feminist Sociology*. Toronto: University of Toronto Press.

Squires, T. 1995. "Men in Nursing." *Registered Nurse* July:26-28.

Stallard, Karin, Barbara Ehrenreich, and Holly Sklar. 1983. *Poverty in the American Dream: Women and Children First*. Boston: South End Press.

Suryamani, E. 1989. *The Organization and the Semi-Professional*. New Delhi: Jainsons Publications.

Travelbee, J. [1966]1977. *Interpersonal Aspects of Nursing*. 2d ed. Philadelphia: F.A. Davis Company.

Valentine, P. 1992. "Feminism: A Four Letter Word." *The Canadian Nurse* 88(11):20-23.

Viens, D. 1989. "A History of Nursing's Code of Ethics." *Nursing Outlook* 37(1):45-49.

Wuest, J. 1994. "Professionalism and the Evolution of Nursing as a Discipline: A Feminist Perspective." *Journal of Professional Nursing* 10(6):357-367.

Williams, C.L. 1995. "Hidden Advantages for Men in Nursing." *Nursing Administration Quarterly* 19(2):63-70.

CHAPTER 5

The Potential for Transformative Justice in Nursing

Rebecca Hagey, Lillie Lum, Jane Turrittin, and Robert MacKay

Learning Objectives:

1. Learn about transformative justice.
2. Consider the value of social justice.
3. Note methods for reducing/eliminating racism within the workplace.
4. Discover the dynamics of racial segregation.
5. Define ethnoracial safety.

What Is Transformative Justice?

Transformative justice is a new approach advocated for dispute resolution in the civil justice system, derived from the introduction of restorative justice—mediation, negotiation, settlement, compensation, reparation—in the criminal system. "Transformative justice is a way of handling conflict that recognizes and responds to the variety of harms caused by conflict...and responds...by bringing individuals together in a process that encourages healing and growth" (Law Commission of Canada 1999).

Restorative justice advocates a number of requirements. Those selected for this model include: (1) the complainant, respondent, and community being involved in a consensus building process; (2) the inquiry process providing an opportunity for the person(s) involved in a breach to take responsibility for the rupture in relationships; (3) the complainant, respondent, and community identifying what standards are appropriate and how the breach will be compensated and standards maintained; and (4) decisions about restoring parties to the community are made with respect to the parties and their circumstances and ethical standards (Law Commission of Canada 1999). All parties in conflict are assumed to have historical realities and ideologies that inform their conflicting perspectives.

Also, the restorative justice idea that disputes offer opportunities for changing relationships is compelling in the context of race relations where the conflict that perpetuates racial stratification is often covert in nature (Essed 1991; van Dijk 1993). Opportunities for talking about perceptions are reported to be rare in nursing settings in the Greater Toronto Area where tensions smolder and the racial hierarchy is spoken of colloquially in metaphors and images (Hagey 2005; Ornstein 2000). For example, "nursing is like a cappuccino. White on top and brown on the bottom. It needs stirring up." The colour layering in these images refers to segmented group realities where advantage is levied resulting in a hierarchy perceived to be unjust and unaccountable (Calliste 1996; Hagey et al. 2001a; Marshall 1996). Rather than fearing conflict, restorative justice takes an assertive approach:

> The most effective response to conflict is to repair the harm done by the wrongful act...For wrongdoers, restoration involves accepting responsibility for their action by repairing any harm that they caused and dealing with the issues that contributed to the wrongdoing...the restorative justice approach responds to the immediate conflict and encourages the development of respectful relationships among those who are wrongdoers, those who have suffered harm and members of the community. (Canadian Council on Social Development 2000:5)

Strategies for repairing relationships appear to be lacking in the formal complaints proceedings of non-unionized nurses and grievances of unionized nurses that we have attended in earlier research funded by the Centre for Excellence in Research on Immigration and Settlement (CERIS) (Collins 1998; Hagey et al. 2001b). In the absence of overt racial slurs or attacks, employers and unions are loath to consider subtle forms of wrongdoing. In current race cases, union officers, lawyers, and arbitrators alike avoid questioning the presumption of innocence and tenaciously seek other possible explanations of events to frame the complaint or grievance (Mactavish and Lenz 1996; Brown 1996).

Events that ensue when racism is named tend to cast the complainant as a wrongdoer. As June Veecock, former educator with the Ontario Federation of Labour noted after consultation with numerous grieving nurses:

> When we remain silent, what in effect we are doing is contributing to our own oppression. And I know that once you begin to speak, you have to be prepared for what comes. People are accused of making false claims of racism. They are accused of being incompetent and of using racism as an excuse for their incompetence. So that immediately the focus is shifted. The accuser becomes the accused. The victim is then faced with the additional burden of not only having to prove that she is experiencing racism, that this is a racist environment, but also that she is competent. (Calliste 1995:60-61)

Justice is surely lacking when the complainant is treated as the wrongdoer and is left as prey for further wrongdoing. The Ontario Human Rights Code (Section 8, 1981) is violated when reprisals are enacted for making a complaint. Yet, all nine of the participants in our CERIS-funded study said they experienced reprisals (Collins et al. 1998). This issue was not dealt with in any of the proceedings they were party to. Reprisals stopped for those who got a white person to support them. Only those with a white person supporting them had their grievance upheld. One informant from the OHRC stated that cases will only get to a hearing if supported by a white person. (ONA 1998). Such reports suggest there may be inadequacies in the current arrangements for legal redress in race cases.

What is Ethnoracial Safety in the Context of Judicial Proceedings Contesting Racism?

Donna Young (1992) has argued that the "normalcy" of racism should be recognized, instead of conceiving of it as a rarity. In her review of race discrimination cases handled by the Ontario Human Rights Commission from 1980 to early 1992, she found that "race discrimination complaints for the most part are dismissed based on the assumption that respondents are rarely 'guilty' and that complainants are oversensitive" (p.7). Recognizing the issue of presuming innocence until proved guilty as a sacred principle in the law, she nevertheless urges that at the investigation stage the complaint should be taken as legitimate until its illegitimacy is established. Her case studies of reasoning applied and recorded suggest that complaints were disposed of on the presumption of innocence and this is illustrated throughout her findings of cases dismissed, despite racially laden negative images evident in language used by the respondents in the cases (p.3). Clearly, the presumption of innocence under the law is a major challenge for justice in racial disputes and it raises the question of Ethnoracial Safety for those feeling violated by racial discrimination (MacKenzie 1990:3; Young and Lio 1992).

Could it be possible that the courtroom model for civil hearings derived from criminal law requiring burden of proof, assignment of guilt and issuing of reasons to fix or clear liability actually interferes with the goal of Ethnoracial Safety in a racial dispute (Tarnopolsky 1999:86-88.2)? For example, could de-escalation or non-blame approaches readily allow respondents to reflect on their input into a situation and have good will about working to repair relationships, correcting problems and providing compensation? As Braithwaite (2000:189) suggested, there is the possibility of enhancing social justice and shifting from a culture of denial to a culture of apology. But, can we assume that this is the desired goal of all employers and employees? Would the practice of forgiveness of wrongdoers be abused? How can we create an environment where offenders will have a "learning moment" and rectify their behaviours that are offensively making complainants feel unsafe in their workplaces? By being non-accusatory will we avoid a denial response in the offender?

The Law Commission suggested that restorative justice principles could be applied to labour relations to build transformative justice in this civil arena (Canadian Council on Social Development 2000:3-4). It suggested the approach would be more responsive to the law, would orient to how people experience conflict, would provide adequate redress for those who have been harmed, and would be less time consuming, costly, and confusing than approaches based on the criminal law model. The latter has guilt and punishment orientations.

We caution the carte blanche application of these suggestions because of the onus placed on the employee who is already vulnerable in the employer/employee power relation. But, would there be a time—say early in the dispute process—when Transformative Justice would be ideal for framing questions of racial discrimination in the employment context? Would questions that are sensitive to how racial discrimination works—often unconsciously taking advantage—be proactive toward healing damaged relationships and ensuring equal opportunities based on valuing diversity of contributions in a multicultural society? Would accountability and commitment to the value of social justice in nursing alter documented practices such as scapegoating, set-up, and backlash (Hagey et al. 2005)?

Critical anti-racism scholars call for changes in institutional practices and in the quality of dispute proceedings (Aylward 1997:34; Delgado and Stefancic 1997). Aylward in particular recommends methods that validate experience, provide restitution—asymmetrical equality—for racial discrimination and pay attention to narratives as accounts of the construction of race relations. All of these methods are intrinsic to transformative justice approaches. With respect to Aylward's position that it is necessary to go beyond a focus on rights, we point out that transformative justice can orchestrate the discussion of multiple interests—rights, power, privilege, duty, liability, immunity—affording the law a presence in collegial and administrative relationships (Hofeld 1920; O'Reilly 1999).

The visual model below, allows us to ask the questions: Can transformative justice offer alternatives to current legal dispute mechanisms addressing racial disputes? Can it introduce new forums for a localized presence of the law in employment contexts, still subject to enforcement?

Process Model for Transforming Racial Disputes in the Canadian Health Care Context

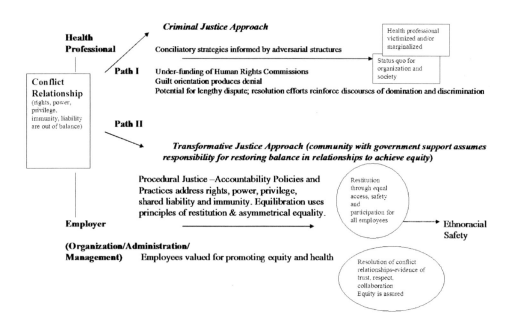

Literature on Racism Complaints in the Employment Context

The most interesting finding in research that takes stock of employment equity initiatives is that by Stryker (2001) who demonstrates that numerous furtive legal arguments continue to evolve around the burden of proof in human rights cases in the

United States federal justice system. However, it was not clear in his review of cases that all avenues for transformation were exhausted before the escalation of proceedings. Since the Canadian human rights proceedings are set up to be more conciliatory in nature, we are posing the question of whether innovative approaches should avoid dwelling on retribution and accusations and, instead, focus on restitution and early compensation for systemic disparities in employment relations that are often invisible to those who do not experience discrimination.

Regarding the justice system as it affects employment relations, there have been serious problems with the treatment of race in tribunal proceedings. Young and Liao (1992) argue that the human rights arbitration system is both structurally and institutionally racist, and is inherently intolerant of the victim's plight. They point out grave problems with assuming neutrality of the arbitrator on this issue. They argue that details about workplace abuse are often not made accessible to the arbitrator as evidence. The cases they review show a very uneven and discouraging record of fairness in arbitration proceedings which appears to be changing. A recent review of human rights race cases shows almost a fifty percent average in upholding the complainant's allegations (Agocs and Harish 2001).

Mackenzie (1990) addresses the perspective that should be adopted to assess if racial harassment has occurred in race cases where redress is sought. He argues that it is crucial to consider evidence about the climate and provide remedies that address a racist environment and promote equality in the workplace. He advocates for greater emphasis on the remedial nature of human rights law, as adopted by the Supreme Court of Canada, to apply in allegations of racial harassment in the workplace, as it does in sexual harassment cases.

Duclos (1993) asserts that human rights law does not provide remedy for racism intersecting with sexism due to the fact that it does not address all objectively discriminatory acts and ignores how racism and sexism factors are linked.

Calliste (1998, 1999) and Flynn (2000) have outlined the history of racist immigration policy as it has impacted on the profession of nursing, as well as the subsequent human rights organizing. The latter indicates the particular relationships these minority individuals, mostly women, have with the Canadian state (Flynn 2000).

MacPherson (1996:118) notes that Canadian nursing has demonstrated a colour bar in various contexts throughout the past century making diversity a major challenge. She also points out that a critical analysis of how race shapes nursing labour has been absent from the discussion of professionalization in nursing.

Das Gupta (1996) has shown how black nurses in particular have been subjected to discriminatory treatment in performance appraisals and disciplinary measures, such as targeting and over-documentation, as well as lack of equal access and participation throughout the gamut of professional privileges. For example, when black nurses spoke critically about patient care issues they were responded to as if they were making threats while this was not true for white nurses. Das Gupta (2002) also reports that racialized nurses perceive harassment coming from patients, colleagues, supervisors, and doctors.

Our interdisciplinary network of researchers is reporting findings from the CERIS-funded study which documented the lived experiences of visible minority nurses (Collins 1998). (Also see Turrittin et al. 2002; Jacobs 2002; Hagey, Turrittin, and Brody 2002; Collins 2003; Hagey et al. 2004).

Since the study participants taught us about the legal procedures and venues, we do not believe the problems we observed in our investigations stem merely from a lack of public education about how to use the legal means currently in place to redress grievances (Hill and Schiff 1998). We concur with Walker (1997) that particular strategies for change are needed to overcome the racism within the justice system in order to have legal mechanisms that promote equality. However, we also believe that much can be done to alter the pattern of resorting to legal remedies that can result in prolonged unresolved disputes. Lowe (2002) has reported unresolved disputes as one of eight key issues requiring coordinated attention in nursing in Canada.

This review of the literature suggests that the multigenerational legacy of racism in Canadian nursing reflects the situation at large in society. Conversely, the means for addressing grievances rests in the mechanisms of the larger society and the levers it can put in place to dismantle racial discrimination and stratification in employment. Given the problems alluded to above with human rights proceedings we see administrative policy and practice and union innovations promoting diversity and equity as among those with the most potential for influencing positive changes in the workplace.

A Discourse Framework that Conceptualizes Power and Privilege

We are constructing the concept of ethnoracial safety to build a discourse framework—an organized way of reflecting on talk, texts, and silences and to locate these in sites of contest for power and privilege where racial disadvantages result in barriers and harm to racialized nurses. The framework helps draw attention to:

(1) White privilege in nursing that is evident in manifest racial differences in advancement opportunities (Marshall 1996; Nestel 2000; Das Gupta 2002).
(2) Set-up to fail, backlash for complaining and health effects experienced by racialized nurses (Zacfilm 1998; Hagey et al. 2001a; Hagey et al. 2004).
(3) The need for procedural justice in the context of systemic racism, i.e., for equilibration, inclusive collaboration, transparency, accountability and restitution in everyday relations in the workplace (Hagey et al. 2001b).
(4) The need for consensus building in nursing to address imbalances in power

and privilege, ingroup and outgroup phenomena and historical antecedents that are reproduced by media in everyday racial dominance (Henry and Tator 2002).

(5) The need for changing exclusionary discourse in mainstream nursing that contrasts with the inclusionary discourse of the racialized nurses we interviewed (Hagey et al. 2001a).

(6) The goal of social cohesion in reconstructing race relations and reforming dispute proceedings (Hagey et al. 2001b).

(7) Employing the new concept of agency—creating participation capacity, including mentoring and supporting diversity of leadership (MacKay 1998).

Accordingly, we are initiating dialogue on whether transformative justice that operates in and through language can transcend some of the problems with the current legal proceedings in race cases.

Several scholars have presented evidence establishing that racial discrimination is a phenomenon of racially-based power and privilege in society that sustains, and is sustained by, discourse (van Dijk 1993; Frankenberg 1993, 1997). Our earlier research examining the lived curriculum of a nursing school shows how racial discrimination is subtly expressed in discourse. The language produces and reflects social segmentation and these processes may not be apparent to the person speaking:

> We are theorizing a category of whiteness, which is distinct from a category of otherness. Whiteness carries certain privileges of a normality, authority or dominance, freedoms for flexibility, capacity for voicing and likelihood of being heard, opportunity for being in control, events being orderly, having information about the correct means and channels, etc. By contrast, otherness carries respectively, marginalization, subordination, disadvantaging, restriction, being silenced, lacking information or cooperation for control, events being in chaos, lacking information about correct means and channels, and so on, which are consistently disadvantages in comparison to the privileges associated with whiteness. (Hagey and MacKay 2000:48)

Given that power and privilege are integral to our discourse findings, we believe these categories may be useful for making the shift from defending rights to new administrative methods of equilibrating privileges, power, and agency using transparency, accountability, and asymmetrical equality. Without equilibration, segmentation is a response of resistance that reinforces images of whiteness and otherness sustaining relations of we/they and us/them thus creating racial dominance and segregation.

Balancing the Dynamics of Racial Segmentation

Bannerji (2000) provides numerous examples where whiteness versus otherness is at work in the discourse of Canadians. We believe with Henry, Tator, Mattis, and Rees (2000) that segmenting discourse is generally operative and determines who is likely to be seen in a positive versus negative light. Pivotal categories can be observed not only in discourse about curriculum, but in discourse in the workplace. In both settings, normative regulation is accomplished in discourse. In both settings, racial discrimination produces negative effects (Canadian Council on Social Development 2000). We are interested in future research that can employ items from this set of categories in assessing the substantive basis of racial discrimination in disputes.

Our present task is to alert the reader to the importance of racialized categories in covertly proliferating conflict that segments US from THEM and triggers disputes that escalate when the offender and/or the victim is oblivious to racializing discourses and what to do about them. A dispute is a special type of intense relation where disagreements can either be addressed or not, where intensity can either escalate or not, where balance in relations can either be reached or not.

A grievable complaint of racial discrimination in Ontario, for example, is determined by the presence of one or more of direct, indirect discrimination or discrimination by association or with adverse effects (Tarnopolsky 1999:86-88.2). Procedures specify who may complain, time limitations and what form the complaints must take. In the complaint process, evidence is based on the presence of race, colour, national or ethnic origin.

By contrast, under transformative justice, a racial dispute is an opportunity—a duty for the employer, we argue—to teach personnel about racial discrimination as a social process, about anti-racism discourse, relationship, equity, asymmetrical equality, transparency, and accountability. A general rule would be that if someone says they are experiencing racial discrimination, the issue must be addressed. Although there have been exceptions, a grievable complaint does not entertain "reverse racism" (Tarnopolsky 1999:14). In anti-racism policy, however, the allegation of reverse racism is a sign that knowledge is lacking and reparative measures of transformative justice are needed. So, we argue, in contrast to conventional procedures, transformative justice interventions can and should address claims of reverse racism and treat the contact time with the complainant of reverse racism as an opportunity for education. Also problematic are relational issues where nobody is naming racial discrimination and yet respect is patently lacking and inappropriate encounters are prevalent, requiring some intervention that can break through to new, mutually accountable relating. It should be noted that transformative justice views whole communities or workplaces as victims in such environments often described as poisonous (Hagey 2003).

Before employer representatives can be accountable for supporting informal problem solving in race relations and racial disputes, they require substantive knowledge and skills. Perhaps more importantly, instruments of administration must be in place to support formal and informal discourse (policy) and procedures that systemically and directly counteract racial discrimination. Racial disparity indicators need to be monitored toward balance in hiring, promotions, shift-work, training opportunities, separation packages, and so on.

Relations can either be moving toward balance or moving toward imbalance, and practitioners skilled in balancing dynamics argue that balance can only be achieved if the underlying conflict is addressed (Mayer 2000). Supporters of visible minorities often experience discrimination because their reform agenda is seen as threatening to the organization (O'Day 1974).

The Law Commission of Canada (LCC) lists aggression, avoidance, and toleration as the common sense methods used in managing conflict that will have to improve if we are to have a more cohesive, civil society (Law Commission of Canada 1999:26).

Ethnoracial Safety as a Justice Concept of Balance

Maori nurses in New Zealand have formulated the concept of cultural safety as a principle of community relations and social justice that honours Maori people's sovereign rights (Author 1988; Ramsden and Spoonley 1993; Hagey 2000). Cultural safety recognizes that governance impacts on subjectivity and identity and that violations in the relations of governance have deleterious effects on racialized people's health, well-being, and ability to function and participate—their personal and collective safety (Hagey 2000). Cultural safety, as interpreted by Aboriginal people in Canada, includes balance in the four directions paralleling the forces of mind, emotions, body, and spirit: (a) social images and identities, (b) relationships and feelings, (c) employment opportunity and agency, as well as (d) political power and responsibility/spirituality (Nabigon and Mawhiney 1996; Nabigon, Hagey, Webster and MacKay 1999; Hagey 2000).

We are building on the concept of cultural safety to focus on the problems of ongoing racial conflict in the profession of nursing that disadvantages racialized nurses. By extending the concept to address the plight of all racialized people and their supporters in Canada, we are altering the term to "ethnoracial safety." The term ethnoracial safety also carries empathy for the offender and outlines transformative justice procedures espoused by Ruth Morris (2000).

We see the problem of racialization of people as stemming from the European concept of race, which since the time of slavery has provided a way of organizing work (van Dijk 1993). The biological indicator of race signifies a cultural rule that accountability or transparency in the relationship is not necessarily required

(Hagey et al. 2004). Thus, information accessible to others may be withheld and the racialized person(s) can be marginalized, problematized, contained or excluded with impunity. (See Essed (1991) for the effects of everyday racism.)

Taking seriously the concept of ethnoracial safety embedded in Aboriginal theory, one has to question the LCC's vision of transformative justice which is to leave aside the negative apparati of "law as a means of social control" and switch to a more positive approach of "law as a means to facilitate harmonious social interaction" (Canadian Council on Social Development 2000:26). According to Aboriginal theory, one would not abandon one and embrace another. A system of balance is called for that levies social control to ensure safety as a foundation for harmonious interaction in all relations within the institution and between the individual and the various jurisdictions of the state. Under Aboriginal theory, we see that relations are governed by the north/south directions of justice and power (emotional health and spirituality) as well as east/west directions of education and employment (mind and body).

State-supported interventions may be required for regulation of, for example, racist media (east) and racialized labour pools (west). (See LCC (2003: 202-203) for the ways advocated by the LCC for governments to work in partnerships with communities.) We would envision, for example, developing anti-racist or diversity secretariats crosscutting ministries of health and other ministries. In sum, we need to be able to resort to Human Rights legal proceedings, but we can certainly strengthen everyday relations and practices in the major institutions of society to make them more just, healthy, and safe.

Summary

Transformative justice is the basis of a proposed model that is also committed to procedural justice—accountability and transparency—administering restitution (accommodation) and requiring employers and employees to share responsibility for ensuring equity and ethnoracial safety. We develop an anti-racism approach to ethnoracial safety advocating a new definition of agency—the socially constructed capacity for participation—that helps us rethink equality of access, participation, and leadership development. Ethnoracial safety is a new concept, derived from work on ethnoracial competencies and Aboriginal cultural safety theory/practice confronting colonization processes in nursing education in New Zealand (Meeks 2003; Author 1988). The present framework is designed to enable conversations that can arrive at new normative standards of relating that are consistent with existing legal standards on human rights and racial discrimination (Author 2005).

Together the concepts and principles in our transformative justice/ethnoracial safety framework hold potential for reforming the grievance processes of racial discrimination according to anti-racism ideals. By promoting ethnoracial safety, a non-accusatory approach to anti-racism, we support culture change toward self-reflection and relational practices oriented to racial integration that are critical and accountable for racial discrimination which we have identified as a barrier to recruitment and retention in the profession of nursing (Hagey et al. 2001b; Hagey et al. 2004).

For ethnoracial safety to be realized, employers and employees alike must learn anti-racism discourse/practice. The ethnoracial safety stance is critical of inequities in power and privilege that impact on relationships, on the nature of collaboration and on the capacities for participation that are sustained by ingroup/outgroup dynamics. Ethnoracial safety, requires supporting resilience (rather than resistance), reclamation, and restitution, and invites people to voluntarily engage in anti-racism within any profession. It initiates connections with individuals and groups who are asking for inclusion and equal participation. It requires advocating for a holistic jurisprudence that sees an important role for state support against racial discrimination to foster voluntary cultural change in employment organizations. While critics of the restorative justice movement are wary of "harmony ideology," we can argue from our research that everyone involved in racial disputes—employers, complainants, respondents, unions—is interested in pursuing innovations that may improve social cohesion, fairly diversify workplaces at all levels, and avoid long, difficult, expensive proceedings (Nader 1980).

References

Agocs, C. and J. Harish. 2001. *Systemic Racism in Employment in Canada: Diagnosing Systemic Racism in Organizational Culture.* Ottawa: The Canadian Race Relations Foundation. Available at (www.crr.ca).

Author. 2005. *Policy and Guidelines on Racism and Social Discrimination.* Toronto: Ontario Human Rights Commission.

Author. 1988. Kawa Whakaruruhau (cultural safety in nursing education in Aotearoa) (Otautahi [Christchurch]: Hui Waimanawa [Conference on Maori Education].

Aylward, C. 1999. *Canadian Critical Race Theory: Racism and the Law.* Halifax: Fernwood.

Bannerji, H. 2000. *The Dark Side of the Nation: Essays on Multiculturalism, Nationalism and Gender.* Toronto: Canadian Scholars' Press.

Braithwaite, J. 2000. "Restorative Justice and Social Justice." *Saskachewan Law Review* 63(1).

Brown, R. 1996. "Human Rights in Employment: of Participation and Compensation." *Canadian Labour and Employment Law Journal* 4:283-309.

Calliste, A. 2000. "Resisting Professional Exclusion and Marginality in Nursing: Women of Colour in Ontario." In *Perspectives on Ethnicity in Canada*, edited by M. Kalbach and W. Kalbach. Toronto: Harcourt.

_____. 1998. "Immigrant Nurses, Human Rights and the State." Paper presented at the Robert Harney Lectures, Program on Ethnic Studies and Pluralism, Department of Sociology, University of Toronto, March, Toronto, ON.

_____. 1996. "Antiracism Organizing and Resistance in Nursing: African-Canadian Women." *The Canadian Review of Sociology & Anthropology* 33:3.

_____. 1995. "Congress of Black Women of Canada Conference Report. End the Silence on Racism in Health Care: Build a Movement against Discrimination, Harassment and Reprisals." A conference for black nurses and other health care workers. Ontario Institute for Studies in Education, May 25-26, Toronto, ON.

Canadian Council on Social Development. 2000. "Unequal Access: A Canadian Profile of Racial differences in Education, Employment and Income." Report Prepared for Canadian Race Relations Foundation. Toronto. Available at (www.crr.ca).

Collins, E. 2004. "Career Mobility among Immigrant Registered Nurses in Canada: Experiences of Caribbean Women." Ph.D. dissertation, OISE/University of Toronto, Toronto, ON.

Collins, E. A. Calliste, U. Choudhry, J. Fudge, R. Hagey, R. Lee, J. Turrittin, and S. Guruge. 1998. "Project Report to the Centre of Excellence for Research on Immigration and Settlement (CERIS): Research Toward Equity in the Professional Life of Immigrants. Phase I: "Making Racism See-able: The Complaints/Grievances Filed by Women Immigrant Nurses who are Members of Designated Minorities." The Culture Care Nursing Interest Group Newsletter 1(3).

Das Gupta, T. 2002. "Racism in Nursing: Executive Summary." Report Sponsored by the Ontario Nurses Association. Toronto, ON.

_____. 1996. *Racism and Paid Work*. Toronto: Garamound Press.

Delgado, R. and J. Stefancic, eds. 1997. *Critical White Studies: Looking Behind the Mirror*. Philadelphia: Temple University Press.

Duclos, N. 1993. "Disappearing Women: Visual Minority Women and Human Rights Cases." *Canadian Journal of Women and the Law* 6.

Essed, P. 1991. *Understanding Everyday Racism: An Interdisciplinary Theory*. Newbury Park: Sage Publications, Inc.

Flynn, K. 1999. "Proletarianization, Professionalization and Careers of Immigrant Nurses." In Canadian Women's Studies: An Introductory Reader," edited by N. Amin, F. Beer, K. McPherson, A. Miles, and G. Rezai-Rashte. Toronto: Inanna.

Frankenberg, R. 1993. *The Social Construction of Whiteness: White Women, Race Matters*. Minneapolis: University of Minnesota Press.

_____. 1997. Local Whitenesses, Localizing Whiteness. *Displacing Whiteness: Essays in Social and Cultural Criticism*. R. Frankenberg, ed. Durham, N.D.:

Duke University Press.

Hagey, R. 2000. "Cultural Safety: Honoring Traditional Ways." *Alternative and Complementary Therapies* 6(4):233-236.

_____. 2003. "What is a Racial Dispute? How Can We Reach a Level Playing Field?" Toronto, ON: Nursing Leadership Network of Ontario.

_____. 2005a. "Highlights of the Report to the Canadian Race Relations Foundation." Toronto: CRRF.

_____. 2005b. "Implementing Accountability for Equity and Ending Racial Backlash in Nursing. Report to the CRRF." February, Toronto, ON.

Hagey, R., U. Choudhry, S. Guruge, J. Turrittin, E. Collins, and R. Lee. 2001a. "Immigrant Women Recommend Interventions to Address Racism and Achieve Inclusion." *Journal of Nursing Scholarship* (fourth quarter): 389-394.

Hagey, R., M. Jacobs, J. Turrittin, M. Purcy, and R. Lee. 2004. "Moving Towards Accountability for Equal Access and Participation." Final report. Toronto: Canadian Race Relations Foundation.

Hagey, R., L. Lum, R. MacKay, J. Turrittin, E. Brody. 2001b. Exploring Transformative Justice in the Employment of Nurses: Toward Reconstructing Race Relations and the Dispute Process. Report to the Law Commission of Canada.

Hagey, R. and R. MacKay. 2000. "Qualitative Research to Identify Racialist Discourse: Towards Equity in Nursing Curricula." *International Journal of Nursing Studies* 37:45-56.

Hagey, R., L. Lum, J. Fudge, R. MacKay. 2000. Toward Alternatives to Arbitration and Human Rights Strategies to Achieve Racial Equity in Employment. Grant proposal to SSHRC/Law Commission of Canada.

Henry, F. and C. Tator. 2002. *Discourses of Domination: Racial Bias in the Canadian English-Language Press.* Toronto: University of Toronto Press.

Hill, D. and M. Schiff. 1998. "Human Fights in Canada: A Focus on Racism." Canadian Labour Congress & Human Rights Research and Education Centre, University of Ottawa, Ottawa, ON.

Hohfeld, W., ed. 1920. *Fundamental Legal Conceptions as Applied in Judicial Reasoning and Other Legal Essays.* New Haven: Yale University Press.

Jacobs, M., R. Hagey, J. Turrittin, and E. Brody. Forthcoming. "Advocating for Diversity: The Problem of Racism in Nursing in the Context of Corporatization." *Women and the Urban Environment.*

Law Commission of Canada. 1999. "From Restorative Justice to Transformative Justice." Discussion Paper. Ottawa: Law Commission of Canada. Available at (www.lcc.gc.ca/en/themes/ sr/rj/2000/paper.html).

Law Commission of Canada. 2003. *Transforming Relationships through Participatory Justice.* Ottawa: Law Commission of Canada.

Lowe, G. 2002. "Quality of Worklife Indicators for Nurses in Canada." Workshop

Report for the Canadian Council on Health Services Accreditation. Canadian Nurses Association. Ottawa, ON.

McTair, R. and J. Crooks. 1996. "End the Silence on Racism in Nursing." Toronto: Zacfilms.

MacKay, R. 1998. "Visible and Invisible Disability. Senior Common Room Talks." University College, March, Toronto, ON.

Mactavish, A. and J. Lenz. 1996. "Civil Actions for Conduct Addressed by Human Rights Legislation—Some Recent Substantive and Procedural Developments." *Canadian Journal of Labour and Employment Law* 4.

MacKenzie, I. 1990. "Racial Harassment in the Workplace: Evolving Approaches." *Canadian Labour and Employment Law Journal* 3.

Marshall, K. 1996. "The Diversity of Managers." *Perspectives.* (Winter):24-30. Ottawa: Statistics Canada.

Mayer, B. 2000. *The Dynamics of Conflict Resolution: A Practitioner's Guide.* San Francisco: Jossey-Bass.

McPherson, K. 1996. *Bedside Matters: The Transformation of Canadian Nursing 1900-1990.* Don Mills, ON: Oxford University Press.

Meeks, D. 2003. Deconstructing Romanow: Concurrent Session at the Canadian Race Relations Foundation Award of Excellence Symposium, entitled Racism: Breaking Through the Denial. March 28, Sheraton Hotel, Toronto, Ontario. (Glossary on ethnoracial competencies shared with the author.)

Nader, L. 1980. *No Access to Law: Alternatives to the American Judicial System.* New York: Academic Press.

Nabigon, H. and A. Mawhiney. 1996. "Aboriginal Theory: A Cree Medicine Wheel Guide for Healing First Nations." In 4th ed., edited by Frank Turner. Toronto: Toronto Free Press.

Nestle, S. 1996. "Proletarianization and Facilitation: Constructing the Nursing Labour Force in Ontario." Sociology and Equity Studies in Education, OISE/University of Toronto, Toronto, ON. Unpublished manuscript.

O'Day, R. 1974. "Intimidation Rituals: Reactions to Reform." *Journal of Applied Behavioral Science* 10.

Ontario Nurses Association. 1998. Focus Group Discussion. July, ONA, Toronto, ON.

Ontario Human Rights Code. 2001. Ontario Human Rights Commission, Toronto, ON.

O'Reilly, D. 1999. "Are There Any Fundamental Legal Conceptions?" *University of Toronto Law Journal* 47(2):271-279.

Ornstein, M. 2000. "Ethno-Racial Inequality in the City of Toronto: An Analysis of the 1996 Census." Toronto: University of Toronto, CERIS, United Way of Greater Toronto. Available at (www.city.toronto.on.ca/accessandequity).

Ramsden, I. and P. Spoonley, P. 1993. "The Cultural Safety Debate in Nursing Education in Aotearoa." *New Zealand Annual Review of Education* 2:161-174.

Stryker, R. 2001. "Disparate Impact and the Quota Debates: Law, Labor Market Sociology, and Equal Employment Policies." *Sociological Quarterly* 42:1:13-46.

Tarnopolsky, W. 1999. *Discrimination and the Law.* Toronto: Carswell.

Turrittin, J., R. Hagey, S. Guruge, and E. Collins. 2002. "Experiences of Professional Nurses who have Migrated to Canada: Cosmopolitan Citizenship or Democratic Racism?" *International Journal of Nursing Research* 39:655-667.

van Dijk, T. 1993. *Elite Discourse and Racism.* Newbury Park: Sage Publications, Inc.

Walker, J. St. G. 1997. *Race, Rights and the Law in the Supreme Court of Canada: Historical Cases.* Kitchener. The Osgoode Society for Canadian Legal History and Wilfred Laurier University.

Young, D. 1992. "The Donna Young Report: The Handling of Race Discrimination Complaints at the Ontario Human Rights Commission." Toronto: Ontario Human Rights Commission, October 23. Unpublished report.

Young, D. and K. Liao. 1992. "The Treatment of Race at Arbitration." Labour Arbitration Yearbook, Vol. 67.

CHAPTER 6

Crossroads in Anthropology's Professionalization: The Contrasting Pathways of Horatio Hale and Franz Boas

David A. Nock

Learning Objectives:

1. To understand that the current system of university-based professionalization of academic disciplines has alternatives.

2. To describe the emergence of North American anthropology as a serious discipline at the turn of the twentieth-century.

3. To illustrate how Franz Boas was influenced by, but came to ignore, the contributions of Canadian resident Horatio Hale.

4. Discover that this erasure of Horatio Hale's contributions was due to Boas' denigration of "amateurs" and a high evaluation of his own professional training.

5. Note that strategies exist to enhance "private scholars" who pursue their studies without dependence on the research multiversity which has emerged out of the professionalization process.

The Professionalization of Anthropology and its Amateur Antecedent

The history of anthropology in North America is generally written as a transition from an amateur or pre-professional era to a professionalized discipline characterized by long socialization and eventual employment in a university setting. The entire process of professionalization has been explored explicitly by Regna Darnell (1971:83-103) in her article "The Professionalization of American Anthropology." The move to professionalization is generally seen as progressive in nature, with employed career scholars replacing "the amateur element" (Stocking 1960:3) and "gentleman scholars" (Darnell 1971:92). Despite writing a praiseworthy article on "The origins of Canadian anthropology, 1850-1910," Cole's (1973) conclusion represents a commonly held view. He writes that the "abrupt close of the amateur period of Canadian anthropology…was not premature" and that the subject "could not continue as the preserve of part-time hobbyists and interested dilettantes" (p.43).

This transition from the pre-professional to professionalized discipline is usually associated with Franz Boas, a German immigrant to the United States in the 1880s who eventually found employment at Columbia University in 1896, rose to full professor in 1899, and is the single figure most associated with the foundation of modern American anthropology. If this transition is usually celebrated by the historians of the discipline, the reason why is hardly a mystery. The very foundation of the American Anthropological Association generated a controversy on this very issue.

Just before and after the turn of 1900, there was active debate on the grounds of such an organization. Boas was now prominent with a secure position at an important research university, although this security was quite recent. However, his growth to prominence had not reached its apex and he still had to contend with a field of other notables. One of these was W.J. McGee, acting chief of the Bureau of American Ethnology who actually took the initiative to organize the AAA. Discussions soon came to a conflict over whether the new organization should provide membership for amateurs, and if so, on what basis. McGee supported the "inclusive" principle, Boas the "exclusive" one which would limit membership mainly to professional anthropologists, normally employed in universities, museums, and other organizational settings.

Stocking (1960) points out that McGee's own background recapitulated the arguments in favour of a more inclusive policy. He had been born in pioneering Iowa in 1853 and had attended "a country district school irregularly" until he was fourteen. Thereafter he had "made his way without formal education." His involvement in the U.S. Geological Survey as a geologist (on the basis of "self-training and experience as a surveyor") had introduced him to a key player in nineteenth-century American anthropology, Major J.W. Powell. Powell brought him along to the Bureau of American Ethnology in 1893 with the title of "Ethnologist in Charge." Despite his lack of formal academic training, Stocking suggests that "By virtue of his position, McGee was the organizer of much of the anthropological work in this country." Given these factors of his up-by –the-bootstraps "auto-didactic" formation, Stocking points out that "…McGee was hardly likely to be receptive to arguments for professional exclusiveness" (Stocking 1960:8).

Stocking does not trace the path of Boas' formation in a similar manner, perhaps because in 1960 most American anthropologists were expected to know a lot about the man acknowledged as the founder of their discipline. The key here is that he was a product of the German university system, which was generally admired (until the advent of the Nazis) as the leading academic research institution in the world. He had attended four German universities (Heidelberg, Bonn, Kiel, and Berlin) and attained the German doctoral degree and its very important successor, the habilitation thesis which actually entitled the holder to undertake academic employment. It is true that Boas' doctoral degree specialized in physics and in particular the properties of water. However after that, he had moved to geography (which had recently attained a solid footing in German universities), and more tentatively to the emerging subjects of ethnology and anthropology. Moving to the United States, Boas had taken years to find secure employment in a setting he considered appropriate to his aptitudes and training. However, given the importance of the university as an institution in Germany, the thought of a university appointment had never been far from his mind.

Even in Germany, he had dreamed of it. Douglas Cole (1999) writes that as early as his years at Bonn, studying undergraduate mathematics and physics, Boas "foresaw a future for himself as a university teacher" (p.48). This aim was frustrated in Germany. He did become qualified as a "privatdozent" at Berlin after his habilitation. He could now lecture at the university on the basis of student fees received (however, privatdozents did not receive a university salary and were not part of the governing professorial structure). Boas quickly became frustrated with the German system and the blockage in senior hands it provided (his own status as a Jew would not have helped as witnessed by the anti-Semitic agitation at Kiel when Boas was a student there). However, it was several years before Boas was able to land an academic appointment in the United States, at Clark University. Clark provides an experiment of trying to build an instant research university, an experiment resulting in failure. Boas quickly departed after three years and was again left in career uncertainty.

In 1896, Boas was offered a low-rank position as lecturer at the major university in New York, Columbia, on the basis of annual appointments which were quite precarious (Cole 1999:212). Although now favourably located at a major university and city, Boas did not achieve a senior professorial rank, and an improved salary until 1899 when his position was converted to that of a full professor. Perhaps he would have been mortified to know that these Columbia positions were only landed on the basis of financial guarantees to underwrite his salary provided by his uncle who lived in New York, Abraham Jacobi. The advantage of Columbia was its great emphasis on graduate studies. Boas soon came to assemble an appreciable team of doctoral students whom he could train in the image he endorsed. On the basis of this training, they proceeded to dominate the expanding opportunities in American anthropology.

Almost from the beginning, Boas had seen himself as a serious career professional in the German academic mold, and he did not empathize with others who did not measure up to his sort of background. Thus, when McGee started his planning to organize the AAA, Boas fulminated for an exclusivist policy from which "the amateur element is rigidly excluded" (quoted in Cole 1999:236). Stocking (1960) refers to Boas' "firmness" and "intransigence in his own position which McGee had not, I think, originally expected" (p.8). Boas actually delivered a speech on the issue, printed in the periodical *Science* (with which Boas had been employed in the 1880s). Here Boas started to frame the issue as one of amateur deficiency which would lead to such associations "popularizing the subject matter" and "lowering the scientific value of discussion." He referred to this as a danger and demurred from an association whose meetings might resemble "the character of popular lectures" perhaps thinking of the Chatauqua and vaudeville circuits of the day, or even the Barnum-like circuses and carnivals with their displays of exotica. The tone is unmistakable, and Stocking (1960) refers to "Boas' rather dim view of the participation of interested amateurs" (p.11).

In the event, Boas actually failed to enforce his exclusivist tendency. McGee's more inclusive policy generally carried with slight modifications. Yet in Stocking's (1960) view "there seems to have developed no great problem of amateur control" (p.13). Stocking reviews McGee's position and concludes that "if he was not right in his dispute with Boas…[he] was at least not seriously wrong" (p.14). Stocking provides some backing that McGee's position, although at odds with the man acknowledged in 1960 (and perhaps today) as the heroic founder of American anthropology, *did* possess some shred of rationality in not excluding the amateur element. Yet Stocking's article ends not on this note but ultimately on the side of Boas commenting that "this episode in the history of American anthropology was part of a general contemporary process of professionalization in the social sciences in this country. The really important aspect of this process within anthropology was the growth of academic anthropology. It was this growth that was to guarantee the professionalism of the American Anthropological Association. Boas saw this process quite clearly and was himself a major factor in it" (p.14). Thus Stocking ultimately sides with the hegemonic view of 1960 (and no doubt today), that if McGee's inclusionist policy actually did no harm, it was nevertheless doomed in the longer run by the academic professionalization of anthropology.

Going beyond Stocking's acknowledgement that McGee's view was a reasonable one, I would suggest the possibility that we may have actually lost something in the drive to professionalization. Monolithic government and business corporations increasingly sponsor university research providing yet another reason to re-examine this controversy.

Horatio Hale: Gentleman-Specialist of the Pre-Professional Era

Interestingly, the debate with McGee was not Boas' first debate with an interested amateur gentleman scholar. This had already occurred when Boas complicated the plans of his research director of the 1880s and early 1890s, Horatio Hale. Eventually, the dispute was patched up and when Hale died at the end of 1896, Boas paid a fulsome tribute which promised that Hale's memory would never be forgotten (Boas 1897). Yet after his full ascension to anthropological hegemony, Boas rarely made any further mention of Hale (Gruber 1967:32) despite the fact that many of Boas' key contributions, such as the rejection of evolutionary stage theory and the espousal of cultural relativism, were anticipated by Hale in advance of Boas' writings on these matters.

It is likely that if Boas had repaid the debt he owed Hale, Hale's memory would be more alive among anthropologists and cognate social scientists. Instead, that memory has slowly faded. It has been kept alive in the pages of the *Encyclopedia Britannica* where every hardcopy edition from at least 1911 through 1998 and onto the online edition of 2005 has contained entries on Hale.

Hale's important book *The Iroquois Book of Rites* (1883) has been reprinted several times, once in a scholarly edition (1963) and once in a collection of Canadiana (1972). The editor of the scholarly edition, William N. Fenton, wrote a useful survey of Hale's life in the 1963 scholarly edition, and much later, an entry in the *Dictionary of Canadian Biography* (1990). Douglas Cole engagingly covered Hale's contributions in his admirable survey on "The origins of Canadian anthropology" (1973). Jacob W. Gruber wrote what remains the best sustained coverage in a 1967 article which appeared in a journal quite appropriate in the circumstances but one which anthropologists might overlook. Recently I have become interested in Hale's career and have written several articles on Hale, including one which simply emphasizes the details of Hale's career and his emphasis on aboriginal giftedness (Nock 2005). My overall point is that this literature on Hale does not amount to much, and no full-scale biography yet exists. If Hale's memory has been unjustly neglected by Boas and his disciples, I believe the reasons can be traced to several factors. Among these was the temerity of an undoctored gentleman amateur directing and contradicting the operations of a fully-certified academic German "doktor," very much aware of his worth as the product of the esteemed German university system.

Before we go into the specifics of Hale's formation, it may be important to remember that the serious amateur scholarly gentleman was an important feature of the nineteenth-century research scene. This has been noted by various observers. Eleanor Burke Leacock in her introduction to Lewis Henry Morgan's *Ancient Society* (1877), points out that while Morgan attained several prestigious scientific leadership roles, "he never took a university position. Like many nineteenth century thinkers, he remained an 'amateur,' and sandwiched periods of intense scholarly activity between periods of devoting himself to practical affairs as a successful lawyer and railroad investor" also serving for a number of years as a New York politician (Leacock 1963: v). Robert Stebbins (1992) (who has written extensively on the distinction between amateurs and professionals in a variety of undertakings), points out that before professionalization occurs, "in the early days of the activity, all participants were so-called gentlemen amateurs, usually independently wealthy individuals who had time to devote to leisure interests" (p.14).

Earlier discussions of this topic from the 1960s and 1970s probably used masculine terms such as "gentlemen" out of the then reigning convention that masculine words subsumed females (thus female scholars such as Burke Leacock (1963) and Darnell (1971) shared in this convention alongside male scholars). Writing in the 1990s (by which time this convention had crumbled due to recognition of its sexism), Stebbins (1992) carefully points out that "very few [of the gentlemen amateurs] were women" to justify continuing use of the masculine terminology (p.9). However, this point may be overdone. While men may have been the majority of the genteel amateurs, the category did include women. One nineteenth century example would be Matilda Stevenson who became one of the earliest ethnographers of the celebrated Zuni Pueblo (McFeely 2001: 43-74).

Another work which emphasized the importance of the gentleman amateur in serious scientific research was Martin J. S. Rudwick and his 1985 book on *The Great Devonian Controversy: The Shaping of Scientific Knowledge among Gentlemanly Specialists*. The somewhat mysterious title (to a North American) refers to a scientific controversy in the field of geology which centered on findings in the county of Devon in England's southwest; these findings were contested by other scholars who developed an alternative viewpoint based on evidence from rocks in Wales. The point here is that many of the participants were gentlemen specialists who had inherited fortunes or depended on non-related professions. Others were in fact relatively "impecunious amateurs on the spot who pursued their local geology as a hobby" (Ross 1997:4). In another case, one of the gentleman amateurs was eventually reduced to government employment as an official of the Geological Survey.

Rudwick's research on this matter had been pre-dated by his work on Charles Darwin who was a celebrated example of the gentleman amateur in an age and era which esteemed them. Rudwick prefers to use the term "gentlemen-specialists" and points out previous work drawing on this theme such as Morrell and Thackray's *Gen-

tlemen of Science: Early Years of the British Association for the Advancement of Science (1981) and Roy Porter's "Gentlemen and Geology" (1978). Rudwick (1982) outlines at length "The Social World of Geology" as it stood in the 1830s. He suggests that talking of "a 'scientific community' of geologists in the 1830s is misleading because it suggests anachronistically a strong-boundaried professional group marked by standardized training and certification, with only the uninitiated public outside" (p.190). Instead, Rudwick suggests "it is more accurate to depict the social topography of the science at that period as a series of graduated zones of 'ascribed competence' that shade insensibly into one another" (p.190). These overlapping zones include the elite of the science, the "accredited geologists," the "amateur geologists," and the general public, although I would find the term "amateur geologists" confusing as Rudwick is using the term amateur as a synonym for those who possessed a lower standard of competence in the subject. Rudwick goes on to discuss the membership of the Geological Society as it stood when Darwin joined (810 members in 1836) and he points out that "the great majority…were clearly amateurs" (p. 192). In the sense of being a gentleman-amateur, not dependent on the income derived from professional employment, many of the top two categories of scientific elite and accredited geologist still qualified as the example of Darwin himself makes clear.

This mapping of the English geological field is relevant to our discussion of Horatio Hale since by virtue of his birth in 1817, he grew up in this same decade of the 1830s as we have been discussing. Interestingly, Hale had two distinct "careers" in what we might anachronistically call anthropology (perhaps truer to historical accuracy, philology and ethnography). The first occurred in this earlier period of the 1830s and 1840s; the second started in 1868 but only produced the fruit of publications and academic recognition in the 1880s and 1890s.

Thus, the "role model" of the scientist in Hale's mind was likely to be that of a Charles Darwin or his contemporary Lewis Henry Morgan, gentlemen with incomes from family inheritances, private professional practices, and personal investments which allowed them the luxury of research and publication.

However, by the second era of the 1880s and 1890s, the German university system had become admired for its sophistication beyond the German-speaking world itself and starting with Johns Hopkins in 1876, and then Chicago, Columbia, and Clark, was being enthusiastically imported into the United States.

Hale was born on May 3, 1817 in Newport, New Hampshire. His father died when he was five. Hale was raised by his mother Sarah Josepha Buell Hale who earned a living for herself and her son as a distinguished journalist, editor, and author, editing the leading periodical for women in the United States, *Godey's Magazine and Lady's Book* for the entire period from 1837-1877, and a predecessor for ten years before that. She also authored an important book on the lives of distinguished women. Hale's formal education was received at Harvard where he studied

Asian languages and literature. This interest in philology led to his serendipitous and unexpected first publication when a band of American aboriginals camped in Harvard's vicinity. Hale studied their language and it led to a self-published monograph in 1834 at age seventeen. Charles Darwin had joined the expedition of HMS *Beagle* as an "unofficial gentleman-naturalist…to observe and collect anything of interest throughout the realm of the natural history sciences" (Rudwick 1982:189). A similar opportunity came with the United States Exploring Expedition to the Pacific under Captain Charles Wilkes which traveled all over the Pacific Ocean with a stop at present-day Oregon. Hale was appointed as philologist at the tender age of twenty and Fenton (1963) notes that he received "an annual salary of $2,000, which is a measure of the importance attached to the task" (p.viii). Thus, he may have qualified as a gentleman but certainly not as an amateur. The expedition led to his book of 1846 *Ethnography and Philology*, which was a well-received summary description of the many aboriginal societies and languages in the region, "immediately acclaimed by scholars here and abroad as indispensable" in Fenton's words (1963:ix).

Fenton (1963) clearly regrets that Hale did not build on this success through a university appointment. He states that Hale's acclaim for 1846 "makes it difficult to understand why an academician of this promise and accomplishment was not summoned to the faculty of one of the great universities" and describes it as "a tragic footnote to the history of American science that a mind of this caliber could not be devoted completely to the pursuit of ethnological and linguistic studies" (p.ix). However, these statements may misunderstand the possibilities open at the time and the aspirations held by young scholars.

Certainly the 1840s and 1850s was an era before the German-style research university had taken hold in the United States. Before that date, graduate studies were rarely available and even the first American Ph.D. had to wait until 1861 (Darnell 1998:101). Moreover, most universities still specialized in a small number of traditional topics, from which Hale's specialties were excluded. Darnell has thoroughly traced this university specialization. She points to D.G. Garrison, publisher of Hale's *The Iroquois Book of Rites*, as holding the "first professorship in anthropology in America [1886], although he received no salary and attracted no students" at the University of Pennsylvania (Darnell 1998:105). She points to the "false starts in academic anthropology" including Brinton's appointment, F.W. Putnam's at Harvard in 1887, and Boas himself at Clark as of 1889 (pp.104-105).

Perhaps the best Hale could have made of the situation was to emulate his contemporary Francis James Child (Winick 2004). Hired to teach mathematics (and later history and economics) at Harvard in 1846, his own research gravitated to the history of English literature in the medieval period, later to the German languages and literature, and finally to the newly emerging subject of folklore. Child was an early example of the American scholar going to Germany (on a leave of absence) to earn his doctorate. On his return, he was appointed to a professorship in rhetoric, concentrating his research on late medieval literature (Chaucer and Gower) and developing a course on Shakespeare. Today, however, Child is chiefly remembered for his collection of ancient English and Scottish ballads, known to most folklorists and "folkies" simply as "Child ballads," each one numbered. It was only in 1876 that Child became "America's first English professor" with the establishment of a professorship at Harvard; in 1888 he became the first president of the American Folklore Society, of which Hale became a successor in 1893. In other words, Child accepted a university appointment in fields which did not reflect his own research interests and developed appointments more to his own tastes as opportunities beckoned.

Given the unpredictability of such a strategy, and given the existing role model of the gentleman scholar, it remains unsurprising that Hale chose to undergo training in law in imitation of his father and brother's profession (not at a university during this era but by articling and apprenticeship). In 1855, he was admitted to the bar of Illinois. He moved to Clinton, Ontario in 1856 as the result of his marriage to Margaret Pugh and as a consequence Hale was appointed administrator of his father-in-law's estate which he thought would take a short time. Instead, Clinton became incorporated as a town in 1858 and Hale became involved in real estate, insurance, and as an estate executor. Hale spent about twenty-five years away from ethnography and philology. Fenton (1990) reports that "Hale was 50 when his original interest in linguistics and ethnology was requickened by his encounter with Iroquois speakers at nearby Brantford…[and] Huron-Wyandot sources at Amherstburg" (p.401). He spent over a decade, from 1867-1880, working with residents of the Haudenosaunee of the Six Nations Confederacy. He entered into a correspondence with Lewis Henry Morgan in 1869 and the two men met in 1880. Despite this initial period of research in the 1860s and 1870s, the publications awaited the 1880s and 1890s. From then until his death he published his major book on *The Iroquois Book of Rites* and several dozen articles (Chamberlain 1897 enumerates thirty-eight publications from 1881 through 1897).

Hale already possessed a substantial scientific reputation on the basis of his earlier work in the 1830s and 1840s, but as decades passed and he absented himself from scholarly involvement it was natural that he risked being a half-remembered footnote of an earlier era. As his second research career began so did his willingness to "network" with other scholars, as witnessed by his correspondence with Lewis Henry Morgan and his taking on amateur enthusiasts such as the Rev. E.F. Wilson (Nock 1982). He became willing and able to become involved in the scholarly associations of the day, and they in turn, recognized his achievements by various appointments to academic office. He became a member of the American Philosophical Society in 1872 (which was much wider in its scope than today). In 1886, he became vice-president of Section H of the American Association for the Advancement of Science. In 1884, he was the secretary and later research director of the committee established by the British Association for the Advancement of Science to investigate the tribes of the Canadian Northwest before their culture was changed by the advent of the railroad and subsequent settlement. In 1889, he became a fellow of the Royal Society of Canada. In 1893, he was the President of the American Folklore Society. Shortly before his death, he was chosen vice-president of the anthropology section of the BAAS for 1897 but declined on grounds of his failing health.

We have seen that gentleman specialists and amateurs were more the rule than the exception in much of the nineteenth-century. Since the word "amateur" is sometimes used in such a way as to imply lesser skill instead of someone who pursues an interest out of love for it instead of for a salary, it may be useful to outline Robert Stebbins' (1980) typology of avocational scientists. The first distinction he makes is between *observers* and *armchair participants.* Observers "directly experience their objects of scientific enquiry." Armchair participants "pursue their avocation largely, if not wholly, through reading." This proclivity of armchair participants may occur "because they prefer it over observation or because they lack equipment, time, opportunities, or physical stamina to observe" (p.35). Thus Herbert Spencer, a gentleman-specialist in sociology, devised elaborate synthetic conceptual schemes on the basis of studies of specific societies undertaken by others.

In the case of Horatio Hale, he clearly was an observer in his first career in the 1830s and 1840s, and then again in the 1860s and 1870s. As he got older and infirm, his direct observational activities waned. For example, Hale, at almost seventy "was supposed to have visited the Indian tribes of the Northwest Coast area in 1886, but was unable to do so" (Gruber 1967:23). Rather than simply retreat to armchair status, his experience as research director of the BAAS' undertaking to examine the tribes of the Canadian northwest presented him with another option: to utilize surrogates who would follow his directions as closely as possible. Gruber (1967) comments that "Hale's continuing role as an active supervisor of the field work of his surrogate is suggestive not only of his own disappointment in his inability to pursue a problem in the field once more, but also of his definition of his successor as an agent rather than as a replacement" (p.24).

Stebbins (1980) further delineates the scientific *apprentice* who is a learner of the discipline itself, its research procedures, its conceptual and theoretical language and assumptions. Next is the *journeyman* who is "a knowledgeable, reliable practitioner who can work within one or a few specialties" and has learned enough "to make an original contribution to…science" (p.36). Finally, the *master* collects "original data on his own which advance the field" and is aware of the "major knowledge gaps in his specialty" and who has their status as masters validated by others' invitations to speak, publish, network, and lead.

This transition in categories is easy to see in Hale's career. During his second research career, he made the transition from journeyman to master, and this latter status is seen in the various obituaries published after his death such as the ones by D.G. Brinton, publisher of *The Iroquois Book of Rites* (1897); by Franz Boas (1897); and finally that of A.F. Chamberlain (1897).

As far as acknowledgement of Hale's status as a scientific master is concerned, Boas' obituary would be hard to outdo with such statements as: "Many are his contributions to science, and they rank among the best work done in America" and that Hale "contributed more to our knowledge of the human races than perhaps by any other single student." In fact, the various phrases utilized by Boas (1897) to praise Hale's work include reference to the latter's "masterly treatment." (p.vii-viii).

Despite this generous assessment of Hale's status as a scientific master and over-the-top phrases referring to Hale's "wise counsel, his amiable guidance, [and] his kindly friendship," Boas had been bitterly resentful of Hale's direction when the latter acted as research director of Boas for the BAAS' Northwest tribes project. Hale and the BAAS had wanted its researcher to visit, map, and gather information on as many of the tribes and nations as possible. Boas already wanted to concentrate on one or only a few selected peoples. Gruber and Cole have extensively documented this dispute and quoted Boas' correspondence. Gruber (1967) quotes a lengthy passage in which Boas uses such words as "childish," and refers to Hale's "vanity, pedantry, and sensitivity" and to his constant "pestering" (p.31). However, it is unlikely that it was these alleged personality defects that hit Boas the hardest. Rather we must look to this comment in which, after Hale had acknowledged Boas' "ability, learning, and industry," he observed: "As well we know, no man, however able, can be a specialist—a *magister*—[master] in more than one branch of science. In other branches, he must be content to be guided by those who have made a special study of each" (March 11, 1889, as quoted in Gruber 1967:30). No wonder Hale (1889) remonstrated with his letter stating: "I cannot understand why you should persist in causing me an immense amount of useless trouble, as well as much annoyance, by objecting to my instructions which you are expressly engaged to carry out."

What seems striking is how vituperative Boas could be when he was, in fact, a research employee and Hale already had achieved a reputation as a scientific master. Gruber (1967) draws attention to these factors in his statement that "one must remember that this was a man of seventy-two, with some fair distinction in the field, addressing a Boas of thirty whose work had not yet found him a position in the establishment" (p.31). However, Boas (1967) was not content to attack Hale's personality but moved to academic matters when he characterized him as "know[ing] nothing about general ethnology" (p.31).

Douglas Cole (1999) states that "The Hale-Boas conflict is a little hard to evaluate" (p.117), and he gives a nuanced interpretation which places some importance to Boas' "unhapp[iness] with subordination" as evidenced by the fact that "his previous experience with superiors had not all been happy ones" (p.117). However, I believe that this dispute must be seen in the light of a Franz Boas who was proud of his strong university formation from the world's leading university system, very aware of his own nascent professionalization, and his lack of empathy with the gentleman-specialists and amateurs, even ones who deserved recognition as scientific masters. This focus on academic and intellectual matters, rather than personality characteristics, is, I think, justified on the basis of Boas' characterization of Hale knowing nothing about general ethnology. There speaks the voice of the university professional specialist who looked with something akin to contempt to those lacking a similar formation. We have seen the same general attitude expressed toward avocational scientists in his remarks to W.J. McGee about the formation of the American Anthropological Association. Douglas Cole (1999) also detected "a whiff of intellectual, even cultural arrogance in Boas's regard for American anthropologists, that too was due to his scientific professionalism. Science required disciplined education and training, which he felt was not appreciated enough in North America" and Cole goes on to suggest: "This opinion was doubtless sensed and resented by those in his field…who had arrived at their anthropological careers in quite a different way and were proud of their accomplishment" (p.284). Already on April 20, 1900, Boas had written to his mother, "Actually it is very easy to be one of the first among anthropologists over here" (Cole 1999:222). Before we conclude with a few words about what may have been lost as well as gained by the process of professionalization, we shall address a few more words to Boas' own university training in the German system and his aspirations for a university post which as we have seen, he had entertained from an early age.

Franz Boas and the Long Arm of the German University System

As mentioned, the German university system was held in esteem until the advent of the Nazis. Robert Lowie (1945), one of Boas' prominent doctoral students, writes, "What roused the admiration of foreigners, above all, however, was the scheme of higher education" (p.42). Lowie (1945) quotes British author Michael Sadler from a 1915 book chapter as stating: "From 1870 to the present day its development has been one of the intellectual wonders of the world" (p.42). Later in the chapter, Lowie once again refers to the German universities and "their long-maintained pre-eminence in Europe" (p.45).

Lowie attributed this pre-eminence to two factors. The first, quite relevant to Boas, was that "the professor was, above all, an investigator valued according to the quality and quantity of his research" (p.45). This Lowie contrasts to the German professor's "American brethren" whose energies were often diverted by administration and teaching. In reference to the second, Lowie makes the point that some German professors might possess "marked pedagogical aptitude" and that this might result in "brilliant lectures," but such factors were "not normally the reason for their appointment and prestige. A philologist, first of all, was expected to advance knowledge and to train devotees of scholarship who would do likewise" (p.45). The result of such a system, according to Lowie, was:

> that the amount of productive scholarship was incomparably greater than in other countries where professors were...primarily appointed to teach what was already known rather than to indicate how the boundaries of knowledge were to be pushed back. (P.46)

This emphasis on the German university as a site of cutting-edge research, and its fostering of graduate students meant that anyone with serious research interests in the German-speaking world gravitated to the universities.

There were a fair number of German universities, and according to Lowie, "far more men (*sic*) attended the universities than in other European countries" (p.46), thus making a university career more normative and routinized. In contrast, some of these supportive factors for universities were absent in England, a condition which encouraged the continuance of the gentleman-specialist and avocational scientist. Lowie (1945) notes:

> whereas in England there have been many scholars of note who remained unconnected with [universities], such instances of *Privatgelehrten* [private scholars] are rare in Germany. This implies that whereas some of the most distinguished scientists, say Darwin and Galton, were not in a position to stimulate a corps of young workers, the reverse held true in Germany. (P.47)

Darnell (1998) points out the importance of the research-oriented German university system in inspiring American university anthropology. As she points out, "Graduate training...did not become a requirement for most scientific professions until the end of the 19th century" and that "major changes" in the American university system had been "necessary...for the university to become a plausible institutional framework for anthropology." The changes derived from "The European, particularly German, model for graduate education" which "was readily available at precisely the right moment" (p.100). Although the German-style research-oriented university became institutionalized with Johns Hopkins in 1876 and quickly adopted at new or older institutions such as Chicago, Clark, Columbia, and Harvard, the prestige of having attended a German university for graduate work remained for many decades symbolized by the term "German-returned" (p.101).

A further appealing characteristic of the German university system was the status its attendance conferred and especially the acquisition of a university appointment. Friedrich Paulson, in passages quoted by Fritz Ringer, suggested:

> The academically educated constitute a kind of intellectual and spiritual aristocracy in German...something like an official nobility...Conversely, anyone in Germany who has no academic education lacks something which wealth and high birth cannot fully replace. (Paulson 1902, as quoted in Ringer 1967:138)

Ringer (1967) himself states: "There is...much evidence that to be certified as highly learned in nineteenth-century German was to be accorded a great deal of formal respect." Further, "The proud wife of an impoverished university instructor was still a *Frau Doktor*, and this meant something" (p.127).

Moreover, if one could make it above the bottom rank of *Privatdozent* (which received no university salary and few rights and privileges) to full professor *(ordentlicher Professor, Ordinarius)* or at least to associate professor (*ausserordentlicher Professor, Extraordinarius*), one could receive high salaries, prestige comparable to higher civil servants, and full membership in faculties and Senates (Ringer 1967).

Given this orientation to research and the kinds of material and psychic rewards it offered, it is scarcely surprising that Boas from early on, sought a university position of this kind. As we have seen, he had already entertained such thoughts about a university appointment during his days in the 1870s at Bonn. In the 1880s, after he had received his second graduate degree, the *venia legendi* (which qualified the holder to lecture at a university, hence *habilitiert* or *habilitation*) Boas had become disillusioned with his prospects at the University of Berlin in his new subject of geography where several others stood in his way, including the senior professor in geography Heinrich Kiepert, a new and rare second professorial appointment Ferdinand von Richtofen, and Alfred Hettner, "an up-and-coming young man" who had studied with von Richthofen. William A. Koelsch has pointed out that five other reasons have been advanced by scholars to explain Boas' decision to abandon his junior post at "Germany's leading university" in favour of opportunities in America. Particularly before the advent of Richtofen and Hettner, Boas had several times emphasized in letters that once he had been a *privatdozent* for three or four years that he would "readily be appointed professor extraordinarius" and in a letter to his parents he enthused that his career might follow the path of his mentor in geography Theobald Fischer, who had risen to a professorial chair in geography (albeit at the less desirable university at Kiel) after only five terms as *privatdozent* at Bonn. Now, however, Boas perceived that his rise might be significantly delayed at Berlin. As Koelsch points out, "Richthofen's professorship foreclosed any early opportunity Boas might have had...Clearly there would be no leap from docent to professor in Fischer's five terms" (Koelsch 2004:9-10).

When Boas came to the United States, he immediately and persistently turned to the university system for his career opportunity. The universities he sought out were the research-oriented universities which were quite new in the United

States. As early as 1882, Boas "had unsuccessfully applied for a position at the then new Johns Hopkins University, whose president was [a] geographer" (Koelsch 2004:7). He continued to foster ties to that university and its president, Daniel Coit Gilman and sought out a position there a second time in the mid-1880s but once again, this did not happen (p.9).

The academic entrepreneur, innovator, and pioneer psychologist G. Stanley Hall at the newly established Clark University, turned out to be a better bet than Gilman, "an ineffectual patron" in Koelsch's (2004:15) words. Hall and Boas had met in August of 1888 as the two men traveled to Cleveland for the meetings of the American Association for the Advancement of Science. Some reports have it that Hall offered Boas a position at this time, in August 1888, but Koelsch insists that no offer was finalized until Boas received a letter in September 1889 while in Victoria, British Columbia. Boas finally had an appointment at an American university with research aspirations. The German inspiration for Clark is indicated by Boas' stipulated rank as "docent" (taken from the German system) dealing with anthropology, rather than geography. His position was still junior, low in salary and precarious. It also ended unhappily when Clark University did not live up to Hall's vision for it (Cole 1999:144-45) and Boas, with two-thirds of the faculty, resigned. Boas was, once again, without a university position. Most of the Clark faculty had been taken on at the newly opened University of Chicago, but Frederick Starr had already been appointed as assistant professor of anthropology.

It took several more years before Boas found an appointment at Columbia University, now a satisfactory research-oriented university in Boas' eyes. Once again, the appointment was not at the professorial level but as a lecturer and was only annual in nature. Although the appointment was continued, it was at the low lecturer's level which not only impacted on the level of his salary but also restricted Boas from the academic governing bodies of the university and thus barred him from "influence on policy and curriculum" (Cole 1999:213). In the third year, despite a noticeable raise in pay, Boas' rank continued as lecturer and his dissatisfaction rose as indicated by his statement, "I am sick and tired of this annual bargaining and will try finally to get a secure position" (p.213). The University of Vienna beckoned, and perhaps this Austrian prospect further emboldened Boas' wealthy and influential uncle, Abraham Jacobi who offered Columbia half of Boas' professorial salary on the condition "that Dr. Boas should never know of this" (p.213). Finally, Boas had the professorial rank, an adequate salary, and secure employment at a research-oriented university where he could hope to attract a coterie of graduate students. The Boas who was to reshape anthropology in the twentieth century had "arrived" after a long period of post-doctoral uncertainty.

While Boas had to endure a precarious variety of jobs, his hankering after a university appointment from the 1870s on is clear. As Darnell (1998) explains:

> Late 19th century German scholarship was organized around academic professional training at the graduate level. This was the model upon which Boas and his first generation of students would differentiate professional anthropologists from their amateur contemporaries. (P.101)

Boas had trained Chamberlain to become the first American-awarded Ph.D. recipient during his stay at Clark. However, the Clark episode was brief and it was not until his professorship at Columbia in 1899 that Boas was in a position to train large numbers of students in his own mould.

Second Thoughts about Professionalization

In the years since the McGee-Boas debate, professionalization has become accepted as a deeply entrenched process, so much so that we may take it for granted as the only template. We have seen that this is not so and that an alternate route existed that was only slowly eliminated in the years after the importation of the German research model to the United States in 1876, and more specifically, after Boas' professorial appointment at Columbia in 1899.

We might conclude by asking ourselves whether the alternate routes had any advantages and whether the current university-research-graduate student mode of professionalization possesses any drawbacks. The answer, of course, is yes. Kelley L. Ross (1997) has written about the British organization of science in the first half of the nineteenth century that "this kind of mix [of amateurs, gentlemen-specialists and the occasional government funding for the Geological Survey] was much healthier than the post-World War II dominance of government funding and government control in education and science" (p.4). Ross fears that this government underwriting of education opens the possibility of "political and totalitarian control" and laments that "the previous safety valves of considerable local control and of the ability of private fortunes (Carnegie, Rockefeller, Ford) to independently finance education and research, has gradually been undermined" (p.4).

Written in an American context, it may be necessary to reflect upon these comments in our own Canadian milieu. Certainly it is true that Canadian universities have largely adopted the Germanic research orientation and this research orientation is almost entirely funded by grants through two organizations which depend on government money, the NRC and SSHRC (the former for the natural sciences and the latter for the social sciences and humanities). Increasingly (even since my full-time university employment in 1976) faculty are instructed that they must apply to these specific two agencies for funding. Persons who are able to do research without publicly-generated money (and to a lesser extent, those who raise money from other sources of funding) are looked upon as not really doing research. This leads to situations where persons could engage in research and scholarly writing without research grants but apply for them anyway to please the academic bureaucrats who staff the system. Universities are often rated for their research not on the basis of publications and still less on the significance of publications, but in terms of research dollars obtained from the two relevant agencies, and to a lesser extent, how many refereed articles a professor publishes in low-circulation severely professionalized academic journals which are read by small numbers of like-minded researchers only. Striving to be a "public intellectual" who writes for the general public is not a strategy which guarantees success.

As far as relying on large private philanthropic organizations of the economic elite of capitalists, I am less sanguine than Ross. While some excellent research has been done under such organizations (one thinks of the series on Social Credit and allied topics funded by the Rockefeller Foundation in Canada), control of research is once again placed in the hands of an undemocratic structure which answers, in the final analysis, to the power of money. One can easily imagine situations in which large capitalist families (or their deployable academic agents) would seek to fund certain research topics rather than others, out of vested interests.

Rather more appealing, I would suggest, is to derive programs which would encourage suitably trained or expert private scholars through schemes such as tax breaks (one recalls the tax relief extended to writers in Ireland, for example). In the nineteenth century, there were many middle and upper-middle class occupations and "professions" which were not so demanding that a dedicated gentleman-amateur could not take on a serious avocation. Examples we have met include lawyers such as Hale and his scholarly friend and correspondent Lewis Henry Morgan. In Victorian times, many such examples came from the ranks of the clergy. The Cuban world chess champion, Capablanca, was given a sinecure as a diplomat.

In this day and age, such sinecures and undemanding professions are rare, and it would be good if the private scholar (*Privatgelehrten)* was encouraged. A simple way to do this would be to eliminate the practice of placing a scholar's university affiliation on title pages (Agger 1989:42). Some journals such as *Telos* have done this precisely so as to encourage the private, amateur, and unemployed scholar (p.10). Tax breaks and journal etiquette are only two ideas. These hardly exhaust the possibilities. The point is that "brainstorming" and taking the issue seriously would lead to many other ways to encourage private scholars.

Another program which may have helped somewhat in Canada is the Public Lending Rights Commission which ensures that writers get some remuneration for libraries holding their books (of course, libraries holding such "intellectual property" may be assumed to lead to a loss in sales by bookstores). However, this program has suffered in its good intentions somewhat by the vagaries of government support and by shifting and sometimes punitive changes in rules by which it is governed. Nevertheless, it has some potential for encouraging the private scholar especially if the private scholar was deemed as a targeted recipient of its largesse. As one who has benefited from the fund, I would suggest that full-time private scholars and creative writers ought to benefit more and might be the sole beneficiaries from the program, rather than reimbursing persons (such as salaried professors) whose books are part of their professional career development. In other words, the PLRC is an excellent program with good intentions but could benefit from a more careful targeting of those writers who genuinely depend on its support.

A final critique of university-fueled research professionalization has been voiced by celebrated Canadian philosopher and social critic George Grant (1986; see also David Cayley's (1995:161-171) interviews with Grant). Grant (for biographical background see Christian 1993) had become a convert to a real, rather than nominal, Christianity in World War II. He became convinced that the aim of a university education was to lead students to an appreciation of wisdom, rather than control over others and the environment. Grant was employed as a university professor for his entire adult career but what is important here was his vision of the university and how it had become corrupted by the research model. He recognized that professors might seek to publish, as he himself did throughout his career, but the aim of such publication should be to foster wisdom and discernment of moral values. As Grant (1986) stated, "Previous scholarship was a waiting upon the past so that we might find in it truths which might help us to think and live in the present" (p.99). In another eloquent statement he wrote, "In any sane educational system (and I am not implying that the North American system is that), scholarship must see itself not as an end, but a means in the journey of minds towards the truth concerning the whole" (p.83).

Grant (1986:100) was particularly concerned when the nineteenth-century German-derived university research paradigm was imported into fields such as religion where he felt it had no place. He winced at departments of religion (in which he was employed at McMaster for many years):

> taken over by people who just did research about the great religions...without caring an iota whether what you've written has anything to do with the truth that is given in the Bible; you can write endless books about old Sanskrit texts without knowing anything about the truth of the Vedanta. (Cayley 1995:165-67)

Grant (1995) emphasized that although what he termed "enormous experts" might be necessary at times, it was more important that the "truth" of various religious, philosophical, and moral traditions be emphasized (pp.165-67).

Although not everyone will sympathize with Grant's views on religion, his analysis has been influential with many who see in it the elements of a critique of just the very sort of professionalized research-oriented university system, in which accumulation of knowledge (defined by Grant as the search for mastery over humans and over nature) becomes an aim in itself, rather than as a means for fostering insight, wisdom, and discernment. We learn more and more about how to manipulate people and objects than about the goal of ancient Greek philosophy of finding the most appropriate mode of living.

Whether another paradigm for anthropology was possible in the wake of professionalization no doubt remains a subject for debate. I have advanced arguments showing that a different tradition had existed in the nineteenth-century and was associated with the avocational scientist and with the amateur (defined as lover of a subject who earns a living from other sources rather than one who is paid a salary). I have also advanced some suggestions for fostering the private scholars who might revivify this earlier tradition while recognizing that these suggestions are only a few of many more which would be needed. The need for fostering such an alternative to the professionalized research model in subjects such as anthropology and sociology is signaled by Grant who warned that "the worst abuses of the modern university, it seems to me, have happened in the social sciences" (Cayley 1995:165).

References

Agger, Ben. 1989. *Reading Science: A Literary, Political, and Sociological Analysis.* Dix Hills, New York: General Hall, Inc.
Boas, Franz. 1897. Obituary of Horatio Hale (reprinted in full from *The New York Month*). *Proceedings and Transactions of the Royal Society of Canada.* VII-VIII. Ottawa and Toronto: John Durie and Son and The Copp Clark Co.
Brinton, D.G. 1897. "Horatio Hale." *The American Anthropologist* 10:25-27.
Cayley, David. 1995. *George Grant in Conversation.* Concord, ON: Anansi.
Chamberlain, A.F. 1897. "In Memoriam: Horatio Hale." *The Journal of American Folklore* 10:60-66.
Christian, William. 1993. *George Grant: A Biography.* Toronto: University of Toronto Press.
Cole, Douglas. 1973. "The Origins of Canadian Anthropology, 1850-1910." *Journal of Canadian Studies* 8:33-45.
Cole, Douglas. 1999. *Franz Boas: The Early Years, 1858-1906.* Vancouver: Douglas and McIntyre.
Darnell, Regna. 1971. "The Professionalization of American Anthropology: A Case Study in the Sociology of Knowledge." *Social Science Information* 10:83-103.
Darnell, Regna. 1998. *And along came Boas: Continuity and Revolution in Americanist Anthropology.* Amsterdam/Philadelphia: John Benjamins Publishing Company.
Encyclopedia Britannica, 1910, New York: Cambridge University Press; 1998 Chicago: Encyclopedia Britannica Inc; *Britannica Online* 2005. Retrieved

June 25 (www.britannica.com).

Fenton, William N. 1963. "Horatio Hale M.A. (Harvard), F.R.S.C. (1817-1896)." In Horatio Hale, *The Iroquois Book of Rites*. Toronto: University of Toronto Press.

Fenton, William N. 1990. "Horatio Emmons Hale." Entry in *Dictionary of Canadian Biography Vo. XII, 1891-1900*, pp.400-403. Toronto: University of Toronto Press.

Grant, George. 1986. *Technology and Justice.* Toronto: Anansi.

Gruber, Jacob. 1967. "Horatio Hale and the Development of American Anthropology." *Proceedings of the American Philosophical Society* 111:5-37.

Hale, Horatio. [1846]1968. *Ethnology and Philology.* [Lea and Blanchard] The Gregg Press.

_____. 1883. *The Iroquois Book of Rites.* Philadelphia: Library of Aboriginal American Literature, vol. 2. Reprinted in 1963 by the University of Toronto Press (see listing above under Fenton 1963) and in 1972 by Coles Publishing Company of Toronto in its Coles Canadiana Collection imprint.

Koelsch, William A. 2004. "Franz Boas, Geographer, and the Problem of Disciplinary Identity." *Journal of the History of the Behavioral Sciences* 40:1-22.

Leacock, Eleanor Burke. 1963. "Introduction to Part I" of Lewis Henry Morgan, *Ancient Society, Or Researches in the Lines of Human Progress from Savagery Through Barbarism to Civilization* [1877]. Cleveland: World Publishing Co.

Lowie, Robert H. 1945. *The German People: A Social Portrait to 1914.* New York/Toronto: Rinehart and Company.

McFeely, Eliza. 2001. *Zuni and the American Imagination.* New York: Hill and Wang.

Morrell, Jack and Thackray, Arnold. 1981. *Gentlemen of Science: Early Years of the British Association for the Advancement of Science.* Oxford: Oxford University Press.

Nock, David A. 1982. "A Chapter in the Amateur Period of Canadian Anthropology: A Missionary Case Study." *The Canadian Journal of Native Studies* II: 249-267.

_____. 2005. "Horatio Hale: Forgotten Victorian Author of Positive Aboriginal Representation." In *With Good Intentions: Euro-Canadian and Aboriginal Relations in Colonial Canada,* edited by Celia Haig-Brown and David A. Nock. Vancouver: University of British Columbia Press.

Porter, Roy. 1978. "Gentlemen and Geology." *Historical Journal* 21:809-836.

Ringer, Fritz K. 1967. "Higher Education in Germany in the Nineteenth Century." *Journal of Contemporary History* 2: 123-138.

Ross, Kelley L. 1997. Review of Rudwick's The Great Devonian Controversy. Retrieved December 30, 2004 (http://www.friesian.com/rudwick.htm).

Rudwick, Martin J.S. 1982. "Charles Darwin in London: The Integration of Public and Private Science." *Isis* 73:186-206.

———. 1985. *The Great Devonian Controversy: The Shaping of Scientific Knowledge among Gentlemanly Specialists.* Chicago: University of Chicago Press.

Stebbins, Robert A. 1980. "Avocational Science: The Amateur Routine in Archaeology and Astronomy." *International Journal of Comparative Sociology* XXI:34-48.

———. 1992. *Amateurs, Professionals, and Serious Leisure* Montreal/Kingston: McGill-Queen's University Press.

Stocking, George W. Jr. 1960. "Franz Boas and the Founding of the American Anthropological Association." *American Anthropologist* 62: 1-17.

Winick, Steve. 2004. "The Child Ballads: What Child Is This?" *Dirty Linen* 110: 29-33, 88.

Chapter 7

Obstacles Faced by Women in the Criminal Justice Professions

Tammy Turner and Stephen E. Bosanac

Learning Objectives:

1. Note some of the challenges facing women in the criminal justice professions.

2. Consider the social construction of gender and gender roles and how these processes are experienced in the workplace.

3. Examine ideas of gender-based professional/occupational segregation.

4. Think about ideological resistance to a gender/sex balanced work environment.

5. Learn about some of the societal reactions and professional obstacles faced by women working in criminal justice professions.

Introduction

Since the enactment of various pieces of civil rights legislation in the United States, including *Title VII* in 1964, and the *Civil Rights Amendment* of 1972, women have been entering male-dominated professions in the United States at a notably increased rate. However, women have not been readily welcomed into those professions, especially within the criminal justice field. Society's reinforcement and maintenance of systemically entrenched institutions regarding traditional, sex-based, patriarchal stereotypes and gender roles continues to challenge women in criminal justice professions. The following discussion focuses on the challenges for women working in the criminal justice professions under these conditions.

Stereotypes and Societal Challenges

Ideologically determined stereotypes and gender roles that have been constructed, defined, and reinforced throughout history produce the challenges that women face in their daily lives, both professionally and socially. Stereotypes are monolithic generalizations that are often overstated and represent a prejudicial view of a particular group of people within a society. Often, they define an inappropriate "ideal" model of a person or group that, generally, does not actually exist within a society. Stereotypes are usually resistant to change because they provide social cohesion and solidarity. Stereotypes for women include such characteristics as weak, subservient, passive, nurturing, friendly, liberal, gullible/naïve, and amiable; and such roles as confidant, peacemaker, rescuer/savior, and sympathizer (Etheridge, Hale, and Hambrick 1984).

Gender roles can be thought of as the positions society has assigned to people on the basis of their social construction as a man or woman. They are based on norms and values regarding activities and aptitudes that are deemed appropriate for each respective gender. Sex is biologically determined; gender, however, is a socially and culturally constructed phenomenon. Accordingly, "appropriate" gender roles are also socially constructed. Male gender roles include father, provider, protector, and disciplinarian. Examples of female gender roles include homemaker, mother, caregiver, girlfriend, and daughter. Professional gender roles for women include nurse, teacher, and librarian. Typically noted male professions include doctor, policeman, fireman, and lawyer (Jurik and Martin 2001).

Intrinsic to each of the previous gender roles is the idea of sexuality:

Sexuality is defined in so many different ways that it is difficult to find any aspect of life that is excluded from such a powerful force...definitions include various aspects of sexuality including gender, historical, private, attractiveness, activity, romance, threatening, stereotyping, biological, physiological, psychological, fantasy, power and political...Sexuality is diverse and can mean sexual orientation, sexual intercourse, sexual behaviour, sexual activity, sexual desires, sexual identities, sexual practices, sexual violence, sexual harassment, sexual fantasies, sexual experience(s), sexual domination, sexual abuse, sexual dynamics, sexual politics, sexual games and sexual discrimination. (Civil 1998:33-34)

Simply put, sexuality is defined as the state of being distinguished by perceived divisions of biological sex and culturally associated desires and behaviors. But, sexuality also represents a significant element of a person's core identity (Burrell and Hearn 1989). Female sexuality in Western culture is often stereotyped as promiscuous, girlfriend, wife, whore, tease, lesbian, and/or man-hater (Pollard and Sorbello 2000). Men are often classified as virile, visual, less emotionally invested, and "players" or Casanovas.

The combination of stereotypes (cultural and sexual) and gender roles (general and professional) can be complex, and feature myriad points of interaction that are manifested socially. Without some realization of these issues, people tend to act according to these socially constructed, culturally established norms and patterns of social interaction or "appropriate" behavior. These notions are reinforced continuously throughout the lifecycle of each member of a society. Consequently, it is somewhat rare, in the transformation from adolescent to adult to professional, to witness patterns of female/male interaction that fall beyond the ideological norms of a society. That is to say, many male/female interactions are based on normative assumptions of interpersonal interaction binaries between the sexes including father/daughter, mother/son, boyfriend/girlfriend, and rescuer/victim. These relationships are generally rooted in cultural standards of patriarchy and paternalism and do not include a model of "ideal" professional interaction between genders.

With no established, culturally acceptable model of professional relations between genders, a team consisting of a female and a male police officer is left to perceive one another in roles that they can negotiate comfortably. This can result in gender role displacement/transference. In gender role displacement/transference, a person applies a gender role with which they are familiar to a point of social interaction with which they are unfamiliar or unequipped to navigate.

Perhaps the male police officer will apply the brother/sister binary to his relationship with a female partner. Perhaps the female police officer will apply the mother/son binary to their relationship. This would create a dissonant situation wherein each partner has differing expectations of the other based on divergent values and needs. In the end, none of these expectations are associated with the professional relationship that should stand as the primary influence on their patterns of interaction.

The misapplication of these binaries serves to establish the division of power between the partners in an already value-laden schema. The male may envision his role when interacting with a sister as that of protector. The female might see herself as a caregiver or nurturer. These perceptions assume certain elements in their relationship and set potentially dysfunctional boundaries. Perhaps the male partner would expect less professional assistance from the female than he would from a male officer. If the male officer feels compelled to protect his female partner, will the female officer, in turn, become dependant upon that protection? The expectations developed because of gendered perceptions rather than professional expectations create a multitude of problematic situations for consideration.

The acceptance and errant application of gender-based stereotypes is a barrier for women in most occupations and professions (Betz and Fitzgerald 1987). Within the corrections and policing branches of the criminal justice professions, the perceived attributes of the stereotypical male are favoured, which include dominance, physical strength, and the protector role (Wilkinson and Froyland 1996; Zupan 1992). The legal branch of the criminal justice professions prefers other attributes generally associated with males including aggression, toughness, and the lack of emotionality (Blodget 1986). These perceived attributes are generally described and/or assessed as valuable skills and abilities.

The stereotypical female traits mentioned throughout this discussion are not valued equally with so-called male traits in the criminal justice professions. Consequently, these traits are not consistent with the previously mentioned, preferred male-centric attributes in considerations of employment in the criminal justice professions. This corresponds to the ideology that reinforces these normative values, and this has a negative effect on the employment of persons displaying so-called female attributes in criminal justice careers. Therefore, women often find it difficult to enter these professions or, once employed, find themselves relegated to certain positions that are compatible with the previously described feminine qualities. They are confronted by glass walls and glass ceilings that prohibit them from moving into certain specializations within criminal justice professions.

Gender stereotypes profoundly influence how women are treated in the workplace (Martell 1996). Supervisors' behaviors and attitudes are affected when they project gender roles onto female workers, thinking of them and treating them as daughters, wives, mothers, or sexual objects as these are the female roles that are most easily understood and employed (Etheridge et al. 1984). This occurs without regard for the appropriateness of the application of these templates. Consequently, the job performance of women is often inappropriately contextualized and measured through the filters of socially constructed femininity. Of course, this often results in lower standardized performance scores and lower employee ratings for women (Etheridge et al. 1984; Pollard and Sorbello 2000). These ratings affect personnel records and decisions, morale, and promotional opportunities (Zupan 1992).

Generally, management does not allow for the accommodation of differences in work styles, nor does management attempt to reconcile the socially constructed nature of negative perceptions of the qualities that are generally associated with female employees. This can negate the reality of female performance in the workplace and the effects of a gendered workplace environment on perceptions of female performance therein.

The categorization of women through gender-based stereotypes is detrimental to the professional workplace environment. It results in discriminatory behaviour, regardless of the latent or manifest intent of management, supervisors or co-workers. In turn, discriminatory behaviours contribute to a negative atmosphere in the workplace environment (Zupan 1992). Differential assignments wherein women and men fill different positions and perform dissimilar duties within the same workplace based solely on gender are one possible result of unchecked adherence to the social construction of gender.

Differential assignments can result in low employee ratings/evaluations, differing levels of experience, fewer opportunities for advancement and professional development, and reduced networking opportunities. For example, assigning a female corrections officer to front desk or reception duties because of her perceived friendly, service oriented nature would significantly limit her field experience. Field experience is a pivotal factor in promotion in many criminal justice professions.

Another example is the tendency for assigning males within the criminal justice professions to restricted housing units in penal institutions, to "dangerous" clients in halfway houses, and/or tactical response teams on police forces (Zimmer 1986; Zupan 1992). These assignments provide experience that is highly valued and a criminal justice professional that can lay claim to familiarity with these respective work environments garners credibility and respect. In other words, differential assignments and the associated stereotypes can prohibit men and women from treating each other in an unbiased, professional manner and males are often the beneficiaries of this phenomenon.

Conversely, women often face greater demands and expectations in a work environment shaped by ideologies rooted in sex and gender stereotypes (Lerner 1988). For example, consider the professional atmosphere of a contemporary courtroom. Female stereotypes can affect the outcome of a trial and the respective work experiences of the professionals who come together to meet the goal of completing a trial. An enthusiastic female lawyer might be described as hysterical, whereas an equally ardent male lawyer might be described as passionate. Conversely, in comparing a calm female lawyer to a similarly composed male lawyer, the female might be described as detached or unsupportive while the male might be described as professional (Blodget 1986). All of these stereotypical perceptions have the ability to influence opinions and proceedings and might serve to undermine the female counsel's credibility and professional stature (Blodget 1986).

In fact, in the United States prior to the American Bar Association's House of Delegates adopting recommendations which promoted the full integration of women into the legal profession, women were only assigned to "specialized" areas of practice. These feminized subfields included probate law, domestic relations, and real estate law, which were defined as being appropriate for women (Bernat 1992; Patterson and Engleberg 1982). This limited experience led to restricted occupational mobility and reinforced the belief that women were unable to successfully hold positions of leadership in a law firm (Bernat 1992).

Women were originally recruited into criminal justice professions for the primary purpose of educating female prisoners in the ways of womanhood and how to be a proper lady. These volunteers of the early nineteenth century set in motion the reformation of "wayward" women, concentrating on improving morals and providing life-skills training. These criminal justice professionals, known as "prison matrons," did ultimately improve conditions for female inmates and professionals alike. Despite this pivotal role in the early penal system, an unfortunate side effect was the reinforcement of the traditional caregiver stereotype (Schulz 1995).

Utilization and reinforcement of traditional gender roles also occurred in police work. Policewomen were trained in social work and assigned tasks of a preventative and service-oriented nature (Hale and Lanier 2002). In order to avoid direct competition with policemen for promotions and male-centric positions, including supervisory roles, a separate police bureau was formed specifically for the employment of women (Martin 1992).

Women's roles in the juvenile justice system developed during this same period of time and concurrently with the arrival of feminist advocates for prison reform and supporters of a separate juvenile justice and welfare system. There was considerable public support for the involvement of women in regulating the welfare of children. Women were readily viewed as the most capable of providing the nurturing and care a wayward child "must surely lack." This new penology system welcomed maternal involvement as women were seen as "natural caretakers" and mothers (Platt 1977). Further, women were also thought to be better teachers, more patient, and more influential in handling juvenile disciplinary problems. Opportunities in this new system were viewed as reputable and honorable tasks for women who wanted to extend their housekeeping functions into the community (Platt 1977).

However, this gendering of the criminal justice professions has not substantially diminished over time. Female gender roles seem to correspond with the assignment of positions that ultimately hinder a woman's career (Martin and Jurik 1996). There are several examples of positions across many fields that can be related to normative gender roles (Vosko 2000). In the criminal justice professions these include placing women in areas where the work is perceived as women's work including desk and clerical positions. Women are also assigned to positions that are perceived as nurturing or caregiving. Further, women are often given particular shift assignments perceived to be more beneficial to working mothers (Vosko 2000). Finally, women are assigned to specific positions that are directly based on gender/sex because of privacy issues. These include positions wherein an inmate might be in a state of undress including showering or being searched.

Some of these examples may appear to benefit the employee, the employer, or even the client. Nevertheless, an assignment based on gender roles rather than equitable mutual agreement or operational necessity is fairly categorized as sex discrimination.

Sexuality and Sexual Harassment

Sexuality in prisons is usually "managed" by denial or default (Pollard and Sorbello 2000). The presence of a female in a predominately male environment can represent a challenge for all employees in the workplace, but this challenge often goes unrecognized (Turner 2005). This is particularly true when there is no institutional support system in place for employees to safely share concerns and address issues of discomfort that might arise.

In a total institution, such as a prison or penitentiary, there exists a state of what is best described as forced celibacy. Most of the inmates housed in these institutions are males, and female employees are clearly in the minority. Under these conditions, the focus of the male inmate's sexuality gravitates toward the few women found in that environment (Pollard and Sorbello 2000).

However, this phenomenon is not limited to inmates. Both male prisoners and male staff members project their attitudes regarding sexuality onto female staff members based on both personal experiences and tacitly held stereotypes. As this occurs, women may feel uncertain and confused about why a particular perception or stereotype exists (Pollard and Sorbello 2000). The tacit and unspoken nature of these relationships and the underlying, often dissonant ideologies held by males and females can lead to a breakdown in communication. While female staff members fairly expect to find themselves in a professional, work-based relationship, the males they encounter often seem to view them in accordance with the previously mentioned binaries of father/daughter, mother/son, or boyfriend/girlfriend to list only a few (Pollard and Sorbello 2000). Because of this dissonance, communications fail, job performance falters, and morale suffers.

When sexuality in the workplace is openly considered and discussed, the focus tends to be on the behavior and appearance of female employees. This negates the distinct, perhaps even unnatural, social structure of many criminal justice professions (English 2003). It also ignores the unique patterns of interaction that occur between the genders/sexes in these total environments.

Critically reviewing a woman's behavior based on sexuality issues alone might leave female staff members feeling isolated and unsupported (Pollard and Sorbello 2000). It is common to see latent and manifest social sanctions placed upon an employee who is perceived to have acted inappropriately regarding sexual codes of conduct both written and unwritten (Bosanac 2005). These sanctions are often imposed without knowledge of the actual events that culminated in the perception of wrongdoing. In many cases, the facts of the situation are not shared with co-workers, or they become distorted as they cycle through employee gossip circles. Pollard and Sorbello provide an example:

> A [female] therapist's session with a particular prisoner ran well over an hour, after which the prisoner emerged from the session red faced. Prison staff were concerned that the prisoner and the therapist had sex. In reality, the prisoner had been in tears for most of his session and did not want to return to the wing until it was less obvious he had been crying. (Pollard and Sorbello 2000:6)

In this scenario, suspicions regarding the therapist's actions might not be eased or alleviated and, consequently, negative perceptions of the "accused" might continue unchecked.

Further, in courtroom-based criminal justice professions, female behavior is often negatively interpreted. Female lawyers often find themselves criticized for their use or non-use of cosmetics and their choice of attire (English 2003). They are often subject to sexualized labels or nicknames including "honey," "cutie," and "beautiful." They might also be infantilized through monikers consisting of, but not limited to, "baby," "little lady," or "little girl" (English 2003; Blodget 1986). These labels can also be considered as sexualized given the sexualization of youth that is evidenced throughout Western culture (McOrmand 2004).

Sexual harassment is an equally difficult, but exponentially more inflammatory concept:

> Supreme Court Justice Clarence Thomas defined sexual harassment as occurring when unwelcome sexual advances, requests for sexual favors, and other verbal or physical conduct of a sexual nature, when occurring as a term of employment; when submission/rejection of conduct is basis for employment decisions; or when the conduct interferes with the individual's work performance or creates an intimidating, hostile or offensive working environment. (Muraskin and O'Conner 2002:430)

There are at least four models of sexual harassment that follow from this definition. The first is based on sexual attraction and is generally structured as a *quid pro quo* arrangement, or an exchange of one thing for another (U.S. Department of Justice, Office of Justice Programs (OJP) 1998). This exchange can, at times, be considered consensual and many may argue that this is not truly a form of sexual harassment. In comparison to this, the second model outlines a hostile work environment wherein unsolicited "sexual jokes, suggestive comments, suggestive pictures, obscene gestures, unwanted physical contact and other situations that interfere with an employee's work performance" occur (OJP 1998:70). The frequency of these events is not a factor in either of these models as any evidence of these activities constitutes a form of sexual harassment that ranges on a continuum of negative impact commensurate with each specific scenario.

The third model is a sociocultural model that regards sexual harassment as a reflection of the dominance of patriarchal values within a society. The sociocultural model bestows power, status, and a position of authority on men. In this context, sexual harassment occurs when men try to maintain dominance over women (Summers 1996). However, the most commonly noted model of sexual harassment is the "sex-role spill-over" model. This type of sexual harassment stems from a failure to separate a woman's role as co-worker from her sexual role outside the workplace (Summers 1996). This spill-over can occur for a variety of reasons.

In the criminal justice professions, one primary cause of sex-role spill-over is the widely disproportionate ratio of male to female employees in the work environment (Gutek and Morasch 1982). When this ratio favours men, male employees have less opportunity to interact with female co-workers on a professional level. As a result, it is more likely that female staff members will be treated according to the traditional stereotypes that are more familiar to the males with whom they interact (Summers 1996).

Research shows that anywhere between 42 and 90 percent of working women encounter some form of sexual harassment on the job (Summers 1996). Research also indicates that women are disproportionately represented among sexual harassment claimants in comparison to the proportion of the workforce that they occupy. Further, available data specifies that males are overrepresented among the group of alleged harassers (OJP 1998).

Aside from the personal, moral, and legal issues intrinsically linked to the effects of sexual harassment, it is appropriate to consider the negative effects of this phenomenon on professions generally. Sexual harassment creates an environment that can be intimidating, inhospitable, and uncomfortable for female staff. This poisoned environment can also have a negative effect on male staff members who empathize with marginalized co-workers and maintain professional behavior with all co-workers, regardless of sex/gender.

It is also important to note that although current research identifies sexual harassment rates for males as notably lower than the respective female rates, male employees can be, and are, victims of sexual harassment. The detrimental effects of the negative emotional reactions that stem from sexual harassment easily flow into the work place through the state of mind and emotional/mental/physical health of the employees. This is true for both victims and witnesses of sexual harassment. The quality of work suffers as victims of sexual harassment are less motivated to perform employment-related tasks and have difficulties concentrating on assignments (Jensen and Gutek 1982).

Societal Reactions and Professional Barriers

A significant body of research shows a clear lack of support for females in many professions (English 2003; Alverez et al. 1996; Belknap 1995; Bernat 1992). This is especially true within the criminal justice professions (Turner 2005). Initially, women working in male-dominated fields experienced great difficulty finding mentors, community assistance, and/or co-worker networks (Boni and Circelli 2002). As a consequence, many women felt alienated and were isolated from co-workers, family, and the professional community (Hale and Lanier 2002; Martin 1992; Zupan 1992). In 1984, a survey of female correctional officers showed that less than half had familial support for their careers (Zimmer 1986). Belknap's follow-up report indicates that eleven years later, this number had increased to 54 percent (Belknap 1995). Nevertheless, it still demonstrates an unfortunately low rate of support for these female professionals.

Perhaps this is because we are inundated with an image of the criminal justice professions as violent, brutal, and corrupt: "Even the legitimate television and print news media tend to focus on the negative imagery of corrections" (Shaffer 1997:20). Moreover, the criminal justice professions are clearly framed as male centered. As a result, community and family alike continue to stigmatize many of the women who choose to work within these fields as deviant in relation to the traditional stereotypes of females as delicate, weak, nurturing, and emotionally invested.

Jane Gaskell analyzed the life goals and expectations of 17 and 18 year old male and female youth. The results of this data collection are surprising. Both groups seem to equally expect and believe that their lives will unfold in accordance with most of the gender-based stereotypes we have discussed to this point (Gaskell 1993). This is despite knowing that adhering to these stereotypes is not required and can, in fact, be detrimental to the actualization of human potential. Nevertheless, young people, today, seem to assume and even expect that women will serve as the primary nurturers of children and managers of the household. Conversely, men will be primarily responsible for meeting the financial needs of a family (Gaskell 1993). In other words, both young men and women appear to reflect the tacit nature of gender-based stereotypes and the corresponding societal expectations and reactions to the idea of women in the workplace. Thus, for the most part, this ideology remains relatively unchallenged.

All of these expectations represent monolithic ideals that are neither practically sustainable nor scientifically verifiable. Women do work outside the home and, more often than not, men cannot provide for the full financial needs of a family without some type of assistance given the erosion of the family wage. Further, men do contribute to domestic responsibilities and this has been increasing in recent years. However, this phenomenon can be characterized as a "helping" role rather than a primary one. Moreover, this role is often related to their role as provider (Pupo 1997; Hochschild 1989). Consequently, women are not only charged with the burden of gendered work expectations, but also, as we can see in the data, they often accept the appropriateness of this socially constructed phenomenon without significant questioning.

We do find a slight variation in some research that followed Gaskell's preliminary project. Rhode (2001) explains that currently there exists a "generation of women who grew up expecting equal opportunity in the workplace" and these women are "unwilling to settle for less, or to give up satisfying personal and family lives to achieve it" (Rhode 2001:15).

But, we must also note that in this later research women are still associated with a desire to bear children and to maintain a home life. The primary difference in these findings is that women seem to have greater confidence about entering the workforce, but only to the extent that they can balance their gender-based responsibilities. Whereas the first half of the above assertion might be interpreted as liberating, the conclusion of the statement unequivocally reinforces the idea of the assumed primacy of gendered responsibilities and desires in a woman's life.

This association is not equally applied to males. The majority of established lawyers are male and they equate professional success with long hours of work. They note that this is only possible at the expense of their personal lives. Subsequently, they do not empathize with the younger generation of lawyers and their requests for time to balance home and work more appropriately. They state that "the young generation's expectations of balanced lives are unrealistic and unreasonable" (Rhode 2001:15). In other words, this research seems to state that both genders are currently more comfortable including women in the criminal justice workforce as long as they can still manage their domestic responsibilities without adversely affecting their performance in the workplace environment.

Therefore, women in the workforce struggle with various demands on their time and energy related to stereotypes. First, let us consider childcare. Childcare is a particularly difficult issue for criminal justice professionals as much of their work is performed outside of what are generally considered "normal" or "standard" hours or shifts (Shaevitz 1985). Shift work for female police and correctional officers is further complicated by the rotating schedule commonly used in total institutions that must operate 24 hours a day, 7 days a week. Of course, their scheduled days off change as do the times they are required to work. Another obstacle is found in on-call obligations that require employees in many criminal justice professions to be available for duty in any official emergency situation, regardless of the time of day or night (Wilkinson and Froyland 1996; Rhode 2001).

Additionally, it is possible that the difficulty of obtaining quality childcare is amplified for corrections officers as correctional facilities are commonly placed in rural areas. Therefore, access to childcare facilities and professionals might be limited either geographically or by a supply/demand imbalance. Despite these difficulties, a woman is often expected to ensure that all of her gender-based roles and responsibilities are adequately fulfilled (Shaevitz 1985). The pressure created by this phenomenon is considerable (Hochschild 1989).

The gap between policy and practice in the administration and bureaucracy of many criminal justice professions is a latent, yet vital factor in the continued mistreatment of women who choose these careers. Where formal policies do exist for part-time work or flexible schedules, very few women feel comfortable utilizing these options (Rhode 2001; Wilkinson and Froyland 1996). Why? There is a considerable, substantiated fear that taking advantage of these "choices" will result in stigmatization. Management and co-workers often develop negative perceptions of any employee who opts to enjoy these benefits. When an employee exercises these "special" rights, they are often perceived by co-workers as uncommitted, professionally apathetic, disloyal, unreliable, and/or lacking ambition (Rhode 2001). In turn, these perceptions seem to negatively "influence performance evaluations, work assignments, mentoring relationships, and promotion decisions" (Rhode 2001:16). Under these conditions, opportunities for advancement can quickly disappear.

It is also important to note that poor or inaccessible workplace policies, and the misuse and stigmatization of these policies, affects both males and females negatively:

> Workplace polices that disadvantage men also disadvantage women. By discouraging male[s]...from assuming an equal division of household responsibilities, the policies reinforce gender roles that are separate and by no means equal. As long as work/family problems are seen as problems primarily for women, potential solutions may receive inadequate attention in decision-making structures dominated by men. (Rhode 2001:18)

Finally, Rhode, in her report to the Commission on Women in the Profession, outlined some of the emotional and mental tolls a career in the highly gendered criminal justice professions can take on a woman:

> For employed women, who still spend about twice as much time on domestic matters as employed men, extended hours result in "double binds and double standards." Working mothers are held to higher standards than working fa-

thers and are often criticized for being insufficiently committed either as parents or as professionals. Those who seem willing to sacrifice family needs to workplace demands appear lacking as mothers. Those who want extended leaves or reduced schedules appear lacking as [professionals]. Those mixed messages leave many women with high levels of stress, and the uncomfortable sense that, whatever they are doing, they should be doing something else. "Good mothers" should be home; "good [workers]" should not. (Rhode 2001:17)

This stress can manifest as physical or mental illness, and can contribute significantly to a toxic or negative home environment wherein all members of a household suffer the consequences of an unnecessarily gendered work environment (Vosko 2000).

Conversely, when males opt to take time off to help their family or mention family concerns at work, they are often lauded as caring and devoted or cute and endearing (Rhode 2001). As detailed earlier, females in the same situations are perceived as unreliable and uncommitted.

Contemporary Concerns and Reactions

Women in criminal justice professions also contend with tokenism. Tokenism is the practice, often entrenched in policy, of making obligatory efforts toward the accomplishment of a goal, in this case sex/gender equality/equity in the workplace. This effort is often only a symbolic gesture. In tokenism, a small number of people from underrepresented groups are hired and/or promoted, primarily in order to prevent criticism and/or comply with mandatory affirmative action policies (Kershnar 2004).

Unfortunately, tokenism does not change the ideologically rooted stereotypes of a social system. Instead, tokenism reinforces these generalizations by simultaneously singling out groups and labeling them as deviant or different, while providing the illusion that positive action is being taken to rectify previous inequities. In fact, tokenism makes the token employee highly visible and places the performance of this employee under a microscope (Kanter 1977). The token employee becomes an "ambassador" for the group they represent in the workplace. Success is expected, while failure is unacceptable and negatively marks the entire group represented by the token employee. Consequently, tokens, in this case women, find that they must continually prove themselves as necessary contributors to the work environment (Hale and Lanier 2002). In other words, success represents one woman's success, but failure is a failure for all women (Hale and Lanier 2002; Zupan 1992).

Glass ceiling "is a term coined in the 1970s in the United States to describe the invisible artificial barriers, created by attitudinal and organizational prejudices, which block women from senior executive positions" (Wirth 2001:1). The glass ceiling continues to exist in most fields, and the criminal justice professions are no exception.

Unfair practices in employee advancement and promotion, the lack of opportunities, and limited mentoring opportunities are the primary reasons that the glass ceiling still exists (Carr-Rafino 1993; Gold 2000). Related systemic barriers include the reconciliation of work and family, career path availability, formal and informal networking, and vertical employment segregation.

Unfair promotional practices include gender-biased performance evaluations and performance measurement standards to which females have unequal access. This includes the use of seniority in male-centric careers wherein the clear majority of senior employees are male. It also includes valuing prior military service, which, until recently, held limited accessibility for women. Prior assignments where women have not had equal opportunities are often considered when promotional opportunities arise (National Center for Women and Policing 2004). Additionally, promotions to higher ranks are more subjective than other promotions, and "[r]esearch shows that the more subjective the promotional process is the less likely women are to [be promoted]" (Polisar and Milgram 1998:5).

Glass wall is a contemporary term intended to describe horizontal employment segregation. Where vertical employment segregation, or the glass ceiling, keeps women from being promoted above a certain level, horizontal employment segregation serves to stream women into specific specializations and areas of a company/organization that are deemed gender appropriate. As a consequence, women are disproportionately found in less prestigious occupations (Alverez et al. 1996; Wirth 2001).

Specifically, these forms of employment segregation in the criminal justice professions tend to prohibit women from receiving critical and/or specific training in particular areas including firearms, tactical skills, and self-defense techniques. This leaves many female criminal justice professionals insufficiently prepared for promotion. Employment segregation, and the limited experience that occurs as a result, often facilitates the transfer of women in the criminal justice professions to service-oriented positions as opposed to more desirable male-centric positions (National Center for Women and Policing 2004).

Gender-role conflict reinforces glass walls and glass ceilings. In particular, the gendered perception of a woman's "basic need" to balance work and family, while also acquiescing to the requirements of her husband's career, results in inappropriate generalizations of a woman's career needs and goals as well as her life situation (Figueira-Mcdonough and Sarri 1987). Not all women have husbands or partners. Not all women have children, and currently the number of voluntarily childless females and males is increasing steadily (Vissing 2002). Consequently, the generalized assumptions regarding a woman's desire/need for family in the traditional Western sense are often inappropriate and/or out of context when considered on the micro-level. Nevertheless, these ideas serve to hinder the career paths of many women.

For example, a common occurrence in professional career development is the need to relocate. Women, if married or cohabiting with a man, are expected to pack up the household and follow their male partners as necessary for the benefit of his career (Finch 1983). Conversely, a man is not held to the same standard. Society assumes that a man's work is more valuable than a woman's and this attitude often has a profound impact on this type of decision (Pupo 1997; Armstrong and Armstrong 1978). More importantly, this attitude and the accompanying decisions can be devastating for a woman's career path.

Antiquated ideals surrounding the "cult of domesticity" tautologically reinforce and are reinforced by all of the previously discussed gender-based stereotypes. This ideology often segregates women into careers that are associated with conceptions of "women's work" as opposed to prestigious, male-dominated professions (Alverez et al. 1996). Ultimately, these forms of employment segregation serve to protect, expand, and reinforce the professional dominance of males.

This segregation is often linked to physical safety and personal security and what some errantly describe as the female tendency toward non-aggression. Specifically, there are various male-centric/patriarchal fears surrounding the overall safety of a woman in a total institution, or in a one-on-one encounter with a client/inmate. That is to say, men are concerned that women might not be able to fend off an aggressor as easily as a man, and that when confronted with a situation that requires the use of physical force, a woman might not be able to perform as well as a male (Haarr 1997; Wilkinson and Froyland 1996; Zupan 1992). Another fear is that a woman might be unwilling to apply necessary force because of a misplaced sense of compassion or a fear of physical engagement. Both of these scenarios, if accurate, contribute to an assumption of a lack of physical support from female staff in situations warranting the application of physical force in restraining and subduing someone.

However, concerns over the physical safety and personal security of female co-workers are misplaced. Female criminal justice professionals are proportionally no more likely to be attacked or injured by inmates/clients than their male colleagues (Holeman and Krepps-Hess 1983). In fact, some research shows that female criminal justice professionals are less likely to be assaulted in the line of duty than are male officers (Rowan 1996).

Further, considerable research on safety, security and personal injury in the criminal justice professions demonstrates that

> the overwhelming majority of incidents, regardless of the task engaged in, are not a result of assaults and, of course, do not result in deaths or serious injury. Most injury incidents are as a result of accidents and most injuries,

regardless of how sustained, are relatively minor. Indeed, the most serious injuries are most often due to accidents, most medical treatment is due to accidents, and most days off are as a result of accidents. (Brandl 1996:258)

This stands in direct opposition to the misperception of disproportionate female vulnerability in the criminal justice professions. It also contradicts the belief that inmate/client attacks are the most common on-the-job dangers for criminal justice professionals.

Regarding the alleged female tendency toward non-aggression, research consistently shows that women are equally aggressive in comparison to men, and reactions to

most incidents do not elicit significant gender differences in aggression. Where differences exist, they are in the opposite direction than is commonly assumed—that is, women [criminal justice professionals] tend to be more aggressive than the men...occupational socialization and the demands of the job account for the similarities between genders and the differences result from the gender specific barriers confronting women. (Jenne and Kersting 1996:1)

In fact, some research suggests a provocative alternative to the alleged female tendency toward non-aggression:

[A]ssuming that being a prison guard relieves women of the normal societal prohibition against their aggressing, it is reasonable to suggest that gender differences will disappear in dangerous situations behind bars, alleviating the need for concern about women guards' capabilities. In other words, power relationships are redefined. (Jenne and Kersting 1996:2)

That is to say, upon gaining entry into a criminal justice profession, a woman appears to feel more comfortable displaying aggressive behaviors and, in this respect, she responds to use-of-force situations in a manner commensurate with her male colleagues.

Conclusion

Female pioneers of the criminal justice professions in all fields and specializations met with organized opposition, horizontal and vertical employment segregation, stereotyping, ostracism, harassment, and sex-based discrimination. The intensity and impact of these systemic and institutional barriers falls on a continuum ranging from moderate to severe depending upon which specific field or specialization one considers (Martin 1992; Bell 1982). Evolving, dynamic forms of latent opposition combined with variations of these original overt mechanisms still hinder women's integration into the criminal justice professions.

In policing and corrections, gender integration and opportunities to change public and institutional policies that would facilitate this integration have been more strongly resisted than in the legal professions (Price and Sokoloff 1995). This resistance is detrimental to advancements in the fields generally, as well as to women acquiring the knowledge and skills necessary in order to be successful in the criminal justice professions.

Men often refuse to share work-related knowledge and skills with women. They play pranks on women; they overprotect them and underestimate them in the work environment (Martin 1992). Women were initially deterred from entering into the legal occupations because of the ideologically rooted, patriarchal belief that "law was synonymous with male characteristics and traits" (Bernat 1992:309). It was a commonly held belief that only men should serve as lawyers, court recorders, bailiffs, and judges. Occupational segregations were created and some areas of legal practice were labeled as appropriate for women (Bernat 1992). This resulted in streaming, which is characterized by glass ceilings and glass walls and is still easily evinced today by the preponderance of men in these professions generally and, particularly, within certain specialized areas. Exceptions include positions such as court recorders or other clerical positions currently associated with ideas of women's work (Eyerman 2000).

This discussion provides numerous other examples of challenges women face in pursuing careers in the criminal justice professions. Major challenges include the projection and transference of gender stereotypes, gender role expectations and pressures, sexual harassment, and sex discrimination. The criminal justice professions must continue to correct the injustices in employment equity and promotional practices and break down the obstacles that confront women as they enter and navigate career paths in these fields. The primary means to this end include eliminating gendered work environments, increasing and rewarding teamwork between genders/sexes, embracing and requiring diverse employee demographics, and providing collaborative experiences that allow growth and professional development for all criminal justice professionals.

References

Alverez, R., L. Robin, M. Tuan, and A. Shui-I Huang. 1996. "Women in the Professions: Assessing Progress." Pp. 118-122 in *Women and Work: A Handbook*, edited by P. Dubeck and K. Borman. New York: Garland Publishing.

Armstrong, Pat and Hugh Armstrong. 1978. *The Double Ghetto: Canadian Women and Their Segregated Work.* Canada: McClelland and Stewart Limited.

Belknap, Joanne. 1995. "Women in Conflict: An Analysis of Women Correctional Officers." Pp. 404-420 in *The Criminal Justice System and Women: Offenders, Victims and Workers.* 2d ed., edited by B. Price and N. Sokoloff. New York: McGraw-Hill.

Bell, D. 1982. "Policewomen: Myths and Reality." *Journal of Police Science and Administration* 10(1):112-120.

Bernat, F. P. 1992. "Women in the Legal Profession." Pp. 307-322 in *The Changing Roles of Women in the Criminal Justice System.* 2d ed., edited by I. Moyer. Prospect Heights: Waveland Press.

Betz, N.Z. and L.F. Fitzgerald. 1987. *The Career Psychology of Women.* New York: Academic.

Blodget, N. 1986. "I Don't Think that Ladies Should be Lawyers." *American Bar Association Journal,* December 72:48-53.

Boni, Nadia and Michelle Circelli. 2002. "Contemporary Issues Facing Women in Policing." Australasian Centre for Policing Research, 138.3. Retrieved December 28, 2004 at (www.acpr.gov.au/publications2.asp?Report_ID=124).

Bosanac, Stephen E. February 2005. Personal Communication.

Brandl, Steven. G. 1996. "In the Line of Duty: A Descriptive Analysis of Police Assaults and Accidents." Pp. 248-261 in *Readings in Criminal Justice Research,* edited by R. Pope, S. Lovell, and S.G. Brandl. Scarborough: Wadsworth.

Burrell, G. and J. Hearn. 1989. "The Sexuality of Organization." Pp. 1-28 in *The Sexuality of Organization,* edited by J. Hearn, D. Sheppard, P. Tancred-Sheriff, and G. Burrell. Newbury Park: Sage.

Carr-Rafino Norma. 1993. *The Promotable Woman: Advancing Through Leadership Skills.* 2d ed. Belmont: Wadsworth Publishing Company.

Civil, J. 1998. *Sexuality at Work: How does It Affect You?* London: B.T. Batsford Limited.

English, Holly. 2003. *Gender on Trial: Sexual Stereotypes and Work/Life Balance in the Legal Workplace.* New York: ALM Publications.

Etheridge, R.C. Hale, and M. Hambrick. 1984. "Female Employees in All-Male Correctional Facilities." *Federal Probation* 48(4):54-65.

Eyerman, Ann. 2000. *Women in the Office: Transitions in a Global Economy.* Toronto: Sumach Press.

Figueira-McDonough, J. and R. Sarri. eds. 1987. "Catch-22 Strategies of Control and the Deprivation of Women's Rights." Pp. 11-33 in *The Trapped Woman: Catch-22 in Deviance and Control,* edited by J. Figueira-McDonough and R. Sarri. Newbury Park: Sage.

Finch, Janet. 1983. *Married to the Job: Wives' Incorporation in Men's Work.* London: G. Allen & Unwin.

Gaskell, Jane. 1993. "The Reproduction of Family Life: Perspectives of Male and Female Adolescents." Pp. 161-174 in *Family Patterns, Gender Relations*, edited by B. Fox. Toronto: Oxford University Press.

Gold, Marion E. 2000. "Blasting through the Glass Ceiling." *Law Enforcement News*, May 15/31, pp.12-14.

Gutek, B.A. and B. Morasch. 1982. "Sex-Ratios, Sex-Role-Spillover, and Sexual Harassment of Women at Work." *Journal of Social Issues* 38:55-74.

Hale, Donna and Mark M. Lanier. 2002. "The New Millennium: Women in Policing in the Twenty-First Century." Pp. 480-492 in V*isions for Change: Crime and Justice in the Twenty-First Century (3rd edition)*, edited by R. Muraskin, and A. Roberts. Upper Saddle River: Prentice Hall.

Haarr, R.N. 1997. "Patterns of Interaction in a Police Patrol Bureau: Race and Gender Barriers to Integration." *Justice Quarterly* March 14(1):53-85.

Hochschild, Arlie Russell. 1989. *The Second Shift.* New York: HarperCollins Publishers.

Holeman, H. and R. Krepps-Hess. 1983. *Women Correctional Officers in the California Department of Corrections.* Sacramento: California Department of Corrections.

Jenne, Denise L. and Robert C. Kersting. 1996. "Aggression and Women Correctional Officers in Male Prisons." *Prison Journal* December pp. 442-460.

Jensen, J.W. and B.A. Gutek. 1982. "Attributes and Assignment of Responsibility in Sexual Harassment." *Journal of Social Issues* 38:121-136.

Jurik, Nancy C. and Susan E. Martin. 2001. "Femininities, Masculinities, and Organizational Conflict: Women in Criminal Justice Occupations." Pp. 264-281 in *Women, Crime and Criminal Justice*, edited by C.M. Renzetti and L. Goodstein. Los Angeles: Roxbury Publishing Co.

Kanter, R.M. 1977. *Men and Women of the Corporation.* New York: Basic Books.

Kershnar, Stephen. 2004. *Justice for the Past.* Albany: State University of New York Press.

Lerner, Harriet Goldhor. 1988. *Women in Therapy: Devaluation, Anger, Aggression, Depression, Self-sacrifice, Mothering, Mother Blaming, Self-betrayal, Sex-role Stereotypes, Dependency, Work and Success Inhibitions.* Northvale: J. Aronson.

McOrmond, Russell. 2004. "Sexualization of Youth, Internet Censorship, and Media Marketing Monopolists." *Flora Community Web* Retrieved February 23, 2005 at (weblog.flora.org/article.php3? story_id=662).

Martell, R. 1996. "Sex Discrimination at Work." Pp. 329-331 in *Women and Work: A Handbook*, edited by P. Dubeck and K. Borman. New York: Garland Publishing.

Martin, Susan. E. 1992. "The Changing Status of Women Officers: Gender and Power in Police Work." Pp. 281-306 in *The Changing Roles of Women in* the *Criminal Justice System: Offenders, Victims, and Professionals.* 2d ed., edited by I. Moyer. Prospect Heights: Waveland Press.

Muraskin, Roslyn and Martin L. O'Conner. 2002. "Women and the Law: An Agenda for Change in the Twenty First Century." Pp 427-439 in *Visions for Change: Crime and Justice in the Twenty-First Century.* 3d ed., edited by R. Muraskin, and A. Roberts. Upper Saddle River: Prentice Hall.

Martin, Susan Ehrlich and Nancy C. Jurik. 1996. *Doing Justice, Doing Gender: Women in Law and Criminal Justice Occupations.* Thousand Oaks: Sage Publications.

National Center for Women and Policing, A Division of the Feminist Majority Foundation. 2004. "Recruiting and Retaining Women: A Self-Assessment Guide for Law Enforcement." NCJ 185235. Retrieved March 6, 2004 at (www.womenandpolicing.org/sag.asp).

Patterson, M. and L. Engelberg. 1982. "Women in a Male-Dominated Profession: The Women Lawyers." Pp. 385-398 in *The Criminal Justice System and Women, Offenders, Victims and Workers,* edited by B. Price and N. Sokoloff. New York: Clark Boardman.

Platt, A.M. 1977. *The Child Savers, The Invention of Delinquency.* 2d ed. Chicago: The University of Chicago Press.

Polisar, Joseph and Donna Milgram. 1998. "Recruiting Integrating and Retaining Women Police Officers: Strategies that Work." *The Police Chief,* October, pp. 42-53.

Pollard, Jacinta and Laura Sorbello. 2000. "*Whore to Madonna and Back: The Challenge of Being a Female Therapist in a Male Prison.*" Presented at WIC: Staff and Clients Conference, October, Adelaide, Australia.

Price, B. and N. Sokoloff. eds. 1995. *The Criminal Justice System and Women: Offenders, Victims and Workers.* 2d ed. New York: McGraw-Hill.

Pupo, Norene. 1997. "Always Working, Never Done: The Expansion of the Double Day." Pp. 144-165 in *Good Jobs, Bad Jobs, No Jobs: The Transformation of Work in the 21st Century,* edited by Ann Duffy, Daniel Glenday, and Norene Pupo. Toronto: Harcourt Canada.

Rhode, Debra. L. 2001. "Balanced Lives: Changing the Culture of Legal Practice." Prepared for American Bar Association (ABA) Commission on Women in the Profession. Retrieved March 8, 2005 at (womenlaw.stanford.edu/balanced.lives.pdf).

Rowan, J.R. 1996. "Who is Safer in Male Maximum Security Prisons?" *Corrections Today* 58(2):186-189.

Schulz, Dorothy. M. 1995. "Invisible No More: A Social History of Women in U.S. Policing." Pp. 383-397 in *The Criminal Justice System and Women, Offenders, Victims and Workers.* 2d ed., edited by B. Price, and N. Sokoloff. New York: McGraw-Hill.

Shaevitz, Marjorie. 1985. *The Superwoman Syndrome*. New York: Warner Books Inc.

Shaffer, John. 1997. "Life on the Installment Plan: Careers in Corrections." Ph.D. Dissertation, Department of Human Genetics. University of Pittsburgh, Pittsburgh, Pennsylvania, U.S.A.

Summers, R. 1996. "Sexual Harassment." Pp. 260-263 in *Women and Work: A Handbook*, edited by P. Dubeck, and K. Borman. New York: Garland Publishing.

Turner, Tammy. February 2005. Personal Communication.

U.S. Department of Justice, Office of Justice Programs. 1998. "*Women in Criminal Justice: A Twenty Year Update.*" NCJ 173416. Retrieved March 12, 2005 at (www.ojp.usdoj.gov/reports/98Guides/wcjs98/).

Vissing, Yvonne Marie. 2002. *Women without Children: Nurturing Lives*. New Brunswick: Rutgers University Press.

Vosko, Leah F. 2000. *Temporary Work: The Gendered Rise of a Precarious Employment Relationship*. Toronto: University of Toronto Press.

Wilkinson, V. and I.D. Froyland. 1996. "No. 58: Women in Policing." *Trends and Issues in Crime and Criminal Justice* Retrieved March 12, 2005 at (www.aic.gov.au/publications/tandi/tandi58.html).

Wirth, Linda. 2001. *Breaking through the Glass Ceiling: Women in Management*. Geneva: International Labour Office.

Zimmer, Lynn. 1986. *Women Guarding Men*. Chicago: University of Chicago Press.

Zupan, L. 1992. "The Progress of Women Correctional Officers in All-Male Prisons." Pp. 323-340 in *The Changing Roles of Women in the Criminal Justice System: Offenders, Victims, and Professionals*. 2d ed., edited by I. Moyer. Prospect Heights: Waveland Press.

CHAPTER 8

Equity and Work

Merle A. Jacobs

Learning Objectives:

1. Discuss how female professions deliver equitable employment in uncertain economic climates.

2. How can you identify macro, meso, and micro levels of discrimination in the area of occupations?

3. There are task forces appointed from time to time to look into shortages concerning health workers. Have politicians and associations used this method of social discussion to avoid new funding in the area of health professions? Have goals from these discussions helped professions?

4. Are nursing organizations such as the CNA responsible for standards within the profession, such as equity for nurses?

5. Discuss legislation promoting equity in Ontario, Canada.

The ideology of our liberal capitalist society has been based on inequality from the very beginning. This chapter traces inequality in the workplace. We usually know what we do not like and it is this routine interaction within the self that can lead us to an understanding of concepts such as equity. Like ethnicity, inequality is a broad and over employed term. However, when we view this term in relationship to access to resources it provides a road map to understanding the relationships that take place in our work lives.

Technology has made our world smaller, and yet, in many areas our lives are more similar in how we relate to family and friends. The technology revolution has made not only communication easy and accessible to the masses, but provided the outsourcing of work and in health care it has taken over from direct interaction with the client/patient to computer based communications. Health care workers can be seen in hospitals staring at computer screens instead of being with their patients. Downsizing and outsourcing are methods in North America to compete with developing countries whose workers are grossly under paid and work in less than desirable environments. A major focus in the area of technology in North America is the compensation for workers and the destruction of the middle class economy, and consequently, the middle class family. Public Policies relate to families and impact the family. The changes in work life and the shift of jobs to the developing countries have a direct relationship to the well being of families in North America. In the economic down turn of 2008 it was the middle class that were more venerable to economic loss. University age children could not find work and returned home to live with their parents. Compensating elites is not considered as part of the ideology of liberal capitalism, which allows for such inequalities to occur; after all, industrialized societies are based on the assumption that hard work must be rewarded. Never mind if that hard work is based on another's work–the other who does not get due compensation for the work done. In the United States, compensation for CEO's has become an issue in the last few years. Yet, managers of hedge funds are raking in huge incomes by gambling on the stock market. They buy up bad debts and wait for the turnaround in the economy. In Ontario, the salaries of CEO and Presidents in hospitals have become a concern of the government. For example, in 2008, Joe Mapa, president of Mount Sinai Hospital, received $702,560 in salary and benefits. Yet, he and his counterparts will have to reduce front line workers that provide care to patients. The Ontario government has frozen the wages of non-unionized, public-sector workers for two years, while the CEO's pay is only tied to performance, for instance, patient satisfaction surveys (Howlett 2010). When society rewards certain types of work and certain behaviours, we ask ourselves when we encounter a shortage of certain workers, such as nurses, if we need to look at societal values, government policies and the media coverage of issues for reasons that allow for behaviours to occur over and over again without cost to politicians and other elites who have power to enforce change.

Equity and Work

Before we can apply equity to work, it is the professional model that separates those who can and those who cannot work within a certain scope of practice. Society views this separation as important to make sure that professional practice is guaranteed and risks are minimized. Differences in the extent to which men and women of various races and ethnic groups participate within the different professions and occupations have been studied (Das Gupta 1996; Galabuzi 2006; Jacobs 1999, 2002) and reported. The inequality and the discussion around these issues have not changed the dynamics in practices related to the hiring of certain groups at certain levels of work.

Race-ethnic groups, because of differences in human capital and discrimination, have different occupational structures and find it difficult to obtain work in their areas of expertise. In spite of the right education and training, these workers compete with others from the dominant group with similar or less education and training. Who gets work and what type of work? This is an important question when we look at equity and work. We cannot just look at changes in work organization arising from heightened competition due to downsizing and job losses and use that for an answer. There are macro, meso, and micro levels of discrimination in the area of occupations. Macro levels decisions are made in the name of globalization and new technology and has a larger effect because of the economic, institutional and cultural dimensions that enter the workplace from a global perspective. Meso level decisions are less omnipresent but still manipulate the structures and process of any transnational production, which then effects local behaviours. Micro level decisions effect local institutions in organizational structures, management behaviour and employment practices. These local dynamics affect equity and work. Political measures at the local level to provide equity for gender and ethnic groups in Canada have focused on how to engage professions and occupations to hire and have policies that are inclusive. Legal measures to abolish discrimination and hiring agendas to equalize the work force is focused more towards a group rather than looking at the practices of how hurdles to equality of opportunity are experienced in the workplace and in hiring practices.

Nursing an Example of Equity and Work

Like the financial disaster in 2009, the shortage in the field of nursing is a complex global nursing issue. There is also a noticeable shortage of doctors, pharmacists, and physiotherapists. If nurses are the backbone of the health care system in Canada, then why has the government not taken a stronger stand and made sure that this issue was corrected over the last 50 years? With other employment available to women they no longer need to participate in care giving roles. Women's paid work can be reviewed and discussed in ways that were not available to researchers in North America in the past. Nursing has been discussed since E. Hughes (1958) in the 1950s, and nursing work was viewed as one of the main employers of women in North America (Jacobs 1999). Nursing work life was described as one of subordination and viewed as semi-professional. These women lacked power and prestige within the system. Nursing moved itself from the position of being a semi-professional occupation into a professional position wanting equity within the system. I have argued that equity for the profession did not always mean equity within the profession.

The Ontario government's nursing task force in 1999 on "Good Nursing, Good Health" was mandated to seek out and hear the views and the ideas of key stakeholders within the health care system, including nurses, nursing students and educators, employers and consumers. Apart from the president of the Ontario Nurses' Association (ONA), the task force included one staff nurse (RN) and one RPN out of the fifteen members. This tokenism in my analysis does not provide for the views of the nurses who are the backbone of the profession. The composition of the task force re-enforced my argument that the voices in nursing are not that of staff nurses but that a small group of elites within the profession. In discussing nursing with state holders, of the 59 individuals who participated in this exercise, the reports states that 25 were nurses (break down not provided). These nurses indicated that "they faced a number of barriers, including heavy workloads as a result of the increased acuity of patients, the nurse-to-patient ratio, and the elimination of the front line nursing supervisors. Many stated that the current focus on task-specific versus holistic nursing has affected patient care and is adding to their own stress levels." Moreover, they pointed out that "the lack of a nursing voice on the boards and senior management teams of many health care organizations continues to give rise to the issue of marginalization" (p.1-2). Eight recommendations were made to the Minister of Health. The Task Force stated that they arrived at their decisions based on evidence, from existing or commissioned research and from what they heard from the key health care stake holders. The Task Force did not deal with racism and the views of ethnic minority nurses, abuse and harassment. Forgotten in this research is the changing face of the residents of Ontario, especially within Toronto. To ensure effective change, ethnic and racialized minority stakeholders input needs to be included within the developing stage of change. Most nurses encounter abuse from multiple sources including clients and their families, colleagues (nursing and others), and systems and structures within the workplace. However, newcomers and racialized nurses are more at jeopardy as they may not have structural information to address these concerns. Rather than participating fully in their profession they do not take the risk to change the system or encourage others to join the profession.

In 2004, once again the Ontario government acknowledged that nurses were not fully employed and there was a shortage of nurses in hospitals. The government recognized that:

- Only 55 percent of registered nurses in Ontario hospitals have full-time jobs.
- Nurses put in 2.7 million hours of overtime in Ontario hospitals in 2002-2003.
- Hospitals purchased two million hours of services from nursing agencies in 2002-2003, sometimes at more than double the cost of employee nurses.
- Nurses are at a high risk of workplace illness or injury. In 2002 alone, nurses filed nearly 1,500 Workplace Safety and Insurance Board claims.

With the identification of the above points, the Ontario government requested a new era of accountability. These statements are not new and have at least since the 1970s in Ontario been verbalized by governments of all political stripes. What politicians promise and what they deliver in terms of true job growth has to be viewed in terms of outcomes, not press releases. The Ontario government has promised full-time work for up to seven and half months to new graduates and offers older nurses less physically demanding duties. The government says it invested in 900 new nursing jobs in 2009-10.The promises for more hiring, more spending and other promises must reviewed in the light of what is occurring in reality. However, we read reports that CEOs in hospitals are cutting back on professional nursing staff (2,045 nurses were laid off from hospitals, see *CTV* 2010) and replacing their work with less skilled nurses or Personal Support Workers (PSW). The lack of accountability and the lack of transparency around decision making in hospitals and the government allowing these decisions leaves little room for equity in the workplace to exist. The issues related to this profession revolve around equity as it relates to gender, class and race. Nursing history, similar to women's history correlates with socioeconomic status. In terms of wages, nurses are paid much higher today, but they are still not in control of their work lives as are physicians who earn far more than nurses. Not only is there a lack of equity in earnings, there is also a lack of equity in job security. The promises that government provides to the population around nursing care employment have not been fulfilled.

The Ontario government promises and forecastes by the Canadian Nurses Association (CNA) reveal that the power elites in Ontario are not serious about nursing work and equity. The CNA states there will be a shortage of 78,000 nurses in the year 2011. By 2016, the expectation is that there will be 113,000 unfilled nursing jobs in Canada. Nurses are still targets of downsizing when governments and hospitals struggle with deficits. The enrolment shortage in Canada in 2004-05 resulted in lower graduates in 2008. This shortage (along with the aging nursing work force, the closure of hospital beds, the increase in patient acuity and shortening of length of stay, ambulances diversions, and emergency centres over crowded with patients) makes nursing work a strategic consideration. For the public and the profession this news around health care is foreboding. For their solution on this important issue, the CNA (2010) states six points. They are:

- Increasing RN productivity by one percent a year would reduce the shortage by close to half by 2022, giving the best results in the shortest time.
- Reducing annual absenteeism from 14 days to seven days for three years.
- Increasing enrolment in education programs by 1,000 per year from 2009 to 2011, with the benefits starting in 2015.
- Improving retention of practising RNs to two percent except for those aged 60 and over.
- Reducing attrition rates for new RNs from 28 percent to 15 percent over the next three years.
- Reducing international migration of nurses actively recruited to come to Canada by 50 percent would affect shortages by less than 10 percent in the long term.

Like the government, the CNA provides information but has not achieved equity for nurses. In fact, the first point is harmful as nurses are already overworked. These six solutions looks at the nurse but does not look into the behaviours of the political class, the hospital administrators as well as the media who do not bring this issue to their audience's attention until there is a crisis. There is no mention of a toxic work environment, racism, and abuse (Das Gupta 1996, 2002, 2003; Hagey et al. 2001, 2005; Jacobs 2007, 2008; Collins 1999) by the CNA, and they miss pointing out the inequity that occurs within the profession of nursing.

The right to certain work areas among nurses is one way where employees find out who is entitled to these limited spaces in times of economic downturns, technology changes or when employers request increasing productivity. Who picks up "the job" at these times provides insight into equitable behaviour. Canada does not practice true social equality when we examine full time vs. part time positions, mentoring, promotions, wages, aboriginal peoples, welfare, unemployment benefits and workplace safety. Like Canada, the CNA also does not pay attention to equity issues other than gender. There is legislation promoting equity, but it is the true enforcement of these laws that is questioned. In the current era of downsizing and job insecurity in the hospital sector, staff nurses and especially minority nurses will be armed with arguments from their nursing organizations, yet they will still be downsized out of their jobs, like they were in the 1990s (Jacobs 2000).

The entitlement of work is very much one of power and under the influence of the dominant group's values and control. In spite of our multicultural society, our laws under the human rights code regarding equity and values of social justice, we in Canada still have social attitudes and arguments that allow for inequity in the workplace. Racism has a negative impact on the health of individuals (Hagey et al. 2001) and the nursing profession. Nurses may encounter racism from multiple sources including clients and their families, colleagues (nursing and others), and systems and structures within the workplace. Rather than looking at racism and racist attitudes, major institutions and the general public still like to use the word diversity.

The 'R' (race) word when used encounters pushback from elites in society. A complex societal problem produces simplistic wars of words to attack the "other" in the workplace and in the media. Living so close to the United States brings with it the war of words that takes place in the areas of race, gender and class within their talking class. The Walmart mentality is linked to the lack of job entitlement, and the cultural side of personal vulnerabilities can be used for our analyses to understand the impact of equity and work. What we can view in the six recommendations by the CNA as once again the view of the dominant group which controls the profession of nursing. The six points especially is troublesome in view that this organization cannot stop Canadian nurses from working in the USA, Europe and Australia. Yet, the CNA in a brief to the Canadian government requested that nurses from developing countries not be induced to come to Canada due to the shortage in their own countries. This double standard is not only troubling but can be labelled as racist. Both the government and nursing organizations have difficulty in understanding the issues around the shortage of women willing to work in nursing and the lack of equity within the profession. Organizational practices and politics and the analysis of inequality in workplaces is tied to the inequalities in the distribution of rewards. Race and ethnic employment segregation in nursing is well documented (Das Gupta 1996, 2003; Collins 1999; Hagey et al. 2005) and tied to not only rewards but to toxic work environments (Jacobs 1999, 2007, 2008).

Understanding the Causes of Inequity

In Canada, we have legal anti-discrimination laws and most economists and legal scholars can agree that employment discrimination is a human rights issue. Employers and professional organizations may treat individuals differently without realizing that they are involving prejudice and stereotypes in their judgments. The issue of balancing rights, protecting employees against employers is difficult given that racial, sexist tensions may lie just beneath the surface of interactions and policy statements. It is not in the policy but in the practice and process of work that this tension comes to the surface. For many researchers these issues go beyond equity and rewards, they reach the level of societal integrity.

In many organizations, authority relations appear to have an impersonal character because of the rational type of standards and rules which appear on paper. For the majority of nurses, these rules and standards impose discipline and control, and leave little room for discretion and individual initiative and allow the employer as well as their professional organizations power over them. The way that those standards and rules are applied is not equal and reports (Das Gupta 1996, 2003; Hagey et al. 2005, 2006; Jacobs 1999, 2007, 2008) show that prejudice and racism is the root cause for inequitable behaviours. Many hospitals provide the public a positive corporate image that promotes diversity and social justice, yet have informal circles of communication and interaction by those who hold positions of power to accommodate decisions that have positive outcomes for this group. Within nursing, actions and interactions are like the "old boys' network." This network cuts out the staff nurse as well as minorities in management from significant information that flows through these networks. Those in power and those close to them exchange information about data, services, job prospects and advancement possibilities (Jacobs 1999). These behaviours are not progressive but retain old ways of distributing resources.

For many organizations, maintaining a diverse workforce at the lower levels of power proves publically that they do not discriminate and have improved access to the job market. Legitimizing the employer's reputation we see a few racialized nurses and other minority employees in positions of power. However, minority nurses at the staff level and in management have reported racism by peers, hospital staff, physicians, patients and visitors; as well when economic downturns occur they are the first to be let go. Last in, first out. The reinforcing patterns of the workplace that discourages staff nurses in reporting abuse, tolerating physicians who abuse staff nurses, and not following thought on harassment, and racism policies by institutions show these employees that administration does not view abuse as an important issue. The public only sees the face that is provided to them via the media. Minority nurses are in most pictures on reports that are published, but we see that management and senior administrators are mainly from the dominant group. The Ontario media does not investigate the percentage of ethnic minority or racialized nurses in advanced nursing positions or in senior management positions. It is the role of the media to expose the issues that allows for inequity to exist in the workplace, yet they avoid the challenge. The media with multiple stories to cover have not viewed inequity in the workplace and this toxic environment as more important that the sex scandals they cover over and over again. Or, is it that the media like the health care system is governed by the same elites or the same dominant group in society. The issue of racism is important to discuss in the area of equity. Those from the dominant group who are powerless still have more power than racialized workers at the same socioeconomic levels. Therefore, race and white privilege must be discussed and reviewed when we speak about equity and work.

Racism and discrimination are alive and well in nursing. However, there still lacks responsible institutional policies to prevent inequitable behaviours from happening. To break the silence we need the media, the power elites to have a real understanding of racism and discrimination and the impact on nurses' lives. The Ontario and Canadian governments needs to have racialized researchers look into how women are streamed into educational programs in nursing; who gets to become a PSW, who is talked into becoming a Registered Practical Nurse and who is provided with the opportunity to become a Nurse Practitioner or take the Ph.D pathway in nursing. A learning experience that is fully accessible and is colour blind would make a difference to racialized men and women entering nursing. The two government documents and the CAN's document do not look into these issues and as I stated earlier, they do not consider inequity in nursing work. Nursing is only one example of inequality within a profession or in the workplace.

We cannot always get numbers to state what is occurring in many workplaces. Most often it is the reporting of one person that engages the researcher to start asking questions around the issue of equity and work. History is another area that informs us of practices that occur in the workplace. New immigrants and the economic disadvantaged who need work will work in areas that are unsafe or abusive in practice. As we work or engage in educational activities we need to ask question related to the relationships of people who are wronged, and who are the people involved in the action, and who gains from these behaviours. What is occurring? Is it a single isolated act or is it part of a pattern? There is a sequence of events that presents itself when asking and answering questions about equity and work.

Conclusion

Equity cannot be achieved in the workplace if it is not a true social value in society. Unfair practices related to work depends on the tolerance that society has to inequality. The problem is not about white privilege or how the dominant groups use parameters. The problem is reliance on trust of others: "if I behave in an equitable way so does the other person." The exclusion of anyone person or group from specific work or profession represents the extent of workplace inequality. There is no real discrimination test that employers take to prove or provide proof that they are equitable and fair. They may have some numbers to show that there are employees who self disclose that they are part of the designated affirmative action groups. Bureaucratic structures and practices help obscure inequitable practices. The belief we have in meritocracy and universal fairness obscures the "the old boys' network" and other reasons recent immigrants, women and minorities have limited access to critical resources to advance within the organization and society. Individuals who achieve success are the poster "girls" and "boys" for the organization or media success stories.

The discussion in this chapter implies that inequality is enormous. I would like to point out that even if it was one person, we as a society need to have this discussion. In this action we espouse positive values such as equity and work, social justice in society, as well as non-supportive organizational culture that allows for inequality. In the face of several predicted crisis in nursing and other health professions, conditions such as racism and abuse displace some nurses to the margins. Like embracing health disparities for patients, nurse leaders, hospital administrators and politicians need to include prejudices, systemic factors, stereotypes, and influences that create a toxic work place when dealing with the inequity in the workplace for nurses and other employees. Dealing with racially, ethnically, and linguistically diverse patient populations means hospitals have the same diversity among their employees in their organizations. Only when they embrace true diversity and understand will those in power be able to make the necessary changes to declining enrolments in nursing education, manage the ageing of the profession, and foster the ability of women to find work in other areas. Using women's work, such as nursing, as a way of discussing equity and work allows us a space to discuss why there is systemic discrimination, lack of accountability, lack of true action by those in power within Ontario. Advocacy is the only tool that most nurses have who wish to engage the public. Remaining silent will maintain the same levels of inequity.

References

Canadian Health Services Research Foundation. 2005. "A Commitment to Nursing, Nursing Leadership, Organization, and Policy Theme." Report prepared to highlight the Canadian Health Services Research Foundation's commitment to nursing. Ottawa. Available at www.chsrf.ca.

Hospital CEO. 2010. "CEO's Salary and Benefits." Available at http://www.hospitalceo.com/ontario-salary-comparison-2009/2010/04/.

Howlett, Karen. 2010. "CEO's Pay to Performance such as Patient Satisfaction Surveys." *The Globe and Mail.* Available at http://www.theglobeandmail.com/news/national/ceos-at-ontario-hospitals-to-face-pay-for-performance-rules/article1525562.

Canadian Nurses Association (CNA). 2010. Available at http://www.cna-aiic.ca/cna/.

Collins, E., R. Hagey, J. Turrittin, U. Choudhry, J. Fudge, and R. Lee. 1999. "Study of Nursing in the Metropolis: Making Racism See-Able. The Grievances/Complaints Filed by Women Immigrant Nurses of Designated Minority Groups." Toronto. Unpublished Paper.

CTV. 2010. "Ontario Nursing Layoffs Hurting Patients: NDP." Available at http://ottawa.ctv.ca/servlet/an/local/CTVNews/20100426/ont_health_100426?hub=OttawaHome.

Das Gupta, T. 1996. *Racism and Paid Work.* Toronto: Garamond Press.

_____. 1996. "Anti-Black Racism in Nursing in Ontario." *Studies in Political Economy* 51(Fall):97-116. Available at http://www.ona.org/pdflib/dasgupta.pdf.

_____. 2002. "Racism in Nursing. Executive Summary." Report. Toronto: Ontario Nurses Association.

_____. 2003. "Racism in Nursing." Available at http://www.ona.org/pdflib/dasgupta.pdf.

Work, Health and Safety Centre. 2010. "Day of Mourning April 10, 2010." Available at http://www.whsc.on.ca/whatnews2.cfm?autoid=621.

Galabuzi, Grace-Edward. 2006. *Canada's Economic Apartheid: The Social Exclusion of Racialised Groups in the New Century.* Toronto: Canadian Scholars' Press Inc.

Hagey, R., U. Choudhry, S. Guruge, J. Turrittin, E. Collins, and R. Lee. 2001. "Immigrant Nurses' Experience of Racism." *Journal of Nursing Scholarship* 33(4):389-394.

Hagey, R., M. Jacobs, J. Turrittin, R. Lee, M. Purdy, M. Chandler, B. Cooper, A. Brathwaite, and T. Das Gupta. 2005. *Implementing Accountability for Equity and Ending Racial Backlash in Nursing.* Toronto: Canadian Race Relations Foundation. Available at www.crr.ca.

Hagey, R., L. Lum, J. Turrittin, R. MacKay. 2006. "How the Profession of Nursing can Achieve Ethnoracial Safety through Transformative Justice." Pp. 144-164 in *The Professionalization of Work,* edited by M. Jacobs and S. Bosanac. Whitby: de Sitter Publications.

Hughes, E.C., H. Hughes, and I. Deutscher. 1958. *Twenty Thousand Nurses Tell Their Story.* Montreal: J.B. Lippincott Company.

Jacobs, M. 1999. "Staff Nurse Collegiality: The Structures and Culture that Produce Nursing Interactions." Unpublished doctoral dissertation. Department of Sociology, York University.

_____. ed. 2002. *Is Anyone Listening: Women Work and Society.* Toronto: Women's Press.

_____. 2007. *The Cappuccino Principle: Health, Culture and Social Justice in the Worplace.* Toronto: de Sitter Publications.

_____. 2008 *Women's Work: Racism and Trauma.* Toronto: APF Press.

Jacobs, M. and Stephen E. Bosanac. eds. 2006. *The Professionalization of Work.* Whitby: de Sitter Publication.

Ontario Ministry of Health and Long-Term Care. 1991. "Good Nursing, Good Health." Available at http://www.health.gov.on.ca/english/public/pub/ministry_reports/nursing_roi_04/nursing_roi.html.

Canadian Association of Schools of Nursing. 2008. "Nursing Education in Canada Statistics 2007-2008." Available at http://www.cna-aiic.ca/CNA/documents/pdf/publications/Education_Statistics_Report_2007_2008_e.pdf.

Other Recommended Readings

Canadian Race Relations Foundation Fact Sheet: Acknowledging Racism. Available at http://www.crr.ca/.

Fernando, S. 1996. "Black People Working in White Institutions: Lessons from Personal Experience." *Human Systems: The Journal of Systemic Consultation & Management* 7(2-3):143-154.

Ontario Human Rights Commission. 2005. *Policy And Guidelines On Racism And Racial Discrimination.* Available at http://www.ohrc.on.ca.

CHAPTER 9

Credentialism: What is it and Why Should I Care?

Greg Scott

Learning Objectives:

1. Consider the nature of credentialism and its competing definitions.
2. Note the historical roots of credentialism.
3. Examine the implications of credentialism for social justice.
4. Describe some of the effects of credentialism on today's youth.
5. Analyze some of the ramifications of credentialism for highly skilled professionals, the labour movement and newcomers to Canada.

Introduction

Henry Adams once remarked that "nothing in education is so astonishing as the amount of ignorance it accumulates in the form of inert facts" (Davidoff 1942:75). Adams may have made the comments in jest, but to a growing number of university and college graduates, his words have the ring of truth. According to the Webster Handy College Dictionary, something which is "inert" has no "inherent power to move or act" (Morehead 1981:278). Could it be that, contrary to the promises of academia, Henry Adams was right to suggest, albeit light-heartedly, that education does not necessarily empower? It is a somewhat troubling prospect, seemingly at odds with conventional wisdom, but is there merit to the argument? Students and professionals, urged more and more to become highly specialized and to seek out refined training and certifications in areas where "demand exists," are quickly learning that in today's competitive workplace, competence and knowledge are not enough. It would be folly to suggest that this is a simple problem with simple solutions. Yet, to root out the real causes of the problem, it is imperative to examine the issue of credentialism, which has gained a foothold on a scale not seen before, and shows no signs of diminishing.

What is Credentialism?

What is credentialism and why is it having such a dramatic effect? Various definitions have been put forward, often grounded in and influenced by where the writer is situated ideologically. Greg Cutbrush and Greg Martin define credentialism as follows:

> Credentialism is a term sometimes used to describe the promotion of formal qualifications above and beyond those necessary to perform a job. It amounts to promotion of over-training. The required additional training serves as a barrier to people obtaining jobs which they could otherwise obtain and do successfully. This can create a kind of low-skill unemployment trap which falls most harshly on the least fortunate sections of society. (ACIL Consulting Pty Ltd 2000:16)

The definition offered up by Cutbrush and Martin captures both the nature of credentialism and the dilemma which it raises. However, there is considerable dissent amongst scholars, as to whether or not the credentialism phenomenon should be embraced enthusiastically, or combated with extreme prejudice. The pursuit of academic qualifications, certifications and higher education–or credentials–has gained prominence on a national and an international scale. A recent study by Statistics Canada revealed that enrolment in post-secondary education hit a record high in 2004, with growth in virtually every demographic (University Enrolment 2004).

Credentialism Vs. Social Justice

Many would argue, from a social and economic perspective, that increasing levels of education and training in the general population offer numerous tangible benefits to society. Indeed, it is certainly a compelling argument, which few would attempt to dispute. On the other hand, the implications for social justice are equally difficult to refute. Diana Kendall, Jane Lothian Murray, and Rick Linden (2004) have defined credentialism as a "process of social selection in which class advantage and social status are linked to the possession of academic qualifications." Few people would disagree that basic education and literacy, as well as a high levels of enrolment in post-secondary institutions are noble and worthwhile goals. The controversy only arises when credentials are overvalued and overemphasized. Assuming that Kendall, Lothian Murray and Linden's somewhat provocative definition has merit, it raises several important questions. First, if credentialism breeds social inequality, is this a price society should be willing to pay to achieve increased levels of education and training? Second, if credentials are as important as they are made out to be, are they equally accessible to everyone, regardless of gender, race and socioeconomic status? Finally, if, as Kendall, Lothian Murray and Linden argue, class advantage and social status are awarded on the basis of the possession of credentials, how vital are those credentials to on-the-job performance? Can the credentials be demonstrably linked to competence, or are they mere titles which offer few real-world benefits? These are important points for society to ponder. Perhaps the most important of the questions raised by Kendall, Lothian Murray and Linden (2004) is this: Could it be that by underscoring the importance of credentials, society is in fact, propping up existing class distinctions and fuelling injustice? To those who have voiced concerns about the practical implications of widespread credentialism, these are deeply troubling questions.

Based on the varying definitions that have been put forward for the phenomenon, it is fair to say that credentialism has several key characteristics: It is a process where social empowerment, status and privilege are bestowed upon individuals who possess a certain pre-determined level of formal training. Furthermore, a lack of such training represents a barrier to employment, and socioeconomic success, even though it is an open question whether or not it would be an impediment to on-the-job performance to lack such credentials, training or certifications. Credentialism becomes enshrined in most professions when there is widespread acceptance, reasonably or not, that certain credentials are necessary to success in those fields.

The Early Roots of Credentialism

While it is a worthwhile exercise to examine the impact of credentialism on social justice, any analysis of the issue would be incomplete without a closer examination of the history of the phenomenon. Credentialism has had a quantifiable influence throughout the ages and is, by no means, a new phenomenon. Unfortunately, the history of credentialism is not well documented and no concrete timeline exists. It is difficult to pinpoint specific historical examples of credentialism without neglecting other instances, which may or may not be more worthy of consideration. Nor is it an easy task to point out a specific moment in history, which marked the beginnings of credentialism, per se. That said, there is no shortage of information about the influence of credentialism throughout history.

Although it by no means sparked the emergence of the age-old trend toward credentialism, the guild movement was key in putting forward arguments about the importance of credentials. In 14th century Europe, guilds emerged as a "means to ensure that non-members could not practice in the trade within their territory" (http://renaissance-faire.com 2004). Accordingly, guild membership became the predominant "credential," which allowed individuals to practice a particular trade. As is the case with modern-day unions, the direct descendants of guilds, the movement had a dual role to play. On one hand, the guilds regulated quality standards for the merchandise produced and sold by guild-members and invoked penalties for inferior merchandise. At the same time, they generally provided some degree of financial recompense for the care of sick and disadvantaged members, their widows and their orphans (2004). The guilds offered their membership tangible benefits and fuelled the growing labour movement.

While guild affiliation offered real benefits to it members, the guilds also tightly controlled who could join them. Guild officials enforced rigid membership requirements which were, arguably, unrelated to competence and job performance (http://renaissance-faire.com 2004). The achievement of full participation was, more often than not, the result of having the right personal connections, and networking with influential friends and family members (2004). In fact, the preponderance of evidence seems to suggest that affiliation with a guild, which was often a pre-requisite for full participation in the economy, was based on arbitrary requirements for training, certification and accreditation:

> Qualifying for membership in a guild involved a long and underpaid (if paid at all) apprenticeship. The apprentice was bound out by parents [of the aspiring guild member] to an employer for approximately seven years. The employer committed to feed, clothe, and lodge the apprentice with his family above or behind the shop in exchange for the apprentices labor. When the apprenticeship was completed, the apprentice was free to pursue their craft and work for daily wages (sic). (http://renaissance-faire.com 2004)

Despite some trials, it was generally worthwhile to pursue entry into a guild. Participation in the guilds offered manifold social advantages and protected workers' at a time when workers rights were rarely taken into consideration.

Despite the benefits for their members, many assailed the early guilds for offering protection and market access to a select few individuals who happened to have the right connections. Influential members of high society could easily dole out favourable treatment to individuals with personal or professional links to them. It is an argument which holds up, even to this day. Nonetheless, the primary objective of guilds was to ensure that only "qualified" practitioners could operate within certain realms of the labour market (http://renaissance-faire.com 2004). The concept was revolutionary. In and of itself, shutting out unqualified individuals did not seem objectionable to the layperson. On the contrary, it seemed to be one practical method of ensuring the quality of the wares produced. Taken at face value, it appeared to guarantee maximum competence within the respective professions. Yet, the guilds rarely considered the plight of those who may have fallen to the wayside as a result of guild monopolization. Guilds rightly protected their membership. Whether or not membership and competence were interconnected, was a moot point. It would only be in later years that professions would begin to build a case for credentials as a means of controlling access to the labour market and ensuring high-calibre on the job performance.

Credentialism and Canada's Youth

Although the implications of credentialism have been felt throughout history, in today's ultra-competitive job market, the problems it poses seem particularly acute. The effects on Canada's youth are numerous. In his article entitled, "Why We All End Up Living With Our Parents," published for the University of Regina's student newspaper, *The Carillon*, writer Federico Barahona (1996) illustrates the real-world implications of credentialism on today's job seekers and students:

> Canadian studies have shown that 66 percent of all jobs in the market require less than twelve months of specialized training. When workers themselves were asked, 44 per cent thought their jobs could be learned in less than a month, suggesting that university degrees are irrelevant for most jobs. But if enough people believe that a university degree is necessary to be a manager at the GAP, then a university degree will become necessary to fill that position. Credentialism becomes a self-fulfilling prophecy.

Barrahona's comments are strikingly personal. This is probably because, as a student himself, he is a member of the demographic most affected by society's increased emphasis on credentials. This new reality presents Barrahona and a host of other young Canadians, with a number of daunting challenges. The consequences of credentialism are both real and broad for contemporary students (Barrahona 1996). The prospect of being relegated to the confines of their parents' basements is one which resonates with college and university students, many of whom are enjoying, for the first time, the taste of independence from their parents. In Barrahona's words, critics of credentialism may have found the rallying cry necessary to reverse a trend with which they are increasingly pre-occupied. On the other hand, like many of the other dire predictions about future employment for Canada's youth, his comments may also prove unfounded.

On a practical level, of more serious concern are the measurable impacts of credentialism on newcomers to the labour market. In May 2010, according to Statistics Canada *Labour Force Survey* 435,000 Canadians between the ages of 15 and 34 were unemployed. The unemployment rate stood at 15.1 percent, a full 6 percent higher than the figure for both genders 15 years and older, which stood at 8.1 percent. Statistics vary from year to year, but the simple fact is that unemployment rates for young Canadians are dramatically higher than they are in the rest of the population, as evidenced by Table 9.1, which tracks unemployment in a number of demographics.

A 1996 study by the Government of British Colombia exposed several trends which are very disconcerting for the demographic in question, not the least of which is an increasingly competitive environment facing young people in all sectors of the job market:

> [Y]outh today without secondary completion [are] running up against other job applicants with significant amounts of post-secondary training and education in competing for jobs. Often employers use education/training credentials as a first screening criterion, even for positions which in practice require little specific amounts of training. In an earlier era where the share of the population with post-secondary training was much lower, this device was seldom used for lower skilled positions. (Government of British Colombia 1996:43)

This observation points to a relationship between increasing credentialism by employers and increased levels of post-secondary education. Economies change and evolve and to some, there may be welcome news in these findings. While the Government of British Colombia's report underscores the importance of educational attainment before entering the job market, this could be seen as an impetus for students to obtain higher and higher levels of education. While this is certainly an expensive proposition for students, increasing levels of education also help make the province and the country more competitive in the global economy (Commonwealth Centre for e-Governance 2001). Still, given the rising cost of education and the many challenges facing students in post-secondary education, the fixation with credentials can be an unwelcome one.

Table 9.1: Labour Force Characteristics by Age and Sex

	April 2010	May 2010	April to May 2010	May 2009 to May 2010	April to May 2010	May 2009 to May 2010
	Seasonally adjusted					
	thousands		change in thousands		% change	
Both sexes, 15 years and over						
Population	27,618.4	27,651.8	33.4	401.8	0.1	1.5
Labour force	18,570.3	18,603.0	32.7	226.9	0.2	1.2
Employment	17,071.9	17,096.6	24.7	284.0	0.1	1.7
Full-time	13,768.4	13,835.7	67.3	263.8	0.5	1.9
Part-time	3,303.5	3,261.0	-42.5	20.3	-1.3	0.6
Unemployment	1,498.3	1,506.4	8.1	-57.0	0.5	-3.6
Participation rate	67.2	67.3	0.1	-0.1	...	...
Unemployment rate	8.1	8.1	0.0	-0.4	...	...
Employment rate	61.8	61.8	0.0	0.1	...	...
Part-time rate	19.4	19.1	-0.3	-0.2	...	...
Youths, 15 to 24 years						
Population	4,403.5	4,404.2	0.7	12.0	0.0	0.3
Labour force	2,874.6	2,871.8	-2.8	-27.1	-0.1	-0.9
Employment	2,438.1	2,436.8	-1.3	-20.1	-0.1	-0.8
Full-time	1,249.9	1,271.5	21.6	-23.0	1.7	-1.8
Part-time	1,188.1	1,165.3	-22.8	2.9	-1.9	0.2
Unemployment	436.5	435.0	-1.5	-7.0	-0.3	-1.6
Participation rate	65.3	65.2	-0.1	-0.8	...	...
Unemployment rate	15.2	15.1	-0.1	-0.1	...	...
Employment rate	55.4	55.3	-0.1	-0.6	...	...
Part-time rate	48.7	47.8	-0.9	0.5	...	...
Men, 25 years and over						
Population	11,355.8	11,372.0	16.2	197.1	0.1	1.8
Labour force	8,308.7	8,346.5	37.8	130.8	0.5	1.6
Employment	7,707.3	7,712.5	5.2	182.5	0.1	2.4
Full-time	7,107.4	7,117.3	9.9	172.9	0.1	2.5
Part-time	599.9	595.2	-4.7	9.6	-0.8	1.6
Unemployment	601.4	634.0	32.6	-51.7	5.4	-7.5
Participation rate	73.2	73.4	0.2	-0.1	...	...
Unemployment rate	7.2	7.6	0.4	-0.7	...	...
Employment rate	67.9	67.8	-0.1	0.4	...	...
Part-time rate	7.8	7.7	-0.1	-0.1	...	...
Women, 25 years and over						
Population	11,859.1	11,875.6	16.5	192.7	0.1	1.6
Labour force	7,386.9	7,384.8	-2.1	123.3	0.0	1.7
Employment	6,926.6	6,947.4	20.8	121.6	0.3	1.8
Full-time	5,411.0	5,446.9	35.9	113.9	0.7	2.1
Part-time	1,515.5	1,500.5	-15.0	7.7	-1.0	0.5
Unemployment	460.4	437.4	-23.0	1.6	-5.0	0.4
Participation rate	62.3	62.2	-0.1	0.0	...	...
Unemployment rate	6.2	5.9	-0.3	-0.1	...	...
Employment rate	58.4	58.5	0.1	0.1	...	...
Part-time rate	21.9	21.6	-0.3	-0.3	...	...

Source: Statistics Canada Labour Force Survey. Data for May 2010 released on June 4, 2010.

If this trend toward obtaining increased levels of formal training persists, it may be inevitable that recent graduates will face growing levels of credentialism in the future. Fortunately, there is some positive news. It is perhaps a bold conclusion to draw, but it seems safe to say that with age comes a reprieve from the spectre of unemployment. However, this is temporary relief only. Of 7,843,600 Canadians between the ages of 45 and 54, 338,600 were unemployed in 2003 (Statistics Canada, Labour Force Characteristics 2003). It is tempting to dismiss the unemployment rate as a factor unrelated to credentialism, as young people, while often highly educated, also lack much of the prerequisite experience employers often seek. Yet given the high rate of participation in post-secondary education today, it would be a stretch to conclude that a fixation with credentials is not one of many impediments facing recent university and college graduates.

The unemployment rate warrants special attention in any discussion of credentialism. There are many other causes for unemployment than a lack of credentials. Yet one of the key barriers for the unemployed is that they often do not possess the training, credentials and skills being sought after in the labour market. To many, the official unemployment rate is seen to be a true reflection of the number of unemployed persons in the job market. This is a mistaken perception. Writing in the *Southwest Missouri Economic Review*, Joe A. Bell (2002) identified one of the fundamental problems with the unemployment rate:

> The problem with the unemployment rate is that it is determined by two different, equally important, measures of employment activity—the labor force and unemployment (i.e., [unemployment divided by the civilian labor force] times 100). The unemployment rate, however, ignores the actual level of employment. If the level of unemployment and the civilian labor force are both increasing, the unemployment rate may increase or decrease, even if total employment is increasing; it is simply a matter of whether employment or the labor force is increasing faster. Similarly, a declining unemployment rate may actually involve fewer jobs or less employment. Examining only the unemployment rate misses the changes in jobs or employment in any labor market.

This is not a small problem. Minor fluctuations in the size of the labour force could skew the calculation in such a way that actual job losses are not reflected in the published unemployment rate.

In addition to the questionable utility of the unemployment rate, it is also important to remember that not all unemployed individuals are included in the tabulation. In Canada, only persons who have met the eligibility requirements for employment insurance are included in the calculation (Skills Development Canada 2005). These are primarily individuals who before becoming unemployed, worked the minimum amount or hours required to qualify for employment insurance. Persons dismissed from their jobs, or unemployed for any other number of reasons, are not included. Similarly, one is only eligible for employment insurance for a fixed number of weeks before being removed, and thereby not included in the equation (Skills Development Canada 2005). Even if one meets these specific requirements, he or she must also be currently looking for work full time. In essence, the unemployment rate only captures a small percentage of real unemployment, although it is often perceived as an accurate gauge of total joblessness. Because the requirement for credentials in certain professions is a major barrier to job-seekers, it is important to understand the complex nature of the how unemployment is tracked and measured. In particular, one must be aware that because of these problems with the unemployment rate, it is even more difficult to assess the true impact of credentialism in terms of access to the job market by workers who lack particular credentials.

Pragmatism or Academic Favouritism?

While the subject of credentialism divides academics and scholars, it has far-reaching consequences for participants in the labour market. Unwisely perhaps, credentialism is all-too often dismissed as just another example of so-called "academic snobbery." That said, credentialism touches a vast cross-section of society and the effects are anything but trivial. Writing in *Washington Monthly*, journalist Michelle Cottle (1998) recounted an experience which illustrates how it manifests itself in her profession:

> [C]redentialism is still alive and well in a variety of professions, including law, finance, business consulting - even the media. (Just recently, a New York reporter half-jokingly asked me how I had managed to get a Washington journalism job without having attended Harvard.) Such misplaced priorities do a disservice to our society, and particularly our students. As people become more and more desperate to attend a handful of prestigious schools, they become less objective about those universities and less demanding about what they receive for their education dollar.

Cottle's example speaks volumes about the degree to which credentialism has been enshrined in contemporary thinking. Often, students are more interested in having the names of prestigious schools on their résumés than they are in obtaining the top-notch education that Ivy League schools purportedly offer. Although Cottle's (1998) journalistic colleague was clearly making an attempt at humour, it is no secret that a degree from Harvard's school of journalism is advantageous to any reporter on the job market. It may be the case that many smaller community colleges or state universities offer wonderful training programs for aspiring journalists, but chances are, they will not catch the eye of a human resources manager sifting through candidate resumes quite as quickly as the submission of a Harvard graduate (1998). Perhaps this trend is justifiable. Harvard University has a well-earned reputation as a top-notch post-secondary institution. The same could be said about many other excellent schools, Ivy League or not. Still, this behaviour is symptomatic of a society which practices credentialism.

The "Right to Work" Movement

The question of credentials has become a complex issue for the labour movement and its political opponents. More specifically, a debate has emerged about the necessity and benefit of union certification in certain workplaces. In the past, belonging to a guild or union meant that a worker would enjoy an unprecedented degree of representation and a strong public voice for his or her interests (http://renaissance-faire.com 2004). However, in today's economy, the trend toward outsourcing and contracting, coupled with the diminished influence of the labour movement and growing anti-union sentiment in the general public, have stripped away many of the same protections for which the guild and labour movement fought (Turner 2002). As the influence of labour unions appears to decline, some groups question the utility of affiliating workers, en masse, with unions they deem to be ineffective and unrepresentative.

At a time when unions face unprecedented challenges, labour leaders are convinced that unionization is more important than ever before. Taylor Rogers, of the American Federation of State, County and Municipal Employees (AFSCME), has succinctly articulated the case for organizing workers today: "Because of right-to-work laws, a hamstrung National Labour Relations Board and increasing anti-union sentiment today, organizing only makes sense. It gives you political power and just representation" (Turner 2002). The increasingly influential National Right-to-Work movement, to which Turner makes reference, has become a significant problem for the labour movement. It rejects mandatory unionization in any form (National Right to Work Legal Defense Foundation Inc. 2004). The movement provides legal and financial support to non-unionized individuals or groups seeking access to a workplace, where union certification has occurred. The existence of such a movement suggests that in some quarters, mandatory union affiliation in any workplace is seen as an unacceptable manifestation of credentialism.

Skepticism about the efficacy of unions today is the impetus behind the right-to-work effort. A certain level of doubt has arisen in some parts of society, throughout the twentieth century, about the commitment of the labour movement to the betterment and advancement of society (National Right to Work Legal Defense Foundation Inc. 2004). Unionized workers, or at the very least, labour leaders, perceive right-to-work laws, popular with conservative politicians, as an affront to workers' rights (Turner 2002). As of 2003, to the chagrin of the American labour movement, Right-to-Work legislation, was in place in 22 states (National Right to Work Legal Defense Foundation Inc. 2004). Despite opposition from the union movement, there is little doubt that the right-to-work argument has been well-received in some circles.

Both sides in the contentious right-to-work debate would lay claim to the credentialist argument. Labour leaders emphasize the importance of having the most qualified professionals practising within the respective work environments of the union membership. Not just anyone, they would argue, can join the union. Union leaders have made much of the dangers of having non-affiliated employees in the workplace (Turner 2002). While it is not always the case, non-unionized workers often lack the accreditations and in some case, the expertise of their unionized counterparts. The question some would ask of the union movement is whether or not it can prove that this level of expertise can be shown to increase on-the-job performance.

Supporters of right-to-work laws argue that union-affiliation has no bearing on professional competence. In fact, many able-bodied and well-trained professionals are shut out of the job market because they are not represented by a union. Right-to-work supporters question the need for some of the credentials held up by union leaders as necessary (National Right to Work Legal Defense Foundation Inc. 2004). One might argue that this position flies in the face of credentialism. However, supporters of right-to-work laws do not deny the importance of credentials to professional competence. They simply disagree with members of the labour movement, about the necessity of certain specific credentials and in particular, union affiliation, in many professions. For example, advocates of right-to-work laws might suggest that a Ph.D. in history is highly desirable in a high-school history teacher. On the other hand, they would have no issue with a talented teacher who possesses such credentials being in the classroom, even if he or she does not possess a university degree in Education. Advocates of mandatory teacher training feel there are important, over-riding reasons why unqualified teachers must be kept out of the classroom. By contrast, many people feel that credentials are secondary to talent in the classroom. Regardless of which side prevails in the dispute between right-to-work activists and labour organizers, this is a debate with the question of credentials at its very centre.

The Education Battlefield

The debate over the importance of credentials in the public school system is a particularly ferocious one. Because it involves the education of children, it is also a discussion fraught with emotion. In the 1990s, the issue of credentials in education became a politically sensitive one for the Progressive Conservative government of

Mike Harris in Ontario. Almost from the day it took office, the government of the day and Ontario's teachers' unions were at odds with one another over educational policies. The ongoing conflict came to a head when the Harris government introduced the *Education Quality Improvement Act* in 1997. One of the many tenets of the bill which teachers found problematic was the drive to make it easier for so-called "specialists" to teach in the classroom without the usual prescribed teacher-training (Government of Ontario 1997). The government argued that students would benefit from the expertise of these skilled professionals through direct classroom teaching, even though "specialists" would not be required to possess formal training and certification in education and teaching:

> Students can benefit from having access to professional musicians and artists when they learn music and art. Human resource specialists can assist students when they seek guidance counselling. Computer programmers can steer students through the latest computer technologies. The bill would allow the government to ensure students have the opportunity of greater access to specialists with professional expertise. (Ontario, Ministry of Training, Colleges and Universities 1997)

Despite the fact that they were not in a legal strike position, teachers staged a short-lived and ultimately futile work stoppage to protest the proposed legislation. Teachers perceived the proposed changes as a direct attack on the profession. They argued that the move provided evidence that the government considered teacher training dispensable and favoured cheaper, unqualified specialists, over certified educators (Eastman 1998). The dispute between Ontario's teachers, and the government of the day was very much about the value being placed on teaching credentials and qualifications.

In fairness to the teachers, criticisms of the new legislation were not limited to the use of uncertified teachers. The *Education Quality Improvement Act* contained a number of equally provocative and contentious measures. Among other things, the package of reforms included reductions in preparation time, the amount of paid time teachers spend away from the classroom, preparing for future lessons. Additionally, in what the union considered to be a thinly veiled attempt to pit management against the teachers, principals were removed from the teacher's union (Eastman 1998). As a whole, the *Act* was widely perceived in educational circles, as a cost-saving initiative, rather than a genuine effort to improve the system (Eastman 1998). However, it is fair to say that credentialism played a leading role in this labour dispute.

The debate over whether or not classroom teachers should only be professionally trained and certified educational professionals was also coloured by the larger, age-old debate over whether teachers should be subject-matter specialists who disseminate information or holistic trainers who facilitate the learning process.

For example, a gifted pianist is undoubtedly a subject matter specialist, but is it fair to say that all gifted pianists make good piano teachers? Many would argue that the answer to the question is "no." Talented as they may be, many excellent pianists do not have the necessary didactic skills required to be a teacher. On the other hand, advocates of subject matter experts in classroom would argue that not all graduates of reputable teacher's colleges are successful educators either. The basic issue at play in this debate is a seemingly simple one: Is formal education in pedagogy (the teaching of children) or andragogy (the teaching of adults) a reasonable minimum standard for entrance into the teaching profession? If society values medical school training for all doctors, can it not also demand a similar standard for teachers? Simple as the issue might seem, there is, as of yet, no consensus on the topic. While the Education Quality Improvement Act may have highlighted the issue of unqualified teachers in the classroom, it is merely an extension of an ongoing debate.

Credentialism as a Means of Personnel Selection

In some cases, the net effect of credentialism can be quite positive. However, more often than not, the phenomenon has tangible real world effects which can only be described as negative. Credentialism is manifested in its most controversial form when credentials are used as an arbitrary means of personnel selection. Despite an emerging body of evidence that the correlation between credentials and productivity is precarious at best, the trend shows no sign of abating (Buon 1998). Certain definitions of credentialism are so skewed towards its effects on the labour market and employment that it is increasingly difficult to deny the impact, or impacts which credentialism wields in the realms of human resources management and staffing. Tony Buon (1998) has defined credentialism as "the empty pursuit of degrees or other credentials that are not necessarily related to intellectual or educational achievement." Buon's definition of credentialism raises the broader question of whether personnel selection should be based primarily on past performance or rather upon various existing indicators of future potential. For example, would twenty years of exemplary service as a police officer be a more effective indicator of future success than a diploma from a leading police college? The answer that one might give would most certainly be affected by his or her views on the importance of credentials.

An argument can be made that many human resources professionals merely use credentials as a screening tool in order to cut corners and reduce hiring time. Inasmuch as this is a tempting excuse for the unsuccessful job-seeker, it is also clearly an over-simplification. Tony Buon has suggested two principal reasons why employers are prone to use credentials as screening criteria in staffing processes. First, many employers believe that credentials show that the applicant has undergone certain educational training that has made him or her more productive. Buon has dubbed this the "Investment Effect." The Investment Effect is similar in nature to Human Capital Theory, which argues that "greater individual and aggregate investments in learning activities lead to greater individual and societal economic benefits" (Livingston [Date Unknown]). D.W. Livingston takes this even further and draws a somewhat disconcerting conclusion: "The learning efforts of the potential labor force (in terms of formal schooling, further education and informal learning) now appear to far exceed opportunities to apply employment-related knowledge in advanced industrial societies" (Date Unknown). Buon also suggests that education, and hence credentials, indicate certain attributes in the applicant that the employer seeks in an employee. This, Buon (1998) calls the "Screening Effect." In both cases, these perceived attributes, are deemed by the employer to be indicators of future productivity on the part of the employee.

To determine if screening on the basis of credentials is an effective hiring practice, one must consider whether or not the credentials will truly make the employee more productive. Buon's Investment Effect manifests itself with some regularity in the labour market: For example, an employer seeking a skilled professional to test new software products using the C++ programming language probably has a vested interest in ensuring that all new hires have a sound education, and demonstrated mastery of C++ and object-oriented computer programming principles. To accomplish this, why not ask potential recruits for proof of C++ certification when filling such positions? While there are many self-taught "gurus" in the software industry, it is a safe assumption to say that individuals who have received formal education in C++ programming can also become productive employees in the field.

Where staffing practices often go awry is when additional qualifications, with no clear relationship to desired productivity outcomes, are brought into play, simply as a means of volume management in personnel selection. If for example, an employer were to seek employees to undertake software testing using C++ in today's competitive job market, she might find that the volume of applications is overwhelming. With recent job losses in the information technology sector, there is a glut of computer programmers on the market. It would be easy for the hiring manager in question to add other related programming languages to her list of requirements. For example, she might indicate a requirement for training in other object-oriented computer languages, such as JAVA or Visual Basic. While these skills could be construed as related expertise, are they in fact necessary to productively perform the tasks required in this specific role? The example provides an overt illustration of Tony Buon's (1998) "Screening Effect." A human resources officer who knowingly employs this approach is putting credentialism into practice.

Unfortunately, rather than rethinking human resources management strategies, many organizations use this methodology to identify a more manageable pool of candidates and to thereby reduce the time required to staff a position. Using credentials as a tool for volume management in the hiring process certainly saves time in the short term. However, beyond the question of time management in personnel selection lies another important consideration. By using credentials as a means of reducing the number of potential recruits, hiring managers are eliminating candidates who lack certain qualifications, but may in fact possess other highly valuable job skills.

An argument can be made that strict adherence to the principle that credentials equal productivity undermines the more important principle of fairness in personnel selection. Moreover, from an organizational standpoint, it is hard to deny that the net effect of credentialism on the employer is also negative (Buon 1998). Ironically, the area where businesses may suffer the most as a result of this practice is the one of the most important and high profile considerations of the business world: efficiency. Buon (1998) has argued that the obsession with credentials as a means of volume management has an impact on the costs associated with staffing:

> In some areas credentialism may even be of detriment to the areas of work, specifically if credentials required are not related to skill or knowledge requirements for the job. In these cases a demand for credentials may favour the less able with credentials at the expense of the more able without credentials. Moreover, in most situations the cost of hiring staff will increase dramatically where credentials are insisted upon.

If credentialism actually affects the financial bottom line, this may offer the business world sufficient grounds to re-examine the trend.

Interestingly, many organizations, including the Canadian federal government, have recently recognized that staffing processes are often painstakingly slow and inefficient. Some have even acknowledged that an excessive focus on credentials and qualifications may be an impediment to efficiency in personnel selection. In 2003, the Government of Canada passed the *Public Service Modernization Act*, legislation which, among other things, was intended to streamline the hiring process and address long-standing complaints by managers and the public about perceived inefficiencies in the system. One of the stated goals of the *Public Service Modernization Act* would be to "modernize staffing in the public service by...giving a new meaning to merit that moves away from the rules-based concept of 'best-qualified' to a values-based approach that allows managers to hire qualified and competent individuals more quickly" (Treasury Board of Canada Secretariat 2003). The decision to emphasize maximum competency over maximum qualifications seems to be a tacit acknowledgement that the best candidate for the job is often not the one with the largest number of credentials on his or her curriculum vitae. Still, it is a minor victory for critics of credentialism. Many taxpayers will attest to the fact that effectively putting legislation into practice is all too often an insurmountable challenge. Whether or not the federal government will in fact eliminate the practice of valuing credentials and training over personal suitability remains to be seen.

Does Credentialism Empower the Empowered?

Although it is impossible to quantitatively gauge the effects of credentialism on productivity, it seems fair to say that as a direct result of the practice, many talented job-seekers may be denied the chance to contribute to the overall success of the organization. But what of the effects on society? The first and most obvious consequence of this phenomenon is elevated unemployment, particularly among marginalized groups that already face a number of barriers to employment. Specifically, credentialism has a disproportionate effect on individuals of lower socioeconomic status, women and ethnic minorities:

> Using credentials for job selection also supports discrimination against women and other low power groups. As education is often limited to those with power (position, money, gender), low power groups have limited access to educational credentials and hence are kept in a position of powerlessness. The process of credentialism legitimizes inequality by making it appear natural, fair and immutable, due to the distribution of "natural ability" and intelligence. (Buon 1998)

If Tony Buon is correct in his assumption, the only reasonable conclusion to be drawn is that credentialism empowers groups which already enjoy a favoured position in the labour market: the wealthy, men, and those individuals already in positions of power and influence. Although it is a controversial point, if it has merit, it is certainly a disturbing development.

Credentialism and "Developing" Countries

The so-called "developing countries" face a particularly daunting challenge as a result of credentialism. The World Bank (2004) defines developing countries as those "where people live on far less money—and often lack basic public services—than those in highly-industrialized countries [and] where incomes are usually well under $1000 a year." According to the United Nations Development Programme (1999), a lack of access to education in developing countries is one of the lead causes of poverty:

> Insufficient schooling, or worse, lack of access to school education is one of the single most limiting factors in life, preventing people to develop and use their full potential. This human deprivation also limits people's ability to find a job, to access well- remunerated employment, or to develop some of their entrepreneurial skills, and is therefore one of the main causes of income poverty.

Even within these countries, full participation in the economy is a luxury not enjoyed by the majority. The prospects for escaping stagnant local economies by finding work in other countries with flourishing economies is almost certainly an impossibility for people in countries where access to quality education is limited. While formal schooling may not be readily accessible to the general population because of widespread poverty, an elite few can always count on access to the best jobs and can be assured a monopoly on the few relatively lucrative opportunities inside those countries. Those with money and influence often use it to attend the most reputable elementary and secondary schools, which are mostly beyond the reach of the middle and lower classes because they charge highly priced tuitions. Limited access to education is a major obstacle to empowerment.

In developing countries, one avenue which often promises to help people escape the cycle of poverty in their countries of birth is to attend one of the few internationally accredited schools which operate there. It is widely known in the developing world that Western countries are often selective about which educational credentials carry weight when applying for immigration. Likewise, the standard for educational credentials is equally high when applying to study at post-secondary institutions or private schools throughout the industrialized West. To bring prestige to their institutions, many schools in Latin America have sought to obtain accreditation with the American Southern Association of Colleges and Schools (SACS). SACS insists that each accredited school, or American International School, have a contingent of North American trained educators and insists that a set amount of English language instruction time be allotted at each school (Southern Association of Colleges and Schools 2004). Because English is considered to be the language of international business, admission to these institutions is much sought-after in some countries. Additionally, the American-style of educational training is often taken more seriously abroad by post-secondary institutions than the normal educational credentials which are available from local public schools. Accredited international schools often pick and choose their pupils from a pool of applicants, and because most charge tuition for enrolment, education at American International Schools is often out of reach for most people. Perhaps the most important lesson to be learned is that credentialism not only touches professionals, but begins to influence lives even in the formative years of elementary and secondary school.

In a more overt manifestation of credentialism, locally trained teachers find it a challenge to secure employment at American International schools, given the tendency of these schools to give preference to teachers trained in North America. The first locally trained teachers to find employment at these schools are, of course, those who speak English fluently, a luxury not available to most professionals in Latin America. The mission of the Southern Association of Colleges and Schools is the "improvement of education in the South through accreditation" (2004). Given the systematic problems prevalent in South American schools, there is little doubt that SACS has put its mission into practice and there is no question that SACS accreditation has brought esteem to these schools to the benefit of those fortunate enough to attend them. Whether or not most Latin Americans have access to the improved system of education is another question altogether. However, given the increasing focus on credentials, it is clear that many of the world's poorest are at a distinct disadvantage early in life and throughout their professional lives, in the race to obtain much sought-after credentials.

The Public Safety Argument

Credentialism has often flourished when it can be linked to a public safety issue. Perhaps never has the need for rigid training and certification been more pronounced than on September 11, 2001. In July 2004, the National Commission on Terrorist Attacks Upon the Unites States, which had been tasked with looking into the causes and security failures surrounding the devastating terrorist attacks of September 11, 2001, issued its report. The report contained several criticisms of what can only be called a massive security failure (National Commission on Terrorist Attacks Upon the United States 2004). However, lost in the hype was a video, released at the same time as the report, showing how easily several of the terrorists passed through security at Washington's Dulles Airport (CNN.com 2004). The National Commission on Terrorist Attacks Upon the United States, also known as the 911 Commission, deliberately avoided questions as to whether or not the September 11 attacks could have been avoided. The video, on the other hand, speaks volumes. While there is no way airport security officials could have been prepared for such a carefully planned terrorist plot, the sad events of September 11 illustrated the need for common training for all airport security officials to ensure that no similar events occur in the future. This training would need to be formal, standardized and, above all else, consistent. In this circumstance, a strong case can be made for credentialism, as a direct way to protect national security. In fact, no stronger argument can be made for credentialism than the claim that it can save lives.

Perhaps the best way to ensure that airport security is equally effective across the country is to ensure that all airport security officials receive the same standardized security training. Experts agree that there is no excuse for having one set of credentials for security officials in Washington and another set of credentials for officials in North Dakota (National Commission on Terrorist Attacks Upon the United States 2004). Likewise, whether an airport security official is employed by a private security firm, or the state or federal government, he or she should be trained to possess the same level of training and certification. However, it also makes sense to experts and gives peace of mind to air travellers. Could it be that credentialism, at its best, is sometimes required to preserve public safety? While nothing that can be done to change history, or to minimize the impact of the intelligence failings that led to the 911 attacks, one can only wonder if an emphasis on consistent security training might have prevented, or at least reduced the scale of devastation that was experienced on September 11, 2001.

The renewed focus on credentialism in the security field has been put into action in around the world. Several countries have recently made an effort to ensure that airport security officials are state or government employees. Shortly after 911, the US government moved to place airport security under federal control. In late September of 2001, the United States Department of Homeland Security announced a new system of airport security which "will be performed by a combination of federal and non-federal workforce, with federal uniformed personnel managing all operations and maintaining a visible presence at all commercial airports. Notably, the American federal government will also establish new standards for airport security" (White House 2001). Presumably, this means that new security training standards would also be implemented across the board. However, with federal and non-federal employees working in airport security, one has to wonder how consistently the new security training package would be delivered. Highly trained Air Marshals, trained in law enforcement, would also be placed on all flights, despite some objections from the airlines (White House 2004). If orchestrated credentialism is to be justified and put into force, it is important that it be done in a consistent manner.

The Canadian government also moved to take over airport security after September 11, 2001. In April 2002, the Canadian Air Transport Security Agency was formed with the intention of taking over responsibilities for airport security. Similarly, the idea was to ensure that Canadians could be assured of a consistent level of qualifications, certification and security training for all airport security officials across the country (2004). In light of the new reality of terrorism, the increasing demands on the federal government to ensure that security officials receive consistent and rigorous training offer some comfort to the travelling public. This new focus on security credentials may be politically popular. Whether or not it translates into increased levels of security is still an open question.

Credentialism in Public Health Care

The recognition of international credentials has long been considered an economic impediment for highly trained professionals, including doctors, seeking to enter the Canadian labour market in areas where the domestic supply of workers is insufficient. It is a well-known fact that there are numerous areas where demand for skilled professionals outstrips supply (Urbanski 2004). The problem is particularly acute in the Canadian public health care system. Long waiting lines in the system have underscored shortages in certain medical specialties, while ample supplies of well-trained physicians from other countries seek access to practise medicine within the same specializations.

Recently, provincial authorities have acknowledged the need to improve access for internationally trained professionals in the medical field. In July, 2003, the provincial government of Ontario announced plans to address the shortages by easing the educational assessment requirements for physicians with international credentials. The plan would "support…the fast-track assessment and registration of up to 40 internationally trained doctors, who are currently practising outside the province, through a pilot program with the College of Physicians and Surgeons of Ontario" (Ontario Ministry of Health and Long Term Care 2004). Furthermore, in August 2004, the province of Ontario indicated that 200 "assessment and training" positions would be made available for qualified international medical graduates and reiterated its assertion that "the screening and selection processes to access these positions [had] also been improved" (Ontario Ministry of Health and Long Term Care 2004). This action is an acknowledgment that the recognition of credentials has been one of the main stumbling blocks for internationally certified doctors seeking the right to practice in Ontario. The government did not necessarily recognize that these international credentials are often equivalent to those held by doctors trained and certified in Canada. Still, these changes to the screening and selection process for internationally trained doctors constitute an admission that the assessment process and not the credentials themselves, is often at the root of the problem.

If there was any doubt that credentialism was having a detrimental effect on the public health system, it was laid to rest in 1999, when the Canadian Medical Association warned that Canada faces a continual shortage of doctors, both general practitioners and specialists (CBC.ca 2004). Given the urgency of the situation, it is puzzling that it took as long as it did to address the critical shortage of medical specialists in Ontario. What factors are in play which have prevented an influx of internationally-trained physicians, when the need was so pronounced? The answer lies in the assessment and recognition of international credentials, a process which many believe to be draconian and out-dated (Ontario Ministry of Health and Long Term Care August 2004). The problems in assessing international medical training are a reflection of systemic credentialism.

To understand the true nature of the problem, an examination of the complex assessment and recognition system for internationally obtained medical training is required. The medical profession is regulated at the provincial level in Canada, meaning that "the requirements to practise are set by each provincial and territorial medical association" (Canadian Information Centre for International Credentials 2004). Internationally-trained physicians must pass the Medical Council of Canada's Evaluating Examination (MCCEE), which evaluates "general medical knowledge compared to that of graduates of Canadian medical schools" (2004). However, passing the MCCEE is only the first step in what is a lengthy and arduous process for physicians with training obtained outside of Canada. In most provinces, doctors trained at internationally-based medical schools must also undergo two to six years of additional postgraduate medical training at a Canadian university. Physicians must also pass the additional certification examinations administered by the College of Family Physicians of Canada or the Royal College of Physicians and Surgeons of Canada. Some, but not all, Canadian provinces and territories have a form of licensure which simplifies the process somewhat for doctors willing to relocate to under-serviced areas (Canadian Information Centre for International Credentials 2004). Even still, apart from this rigorous and extraordinarily costly certification process, physicians with international medical training face one more significant challenge. According to the Canadian Information Centre for International Credentials (2004), it is the policy of some academic institutions not to recognize international medical training:

> Thirteen accredited Canadian postgraduate medical training programs participate in the Canadian Resident Matching Service. This service matches prospective physicians to a training program. Not all medical schools participating in the matching service accept graduates of foreign medical schools into their postgraduate medical training programs. Applications from graduates of medical schools outside of Canada are processed according to the policies established by each institution.

The arguments in favour of practising credentialism have often been advanced in the name of preserving the public good. The trend in the field of medicine is no exception. Justifiable or not, one of the key reasons for stringent assessment and certification of new doctors to Canada is to ensure that medical practitioners are consistently well-trained and demonstrably competent.

Unfortunately for new Canadians, who often lack the financial resources of Canadian-born residents, the certification processes in medical specializations are often long and costly. Frequently, these requirements are a duplication of previous training and assessment. A sizable number of individuals with internationally obtained medical training choose instead to leave the medical profession. With the Canadian health care system strained by financial pressures and growing doctor shortages, it is indeed frustrating to many medical doctors, and to the public, who are the stakeholders in the system, that few steps have been taken to alleviate these daunting challenges.

Foreign Credentials Referral Office

One of the challenges facing those who seek to reduce the barriers flowing from credentialism is that there are a wide range of organizations involved in recognizing credentials. Among others, key players include provincial and territorial governments, professional associations, regulatory bodies, trade unions, colleges and universities. For those with internationally obtained credentials, the problem is more than just a nuisance. To put this in perspective, According to Citizenship and Immigration Canada, there are more than 400 regulatory bodies at work across the country (2008). In May 2007, Canada's Minister of Citizenship and Immigration, Diane Finley, launched the Foreign Credentials Referral Office (FCRO) within her department. The new organization was created "to help internationally trained individuals who plan to work in Canada get their credentials assessed and recognized more quickly" (Citizenship and Immigration Canada 2007).

While this move was undoubtedly welcome news for many, it is worth noting that the FCRO would not be involved in the direct recognition of credentials. Instead, the new entity would focus on increasing in-person contact, expanding dedicated telephone services, strengthening online tools and increasing awareness activities for potential immigrants and newcomers to Canada, as well as Canadian employers (Citizenship and Immigration Canada 2007). In her first Progess Report on the FCRO for the years 2007-2008, the Minister herself reiterated that the issue is multijurisdictional and very complex:

> The Government of Canada listened to the frustrations of these newcomers, and to employers who want assurance that workers have the necessary education and training. We heard from provinces and territories that face shortages of skilled employees, and from regulatory organizations and postsecondary institutions that must make sure international education and experience meets Canadian standards. (Citizenship and Immigration Canada 2008)

By the time the FCRO released its second progress report for 2009, Executive Director Corinne Prince-St-Amand was able to cite some progress in increasing awareness amongst potential newcomers to Canada about the requirements for credentials recognition in Canada:

> An important innovation in FCR has been the provision of more pre-arrival information and services to prospective immigrants and internationally trained workers. By offering support prior to landing, newcomers are better prepared to integrate into the Canadian labour market (Citizenship and Immigration Canada 2010).

One one hand, the limited scope of the new organization, owing to the multiple players involved and cross-jurisdictional issues, may have disappointed frustrated would-be immigrants and newcomers to Canada. On the other hand, the creation of the FCRO could also be considered a major step by the federal government in recognizing that it had an important role to play in finding a solution to the persistant problem of credentials recognition (or the lack thereof).

Conclusion

Credentialism is a very real phenomenon in society, and there is little doubt it is here to stay. Competing camps will continue to argue for generations with respect to its perceived benefits and/or consequences. Does credentialism safeguard the public good or undermine it? It is an endless, often emotional debate, which will not soon see resolution. However, in light of the fact that credentialism has far-reaching implications for professionals and society, as a whole, it is a trend which requires intense and ongoing scrutiny. As old as credentialism may be, its influence on the world of work is clearly growing. What remains to be seen is whether or not an increasing preoccupation with certification and credentials will become an insurmountable challenge for professionals. To date, the effects of credentialism have had a particularly strong impact on the young, on workers in highly specialized professions and on individuals with international credentials. In assessing the consequences of credentialism, there is an overarching need to weigh the good of society against the good of the worker. This can be a challenge, as the line between the two is often blurred. Assessing what is good for the worker and what is good for society is further complicated by the subjectivity inherent in the debate. Furthermore, it is impossible to judge whether a growing emphasis on credentials has been a positive or negative force. More than anything, credentialism must be appraised on the basis of its distinct history in each and every profession. This will be a difficult task, but an important one. Quite possibly, the most apparent lesson of credentialism is this: credentials, when placed in the proper perspective, add value to the professional milieu and benefit all elements of society. Insistence on credentials with no proven link to on-the-job performance has set a dangerous precedent. That alone, may be justification for swift and immediate action on this issue.

References

Author Unknown. 1999. "CMA Discusses Doctor Shortage in Canada." CBC.ca, August 23. Retrieved October 27, 2004. (http://www.cbc.ca/stories/1999/08/23/canada/doctors990823).

Author Unknown. 2004. "History of Guilds." Renaissance Fair and Festival Guide. Retrieved August 22, 2004. (http://renaissance-faire.com/Renfaires/Entertainment/History-of-Guilds.htm).

Author Unknown. 2004. "Video Shows 9/11 Hijackers at Airport." *CNN.com*, July 22, 2004. Retrieved July 24, 2004. (http://www.cnn.com/2004/US/07/21/attacks.surveillance.video).

Barahona, Federico. 1996. "Why We Will End Up Living with Our Parents." *The University of Regina Carillon* 38(20): March 7. Retrieved May 15, 2004. (http://ursu.uregina.ca/~carillon/mar7/feature2.html).

Bell, Joseph A. 2002. "Springfield and Taney County Employment Cycle." Southwest Missouri Economic Review. Retrieved March 9, 2005 (http://www.smsu.edu/ecocnt/review.2.htm).

British Columbia Ministry of Advanced Education. 1996. "Changing Employment Demand and Skill Needs in British Columbia: Under-Employment, Rising Educational Attainment and Creeping Credentialism." July. Victoria, BC: Canada. Historical Reports & Publications. Retrieved March 27, 2004. (http://www.aved.gov.bc.ca/labourmarketinfo/chgngskills/content/page43.htm).

Buon, Tony. 1998. "The Use of Educational Credentials for Employee Selection." London, England, UK: Eastburn Partnership Inc. Retrieved May 15, 2004 (http://www.eastburnpartnership.co.uk/papers/credential.htm).

Canadian Air Transport Security Authority. 2004. "Mandate." Ottawa, ON: Canada. Retrieved September 23, 2004. (http://www.catsaacsta.gc.ca/english/about_propos/mandat.htm).

Canadian Information Centre for International Credentials. 2004. "Information for Foreign-Trained Medical Doctors." Toronto, ON: Canada. Retrieved September 28, 2004. (http://www.cicic.ca/professions/3112en.asp).

Citizenship and Immigration Canada. 2007. "News Release: Canada's New Government Launches First Phase of Foreign Credentials Referral Office." May 24. Toronto, ON: Canada. Retrieved June 11, 2010. (http://www.credentials.gc.ca/media/releases/2007-05-24.asp).

_____. 2008. ""Progress Report of the Foreign Credentials Referral Office 2007–2008." April 22. Calgary, AB: Canada. Retrieved June 11, 2010. (http://www.credentials.gc.ca/about/progress-report 2007.asp).

_____. 2010. ""Progress Report of the Foreign Credentials Referral Office 2009." Calgary, AB: Canada. Retrieved June 11, 2010. (http://www.credentials.gc.ca/about/progress-report2009.asp).

Commonwealth Centre for e-Governance. 2001. "Tools for the Knowledge Economy: An Overview." Ottawa, ON: Canada. Retrieved March 17, 2005. (http://www.electronicgov.net/pubs/research_papers/tke/chapter2.shtml).

Cottle, Michelle. 1998. "Too Well Endowed? Are Top Universities More Concerned About Money than About Educating Students?" *Washington Monthly* 30(9):September. Retrieved May 15, 2004. (http://www.washingtonmonthly.com/features/1998/9809.cottle.endowed.html).

Cutbrush, Greg and Greg Martin. 2000. "Professional Regulation: It's Impact on Rural Australia." Canberra, AU: ACIL Consulting Pty Ltd.

Davidoff, Henry, ed. 1942. *The Pocket Book of Quotations.* New York, NY: Simon and Shuster, Inc.

Eastman, Jim. 1998. "Aftermath: The Ontario Teacher Protest." Retrieved March 21, 2005. (http://www.bctf.bc.ca/ezine/archive/1997-1998/1998-01/support/after.html).

Government of Canada. 2003. *Public Service Modernization Act* (Online). Ottawa, ON: Canada. Ottawa, ON: Canada. Department of Justice. Retrieved September 23, 2004. (http://laws.justice.gc.ca/en/p-33.4/text.html).

Government of Ontario. 1997. *Education Quality Improvement Act* (Online). Toronto, ON: Canada. Retrieved September 23, 2004. (http://www.edu.gov.on.ca/eng/document/nr/97.09/compende.html).

Kendall, Diana, Jane Lothian Murray and Rick Linden. 2000. *Sociology in Our Times.* 3d CDN ed. Scarborough, ON: Thomson Nelson. Retrieved March 27, 2004. (http://www.sociologyinourtimes3e.nelson.com/glossary.html#credentialism).

Livingstone, D.W. 2004. "Beyond Human Capital Theory: The Underemployment Problem." Retrieved March 21, 2005. (http://tortoise.oise.utoronto.ca/~dlivingstone/beyondhc/).

Morehead, Albert and Loy Morehead, eds. 1981. *The New American Webster Handy College Dictionary.* New York: Signet Books.

National Commission on Terrorist Attacks Upon the United States. 2004. "9-11 Commission Report." Washington, DC: USA. Retrieved July 24, 2004. (http://www.9-11commission.gov/report/index.htm).

National Right to Work Legal Defense Foundation Inc. 2003. "Right to Work States." Springfield, VA: USA. Retrieved August 30, 2004. (http://www.nrtw.org/rtws.htm).

Ontario Ministry of Health and Long Term Care. 2004. "An International Medical Graduate." *HealthBeat: A Weekly Synopsis of Current Health News* 132: July 2. Toronto, ON: Canada. Retrieved March 12, 2005. (http://www.health.gov.on.ca/english/media/healthbeat/archives/hb_04/hb_070204.html).

_____. 2004. "International Medical Graduates." August 27. Toronto, ON: Canada. Retrieved March 12, 2005. (http://www.health.gov.on.ca/english/providers/project/img/img_mn.html).

Ontario Ministry of Training, Colleges and Universities. 1997. "Backgrounder: New Bill Promotes a High Quality Education System." September 22. Toronto, ON: Canada. Retrieved September 23, 2004. (http://www.edu.gov.on.ca/eng/document/nr/97.09/septbcgr.html).

Skills Development Canada. 2004. "Employment Insurance." Ottawa, ON: Canada. Retrieved March 21, 2005. (http://www.sdc.gc.ca/en/gateways/individuals/cluster/category/ei.shtml).

Southern Association of Colleges and Schools. 2004. "Accreditation Standards 2005 for K-12 Public Schools." Decatur, GA: USA. Retrieved September 23, 2004. (http://www.sacscasi.org/region/standards/SACS_CASI_K-12_Standards_InternetVer.pdf).

Statistics Canada. 2004. "University Enrolment." *The Daily*, July 30, 2004. Ottawa, ON: Canada. Retrieved August 15, 2004. (http://www.statcan.ca/Daily/English/040730/d040730b.htm).

Statistics Canada. 2010. "Labour Force Characteristics by Age and Sex." Ottawa, ON: Canada. Retrieved June 4, 2010. (http://www.statcan.gc.ca/subjects-sujets/labour-travail/lfs-epa/t100604a1-eng.htm).

Statistics Canada. 2004. "Labour Force Survey: Data for July 2004 released on August 6, 2004." Survey ID: 3701, Collection Registration: STC/LAB-035-02581, SQC/TRV-03502581. Ottawa, ON: Canada. Labour Statistics Division. Retrieved August 15, 2004. (http://stcwww.statcan.ca/english/sdds/3701.htm).

Treasury Board of Canada Secretariat. 2003. "Backgrounder: President of the Treasury Board of Canada Very Satisfied with Passage of the Public Service Modernization Act." November 4. Ottawa, ON: Canada. Retrieved February 28, 2005. (http://www.tbs-sct.gc.ca/media/nr-cp/2003/1104_e.asp).

Turner, Jimmie. 2002. "Organizations Can Shape History." November-September. American Federation of State, County and Municipal Employees (AFSCME) Publications. Retrieved September 23, 2004. (http://www.afscme.org/publications/public_employee/2002/pend0216.htm).

United Nations Development Programme. 1999. "Education and Vocational Training." Retrieved March 21, 2005. New York, NY: U.S. (http://www.undp.org/teams/english/educat.htm).

Urbanski, Michael. 2004. "What Doctor Shortage?" *The Toronto Star Online*, August 19. Retrieved August 19, 2004. (http://www.thestar.ca).

White House. 2001. "Enhancing Aviation Safety & Security." September 17. Washington, DC: USA. Retrieved July 24, 2004. (http://www.whitehouse.gov/news/releases/2001/09/20010927.html).

World Bank Group. 2004. "About Development." Washington, DC: U.S. Retrieved on March 21, 2005. (http://web.worldbank.org/WBSITE/EXTERNAL/EXTSITETOOLS/0%2C%2CcontentMDK:20147486~menuPK:344190~pagePK:98400~piPK:98424~theSitePK:95474%2C00.html).

Chapter 10

The Foreign Credentials Gap: Understanding the Dynamics of Racialized Immigration in Canada

Lorne Foster

Learning Objectives:

1. Learn about contemporary immigration patterns and the connection between these patterns and globalization.

2. Consider the racialized, downward shift in employment patterns for immigrants.

3. Examine how many highly educated immigrants of colour encounter credential barriers that prevent them from entering their chosen professions.

4. Discuss how credential barriers limit equity for immigrants in the labour market.

5. Think about the impact of rapid social change coupled with growing diversity through immigration, and the significant implications and challenges this poses for race relations and employment within Canadian society.

The Contemporary Social Problem of Foreign Trained Professionals

The issue of equity and fair practice in the contemporary Canadian workplace has a public intersection with the problem of proper assessment and recognition of immigrants' foreign-acquired credentials. Foreign credential barriers, or "credentialism" in an immigration context, can be defined as people not being able to get work within professions for which they are qualified to the same extent as Canadian born candidates. However, a comprehensive understanding of foreign skills accreditation as a social problem requires a focus on both a structural and racial nexus. As the Treasury Board of Canada Secretariat, *Employment Systems Review—A Guide for the Federal Public Service* (1999), states:

> Credential barriers (credentialism) may be found in educational requirements that are constrained by a practice of considering only "recognized" educational institutions, or that do not recognize knowledge and skills acquired through means other than formal education. Credentialism often unjustly excludes visible minorities from the candidate pool.

The social problem of non-accreditation of immigrant skills is made even more insistent by also being segmented along colour lines. Today three quarters of new immigrants come from developing countries and are people of colour. These immigrants are often better educated than native-born Canadians, yet they are having a tougher time finding the work they are trained to do, and their incomes are falling further and further behind.

In 1980, the average newly arrived immigrant man earned about 80 percent of the average Canadian's salary. Twenty years later, he is earning only 60 percent of this average. Foreign-trained immigrants are also more likely to be unemployed, even at a menial job. In 1980, 86.3 percent of immigrant men were employed, compared with 91 percent of Canadians. By 2000, only 68.3 percent of newcomers had jobs, versus 85.4 percent of native-born people (Reitz 2005).

Thousands of individuals, including a disproportionate number of people of colour, who immigrate every year find their university degrees and trade diplomas of little value in Canada, creating a social-economic environment where untapped talent-pools can lie dormant and ineffective. Canada has officially moved towards creating immigration policies that seek to eliminate the use of racially discriminatory admission criteria. Nevertheless, Canada's racially infused hierarchy of power has not been reduced and is still in practice through its active exclusion of racialized immigrants in the labour and educational markets (Sharief 2005). The current credentialism process not only degrades non-Western countries that are likely to be non-accredited, it also forces professionally trained immigrants to take jobs of lower socioeconomic statuses in order to survive. Even more disquieting is that the discounting of immigrant educational qualifications may be increasing in Canada in concert with the increase in the population of people of colour (Reitz 2003). This possibility suggests that institutional and social changes are related to increased social distance and marginalization (Ornstein 2000).

In this chapter, I will begin to explore the social problem of foreign accreditation barriers and the social consequences of this process in the context of Canadian immigration policy and the knowledge-based political economy. In particular, I will explore Canadian immigration policy and the discounting of foreign credentials as an illustration of the link between immigration and the political economy in the context of a colour-coded national and international division of labour. The main objective of this chapter is to examine the hierarchical relationship between racialized individuals and groups as the new recurring theme in Canada's vertical mosaic, and the postindustrial base for class and power. This, of course, is a very large topic and so my treatment of it will be limited. Stated generally and briefly, I argue that race is the new foundation for the social construction of twenty-first century global reality.

In Canada, the increasing urbanization of immigration and lack of effective immigrant settlement polices is resulting in the racialization of poverty (Shields 2002). The racialization of urban poverty warns of a looming crisis of social instability and political legitimacy for Canadian society (Galabuzi 2001). The term "democratic racism" best describes the deep tension between the reality of racism and the ideology of democratic liberalism (Henry and Tator 2000). At the same time, however, the discourse on democratic racism, and race as "foundational" to the creation and maintenance of the contemporary Canadian political economy, is not recurrently acknowledged (Dua 1999). It is my hypothesis that this is caused by the invisibility of Whiteness and the erasure of race in the discourse of political economy. Negating visible minority experiences of racialization in the workplace provides justification for the downward shift in career mobility and income inequality for people of colour. As Hamani Banerji (1995) points out, "the erasure of the factors 'race', racism, and continual immigration prevents an adequate understanding of the Canadian economy" (p.77). Similarly, this chapter will show that overlooking the social fact of international migration flows that are both multicultural and colour-coded is also a kind of erasure that disregards visible minority experiences of racialization in the workplace and prevents a coherent comprehension of Canada's political economy.

Consider that the viability of the prevailing discursive geo-political categories of "Global North" and "Global South" today is only a small indication of the entrenchment of the obscured dialectic between race and political economy operationalized by worldwide capitalism (Brant Report 1980). Yet, this is the contextual referent point for the euphemistic erasure of race in contemporary political economy discourse. There is a persistent effort in contemporary public discourse to classify people along silent racial lines, reconfiguring the world order into a new North-South dichotomy (Brandt Report 1980; South Commission 1990).

The use of disembodied language parameters for an embodied world is where racialization and racism begin because the new world order, geo-political definitions of the situation mask the processes of global empowerment and disempowerment on the basis of the body—"white bodies versus dark bodies." In the contemporary world, race matters, not because of innate characteristics, but because racialized individuals and groups are treated as though certain characteristics of their bodies matter in certain unspoken ways. However, even when race is not spoken in the postindustrial world, it looms large. Moreover, in many cases because it is not spoken it looms even larger.

Canada's Demographic Frame of Reference

For the next several decades, Canada will face two demographic processes that frame the social problem of discounting immigrant skills. First, the population growth rate has dropped to an all-time low. The country's population reached 30,007,094 in 2001, representing a 4 percent increase since the 1996 census, which matches the lowest five-year growth rate in Canadian history. In light of this census data, statisticians forecast that the population will stop growing entirely without increased immigration. Because Canada's fertility rate is just 1.5 children (the average number of children a woman will have over her lifetime), well below the rate of 2.1 children per woman needed to sustain the current population, in order to maintain a zero percent growth rate, Canada must increase immigration every year. Forty-five years ago, the average Canadian woman had 4 children over her lifetime. Today, approximately half of Canada's current population growth comes from immigration. However, given the decline of domestic birth rates, by 2011, newcomers will likely account for all growth in the Canadian labour force. By 2026, immigration will be responsible for all growth in the country's overall population.

The second demographic process is the aging of Canada's population. Again, if current trends continue, there will be relatively few people of working age to support relatively greater numbers of retired people. Projections indicate that the proportion of the total population of the country 65 years and older is expected to increase from 8.7 percent in 1976 to 20.2 percent in 2031. Left unabated, these two demographic processes could have dire social and economic consequences in Canada (Satzewich 2000).

Against this backdrop of potential social and capital accumulation issues associated with declining fertility and population aging, Canada's Minister of Immigration publicly announced that as we move further into the new millennium, the country faces a shortage of up to one million skilled workers within five years. Of course, this presupposes that foreign-trained workers are actually going to be able to practice their professions and contribute meaningfully to Canadian society. While the attraction and integration of skilled professionals and tradespersons to Canada is acknowledged to be central to the success of national development, this objective continues to be jeopardized by the many barriers faced by foreign-trained immigrants in having their skills and credentials recognized. The result is that nearly 40,000 highly skilled immigrants have arrived in Ontario in each of the past 10 years, yet many immigrants with Ph.D.'s have been left driving cabs or delivering pizzas, as opposed to being gainfully employed within their chosen vocations.

A Statistics Canada (2004) census study provides a survey of the characteristics and experiences of recent immigrants residing in Canada's metropolitan areas regarding settlement patterns, labour market experiences, and earnings. The research shows that virtually all immigrants coming to Canada in the 1990s—approximately 1.8 million—have settled in one of Canada's 27 census metropolitan areas. These immigrants tend to have higher levels of education than people born in Canada. Yet, in virtually every urban region, a far higher proportion of recent immigrants were employed in jobs with lower skill requirements than Canadian-born persons. In addition, recent immigrants were less likely to be employed in professions typically requiring a university degree. Recent immigrants with a university degree were much more likely than their Canadian-born counterparts to be working in occupations that typically require no formal education. Further, in most urban centres, recent immigrants were at least twice as likely as Canadian-born workers to earn less than $20,000 a year. They were also much less likely to have high earnings, that is, more than $100,000 a year. This reinforces the findings of several previous labour force studies. The result is a drain on social programs and public transportation in the country's largest cities (Statistics Canada 2004).

Comprehensive policy strategies in the area of immigration and immigrant accreditation barriers are vital in order for Canada to keep pace with the new market challenges set by the changeable and dynamic nature of both domestic and global economies. However, while attracting and integrating skilled professionals and tradespersons to Canada is a central topic in the area of national development, a dramatic contradiction is found in that many immigrants with professional qualifications earned outside of Canada continue to encounter barriers in the workforce. In economic terms, the Conference Board of Canada estimates that over 500,000 Canadians would earn an extra $4.1 to $5.9 billion annually if their experiences and credentials were fully recognized (Committee on Citizenship and Immigration 2003). Similarly, studies collected by the World Education Services (WES) show an annual income loss of approximately $5 billion for underemployed immigrants in Canada, which equates to $1.5 billion in lost income tax revenue, assuming a 30 percent tax rate.

Additionally, WES—a not-for-profit organization that produces evaluations of foreign degrees and diplomas—determined that more than 75 percent of the foreign credentials they evaluated in 2003 in engineering, health care, and information technologies fields matched or exceeded Canadian standards (WES 2005).

This empirical disparity supports contentions that barriers faced by foreign-trained individuals as they attempt to join the labour force in Canada result in a waste of talent, and are strongly influenced by variables including ethnic origin, ancestry, race, colour, and/or gender, and accordingly, these barriers constitute systemic discrimination. Such discrimination is not only unlawful under governing provincial/ territorial/federal human rights legislation and under section 15(1) of the Canadian Charter of Rights and Freedoms, but also leads to debilitating social costs of both an economic and non-economic nature. These costs include: (1) slower movement of professional services, (2) community frustration, (3) weaker immigrant integration, (4) human rights complaints, and (5) macroeconomic costs. All of these societal costs have direct impacts on productivity levels and societal cohesion.

Meanwhile, in the context of Canadian multiculturalism and increasing urbanized ethnoracial diversity, the groups most adversely affected by underutilization of skills are composed of people of colour. According to a 2001 report by the National Anti-Racism Council, racially visible persons born in Canada earn almost 30 percent less on average than other native-born persons:

> [R]acially visible persons, native-born or not, are better educated than the native-born White population, they are underemployed to a disturbing degree, creating a large pool of highly qualified labour, ripe for exploitation...[and] the cost of the low participation of racially visible persons in the Canadian workforce is $55 billion. (Saidullah 2001)

In addition, the Ornstein (2000) report, "Ethno-racial Inequality in the City of Toronto—An Analysis of the 1996 Census," indicates that despite their educational qualifications, unemployment rates for "Africans and Blacks" and South Asians have skyrocketed. Among Ethiopians, Ghanaians, Somalis, and the "other African nations," the overall unemployment rates respectively are, 24, 45, 24, and 23 percent, while the Pakistani, Bangladeshi, Sri Lankan, Tamil, and "Multiple South Asian" groups have unemployment rates above 20 percent (Ornstein 2000). This is in stark contrast to Toronto's average unemployment rate of 11 percent.

There is increasing evidence that visible minority immigrants are at a greater risk than non-visible minority immigrants to experience higher underemployment and unemployment levels and lower incomes due to credential devaluation (Smith and Jackson 2002; Hou and Balakrishnan 2004). One cause of this is thought to be related to institutions which are targeted for non-accreditation are generally, unexplainably non-Western and consequently non-White (Simmons 1998; Sharief 2005). This discrepancy in outcome has not only had a significant economic affect on racialized immigrant professionals, but has taken a psychological toll in terms of the erosion of skills, the loss of self-esteem, and increased tensions within and outside the alienated community (Brouwer 1999).

In light of these formidable public policy and social justice challenges, some observers argue that improving the utilization of immigrant skills must be addressed in terms of both "human capital" and "human rights" needs, and due to the complexity of the task, time pressures, and underlying racial attitudes, major institutional innovations are necessary (Foster 1998; Reitz 2005). This suggests that the issue of immigrant skills utilization must be viewed through the lens of competence and equity rights. This first involves moving away from the current credential or certificate-based system to a competency-based system that reflects clear and concise criteria, and applies the same occupational standards to all people. Secondly, it involves eliminating the double standard between citizens and immigrants in the workplace by moving away from labelling immigrant skills as a regulatory and assessment problem, to envisioning them as an equity problem that requires treating professional licensure of foreign professionals as a right rather than a privilege. Finally, it is argued that implementation of this human capital and human rights format should be a priority of immigrant-settlement policy. Recalibrating Canada's immigration program is the most cogent and cost-effective policy option to augment Canada's institutional capacity to improve the utilization of immigrant skills, and to monitor the administration of equity and fair play (Foster 1998; Reitz 2005).

Postindustrial Canada and the "New" Theme of Race

Once upon a time Canada was described as a White-settler colony (Abele and Stasiulis 1989; Stasiulis and Jhappan 1995). Canada never had a formal "Whites Only" immigration policy as Australia had. However, it is well known that what was lacking in explicit policy was implemented through immigration practices such as the head tax on Chinese immigrants, and the "continuous journey" provision on immigrants from several Asian and African countries. At that time, there were no ships sailing continuously between those continents, so this effectively blocked their entry into Canada. Further, Canada excluded Caribbean immigrants alleging that the Canadian winter would be too harsh on them. The eurocentrism of Canadian immigration was epitomized by Sir Clifford Sifton. As Minister of Interior, responsible for lands administration and immigration from 1896 well into the twentieth century, he uttered the famous words—"When I speak of quality...[immigrants]...I think a stalwart peasant in a sheep-skin coat, born on the soil, whose forefathers had been farmers for generations, with a stout wife and half-a-dozen children" (Dafoe 1931:319). Sir Clifford's words reflected the focus in early immigration policy on racial homogeny. From the very first Canadian Immigration Act of 1869 through to the late twentieth century, the flow of what state officials deemed to be desirable immigrants from preferred countries mainly consisted of White people from Britain, Europe, and the United States. Even after the Second World War, between 1954 and 1967 approximately 83 percent of immigrants to Canada were from Europe, while only 4 percent were from Asia and 1 percent from Africa.

Since the 1960s, following the introduction of the universality of immigration policy which was introduced informally by the Progressive Conservative government in 1962, and formally by the Liberals in 1967, social scientists have documented increases in the demographics and frequency of migration flows around the world. They have analyzed the varying factors that shape immigration policies, and they have recognized the growing complexity of contemporary immigration flows. As Satzewich and Wong (2003:378) have observed, contemporary migration flows in Canada not only involve the sanctioned movement of highly skilled professionals and technical workers who fill well-paying and socially desirable jobs, they also involve the movement of unskilled workers who fill undesirable, low-wage jobs that are hard to fill with domestic labour. The global masses now comprise a variation of the Marxian reserve-army thesis regarding flexible sources of labour. The conception of flexible labour continues to be relevant to contemporary world migration:

> While the phenomenon of "runaway shops" has moved many industrial production sites to places where cheap labour is located, there are now large movements of professional, skilled, and unskilled labour into industrialized, developed countries such as Canada, the United States, and many other European countries. (Satzewich and Wong 2003:365)

While in the past, the "reserve army" consisted essentially of unskilled or semiskilled workers, today it also consists of highly skilled and technical workers.

In the late-twentieth century there was a paradigm shift in advanced Western economies. They evolved from an economic system based primarily on the manufacture of physical goods (cars, television sets, refrigerators) to a system based on "knowledge goods" (computer software, global media and telecommunications information systems, virtual financial and other cyberspace markets) at one end, and personal services (fast-food restaurants) at the other. The knowledge-based economic sector in the primary labour market tends to be associated with relatively high-status, well-paid professions requiring high levels of education and training. While the service sector in the secondary labour market tends to be associated with low-status, low-paying, and dead-end work. This trend towards a dual economic system signifies what many writers refer to as a postindustrial political-economic order with a segmented labour market (Bell 1973; Hage and Powers 1992; Esping-Anderson 1993; Clement and Myles 1994).

The postindustrial economy of the twenty-first century is crosscut by what is often described as the forces of professionalization at the high-end of the scale, and the forces of McDonaldization at the low-end (Ritzer 1998). Although it might seem a contradiction, or merely a function of a transition from an old industrial society based on unskilled or deskilled jobs to a contemporary society based on an increasingly skilled labour force, both trends are indelible features of postindustrialism.

Today, one of the most striking features of contemporary skilled and unskilled immigration flows to postindustrial Canada is ethnoracial diversity. The Global North, primarily the United States and Europe, now provides Canada with less than 30 percent of all immigrants, with the balance coming from the Global South—Asia, the Caribbean, South and Central America, and Africa. Indeed, the list of countries that now constitutes the top ten sources of immigrants to Canada was unfathomable in Sir Clifford's "Eurocentric-social-class-universe"—comprised of English and French charter groups at one end of the social scale, and supplemented by White ethnic peasants in sheepskin coats at the other.

As Castles and Miller (1993) note, virtually all highly-developed countries in the Western World have experienced relatively large-scale immigration since the mid-twentieth century. In comparing these countries they found the following common characteristics: (1) a dynamic process of migration, which transforms the temporary entry of workers and refugees into permanent settlers who form distinct ethnic groups; (2) economic and social marginalization of these immigrants; (3) community formation among immigrants; (4) increasing interaction between immigrant groups and the local population; and (5) the imperative for the state to react to immigration and ethnic diversity (Castles and Kosack 1984).

Accordingly, there are now large movements of multicultural and multicoloured migrants from the Global South into postindustrialized countries such as Canada, the United States and many other European countries in the North, altering and transforming the global territorial format, and challenging nation-states to address diversity issues related to political and economic accommodation (Foster 1998). The 2001 Census of Canada enumerated hundreds of ethnic groups defined by their ancestry. They found that while up to twenty years ago, people of colour made up less than 5 percent of the population, as much as 25 percent of Canada's population could soon be foreign-born (Statistics Canada 2003).

There is another important feature associated with the era of global migration. In most postindustrial countries, including Canada, there has been a general increase in the importance of higher education for access to employment opportunities across a wide range of occupations (Hunter 1988; Hunter and Leiper 1993; Baer 2004). The changing role of education and credentials in labour markets has been referred to as a "knowledge economy," and this is reflected in a range of institutional developments, including changes in the organizational role of personnel and the professionalization of human resources management. This has changed relations between corporations and educational institutions in employee recruitment for certain critical professions, contributed to the rapid expansion of education institutions, and fostered the development of professional schools oriented toward the needs of local labour markets through increased control over professions (Reitz 2003:5).

Many people in Canada's knowledge economy consider the attainment of jobs and social standing in the knowledge economy a reflection of personal talent and effort (that is, a "merit system"). This tends to exaggerate the extent to which people control their own destinies. Reitz (2003) framed the institutional and occupational changes associated with the emergence of today's knowledge economy and flexible labour force, by arguing that the attendant influx of talented, skilled, unskilled, and semi-skilled workers to Canada can be analyzed in terms of three distinct categories—regulated or licensed professions, managerial positions, and professions where employees now have university degrees. He examined differences between professional, managerial, and other occupations in Canada using census data for immigrants arriving between 1970 and 1996. Reitz found that over time, despite increases in educational requirements and professional standards in many professions, immigrants appear to encounter increased skill discounting.

According to Reitz's research, although immigrant education and skills are frequently discounted in professional fields, the extent of such discounting is greater in the management of the growing knowledge-based industries, and greater still in occupations at lower skill levels. This seems to indicate that the underemployment of immigrants is magnified at various skill-levels, and exasperated by an escalating downward pressure and the movement of immigrants from higher to lower skill-level occupations. As a result, in our increasingly knowledge-based economy, the non-recognition of immigrant qualifications is not only a prevailing workplace dysfunction, this phenomenon increases as one moves downwardly within the labour force.

According to the human capital perspective, the promotion of meritocracy in an education-based economy should create pressures toward a more functionally-appropriate assessment of all credentials, including the foreign-acquired credentials of immigrants. At the economic level, human capital theory emphasizes that where education-based skills affect productivity, employers are under competitive pressure to seek the most highly educated skilled workers, and to disregard personal characteristics irrelevant to productivity, including gender, birthplace, ethnic origin, and race. Here, the impact of any prejudice or discrimination against immigrants, and/or visible minority immigrants, would not necessarily be eliminated by competitive pressures, but would be expected to diminish significantly. At the institutional level, codification of hiring and promotion procedures focusing on objective knowledge-based criteria for achievement could guard against arbitrary and potentially discriminatory practices. This would mitigate against the undue and arbitrary dismissal of foreign qualifications, and ensure equitable hiring practices.

However, despite the commonsense notion that contemporary Canada is a society where anyone can get a good job and get ahead if they try hard enough, one of this country's most salient sociological features is that it has historically been highly stratified along ascribed rather than achieved lines. Canada is, in John Porter's (1965) original and instructive terms, a hierarchical consortium of ascribed group status that is both at cross-purposes with and undermines equal opportunity and cultural democracy. Porter (1965:xii-xiii) demonstrated the hierarchical relationship between modern Canada's many cultural groups as a recurring theme in the formation of class and power:

> In a society which is made up of many cultural groups there is usually some relationship between a person's membership in these groups and his class position and, consequently, his chances of reaching positions of power. Because the Canadian people are often referred to as a mosaic composed of different ethnic groups, the title, "The Vertical Mosaic," was originally given to the chapter which examines the relationship between ethnicity and social class. As the study proceeded, however, the hierarchical relationship between Canada's many cultural groups became a recurring theme in class and power. For example, it became clear that the Canadians of British origin have retained, within the elite structure of the society, the charter group status with which they started out, and that in some institutional settings the French have been admitted as a co-charter group whereas in others they have not. The title, "The Vertical Mosaic," therefore seemed to be an appropriate link between the two parts of the book.

Porter's twentieth-century Canada was a system of graduated differential ethnic privilege entrenched in an unequal distribution of valued resources.

It has more recently been suggested, however, that the ethnic group disparities encountered by Porter have decreased continuously in both education and the workplace over the last several decades (Herberg 1990:218). Some subsequent studies have indicated that any privileged position that the charter groups may have historically held in the occupational structure has been effectively challenged by other European ethnic groups (Tepperman 1975; Darroch 1979). The sociological implication is that in the twenty-first century, postindustrial and cosmopolitan world, simplistic claims of ethnic identity as a hindrance to social mobility must be rejected because the causal relationship between cultural identity and social mobility today is minimal (Isajiw, Sever, and Driedger 1993). Nevertheless, it is important to grasp that the sociological objective is still the same as when Porter first introduced the "ethnically blocked mobility thesis" (Hou and Balakrishnan 1996). That is, we must examine any system of privilege where higher occupational levels are preserved, or tend to be preserved, for particular social groups.

In order to unpack the recurrent theme(s) of contemporary cosmopolitan and postindustrial society, some sociologists have hypothesized "the discrimination thesis" (Hou and Balakrishnan 1996). This attributes the inferior position that exists today for some visible minority groups to the socioeconomic structure of society. Discrimination is the actions or practices of dominant group members that have a harmful impact on members of subordinate groups (Feagin and Feagin 1998). For instance, despite the higher educational levels and occupational attainment of immigrants, visibility and social distance manifest themselves in income inequality which impacts the degree and speed of integration into Canadian society. Consequently, it can be hypothesized that visibility has replaced cultural group status as a recurring theme and focus of discrimination and differential rewards in the hierarchical structure of power and class in Canadian society (Li 1988; Reitz 1990). Visibility (or colour) and invisibility (or Whiteness) have replaced ethnic culture as the primary basis for the new system of privilege that exists within contemporary occupational structures.

In postindustrial societies, there is evidence to suggest that the relationship between dominant and sub-dominant groups does not usually extend over diverse ethnoracial relationships in a way that reinforces institutional realms across the society. On the contrary, everyday life does not reflect a "back of the bus" formal segregation and hierarchy, and there are no public spaces designated "Whites Only" or "Coloureds Only." This pattern in social institutions gives contemporary pluralism a non-caste-like public image in which society looks as though it is not resistant to change or to the social mobility of people of colour. Instead, visible minority progress from accommodation to assimilation appears to be, and is presented as, a straightforward "first come, first serve queue" and "point system" proposition—a matter of individual merit and personal initiative. However, the fluidity of social institutions does not necessarily correspond to, or interface with, the political economy where the subtlety of racial domination and discrimination in the workplace is negated by the informality of unassuming policies and practices that are woven into the framework of economic institutions.

Canadian immigration policy is an example of an institution that features specific racialized biases. Like many other social problems, racialized immigration signals a discrepancy between the ideals and realities of Canadian society. While equality of opportunity and freedom for all—regardless of country of origin, body colour, creed, or language—are stated Canadian ideals, many subordinate minority group members experience discrimination on the basis of racializing factors. Although passage of employment equity legislation, human rights legislation, official promotion of multiculturalism, and the introduction of universality in Canada's immigration system are aimed at eliminating overt institutional discrimination in and by Canadian society, people of colour, particularly visible immigrants, are often marginalized (Foster 2002b). Accordingly, in the contemporary workplace, while there are variations in income levels between visible minority groups, research has consistently found that earnings disadvantages are particularly significant for immigrants from non-European backgrounds (Reitz and Sklar 1977).

In the end, colour is the source of the first dialectical tension of the contemporary postindustrial political economy, albeit obscured by the naturalization and normalization of White privilege. Here, discrimination persists in institutional settings created by White people for White people, which are based on White people's experiences, with the result that corporate institutional structures and cultures rarely accommodate the value systems of people of colour, their styles of interacting, or the complexities of their lives. Mainstream institutions are crafted by the dominant group and deliberately or inadvertently normalize dominant values, priorities, agendas, and practices (Fleras and Elliott 1999). As a result, some institutions may limit access to resources through the practice of gate-keeping.

Individual and Structural Barriers

Although the facts may not be in dispute, the reasons for the devaluation of credentials and skills discounting are still vigorously contested (Basran and Zong 1998). The debate in sociological literature revolves around the extent to which individual factors or structural factors contribute to the social problem of the integration of immigrant skills into the Canadian workplace.

The Social Facts: Before engaging in the sociological research debate, we need to review the social facts. In the 1960s, immigration policy reforms eliminated preferences for immigrants of European origin and implemented a points-based system for economic immigrants as a strategy for ensuring quality-control. The points system allowed immigrants to be chosen on the basis of suitability to Canada and labour market needs, and mitigated against discrimination owing to religion, race or country of origin (Foster 1998:72-74). Immigrants gained points for factors including occupational attainment/skills, educational level, knowledge of English/French, and age. Consequently, the source countries of immigrants became more diversified, even while admission requirements became more refined around economic, and/or value-added, criteria. Statistics Canada's (2003) most recent release of the demographic trends from the 2001 census demonstrates that visible minorities now make up 13.4 percent of Canada's population. In total, 58 percent of immigrants arriving since the prior census in 1996 came from Asia, 20 percent from Europe, 11 percent from the Caribbean, Central and South America, 8 percent from Africa, and 3 percent from the United States. Chinese people are now Canada's largest visible minority group, with a population of more than one million. They comprise 3.5 percent of Canada's total population, followed by immigrants of South Asian origin at 3 percent, and Blacks at 2.2 percent. Up to twenty years ago, visible minorities constituted less than 5 percent of the population. However, as previously stated, demographic projections indicate that 25 percent of Canada's population could soon be foreign-born.

Underlying this contemporary social context are questions arising from the interrelation between immigration issues and increasing ethnocultural and racial diversity. Surveys often deal with foreign-trained professional immigrants in general terms that serve to de-racialize discourse. However, it must be noted that visible minority, foreign-trained professionals have distinctive cultural backgrounds and experiences that differ from White foreign-trained professionals. Accordingly, visible minorities may tend to be disadvantaged, even in a contemporary labour market in which meritocratic practices are espoused.

Sociological research has recognized the "social fact" that contemporary immigration to Canada is both urbanized and racially segmented (Durkheim [1895]1964a). That is, a large number of foreign-trained professional immigrants have experienced downward social mobility after immigrating to Canada, and the significant human capital belonging to this immigrant population has been underutilized. Further, it is a well-established social fact that the economic returns on human capital appear to be lower for immigrants who belong to visible minority groups (Baker and Benjamin 1994). Further, Richmond (1984: 253) found that despite high levels of education, visible minority immigrants from "Third World" countries appear to be particularly vulnerable in the Canadian labour market. Subsequently, immigrant skills are significantly discounted in Canada, and the groups affected by this process are primarily composed of racial minorities (Reitz 2005).

The Sociological Debate: A debate has arisen regarding the reasons for devaluation of credentials and discounting of skills (Basran and Zong 1998). This debate has several research sub-sets and is organized around the issue of whether individual factors are mainly responsible for immigrants' occupational disadvantages, or whether this phenomenon might be attributable to structural and institutionalized barriers. Some research accentuates the focus on individual attributes, including the lack of Canadian experience and inadequate command of English as major occupational limitations for immigrant professionals (Ornstein and Sharma 1983; Basavarajappa and Verma 1985).

Still other research features a focus on differences in "achieved" social and economic characteristics, acquired through personal attributes and efforts. In other more structurally focused studies, barriers are depicted as institutions failing to recognize the credentials of foreign-trained professionals, and professional organizations acting as gatekeepers to disadvantage professional immigrants. These studies suggest that control of entry into professions has caused systematic exclusion and occupational disadvantages for professional immigrants (Boyd 1985; Trovato and Grindstaff 1986; McDade 1987; Ralston 1988; Beach and Worswick 1989; Rajagopal 1990; Krahn et al. 2000). A focus on structural and institutional factors in determining occupational disadvantage looks at differences in "ascribed" statuses of individuals, including differences attributed to ethnicity and race.

Hence, the problem for contemporary research is as follows—given that it appears that there are occupational disadvantages for immigrants that cross colour lines, is this phenomenon the result of structural and institutional resistance in society, or is it the result of more complex demographic or motivational factors?

The First Research Theme Stresses Individual Factors: In an open society that sanctions achievement and merit in the form of education-based skills, how do we account for occupational disadvantages across colour lines? Much research suggests that the idea that racial minorities experience greater problems of skill underutilization is not conclusive or unproblematic evidence of racial discrimination. Some would argue, particularly in the context of a diverse multicultural and multiracial society, that the influences of confounding factors on income differences are complicated. Therefore, without careful controls of demographic and motivational influences, structural factors (ethnicity and race) in income differences and discrimination may be exaggerated. Different rates of occupational return may relate more to personal qualifications than to blocked mobility. It is argued that multivariate analysis is essential in adjusting the effects of other influential factors, including schooling, age, sex, nativity, language, occupation, and labour-force activity (Boyd 1992).

One general finding in the literature is that after controlling for various factors that affect earnings, including years of education and labour market experience, immigrants appear to start at a significant disadvantage relative to native-born Canadians, but catch-up over time. This phenomenon is known as the "years since immigration" effect. Virtually, all ethnic groups have experienced overall improvement in educational attainment over the last three decades (Herberg 1990; Shamai 1992). The implication of this is that at some point, the immigrant gap could be eliminated. The expectation of better prospects for second generation immigrant children is based, in part, on the importance attached to education by highly educated immigrants, which they often pass on to their children. Also, employers are more likely to accept this second generation, because their education, unlike that of their parents, will be acquired in Canada. Previous studies on the offspring of immigrants generally confirm this optimism (Boyd 1992). However, there seems to be general agreement that for non-White immigrants who arrived in Canada since the 1980s, the initial earnings gap has widened and the catch-up rate has slowed (Baker and Benjamin 1994). Black men of Caribbean origin, for example, seem to carry a long-term disadvantage and may never reach the wage level that one might expect (Simmons and Plaza 1995).

Alboim, Finnie, and Ming (2005) found evidence that minorities who hold at least one degree from Canada and one from abroad achieve very high levels of income, even in comparison to White immigrants with similar credentials. Further, minority immigrants with multiple degrees do exceptionally well in the labour force, and immigrants of colour with only one foreign degree do very poorly. This is in comparison to similarly educated White immigrants who consistently earn substantial returns for their schooling. There is very little difference between White and visible minority immigrants who obtain their university degrees in Canada, and there is, little difference in the returns for a Canadian degree when comparing White and non-white native-born Canadians. That is to say, both immigrants and native-born Canadians with Canadian degrees—visible minority or White—receive similar rewards in the labour force. In fact, returns are actually estimated to be slightly greater for people of colour (Alboim, Finnie, and Ming 2005).

These results suggest that a foreign degree held by an immigrant who belongs to a visible minority group is heavily discounted in the Canadian labour market. However, they go further to suggest that there is little difference in the returns on degrees obtained in Canada for both immigrants of colour and White immigrants. Additionally, native-born members of visible minority groups holding degrees achieve income levels that are again, a little higher than their White counterparts. From this, researchers conclude that direct racial discrimination seems unlikely to be the reason—or at least the sole reason—for this gap. Finally, researchers cannot discern why non-White immigrants with foreign degrees consistently earn low returns for their schooling, and cannot rule out some discrimination towards foreign education obtained in certain countries. However, differences in the type and quality of schooling, or the inability of Canadians to accurately judge the worth of foreign degrees seem to be more likely explanations (Alboim, Finnie, and Ming 2005).

Interestingly, research has found that while foreign-born visible minority members are at a disadvantage in the wage labour force, those who are native-born and self-employed do substantially better than self-employed Canadian-born persons (Maxim 1992). It has been suggested that the decline of manufacturing jobs and the erosion of opportunities for advancement within the labour force for immigrants are tied to entrepreneurship within an ethnic economy (Satzewich and Wong 2003). This situation is reminiscent of earlier times when entrepreneurship was chosen by members of Chinese and Jewish communities because of blocked mobility in the mainstream labour market.

There is some evidence to suggest that contemporary ethnoracial entrepreneurship is also consistent with the new global formation of the "transnational" actor, and the related formation of the international approach to social life and citizenship (Portes 1999). Previously, international migrants made radical breaks from their ancestral homes to start life afresh in their new homeland. Currently, the new paradigm of transnationalism emphasizes the link that immigrant and ethnic communities retain and cultivate with families, institutions, and political economies abroad (Satzewich and Wong 2003). Ethnic entrepreneurship and related transnational economic enterprises may offer opportunities to immigrants of modest backgrounds for escaping dead-end, menial jobs and making their way into the middle class (Portes 1999:471). This would seem to support the individual factor approach to the examination of immigrant earnings inequality.

Some research has referenced demographic and motivational factors in regard to the selectivity of immigration procedures. For instance, it has been found that Asian immigrants have experienced the greatest social economic advancement in Canada in recent years. This appears to imply that there is a place in Canada's vertical mosaic for the upward mobility of some visible minority groups (Shamai 1992). However, there are studies that attribute this apparent success to the selectivity of the immigration points system and an increase in the number of Asian immigrants over the last three decades (Basaarajappa, Ravi, and Verma 1985:32-35). It has also been suggested that new immigration regulations may have been more stringently applied in the selection of non-European immigrants, thereby increasing entry levels of human capital (Kalbach and Richard 1988). In view of these potential variables, it is possible that some minority groups may have high educational attainments due to the selectivity of immigration, or to high aspirations and individual efforts.

Hou and Balakrishanan (1996) found that the selectivity of immigration only contributes partly to the achievement of visible minorities in education. They argue that income inequality on the basis of qualifications is probably related to discrimination rather than demographic factors. This finding is substantiated in two ways. First, while there is some evidence of variability within both non-visible minority groups and visible minority groups in terms of the effects of various individual factors on their income levels, patterns of integration into Canadian society for non-visible minorities and visible minorities are different and clearly distinct. Second, while income equality has materialized in spite of educational differences for some European groups, it has not for visible minority groups. Specifically, in Canada, differences in income exist between and within non-visible and visible minority groups. After adjusting for variations in educational and occupational distributions, most visible minorities receive less income for equal levels of employment and skills. In this sense, we can say that visible minorities follow a different path of integration into contemporary Canadian society (Hou and Balakrishanan 1996:282).

The Second Research Theme Stresses Structural Factors: Accentuating the importance of higher education in postindustrial societies is thought to be consistent with an "open society" concept based on the principle of meritocracy. This mandates that an individual's accomplishments are basically determined by personal attributes and efforts. Income, for instance, is the reward for an individual's investment in human capital. Therefore, income differences between individuals should reflect differences in education, profession, age, and other achieved social and economic characteristics. The ascribed statuses of individuals, including visible ethnicity and race, should not be factors. Consequently, racialized differences in income may be an important indicator of discrimination.

In this approach, structural factors that contribute to racialized patterns of difference are noted as indicators of discrimination in the recognition of foreign credentials. This suggests, in conjunction with "the discrimination thesis," that control of entry into professions has caused systematic exclusion and occupational disadvantages for professional immigrants (Boyd 1985; McDade 1988; Trovato and Grindstaff 1986; Rajagopal 1990; Ralston 1988; Beach and Worswick 1989). Specifically, Boyd provides an analysis of differences between Canadian-born and foreign-born workers in the acquisition of occupational status. Boyd (1985) argues that Canadian-born people receive a greater return for their education compared to foreign-born individuals because of "difficulties of transferring educational skill across national boundaries" (p.405).

Several studies use census data to demonstrate the difficulties in translating educational achievements into occupational advantage that are faced by selected cohorts of immigrants (Trovato and Grindstaff 1986). Pendakur and Pendakur's research suggests that even when controlling for occupation, industry, education, experience, official language knowledge and household type, visible minorities earn significantly less than native-born white workers (1998:26). Reitz argues that the cause of low earnings among immigrants is overwhelmingly pay inequity, with some underutilization of skills (2003).

Dynamic Interplay of Social Forces and the Collective Experiences of Individuals

Although the individual approach has elucidated some personal difficulties, it cannot explain how structural factors pertaining to policies, criteria, and evaluation procedures also contribute to occupational disadvantages for foreign-trained professionals. In a Durkheimian sense, failure to locate individual barriers in social conditions and structural arrangements tends to blame immigrant professionals for their problems in Canada. However, individual behaviour does not evolve in a vacuum. For example, lacking Canadian experience is an individual attribute, but it is related to employers refusing to recognize foreign credentials and failing to hire immigrants for jobs suited to their training. Samuels (2004) notes that the use of "Canadian experience" is used as a euphemism for racism. From the vantage point of visible minority foreign-trained professionals, it would not be accurate to consider their occupational disadvantages as resulting from these two types of barriers in isolation. Instead, their visible status can have the effect of precluding a smooth transition into Canadian society, while public reaction to their visible status and cultural differences can complicate the settlement process.

Faviola Fernandez, of the Policy Roundtable Mobilizing Professions and Trades (PROMPT), affirmed that earnings disadvantages can be particularly egregious for visible minority immigrants whose physical appearance and cultural backgrounds are most distant from the White mainstream population. Immigrants from non-European, racialized communities face the steepest downward shifts in career mobility and the highest levels of poverty (Second Annual Law and Diversity Conference 2004).

Fernandez recounted her personal baptism in social and economic inequities and the racialization of poverty she encountered in Canada that eventually shocked her into a greater level of community involvement. After immigrating to Canada three years ago in possession of an honours degree in Literature and Linguistics from the University of Singapore and a masters degree in Applied Linguistics from the University of Essex, UK, Fernandez discovered her foreign-acquired degrees where not recognized toward the procurement of an Ontario Teaching Certificate. Instead, since her arrival she has struggled to work in part-time and/or contract positions as a second language (ESL) teacher, an after-school program coordinator, and a recreation project coordinator for newcomer children. As is common among visible minority job seekers, Fernandez first experienced employment discrimination in a unique form of Canadian "low-grade racism," embodied by "people who could be polite even when they were being impolite" (Second Annual Law and Diversity Conference 2004).

Visible minority natives and newcomers are regularly exposed to subtle and informal exploitation in the Canadian workplace that can lead to a demoralizing sense of despair and loss of dignity. However, visible minority newcomers are further exposed to the immobilizing "catch-22" of the "Canadian experience" rule which holds that you need Canadian experience to get a job, but you cannot get a job because you do not have Canadian experience. All of this means that immigrants from racialized communities are typically relegated to the most "vulnerable place in society...where there is a loss of control over your life...with a limited right to participate in the processes to gain a right to participate" (Second Annual Law and Diversity Conference 2004).

Reitz (2003:5-6) argues that even when occupational or educational standards in the immigrant's place of origin are not questioned, traditional prejudice may be operant, and the institutional development of society may present barriers.

Education may be valued for reasons other than its functional relevance, including prestige or authority-enhancing capacity. Some employers may tend to distrust the relevance of foreign qualifications because they lack familiarity with them, and because of the fear involved in taking a chance on the unknown. Bureaucratic procedures in hiring may be tailored to local or conventionally esteemed educational institutions. Since these traditional prejudices and conventional standards of authority tend to breakdown along geographic and colour lines, they represent a form of racialization of skill-recognition that compounds other obstacles faced by immigrants. It has been suggested that the contemporary workplace phenomenon of managerial cloning might be a related tendency which further functions to entrench Whiteness at the level of corporate power and decision-making (Arrow, Bowles, and Durlauf 2000).

"The Voices of Visible Minorities: Speaking Out on Breaking Down Barriers" (2004) summarizes seven focus group discussions with successful immigrant and Canadian-born managers and professionals. Participants in these focus groups reported that organizations in Canada have regularized use of duplicitous terms like "lack of fit" to exclude talented visible minorities from senior positions. Immigrants of colour face particularly daunting, albeit unspoken, barriers to achieving career success that goes beyond psychometric career counseling strategies. These range from lost opportunities because they speak with an accent to non-recognition of their work experience or credentials. Many immigrants felt that in Canada, speaking with an accent or owning foreign credentials is often used by employers as an excuse to screen them out of job competitions. Consequently, many talented immigrants are prevented from working in their fields, even in professions where labour shortages exist.

The low valuation of foreign credentials together with the demand for Canadian experience is ethnocentric and cannot be separated from the ethnoracial dimension of disparity. European and American credentials are easily translatable because they are part of the dominant "whitestream" culture. Furthermore, public perception of visible minority immigrants who are forced to compete for menial jobs is shaped negatively, which in turn serves to negate government responsibility for the problem (Keung 2005). While skilled jobs go unfilled, this vicious circle also creates heightened competition for menial jobs. Immigrants living in poverty could create pressures—or at least the perception of pressures—on the social safety net (Keung 2005). This might result in public demands for a reduction in social programs and other support for immigrants (Keung 2005).

Even those visible minority immigrants who succeed continue to feel undervalued and underappreciated, looked down upon by the dominant class, and torn between the cross-cutting pressures of affirming their distinctiveness while accepting the norms and practices of White middle-class society (Fleras and Elliott 1999:276).

While it is sometimes difficult to separate individual factors from structural factors, ethnoracial stratification must be examined dynamically. We live in a world were the dynamics of human enterprise and social outcomes are primarily filtered through a techno-coloured lens which is not always responsive to individual skills, aptitudes, values, personality traits and/or interests. Objective research consistently reveals that a commitment to social justice must recognize the need for collective as opposed to individual initiatives where appropriate. It also endorses the principle of social intervention for true equality, since equal outcomes in the workplace are unlikely to arise from competitive market forces.

Two Key Approaches used to Study Structural Barriers

The first approach to the study of structural barriers focuses on the policies, regulations, and procedures that control entry and advancement in the workplace. Even when education-based skills are important and meritocracy is espoused in a labour market, immigrants may experience structural difficulties. The first key approach to the study of these difficulties focuses specifically on governmental practices and policies (Task Force on Access to Professions and Trades in Ontario 1989; Reitz 1997). Access to information on accreditation procedures, agencies involved in assessment, and the nature of these evaluations are some of the factors considered through this approach.

Culminating with Ontario's 1989 "ACCESS! Report" and the 1997 federal government "Not Just Numbers Report," most reputable structurally-oriented research now seems to agree on the barriers foreign-trained immigrants face in having their skills and credentials recognized. Particularly, much research notes the problematic nature of the various, confounding rules/regulations/requirements of provincial regulatory bodies, the obtuse requirements of education institutions and the subjective hiring and promotion rules of employers. The current problem is not to be found in identifying barriers, but in establishing effective strategies for eliminating these barriers.

The "ACCESS! Report" (1989) also includes an examination of whether the Charter of Rights and Freedoms applies to regulatory bodies. It contains a review of admissions criteria, appeal requirements, and additional examinations for internationally trained candidates and concludes that the Charter may apply if the licensing practices are found to be discriminatory. The report acknowledges that the primary obligation of professional bodies is to protect the public interest with respect to health, safety, and welfare. However, in fulfilling this obligation the bodies must also consider the duty to respect an individual's right to equality of opportunity and to equal treatment without unreasonable discrimination. The report goes on to review barriers to entry, including:

- the lack of clear information on professional standards and registration requirements;
- the lack of recognition of related academic qualifications and experience;
- inappropriate and/or unfair registration exams that might not provide a fair reflection of knowledge and skills;
- language tests that do not measure the skills actually required for appropriate, safe and effective professional practice;
- the lack of upgrading and bridging training opportunities; and
- the lack of internal appeal mechanisms.

According to the "ACCESS! Report," the assessment of equivalency is the stage that is the least standardized and most difficult for applicants. This report recommends a Prior Learning Assessment Network (PLAN) to address problems in assessing equivalency. The PLAN proposal was recommended as a move away from a certificate-based system toward a competency-based system.

Subsequent analyses into the problem of assessing equivalency have built on this recommendation. For example, in the medical profession, Joan Atlin, Executive Director, Association of International Physicians and Surgeons of Ontario (AIPSO), has emphasized the importance of focusing on the doctor shortage in Ontario through a lens of competence and rights—human rights and the Charter of Rights. The question is, why is medical licensure a right for Canadians and a privilege for internationally trained physicians (Second Annual Law and Diversity Conference 2004)?

At present, internationally trained physicians compete for the limited assessment and training positions available, with only 10 to 15 percent of these professionals finding placement. At the end of this process, those who do succeed in obtaining a license to practice are also required to fulfill a five-year return of service contract with the government. In other words, the present licensure system has created two classes of Canadians. One class has full access, and the other class must compromise and compete before they can gain access to the steps to prove competency. According to Atlin, Canada's doctor shortage is not only a regulatory and assessment problem, but an equity problem that requires a "paradigm shift" to eliminate the double standards that are embedded in the medical profession and society. Internationally trained physicians are "treated like labour market commodities and not like citizens with equality rights" (Atlin 2004). The potential for the development of a self-sufficient health-care system that provides adequate service to all Canadians lies in organizing social policy principles around fair practices that actualize existing human resources (Atlin 2004).

The Council of the College of Physicians and Surgeons of Ontario has recently taken steps toward addressing Canada's health-care problem, and has forwarded recommendations to the health ministry proposing a new assessment program for foreign-trained physicians. This assessment tool was created by Ontario's five medical schools, and includes a fast-tracking process that is to be coupled with other initiatives including location incentives for under-serviced areas and tuition subsidies.

However, Atlin argues for a new "equity rights" action plan as well. This recommends the provision of adequate training opportunities and emphasizes competencies that reflect clear and concise criteria that are equally applied to all physicians. Atlin notes that for many internationally trained physicians, this was the "working assumption" about this country before they emigrated. Only after their arrival did they realized they had been seduced and abandoned by the immigration system (Second Annual Law and Diversity Conference 2004). Some sociologists maintain that the removal of overt and covert systemic barriers in a way that preserves human rights and professional standards would involve the implementation of government administered programs and policies, for example, a "licensing equity plan" for regulatory and licensing bodies and/or the implementation of an "employment equity plan" (Foster 1998).

The second approach to the study of structural barriers focuses on experience and perceptions. An attitudinal survey conducted in 1990 by Decima Research Ltd. showed that 90 percent of Canadians agreed with the statement, "All races are created equal" (cited in Reitz and Breton 1994: 68). Nevertheless, a 2005 Ipsos-Reid poll conducted on a randomly selected sample of 1,001 Canadians found that one in six adults, or 17 percent of those surveyed, had personally experienced racism. The survey also found that 7 percent (1.7 million) of Canadians would not welcome someone of another race as a next door neighbour. Further, 13 percent (3.1 million) said they would never marry or have a relationship with a person of another race, and 15 percent (3.4 million) said skin colour makes a difference in their workplace.

Today most Canadians tend to believe that all races are created equal, and the dominant White majority is generally open to residency, citizenship, and commingling with and among ethnic and racial minorities in public. Nevertheless, studies also indicate that many people are hesitant about minorities marrying into their families, and they strongly resist the admittance of minorities to prestigious professional structures. A report released by the Canadian Race Relations Foundation (2000), entitled "Unequal Access: A Canadian Profile of Racial Differences in Education, Employment and Income," confirmed that ethnoracial diversity is generally seen at the bottom and middle level of the labour force pyramid, but, "the higher the pyramid, the less diverse and the Whiter it becomes."

Further, research also suggests that most professions would prefer to restrict supply so that members can continue to enjoy higher income levels. This seems to be particularly true among physicians, surgeons, dentists, and veterinarians (Samuels 2004).

Basran and Zong's (1998) research emphasized the importance of personal experience and perceptions in understanding both individual and structural barriers. In their study of 404 Indo and Chinese immigrant professionals residing in the Vancouver area, they found only 18 percent of this population to be working in their profession in Canada. Only 6 percent agreed that the provincial government fairly assessed and recognized their foreign credentials. When asked about possible sources of discrimination in the accreditation process, 65 percent noted colour, 69 percent listed nationality or ethnic origin, and 79 percent cited the inability to speak English as issues of concern.

Samuels (2004) interviewed nine foreign-trained graduates of various disciplines from developing countries who now reside in Ontario. Eight of the nine respondents feel that undertones of racism have hindered their ability to become credentialed. Veterinarians and dentists are particularly affected. They stated that there is a "strong element of exclusion" felt by graduates from developing countries since internship positions are very limited and there are not many visible minorities who own animal hospitals. A lack of Canadian experience, combined with accents of varying notability and differences in culture block visible minority immigrants from internship positions, even when their help is offered free of charge. Most of the respondents stated "somewhere race is coming into play" (Samuels 2004).

The Ethnic Diversity Survey (2003) offers a portrait of the experience and perception of discriminatory barriers in Canada. Respondents were asked how often they felt out of place in Canada because of their ethnicity, culture, race, skin colour,

Table 10.1: Population reporting discrimination or unfair treatment in Canada in the past five years because of ethno-cultural characteristic, by generation in Canada and visible minority status, 2002

	Total population	Sometimes or often	Rarely	Frequency of discrimination — Did not experience discrimination
	'000s	%	%	%
Total population	22,445	7	6	86
Not a visible minority	19,252	5	5	90
Visible minority	3,000	20	15	64
First Generation	5,272	13	10	77
Not a visible minority	2,674	5	6	89
Visible minority	2,516	21	14	65
Second Generation or more	16,929	6	5	89
Not a visible minority	16,349	5	5	90
Visible minority	480	18	23	59

Note: Refers to Canada's non-Aboriginal population aged 15 and older.
Source: Statistics Canada, *Ethnic Diversity Survey.* 2002.

language, accent or religion. The findings show several distinctive ethno-cultural patterns. First, visible minorities were more likely than others to say that they felt uncomfortable or out of place at least some of the time. Second, it found that one in five visible minorities experienced discrimination or unfair treatment "sometimes" or "often," while only one in twenty non-visible minorities reported experiencing discrimination or unfair treatment "sometimes" or "often." Further, among indicators of discrimination or unfair treatment, race or colour was the most commonly cited reason for perceived discrimination or unfair treatment. Finally, the research found that discrimination or unfair treatment was most likely to occur in the workplace.

Twenty-four percent of visible minorities in Canada said they felt uncomfortable or out of place because of their ethno-cultural characteristics "all," "most" or "some" of the time. This is almost three times higher than any other reporting group. Generational differences also indicate that visible minorities may feel uncomfortable for a longer period than their non-visible minority counterparts after they or their families arrive in Canada. Twenty-nine percent of first generation visible minorities who arrived between 1991 and 2001 said they felt uncomfortable or out of place in Canada "some," "most" or "all" of the time. This proportion was only slightly lower, at 23 percent, for visible minorities who came before 1991. In contrast, among the population who were not visible minorities, a higher proportion of recent arrivals than of those who had resided in Canada for over 10 years (18 percent versus 9 percent) felt uncomfortable or out of place because of their ethno-cultural characteristics.

Finally, respondents who had reported discrimination or unfair treatment because of their ethno-cultural characteristics in the previous five years were questioned about where the incident took place. Regardless of the location, a significantly higher proportion of visible minorities reported discrimination or unfair treatment in the previous five years in comparison to all other groups. The survey found that approximately 35 percent of people 15 years and older had "sometimes" or "often" been discriminated against. The workplace was noted as the most common location where perceived discrimination or unfair treatment occurred. Fifty-six percent of those who had "sometimes" or "often" experienced discrimination or unfair treatment because of their ethno-cultural characteristics in the past five years said they had experienced such treatment at work or when applying for work.

Figure 10.1: Frequency of feeling uncomfortable or out of place in Canada because of ethno-cultural characteristics, 2002

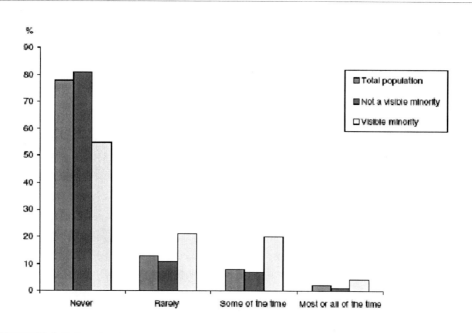

Note: Refers to Canada's non-Aboriginal population aged 15 and older.
Source: Statistics Canada, Ethnic Diversity Survey. 2002.

Figure 10.2: Percentage reporting discrimination or unfair treatment "sometimes" or "often" in the past five years, by visible minority status, 2002

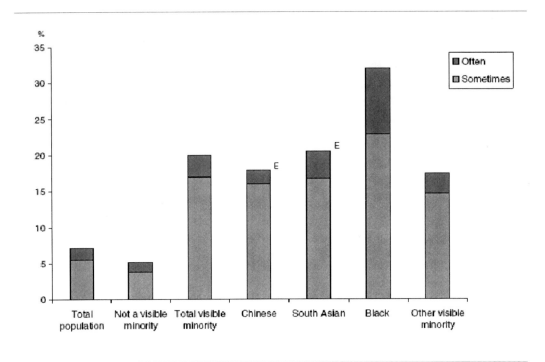

^{E} use with caution
Note: Refers to Canada's non-Aboriginal population aged 15 and older.
Source: Statistics Canada, Ethnic Diversity Survey. 2002.

The Immigration and Refugee Protection Act and the Definition of "Skilled" Worker

According to demographer Joseph Chamie, Director of the United Nations Population Division, immigration will become one of the most crucial issues of the century for countries with declining birth rates. He predicts a "global immigration selection and recruitment contest" in the not so distant future, where Canada will compete for "talented, skilled, unskilled and semi-skilled workers" (Foster 2002a). Nevertheless, the overriding goal of the Canadian immigration system has always been to conscript workers who will supposedly make the greatest contribution to the labour market and have the best opportunities for economic establishment.

In Canada, entry restrictions are authorized by the Immigration and Refugee Protection Act and the accompanying regulations that came into effect June 28, 2002. This act revamped criteria for the admission of skilled workers into Canada. Today, independent immigrant skilled workers are accepted for entry on the basis of the number of points they score out of 100 in the following categories: education (25), age (10), language abilities (20), employment experience (21), arranged employment (10) and adaptability (10). These are some of the changes that have been made to the selection grid for skilled workers: Education increased from 16 to 25. More points have been allocated for applicants with a trade certificate or a second degree. More points have been allocated for language proficiency. The maximum number of points available for proficiency in both English and French combined has been increased from 20 to 24. A new language assessment level that recognizes basic proficiency has been added to the three existing levels (high, moderate, and none). These changes are expected to result in the admittance of more officially bilingual immigrants.

The total number of points available for "experience" has been reduced to 21 from 25, and more points will be awarded for one to two years of work experience. This is expected to attract younger workers who may have higher levels of education but fewer years of experience. The "age factor" has been adjusted upwards, so that workers between the ages of 21 and 49 will score the maximum number of points (10 points). This is expected to make it easier for older workers to gain entry to Canada under the skilled worker class. Finally, the pass mark is currently set at 67 points from previous levels of 70 and 75. This is in response to concerns that higher pass marks cost Canada many skilled immigrants.

Some researchers argue that even though the category of "race" is no longer a formal criteria of immigration control in Canada, and even though there are increasing numbers of immigrant arrivals from outside Europe, questions remain regarding the informal influence of racism on this process. Changes to Canada's immigration policy that place greater emphasis on the selection of immigrants on the basis of their ability to speak English or French have been interpreted by some as "politically acceptable" racial selectivity. The Conference Board (2004) conducted focus groups of visible minority immigrants who reported that proficiency in Canada's official languages and adapting to Canadian cultural norms are required ingredients for success. Many immigrants also felt that speaking with an accent hindered employment opportunities.

Simmons (1998) argues that Canadian immigration policy may be officially non-racist with respect to the formal procedure of immigrant selection. However, the increasing focus on highly skilled immigrants means that people who have low levels of schooling due to racist oppression in their country of origin are less likely to be accepted into Canada. This outcome reinforces racial inequality on a global level, and represents a neo-racist policy element. Racism can covertly influence various aspects of immigration policy including: (1) selection and recruitment of immigration targets, (2) access of foreigners to Canadian immigration information and services, (3) selection of immigrants, (4) settlement and economic integration of immigrants, and (5) the expulsion or deportation process (Simmons 1998). Informal procedures, standards, and practices may also have detrimental effects on visible minorities (Simmons 1998). Accordingly, the impact that racism continues to have on immigration must be examined.

It is worth noting that for the first time in recent history changes in policy regulations incorporate a broader notion of human capital beyond specific occupational designations. For instance, not only have points for education increased, but an applicant can also gain additional points if their spouse has a post-secondary education. However, some observers maintain that even with these slight improvements, Canada's new immigrant selection process does not go far enough in appropriately recognizing the human capital of potential immigrants.

Canadian society is in the process of being re-tooled by an information economy that has produced a state of rapid occupational change where the knowledge base is expected to double every 18 months. Many of the jobs of tomorrow have not yet been invented. Therefore, the ability to adapt to new skills is increasingly more important than the acquisition of existing ones. Because the educational system adapts slowly to the changing needs of information technology and related industries, many sectors experience periodic shortages of trained professionals. In this regard, a premium has been placed on learning-based rather than skill-based immigration and population planning. Future dividends are expected to be reaped through a prevailing focus on life-long learning and human capital development strategies (Foster 1998:76-112). This presupposes a shift in focus to skills development within Canada, as opposed to skills acquisition from abroad. Citizens and newcomers alike will profit from a transferable skills-set that is conducive to a cradle-to-grave learning model for postindustrial society.

Yet, in the face of historical trends and the rapidly changing occupational structure, the latest immigration act actually requires Canadian policy to place greater emphasis on human capital skills-acquisition through refined front-end admission requirements, rather than back-end human capital development. This policy focus is an extension of the neo-liberal restructuring in the 1990s that saw the advent of "designer immigration"—the selection of immigrants who can "hit the ground running" (Foster 1998). In recent years, there has been substantial sociological and economic literature that criticizes the state's view towards "value-added" immigrants in the economic model of designer immigration. For, as is noted, a value-added system where newcomers are required to add to the national skills-pool is limited and potentially counterproductive to effective postindustrial population planning.

In the context of a constantly evolving postindustrial workplace, a continued focus on immigrants' entrance status as opposed to settlement and integration mechanisms is thought to be a form of culture lag—an out-of-date and untimely perspective considered in the context of an expanding knowledge economy. Instead of a value-added immigration system that relies primarily on the importation and recruitment of skills, some researchers propose the shift to a "value-generating" system that reaches out to empower people through effective settlement support programs that contribute to success and performance patterns of immigrants over time (Foster 1998; Simmons 1999).

Also in recent years, there has been substantial literature that criticizes the state definition and understanding of what a skilled worker is. Current definitions do not take into account barriers to formal education and skills acquisition that some groups face in their countries of origin. It also excludes an appreciation of different kinds of professional experience and skills, including those associated with "women's work" such as child-rearing, kin-keeping, small-scale agriculture, and market work.

Further, the state's definition of skilled worker continues to informally reinforce certain kinds of stereotyping and discrimination. This is particularly true for many people of colour, a large portion of whom are women, designated for nonstandard and contingent work. Conceived broadly, contingent work includes forms of employment involving non-standard employment contracts and/or arrangements, limited social benefits and statutory entitlements, job insecurity, poor wages, and low safety standards. Contingent work diminishes standards of living, self-fulfillment, and contributions to the social good. Recent studies confirm that this type of employment is consistently gendered and racialized (Krahn 1995; Ornstein 2000; Zeytinoglu and Muteshi 2000).

The most noteworthy example of this is the continuation of policies regarding the movement of "skill-devalued" foreign domestic workers in Canada including maids, nannies, and Live-in Caregivers who work in private homes. These immigrants are relegated to a tenuous and exploitative status through the racialization of "women's household work." Those admitted are primarily women of colour who generally work long hours for very low wages and frequently experience abuse. Studies of the Live-in Caregiver program have noted the manner in which it is grounded in, and reinforces, sexist and racist stereotypes (Silvera 1989; Calliste 1991; Arat-Koc 1989, 1992, 1997; Macklin 1994). This research reveals the intricate interplay of social forces and the collective experiences of individuals in the context of racialized immigration and an international division of labour. More recent research focuses on resistance and the negotiation of citizenship rights (Stasiulis and Bakan 1997a, 1997b; Fudge 1997). In the case of Filipina domestic workers, participatory and policy-oriented research has emerged which proposes short and long-term policy solutions for addressing the dilemma of this form of labour migration (Grandea 1996; Satzewich and Wong 2003).

In late 2004, eight Filipino community groups in and around the Greater Toronto Area developed and presented a position paper, with hundreds of signatures, recommending widespread changes to the federal program that brings nannies and caregivers to this country. The recommended changes include eliminating two of the federal Live-in Caregiver Program's (LCP) key requirements: (1) that nannies "live-in" the home of their employers, and (2) that nannies complete two years of work within a three-year period in order to qualify to apply for permanent resident status. Eliminating the obligatory live-in requirement and facilitating landed status are recommendations supported by prior research studies and national consultations identifying a number of equality and human rights issues resulting from the LCP. These issues include increased vulnerability to abuse and rape because of the live-in requirement and their temporary immigration status. These abuses often go unreported because the victims are concerned about jeopardizing their immigration status. The paper also calls for a crackdown on unlicensed, unregulated agencies that charge thousands of dollars for their services, and better monitoring of legitimate agencies (Simmie and Leong 2004).

The Racialized "Other"

Sociologists who subscribe to the discrimination thesis have focused on the concept of race as an ideology and a discourse, which is a way of mapping out the world that confers meaning and status. Through discourse, participants develop a shared knowledge about the world. To the extent that there is racial discourse in Canada, it is part of a dominant cultural/ideological discourse that provides conceptual models for people around which they chart the social world. The dominant discourse of race maps a form of polite "social biology" as normative—meaning it is generally assumed, often without malice or intent, that certain "bodies" adhere to certain "patterns of action."

The concept of racialization refers to the assigning of racial connotations to activities and/or places. Many sociologists prefer to use the term racialization as opposed to race in order to emphasize that racial categories are changeable social constructions (Backhouse 1999). For example, in 1901, civil servants charged with conducting the first Canadian census of the twentieth century were instructed to designate the races of men by the use of "w" for White, "r" for Red, "b" for Black, and "y" for Yellow:

> The whites are, of course, the Caucasian race, the reds are the American Indian, the blacks are the African or Negro, and the yellows are the Mongolian (Japanese and Chinese). But only pure whites will be classed as whites; the children begotten of marriages between whites and any one of the other races will be classed as red, black or yellow, as the case may be, irrespective of the degree of colour. (Backhouse 1999:3)

Backhouse further deconstructs the idea of race:

> The primary colour scheme selected by the officials, with bold brush strokes of reds and yellows, was a curious choice. The census palette stretches

beyond these vivid hues right to the margins of the colour charts. It splashes literally off the spectrum to the black tones, representing the absorption of all the colours of the rainbow, and white tones, incapable of colour absorption at all. As most observers would likely have admitted if pressed, the categories are also highly inaccurate. Human beings simply do not come in any of these colours. (P.4)

Canada has a colour-coded legal and immigration history, but race is not a static category. Rather, race is a dynamic relationship integral to the construction of contemporary social life (Backhouse 1999). It is testimony to the strength of the socialization process given that race is often treated as an immutable "thing." However, to see race is to be engaged in a thought process which biologizes people by attaching status to the physical. People are the objects of racialized formations. That is to say, people do not see race, rather they observe certain combinations of real and sometimes imagined physical and cultural characteristics to which they attribute meaning. But, this goes beyond the biological. Race is a social differentiation process of attributing superior-inferior statuses which involves complex relationships of exploitation, control, exclusion, and ultimately gives rise to the ideological construction of the "racialized other."

Sociologists who subscribe to the discrimination thesis have also focused on racism as a form of "othering" that defines and secures one's own positive identity through the stigmatization of an "other." Distinctions of race create "other" people—or make people into the "not-us." When "they" are not-us, they lack something. When they lack something, they are "less than us." To be othered is to be defined as a thing that deviates from the norm. In short, othering is a way of protecting status and depriving others. Othering often involves mental images wherein people who have some distinctive physical attributes and/or associated ethnic characteristics are viewed as different, or less deserving.

Richmond (1990) argues that current immigration policies are designed to protect our borders from the otherness of undocumented migrants. "Restrictions are intended to reduce competition for scarce resources such as jobs and housing, to limit overcrowding in schools and avoid excessive demands on health services or the welfare system" (p.158). He suggests that none of these considerations are premeditatedly racist, but they assume immigration controls are necessary for social harmony. However, these restrictive policies explicitly group and implicitly label non-White immigrants as less desirable and legitimize racist attitudes. Because immigrants are seen as a "problem," policies are directed toward exclusion instead of addressing the root causes of racial prejudice and discrimination.

The concept of the racialized other produces complex interlocking discourses that are used to justify the power wielded by those who do the defining, often in an imperialistic manner. For instance, studies show there is an emerging immigrant underclass in Canada's major cities. This underclass is comprised primarily of visible minorities. During the last two decades especially, this cohort has experienced severe difficulties in the Canadian labour market. For many, it has been a life of underemployment or unemployment, low income or poverty and lost hope. Although between 1991 and 1996 poverty levels increased for all immigrants, visible minorities were most disadvantaged. In Toronto, the destination for almost one-half of all newcomers, visible minorities showed the largest increase in poverty levels in that period as the rate increased from 20.9 percent to 32.5 percent. They are also at higher risk for long-term, persistent poverty (Harvey and Siu 2001).

The discounting of foreign credentials and the skills of visible immigrants is an example of how othering functions to disempower neo-colonialized people. That is to say, neo-racism is a form of ideological colour-blindness in the Canadian political economy that conceals colour-coded social and material consequences, not only for professions, but also for the nation as a whole.

Re-Thinking Accreditation

Anti-racism activists and sociological researchers are now in the process of trying to re-think Canadian society and immigration/emigration in terms of ethnoracial reality. This requires that research provides analyses that come from the standpoint of racialized persons. Additionally, this research must consider other stakeholders including governments, regulating bodies, employers, unions, educational institutions, and credential assessment services.

Alboim (2003) explored the social implications of the under-utilization of immigrant skills at the individual, ethnoracial, and societal level for the design and implementation of public policy. In conjunction with prior research, she found that when large numbers of visible immigrants are prevented from practicing their professions, society experiences higher levels of inter-group tensions, individual and collective alienation, and generalized perceptions of institutional discrimination. Ultimately, Alboim argues for the implementation of a public discourse that moves beyond competency assessment to qualifications recognition.

Accordingly, The Maytree Foundation developed a ten-point action plan for implementation at federal, provincial, and local levels that would better provide for the integration of immigrants and their skills into the Canadian economy:

1. Create an Internet resource that contains employment, certification and educational information to assist skilled immigrants with employment;
2. Improve collaboration on the assessment of academic credentials to increase employer confidence;
3. Provide incentives for educational institutions and licensing bodies to develop competency-based assessment tools;

4. Review post-secondary funding formulas and the statutory framework so that educational institutions are encouraged to provide bridging programs as part of their mainstream services;
5. Expand student loan programs;
6. Fund labour market language training to be delivered by employers and educational institutions;
7. Provide incentives to employers, employer associations, and labour to become more active in the integration of immigrant skills;
8. Sustain the collaborative efforts of self-regulated professions to improve access for international candidates;
9. Initiate multi-lateral discussions between levels of government, regulating bodies, employer's associations, unions, educational institutions and academic credential assessment servers in order to develop agreements on the labour market integration of immigrants; and
10. Support local initiatives to integrate immigrant skills (Alboim 2003).

This plan, provided through The Maytree Foundation, is an example of a holistic and dynamic approach to the contemporary social problem of foreign accreditation barriers. It emphasizes skills utilization and fair practice and assumes an equity paradigm. The equity paradigm states that all qualified persons should be able work within their field. Further, it assumes all regions that adopt this paradigm and a congruent plan of action will reap the many benefits that immigrants have to offer society.

Conclusions

Only the identification of the central bases of social inequality that arise from the exercise of power in Canada and other modern societies can provide the foundation for adequate understanding of professions and the political economy (Krahn 1998:159). I submit that overlooking race prevents adequate understanding of the issue. Where the prevailing discourse on political economy is colour-blind at the ideological level, perception can be blinded to many colour-coded activities and material consequences in the workplace.

At the analytic level, consider that in conjunction with a de-racialized political economy discourse, many sociologists still insist that social inequality and professional hierarchies are by-products of the class exploitation made possible through the control of property and the means of production. Consequently, racialized phenomena are typically conceived of as class-based. Many have consistently argued—even in the conceded wake of what has been called a world "ethnoracial revival"—that inequality and domination between ethnoracial groups can only be understood as rooted in socioeconomic-class conflicts (Smith 1981; Nash 1989). However,

> class is an increasingly outmoded concept, although it is sometimes appropriate to earlier historical periods...Class analysis has grown increasingly inadequate in recent decades as traditional hierarchies have declined and new social differences have emerged. The cumulative impact of these changes is fundamentally altering the nature of social stratification—placing past theories in need of substantial modification. (Clark and Lipset 1991:397)

That is to say, globalization is not only, or even primarily, about class. Consequently, the effect of globalization on the employment of immigrants and adequate recognition of their credentials is not significantly rooted in the problematic nature of class. Rather, it involves a worldwide overlay of Western values, norms, institutions, and practices that sanction White cultural hegemony. The global technological and organizational infrastructure has been established primarily by corporations, governments, and individuals in rich, developed countries to the benefit of White privilege.

Patterns of dependency and underdevelopment are no less devastating today than at the height of European colonialism. However, direct colonial rule is no longer visible. The indirect rule of neo-colonialism now prevails with its minimal political independence, continued economic control, and cultural domination through assimilation. Neo-colonialism is exercised less by physical deterrents and increasingly through the distribution of an elaborate system of norms and imperatives. Accordingly, it no longer requires open articulation in competitive world politics. It is instead a global working assumption, or tacit knowledge. This assumption can be witnessed in the underemployment and failure to recognize the credentials of visible minority immigrants, not only in Canada, but around the world today.

It is the commonsense of reality, propagated by global media conglomerates, that is assumed and normalized as the standard measure of all things. In this process, all communal life is inappropriately subordinated to Eurocentric, whitestream categories as a basis for description and evaluation. We see this process at work in the consistent devaluation of foreign credentials and experience in the workplace. Modern globalism constitutes an elitist, North-based, Western-focused technological form of economic and cultural imperialism (Hedley 2002:37). The North-South bifurcation of the world extends a social-psychological dualism to all people of colour that Du Bois (1969) once designated primarily to the soul of Black folks:

> It is a peculiar sensation, this double-consciousness, this sense of always looking at one's self through the eyes of others, of measuring one's soul by the tape of a world that looks on in amused contempt and pity. One ever feels his twoness,—an American, a Negro; two souls, two thoughts, two unreconciled strivings; two warring ideals in one dark body, whose dogged strength alone keeps it from being torn asunder. (P.45)

In this brave new postindustrial world, people of colour can have double the knowledge, education and credentials, and yet still be ranked as somehow less than whole. This racialized political-economic gap between the Global North and the Global South is drifting toward a kind of "global apartheid" wherein extremes of power and wealth are compressed into increasingly geographically segregated zones to create an "apartness" every bit as punitive and pervasive as apartheid was in South Africa (Richmond 1994).

The reference to apartheid here is a sociological and not merely a metaphorical one. The comparison made by some sociologists recognizes that apartheid is a fundamental principle of race relations, and not merely a system of segregation. The foundational principle of apartheid is "racial hegemony"—managing the presence of large populations of non-Whites without undermining White power and privilege. In this respect, apartheid does not have to be formalized to exist. Rather, it can be preserved as a matter of consequence, and in the absence of an infrastructure of laws and institutions to support it.

The internal logic of a universal global economy ensures that virtually no problem is exempt from its operational dynamics. When corporate globalization destabilizes local economics in the South, indigenous dark populations are displaced from traditional means of production and forced to migrate to the world's cities in search of subsistence and survival. This has resulted in tremendous flows of documented and undocumented migration. As a further consequence, many nation-states in the Global North have mobilized to curtail the very forces they have unleashed by militarizing border enforcement and criminalizing undocumented immigrants.

Meanwhile, public discourse on contemporary immigration is becoming increasingly more defensive and attenuated, taking on a "Fortress North America" mentality bent on harmonizing border security and waging war against the terror of racialized others. The central paradox of this mentality, however, is that the more interdictions there are into international migration patterns, the more egregious the situation seems to become. In other words, the result of restrictive immigration measures around the world is a greater propensity to migrate (Appleyard 1991).

Despite the international marketing tool of multicultural diversity, many Canadians have not confronted the reality and challenges of a racially and culturally diverse society. The need to be more inclusive in our thinking about the importance of immigration for society-building and economic development in the global age is often compromised by public pressure to preserve the entrenched interests of the status quo. Immigrants no longer typically endure legislated racial abuse and overt discrimination. Nevertheless, in the new world order, the furtive de-racialization of political economy discourse disregards visible minority experiences through the discounting of qualifications and restricting access to gainful employment in the professions. This results in social marginalization, alienation, and disillusionment.

It is imperative that future sociological research on professionalization and the associated processes to continue trying to re-think Canadian society and global-international relations from the standpoint of people who are racialized as dangerous, alien, and/or potential threats to civilization, and whose knowledge, education, and credentials are viewed as less than whole.

References

Abele, Frances and Daiva Stasiulis. 1989. "Canada as a 'White Settler Colony': What about Natives and Immigrants." Pp. 240-277 in *The New Canadian Political Economy*, edited by Wallace Clement and Glen Williams. Montreal: McGill-Queen's University Press.

Alboim, Naomi. 2003. *Integrating Immigrant Skills into the Ontario Economy: A Ten Point Plan*. Toronto: The Maytree Foundation.

Alboim, Naomi, Ross Finnie and Ronald Meng. 2005. "The Discounting of Immigrants' Skills in Canada: Evidence and Policy Recommendations." Institute for Research on Public Policy. 11, 2.

Appleyard, R. 1991. *International Migration: The Challenge of the Nineties*. Geneva: International Organization for Migration.

Arat-Koc, Sedef. 1989. "In the Privacy of Our Own Home: Foreign Domestic Workers as Solution to the Crisis in the Domestic Sphere in Canada." *Studies in Political Economy* 28:33-58.

———. 1992. "Immigration Policies, Migrant Domestic Workers and the Definition of Citizenship in Canada." Pp. 229-242 in *Deconstructing a Nation: Immigration, Multiculturalism and Racism in '90s Canada*, edited by Vic Satzewich. Halifax: Fernwood Press.

———. 1997. "From 'Mothers of the Nation' to Migrant Workers." Pp. 53-79 in *Not One of the Family: Foreign Domestic Workers in Canada*, edited by Abigail Bakan and Daiva Stasiulis. Toronto: University of Toronto Press.

Arrow, K., S. Bowles and S. Durlauf, eds. 2000. *Meritocracy and Economic Inequality*. Princeton: Princeton University Press.

Backhouse, Constance. 1999. *Colour-Coded: A Legal History of Racism in Canada 1900-1950*. Toronto: The Osgood Society for Canadian Legal History and University of Toronto Press.

Baer, Douglas. 2004. "Educational Credentials and the Changing Occupational Structure." Pp. 92-106 in *Social Inequality in Canada: Patterns, Problems and Policies*, edited by Curtis et al. Toronto: Pearson Prentice Hall.

Baker, M. and D. Benjamin. 1994. "The Performance of Immigrants in the Canadian Labor Market." *Journal of Labor Economics* 12:369-405.

Bannerji, Himani. 1995. *Thinking Through: Essays on Feminism, Marxism and Anti-Racism*. Toronto: Women's Press.

Basavarajappa, K.G. B. Ravi and P. Verma. 1985. "Asian Immigrants in Canada: Some Findings from 1981 Census." *International Migration* 23(1):97-121.

Basran, Gurcharn, and Li Zong. 1998. "Devaluation of Foreign Credentials as Perceived by Non-White Professional Immigrants." *Canadian Ethnic Studies* 30(3):6-23.

Beach, Charles and Christopher Worswick. 1989. "Is There a Double-Negative Effect on the Earnings of Immigrant Women?" *Canadian Public Policy* 16(2):36-54.

Bell, David. 1973. *The Coming Post-Industrial Society: A Venture in Social Forecasting.* New York: Basic Books.

Boyd, Monica. 1985. "Immigration and Occupation Attainment in Canada." Pp. 393-445 in *Ascription and Achievement: Studies in Mobility and Status Attainment in Canada,* edited by Monica Boyd et al. Ottawa: Carleton University Press.

——. 1992. "Gender, Visible Minority, and Immigrant Earnings Inequality: Reassessing an Employment Equity Premise." Pp. 279-321 in *Deconstructing a Nation: Immigration, Multiculturalism & Racism in 90's Canada,* edited by Vic Satzewich. Halifax: Fernwood.

Brandt Report. 1980. *North-South: A Program for Survival. Report of the Independent Commission on International Development Issues.* Cambridge: MIT Press.

Brouwer, Andrew. 1999. "Immigrants need not Apply: Canada Barring Highly Skilled Immigrants from Practising Professions and Trades." The Maytree Foundation: (www.maytree.com/PDF_Files/INNA.pdf).

Calliste, Agnes. 1991. "Canada's Immigration Policy and Domestics from the Caribbean: The Second Domestic Scheme." Pp. 136-168 in *Race, Class, Gender: Bonds and Barriers,* edited by J. Vorst. Toronto: Garamond Press.

Canadian Race Relations Foundation. 2000. "Unequal Access: A Canadian Profile of Racial Differences in Education, Employment and Income." Canadian Race Relations Foundation.

Castles, S. and M. J. Miller. 1993. *The Age of Migration: International Population Movements in the Modern World.* London: McMillan.

Clark, Terry Nichols and Seymour Lipset. 1991. "Are Social Classes Dying?." *International Sociology* 6:397-410.

Clement, W. and J. Myles. 1994. *Relations of Ruling: Class and Gender in Postindustrial Societies.* Montreal: McGill-Queen's University Press.

Committee on Citizenship and Immigration. 2003. "Settlement and Integration; A Sense of Belonging, 'Feeling at Home.'" Report of the Standing Committee on Citizenship and Immigration. June http://www.parl.gc.ca/InfocomDoc/37/2/CIMM/Studies/Reports/cimmrp05/05-hon-e.htm.

Conference Board. 2004. "The Voices of Visible Minorities: Speaking Out on Breaking Down Barriers." Conference Board's e Library.www.conferenceboard.ca/boardwise.

Cumming, Lee, Oreopolous & Access! "Task Force on Access to Professions and Trades in Ontario." 1989. Queen's Printer for Ontario.

Dafoe, John W. 1931. *Clifford Sifton in Relation to His Times.* Toronto: Macmillan Canada.

Darroch, Gordon A. 1979. "Another Look at Ethnicity, Stratification and Social Mobility in Canada." *Canadian Journal of Sociology* 4:1-25.

Du Bois, W. E Burghardt. [1903] 1969a. *The Soul of Black Folks.* New York: The New American Library, Inc.

Dua, Enakshi. 1999. "Canadian Anti-Racist Feminist Thought: Scratching the Surface of Racism." Pp. 7-31 in *Scratching the Surface: Canadian Anti-Racist Feminist Thought*, edited by Ennkshi Dua and Angela Robertson. Toronto: Women's Press.

Durkheim, Emile. [1964a]1895. *The Rules of Sociological Method.* Translated by Sarah A. Solovay and John H. Mueller. New York: The Free Press.

Esping-Anderson, G. 1993. "Postindustrial Class Structures: An Analytic Framework." Pp. 7-31 in *Changing Classes: Stratification and Mobility in Post-Industrial Societies*, edited by G. Esping-Anderson. Newbury Park, California: Sage.

Feagin, Joe R. and Clairece Booher Feagin. 1998. *Racial and Ethnic Relations.* 6th ed. Englewood Cliffs: Prentice Hall.

Fleras, Augie, and Jean Leonard Elliott. 1999. *Unequal Relations: An Introduction to Race and Ethnic, and Aboriginal Dynamics in Canada.* 3d ed. Toronto: Prentice Hall.

Foster, Lorne. 1998. *Turnstile Immigration: Multiculturalism, Social Order & Social Justice in Canada.* Toronto: Thompson Educational Publishing.

——. 2002a. "Immigration Crucial to Our Future." *Share* 25(16): July 27.

——. 2002b. "The Race Paradox of Our Time." *Share.*25(24): September 19.

Fudge, Judy. 1997. "Little Victories and Big Defeats: The Rise and fall of Collective Bargaining Rights for Domestic Workers in Ontario." Pp. 119-145 in *Not One of the Family: Foreign Domestic Workers in Canada*, edited by Abigail Bakan and Daiva Stasiulis. Toronto: University of Toronto Press.

Galabuzi, G. 2001. *Canada's Creeping Economic Apartheid: The Economic Segregation and Social Marginalization of Racialized Groups.* Toronto: CJS Foundation for Research & Education.

Grandea, Nona. 1996. *Uneven Gains.* Ottawa: North-South Institute and the Philippines-Canada Human Resource Development Program.

Hage, J. and C.H. Powers. 1992. *Post-industrial Lives: Roles and Relationships in the 21st Century.* Newbury Park, California: Sage.

Harvey, E.B. and B. Siu. 2001. "Immigrants' Socioeconomic Situation Compared, 1991-1996." *INSCAN* 15(2): Fall.

Hedley, Alan R. 2002. *Running Out of Control: Dilemmas of Globalization.* Bloomfield: Kumarian Press.

Henry, F. and C. Tator. 2000. "The Theory and Practice of Democratic Racism in Canada." Pp. 285-303 in *Perspectives on Ethnicity in Canada*, edited by M.A. Kalbach and W.E. Kalbach. Toronto: Harcourt Canada.

Herberg, Edward N. 1990. "The Ethno-racial Socioeconomic Hierarchy in Canada. Theory and Analysis of the New Vertical Mosaic." *International Journal of Comparative Sociology* 31:206-221.

Hou, Feng and T.R. Balakrishnan. 1996. "The Integration of Visible Minorities in Contemporary Society." *Canadian Journal of Sociology* 21(3):307-326.

Hunter, Alfred A. 1988. "Formal Education and Initial Employment: Unravelling the Relationships between Schooling and Skills Over Time." *American Sociological Review* 53:753-765.

Hunter, Alfred A., and Jean McKenzie Leiper. 1993. "On Formal Education, Skills, and Earnings: The Role of Educational Certificates in Earnings Determination." *Canadian Journal of Sociology* 18(1):21-42.

Isajiw, Wsevolod W., Aysan Sever, and Leo Driedger. 1993. "Ethnicity Identity and Social Mobility: A Test of the 'Drawback Model.'" *Canadian Journal of Sociology* 18:206-221.

Kalbach, Warren E. and Madeline A Richard. 1988. "Ethnic-Religious Identity, Acculturation, and Social and Economic Achievement of Canada's Post-War Minority Populations." Report for the Review of Demography and Its Implications for Economic and Social Policy. Toronto: University of Toronto Population Research Laboratory.

Keung, Nicholas. 2005. "Immigrants Better Trained, Worse Off." *The Toronto Star*, February 1.

Krahn, Harvey. 1995. "Non-standard Work on the Rise." *Perspectives on Labour and Income* 7(4):35-42.

———. 1998. "Social Stratification." Pp. 154-85 in New Society: Sociology for the 21st Century, edited by Robert J. Brym. Toronto: Harcourt.

Krahn, Harvey, Tracey Derwing, Marlene Mulder, and Lori Wilkinson. 2000. "Educated and Underemployed: Refugee Integration into the Canadian Labour Market." *Journal of International Migration and Integration* 1(1):59-84.

Li, Peter S. 1988. *Ethnic Inequality in a Class Society.* Toronto: Thompson.

McDade, Kathryn. 1987. *Barriers to Recognition of the Credentials of Immigrants to Canada.* Ottawa: Institute for Research on Public Policy.

———. 1988. "Barriers to Recognition of the Credentials of Immigrants in Canada." Ottawa: Institute for Research on Public Policy.

Macklin, Audrey. 1994. "On the Inside Looking In: Foreign Domestic Workers in Canada." Pp. 13-39 in *Maid in the Market*, edited by Wenona Giles and Sedef Arat-Koc. Halifax: Fernwood Publishing.

Mata, Fernando and John Samuels. 2000. *Recognition of Foreign Professional Qualifications with Special Reference to Ontario.* Ottawa: Center for Immigration and Ethnic Studies.

Maxim, Paul. 1992. "Immigrants, Visible Minorities and Self-employment." *Demography* 29:181-198.

Nash, Manning. 1989. *The Cauldron of Ethnicity in the Modern World.* Chicago: The University of Chicago Press.

Ontario Ministry of Citizenship. 1989. "Task Force on Access to Professions and Trades in Ontario 1989." Access! and Peter A. Cummings. Toronto: Ontario Ministry of Citizenship.

Ornstein, Michael D. 2000. "Ethno-Racial Inequality in Toronto: Analysis of the 1996 Census." Prepared for the Chief Administrator's Office of the City of Toronto.

Ornstein, Michael D. and Raghubar D. Sharma. 1983. "Adjustment and Economic Experience of Immigrants in Canada: An Analysis of the 1976 Longitudinal Survey of Immigrants." A Report to Employment and Immigration Canada. Toronto: York University Institute for Behavioural Research.

Pendakur, K., and R. Pendakur. 1998. "The Colour of Money: Earnings Differentials among Ethnic Groups in Canada." *Canadian Journal of Economics* 31(3):518-48.

Porter, John. 1965. *The Vertical Mosaic: An Analysis of Social Class and Power in Canada.* Toronto: University of Toronto Press.

Portes, Alejandro. 1999. "Towards a New World–The Origins and Effects of Transnational Activities." *Ethnic and Racial Studies* 22(2):463-77.

Rajagopal, Indhu. 1990. "The Glass Ceiling in the Vertical Mosaic: Indian Immigrants to Canada." *Canadian Ethnic Studies/Etudes Ethniques au Canada* 22(1):96-105.

Ralston, Helen. 1988. "Ethnicity, Class, and Gender among South Asian Women in Metro Halifax: An Exploratory Study." *Canadian Ethnic Studies/Etudes Ethniques au Canada* 20(3):63-83.

Reitz, Jeffrey. 1990. "Ethnic Concentration in Labour Markets and Their Implications for Ethnic Equality." Pp. 135-95 in *Ethnic Identity and Equality*, edited by Raymond Breton, Wsevolod Isajiw, Warren Kalback, and Jeffrey Reitz. Toronto: University of Toronto.

———. 1997. "Priorities for Immigration in a Changing Canadian Economy: From Skill Selectivity to Skill Utilization." Pp. 189-206 in *New Selection Criteria for Economic Stream Immigrants*, edited by the Ministry of Citizenship and Immigration Canada, Workshop held October 30-31. Ottawa: Citizenship and Immigration Canada.

———. 2003. "Occupational Dimensions of Immigrant Credential Assessment: Trends in Professional, Managerial and other Occupations, 1970-1996." The Monk

Centre for International Studies (http://www.utoronto.ca/ethnicstudies/reitz.html).

———. 2005. "Tapping Immigrant Skills: New Directions for Canadian Immigration Policy in the Knowledge Economy." *Institute for Research on Public Policy* 11(1):1-18.

Reitz, J. G. and R. Breton. 1994. *The Illusion of Difference: Realities of Ethnicity in Canada and the United States.* Toronto: C.D. Howe Institute.

Reitz, J. G. and Sherrilyn M. Sklar. 1977. "Culture, Race, and the Economic Assimilation of Immigrants." *Sociological Forum* 12(2):233-277.

Richmond, Anthony H. 1984. "Immigration and Unemployment in Canada and Australia." *International Journal of Comparative Sociology* 25(3-4):243-55.

———. 1990. "The Income of Caribbean immigrants." Pp. 363-380 in *Ethnic Demography*, edited by Shiva Halli, Frank Trovato and Leo Driedger. Ottawa: Carleton University Press.

———. 1994. *Global Apartheid: Refugees, Racism, and the New World Order.* Toronto: Oxford University Press.

Ritzer, George. 1998. *The McDonaldization Thesis: Explorations and Extensions.* Newbury Park: Sage.

Saidulla, Ahmad. 2001. "The Two Faces of Canada: A Community Report on Racism." National Anti-racism Council. Village Green Communications.

Samuels, John. 2004. *Are There Racial Barriers to Access to Professions and Trades for the Foreign-trained in Ontario?* Canada: Queen's Printer for Ontario.

Satzewich, Vic. 2000. "Capital Accumulation and State Formation: The Contradictions of International Migration." Pp. 51-73 in *Social Issues and Contradictions in Canadian Society*, edited by B. Singh Bolaria. Toronto: Harcourt Brace Canada.

Satzewich, Vic and Lloyd Wong. 2003. "Immigration, Ethnicity, and Race: The Transformation of Transnationalism, Localism, and Identities." Pp. 263-290 in *Changing Canada: Political Economy as Transformation*, edited by Wallace Clement and Leah F. Vosko. Montreal: McGill-Queen's University Press.

Second Annual Law and Diversity Conference. 2004. "Making the Mosaic Work." January 2004. Second Annual Law and Diversity Conference held at the University of Toronto.

Shamai, Shmuel. 1992. "Ethnicity and Educational Achievement in Canada 1941-1981." *Canadian Ethnic Studies* 24:43-51.

Shareif, Sofia. 2005. "Foreign Land and Foreign Trained: A Policy Paper on the Non-accreditation of Foreign Credentials for Racialized Immigrant Professionals." Department of Sociology, York University, Toronto. Unpublished manuscript.

Shields, J. 2002. "No Safe Haven: Markets, Welfare and Migrants." Presented to the Canadian Sociology and Anthropology Association, Congress of the Social Sciences and Humanities, June 1, Toronto, Ontario.

Silvera, Makeda. 1989. *Silenced.* 2d ed. Toronto: Sister Vision.

Simmie, Scott and Melissa Leong. 2004. "Filipino Community Groups Develop Caregiver Position Paper." *Toronto Star*, December 12.

Simmons, Alan. 1998. "Racism and Immigration Policy." Pp. 115-130 in *Racism and Social Inequality in Canada*, edited by V. Satzewich. Toronto: Thompson Educational Publishing.

———. 1999. "Economic Integration and Designer Immigrants: Canadian Policy in the 1990s." Pp. 53-69 in *Free Markets, Open Societies, Closed Borders? Trends in International Migration and Immigration Policy in the Americas*, edited by M. Castro. Miami: North-South Press.

Simmons, Alan and Dwaine Plaza. 1995. "Breaking through the Glass Ceiling: The Pursuit of University Training among Afro-Caribbean Migrants and their Children in Toronto." Presented at the Annual Meeting of Canadian Population Society, Montreal, Quebec.

Smith, Anthony D. 1981. *The Ethnic Revival.* New York: Cambridge University Press.

Smith, Ekuwa, and Andrew Jackson. 2002. *Does a Rising Tide Lift All Boats?* Ottawa: Canadian Council on Social Development.

South Commission. 1990. *The Challenge to the South: The Report of the South Commission.* New York: Oxford University Press.

Stasiulis, Daiva and Abigail Bakan. 1997a. "Regulation and Resistance: Strategies of Migrant Domestic Workers in Canada and Internationally." *Asian and Pacific Migration Journal* 6(1):31-37.

———. 1997b. "Negotiating Citizenship: The Case of Foreign Domestic Workers in Canada." *Feminist Review* 57:112-57.

Stasiulis, Daiva and Radha Jhappan. 1995. "The Fractious Politics of a Settler Society: Canada." Pp. 95-131 in *Unsettling Settler Societies*, edited by Daiva Stasiulus and Nira Yuval-Davis. London: Sage Publications.

Statistics Canada. September 2002. "Ethnic Diversity Survey: Portrait of a Multicultural Society." Catalogue no. 89-593-XIE.

Statistics Canada. August 2004. "Immigrants in Canada's Urban Centres 2001." Catalogue no. 3 89-613-MWE2004003.

Tepperman, Lorne. 1975. *Social Mobility in Canada.* Toronto: University of Toronto Press.

The Treasury Board of Canada Secretariat. "Employment Systems Review–A Guide for the Federal Public Service." (http://www.tbs-sct.gc.ca/index_e.asp 1999-02-01).

Trempe, Robert, Susan Davis, and Roslyn Kunin. 1997. "Not just Numbers: A Canadian Framework for Future Immigration." Minister of Public Works and Government Services Canada. Catalogue no. Ci63-21/1998E.

Trovato, Frank and Carl F. Grindstaff. 1986. "Economic Status: A Census Analysis of Immigrant Women at Age Thirty in Canada." *Review of Sociology and Anthropology* 23(4):569-687.

Van Rijn, Nicolaas. 1999. "Expert Immigrants are Being Left out in the Cold." *The Toronto Star*, February 21.

World Education Services. 2005. (http://www.wes.org/ewenr/research.htm).

Zeytinoglu, Isik Urla and Jacinta Khasiala Muteshi. 2000. "Gender, Race and Class Dimensions of Non-Standard Work." *Industrial Relations/Relations Industrielles* 1:133-67.

Chapter 11

The Community College Con: "Changing Your Life Through Learning"

Randle W. Nelsen

Learning Objectives:

1. Consider the way in which bureaucracy as a form of social organization and professionalism as ideology are made complementary to one another by authorities whose major interest is in blocking fundamental social change.

2. Examine the gatekeeping and disciplining function of the professionals and their professions.

3. Understand the primary role of capitalist socioeconomic arrangements as well as the crucial secondary and supporting role played by technology in reproducing the status quo.

4. Analyze the way in which deviance gets both psychologized and individualized in explanations of "failure" offered by authorities and (sadly) students alike.

5. Note how various con jobs can be, and are usually best, explained as systemic to "the system."

6. Learn the difference between training and educating.

7. Appreciate how "professional" and "professionalization" are best thought of as ideological code for "attitude adjustment."

8. Discover the explanatory power and importance of social research and analysis that emphasizes historical, in-depth case studies.

Indroduction

This chapter is about the norms and the dictates of both professional training and bureaucracy, and the way they are brought together in post-secondary schooling at the college level. While the analysis and the arguments presented can be generalized to most of what goes on in community colleges as a group, the data collected and analysed over the past twenty-five years (1979-2004) are part of a case study of one particular college, which I will call "The College." This examination of its usual practices reveals that the abbreviated name is appropriate, its operations often fitting the commonly-accepted definitions of a con job, "involving abuse of confidence [and/or] to persuade by deception" (Webster's Dictionary 1996:135).

The analysis developed turns on a crucial distinction between training and education. Particular attention is paid to student training, "professionalization" as "attitude change," part of a professional academic culture that is shaped by and reproduces prevailing socio-economic arrangements. It is argued that promoting education as "education that works" or "changing your life through learning" is part of a confidence or con job characterizing bureaucratized training found throughout our school system, and definitely at the college level.

An important focus in this chapter is upon those students for whom The College is education that does not work to change their lives. They do not present "normal cases" to the professionally-oriented bureaucracy, and the bureaucracy is incapable of coping with, not capable of understanding and serving, these students without changing its terms of reference. Special attention, then, is paid to the manner in which schooling treats "deviant" students, attempting to "break" them to the bureaucratic mould.

Finally, the political economy that structures the operations of The College and its counterparts, and schools at all levels, is a constant backdrop to this analysis. Economics, as I tell my students, is the dog that wags the political/educational tail, and the old saying about following the dollar(s) and you will get most of the story remains a truism. The College is no exception, and over the years it has become efficiently successful when it comes to 'the bottom line."

In short, the gold standard has paid off for the College. Its current well-appointed campus is a far cry from its humble beginnings in temporary trailers. However, as the material here reminds us, the price, the heavy social costs of leaving the trailers behind, is marked by a trail of tears affecting not only the individual lives of hundreds of students but the well-being of several communities.

**The Warm-Body Syndrome and the Gold Standard:
"The College" Delivers Distance Education**

During the calendar year 1980, a colleague and I conducted lengthy interviews (in most cases we interviewed each respondent more than once) with the following key informant groups. Three teachers employed by The College in its academic upgrading and training programs, three College administrators of distance and continuing education, and two employees of Canada Employment and Immigration, one of whom used to bear major responsibility for delivering academic upgrading and training programs to the First Nations' people. Through these contacts, I was able to conduct shorter, informal interviews with six students involved in adult education programs offered by The College from 1977 though 1980. These six interviews helped me to further consider some of the information gathered from our original key informants.

The picture that emerged at that time, some 25 years ago, spotlights college-government administration of funding policies that encourages further centralization and the bureaucratic expansion of administrative functions at The College's corporate headquarters. It was an expansion, parts of which continue to characterize The College's current programs, where inadequate attention is paid to the quality of teaching or the material being taught. In this context, decentralized programs created and taught by local residents are discouraged in favour of the supposedly more "efficient" programming and teaching brought to hinterland areas from The College's administrative centre.

One example of the warm-body syndrome occurred in the late 1970s when The College was asked to give a sixteen-week business management course. Originally, an unemployed interior designer, threatened with being "cut-off" by her Unemployment Insurance (today known as Employment Insurance) counsellor was "asked" to teach the course. Two months before the course was to start, she was hired in a job for which she is trained, and immediately withdrew from her college teaching assignment. She would have been paid for two weeks before the class started in which time she was to learn "the academic discipline" and prepare a course. She was told by those who hired her, in an attempt at humour which she felt most of her prospective students might not regard as funny, that "any warm body who will go out there will do."

A second representative illustration of the warm-body syndrome concerns a college agreement to offer an academic upgrading program on a reserve. A young woman is hired who knows little or nothing about the cultures of First Nations and is given almost no orientation as to how to survive in this kind of community. One of our interviewees familiar with this case offers further details:

> She was standing before a class of 20 men, all of whom are married. She's wearing a tee-shirt and no bra. And, all the women in the community decided it wasn't right for an unmarried woman to spend all day in a classroom with married men—not culturally right. So, they tried to work with that and she [the teacher] tried to develop a relationship with these women in the community. The teacher thought she was going to "liberate" the women of the

North and get "women's activities" going. But, she found that she had all this resentment coming her way from all these women and she couldn't understand it. And, then the women in the community decided, well, what we have to do is marry her off and then she won't be an unmarried woman in the classroom. She'll have a responsibility. So, they hired a single guy from the community as a teaching assistant and encouraged him to try and marry her. So then, the pressure was on her to marry him and the pressure was on him to spend time with her, and court her, and marry her. And, this teacher finally ended up in the mental hospital.

It was really unfortunate because something could have been done to remedy this situation early on. Because she was definitely misplaced and upset and in trouble. However, she was forced to stay on in that position about two months longer than she should have because her failure was being used as a "political football" by administrators after each other's jobs and quick promotions. So, they just let her hang and, of course, the program was not successfully delivered.

While this case differs from the first illustration in that this teacher had adequate training in the subject matter she was to teach, still she had no cross-cultural experience or training. The point to understand is that The College made little attempt to provide training or orientation for its workers in the field. These workers and their students are often pawns in a game with much higher stakes and a much larger scope than any single branch or individual–a game played for keeps by 'the big wigs" at the head office. One of our respondents, speaking for several others, elaborates:

> Generally speaking, the college never really supports the people in the field. For example, I know of several cases where people have gotten "cabin fever"—their mental health was in jeopardy. And, what the administrators did in most of these cases was to play ball with the person in that situation. By that, I mean that they would reassign the duties of the person with cabin fever to someone else from the College's administrative team, someone whom organization higher-ups had already fingered for dismissal. Then, when the program went down it was that person's fault and the higher-ups would leave it flaming and let it crash all the way down, rather than bailing the targeted individual out and replacing him with someone who could deliver the program.

However, the warm-body syndrome is not confined to administrators and the teachers they send into the field. To complete the picture it is important to understand that students are also part of the syndrome.

For example, a merchandising course needed three more students to make the minimal student enrolment figure for the program to be offered. The College finds these three on very short notice. Later, Canada Employment officials discover that perhaps at least one of the major reasons these three candidates failed to pass the course is that they were "functionally illiterate"—reading and writing at a grade five level. These people should have been placed in an academic upgrading program before they were put in a skill course.

Similarly, a business program emphasizing accounting was offered in the North. It is a very intensive program–covering a lot of ground quickly. One day, early in the course, the instructor is trying to make the most of the one week he has to spend on the subject of debit and credit, and he finds out that his students cannot spell January. Accordingly, we were not surprised when our informant told us that at the end of the sixteen weeks *only two* of the original twelve students remained in the course. Currently, The College has improved somewhat in this regard by putting in place required upgrading programs that have helped retain a greater percentage of students who are adequately prepared to meet the demands of their program.

Finally, it should be pointed out that the warm-body syndrome described in this case study material from the 1970s is closely related to government funding policies regarding adult education in place at the time, and the large, sparsely–populated area served by The College. However, it remains the case that professional-technical programs continue to be structured by The College's orientation as a corporate and bureaucratic business. While funding policies have changed and private-sector competition has come into play over the past five years, it remains true that these policies continue to generate College profits once the students successfully complete day one of the program. Thus, College administrators continue to be highly motivated to get a course started but are somewhat less concerned about what happens once the course is underway.

The respondents from sponsoring agencies interviewed in the late 1970s were particularly critical of the way in which both educational "standards" and course content were excessively dictated by potential profitability–what one respondent referred to as the "gold standard." Stories from our respondents of The College "hustles" producing training programs of profit to The College which leave in their wake a dozen apprentice electricians and a like number of skilled secretaries and other workers without paid employment (only one or two graduates in each program managed to secure work) were all too common. This discernible pattern in which the metropole profits at the expense of hinterland communities has in today's economic climate been transferred to the metropole itself (Davis 1978:217, 225). Mid-1990s research reveals that "training for what?" remains a troubling question for the government-community college partnership to answer (Dunk and Nelsen 1993). This more recent 1990s re-examination also indicates that the situation may have been exacerbated with the government decision to allow private sector bids to break the community college monopoly on selling educational seats sponsored in whole or in part by government agencies. In brief, it remains the case that when the warm-body syndrome and the gold standard continue to deliver college education programs, the College profits, often at the expense of both the local communities and the students it purports to serve. The following material, drawn from the last decade or so of The College's operations, continues to clearly emphasize this point.

From Warm Bodies to the Disembodied Classroom: Technology Brings Distance Education Home

In the fall of 1995 full-time business students at The College received local media coverage of their protest over being assigned to three-hour video classes where no instructor was present. In describing this incident at the time, I commented as follows:

> College administrators, citing diminished resources, eventually worked out a compromise whereby an instructor capable of answering questions and engaging in dialogue about course material would be provided for the last half hour of each session. The protesting students, who did not know at registration that they were signing up for video classes, only reluctantly accepted this compromise, maintaining that they were not getting what they paid for and bemoaning the video pedagogy's lack of interaction. (Nelsen 1997:188)

However quaint The College students' protest may appear in this age of technology, their notion that post-secondary schooling should provide a heavy dose of student/teacher, in-person interaction is food for thought. In essence these students were protesting The College's idea of progress, movement from warm-bodied to disembodied instructors–flesh and blood teachers replaced by the cold (proponents consider it "cool") efficiency of technology-based instruction.

Their protest goes beyond a simple declaration of being against or for the latest technology, to The College's institutional fascination (and it is joined by nearly all, if not all, post-secondary institutions) with video and computerized learning. It is a fascination that Todd Oppenheimer (2003), in a telling critique of the glitz and glamour surrounding computer-centered instruction, shows is not only enormously wasteful of our resources, but also successful in deceiving most Americans (and I would add Canadians) with a false promise that it can save the schools. What this con of disembodied instruction produces is usually complete disdain and lack of respect for students, and sometimes for faculty as well. As the following case study demonstrates, such objectification of students and teachers, from warm-bodied to disembodied, is part and parcel of The College's instruction in bureaucratized professionalism.

Disciplining Deviance: "Change Your Life Through Learning"

For a certain group of students The College's promise of an education that works to change lives is not fulfilled. Curious about their stories, I conducted interviews (all but two were done during the 2001-02 and 2002-03 academic years) with six students having trouble in their college programs. Three of these were lengthy and involved more than one meeting. The other three were shorter single encounters that I utilized primarily to analyze patterns, and the similarity of experiences seemingly present in the more in-depth interviews. These patterns are best observed in the experiences of one particular interviewee, and I have chosen to focus upon her as a case study that represents the difficulties experienced by many. In closely examining Joyce's (a pseudonym) time at The College, I also had an opportunity to meet with her fieldwork placement supervisor and later, both the major professor and co-ordinator of the program in which she was enrolled.

Joyce completed three years and parts of two others (at least one semester) at The College. She was awarded a General Degree in Arts after her first two years, but failed to complete her certification in the Child and Youth Worker (CYW) program. Joyce was twenty years old when she entered The College and nearly twenty-five when she left. Her high school marks were above average, her attendance award-winning, and she self-reports a lively interest in social studies and especially history.

During the course of her school career Joyce was diagnosed as having an auditory recognition disability which caused her to experience some difficulty with reading/spelling and consequently, attending to course requirements that emphasized completion of written reports. She received some extra help in this regard at both the high school and college levels, and went on to successfully complete her high school diploma after the usual five years, with time and course options to spare in her final grade 13 semester. She also completed the requirements for her college degree within the usual two-year time frame. She did spend a semester prior to entering the CYW program on academic probation but recovered nicely, with probation being lifted. In brief, Joyce was an adequate, and in several cases as her transcript indicates, a better-than-average, general arts student. So, what happened to Joyce that made it impossible for her to complete her certification program?

Before answering this question, it is important to understand college as a bureaucratic business from a student's point of view by referring to academic probation and course failure as part of the prerequisite system employed by community colleges. For many students unable to pass a particular course in this system anchored in prerequisite requirements, they wind up marking time for an extra semester, sometimes a year, while they wait until the course required is offered again and successfully passed. Only then can they move ahead in their step-by-step sequential march toward certification. As one of my interviews disgustedly noted in reference to this situation, "Sheesh! Do they have to make it so difficult?" Later, helped in part by the interview questions and the conversation that ensued, he became light-bulb-like aware that the prerequisite system was/is a great money-maker and that The College turns a handsome profit with the extra semesters of government funding and tuition money forked over by students like himself guilty of just one slip-up.

In sum, it is the ordering, the sequencing of the prerequisites, as well as the frequency with which they are offered that is the centrepiece of The College's bureaucratic business logic. Most of my informants were unable to see any sound pedagogical reasons for most of the decisions produced by this logic, and realized that these decisions had a detrimental effect on their academic progress toward certification.

In Joyce's case, this played a significant and costly role in her college troubles. But now, I shall turn my attention to her Achilles heel, the fieldwork placement. I shall summarize and draw some quotations directly from interviews I had with Joyce's major professor at The College, her fieldwork supervisor, and Joyce herself regarding her placement at a youth detention facility.

The professor's position is that "Joyce was unable to meet professional expectations." He said that she "required direction and guidance beyond what is expected," and the team members (staff at the facility) reported that Joyce had not formed "a professional relationship" with the team. According to the professor, Joyce's "professional growth" was in question:

> Professional growth involves developing an awareness of how transference and countertransference issues affect your [the student's] behaviour and intervention with clients... Being conscious of this is the key to consistently basing intervention on the needs of the client... rather than on the needs of the worker. (CYW Practices Manual)

In short, and in the professor's view, for Joyce, professional growth and the accompanying professional consciousness were missing.

The professor relied on staff reports to tell me that Joyce was having "minimal relationships with the youth," only engaging them at "a superficial level." He made much of her playing cards with the residents, not engaging them "therapeutically" in a manner that would show her awareness of "group dynamics" and differences between staff and residents, as well as her seeming inability to correct youth when they were engaged in inappropriate conversations. This was summed up by the professor's comment that Joyce appeared to avoid confrontation and conflict, and using his professional jargon, that she had considerable difficulty "consequencing youth." Joyce in her several interviews with me interpreted all this as meaning that she had a different, not necessarily an inferior, treatment philosophy from the one espoused by the professor and the program. She admitted that this had led her to treat residents too much as equals, making program staff uncomfortable and suspicious of her professionalism and professional aspirations.

Finally, the professor and colleagues, in a move that can only be termed ironic given her clearly asserted differences with the program's socialization (perhaps indoctrination), required Joyce to take an assertiveness training course with a specific instructor. She did not do this, but it should be noted here that this course was already fully enrolled and therefore not offered during the time she was supposed to sign up for it. The professor also offered "to bridge" Joyce to various counselling services and when she declined he interpreted this as another instance of her non-responsiveness and communication difficulties. On this point Joyce made it clear she was unaware of the importance attached to initiating contact with the field supervisor and the program co-ordinator. She put this both more succinctly and colourfully: "I was not aware that 'sucking up' was a program requirement."

My interview with Joyce's fieldwork supervisor revealed an overall assessment similar to the professor's, although there are some differences and different language is used to describe the situation. The supervisor's main complaint seemed to be that Joyce, to use a well-known Dale Carnegie phrase, did not know "how to win friends and influence people" in a professional manner. He told me, "you have to sell yourself" and Joyce did not. "She was buffaloed" by the institution's clients who were "using her and she didn't know it." Furthermore, "she let one kid monopolize her time."

On the other hand, Joyce's supervisor did admit that she was "beginning to do some good things and was learning on the job." He said she was becoming better at "bed checks" and developing her ability regarding "crowd control," citing a recent fight situation that Joyce defused and for which "she received praise from everyone and positive feedback from clients." (To me this did not sound like the person who the professor had said "appeared to avoid confrontation and conflict.") However, according to the supervisor, overall "the kids (clients) weren't buying her or buying in to what she was doing."

From Joyce's point of view her participation in breaking-up the fight was just one of several instances of improvement, learning the bed-check and reporting routines as well as speaking-up more frequently were others, where she was demonstrating that she could do the job. When I informed her that her supervisor had corroborated much of what she was saying, but remained worried about the speed of her learning, Joyce responded with some pedagogical theory/philosophy of her own.

She noted that The College is supposed to be an institution interested in learning, and she sees learning as a developmental process:

> I was not given enough credit for my learning and improvement. I should have been rewarded for the growth I demonstrated–the changes I was making. Instead, I was penalized in an inflexible way. They didn't give me enough

direction and left me alone and wanting to cry a lot because I did not feel they (the college authorities) were with me.

Furthermore, Joyce continued, The College should be a place where good communication is paramount. She noted that in papers she wrote for her professor she discussed many of the "professional issues" in question (for example, one youth monopolizing her time and how to deal with this). But, what she had written did not seem to get communicated back to the supervisor. (In my meeting with the supervisor, nearly half-way through the semester-long placement, he admitted that he had not yet read Joyce's journals to get her version of the placement experience.) Elaborating, Joyce makes the point that communication between The College professors and the agency supervisor is minimal and weak, and that it only picks up in frequency and quality when trouble puts the student in school jeopardy–in short, when it is too late.

    As an example in her case, Joyce cited the fact that the supervisor had not been told of her learning "disability" or other problems until several placement weeks had passed (this was confirmed by the supervisor). This lack of communication resulted in an embarrassing situation, one that could have been avoided, where Joyce was asked to read aloud in front of everyone. Since this is not her strongest suit, it soon became evident that she was having difficulty with certain passages. As Joyce in one of our interviews asked in rhetorical fashion, "What's the chance of establishing credibility in your position when you have been embarrassed in front of everyone (clients and staff) and feel badly about it? And, what are you going to do after an experience like this?" Of course, as Joyce pointed out, referencing what she saw as the professor's/supervisor's ironic critique of her being non-communicative now supported by this public-reading humiliation, you are likely to "clam-up," "shut-down," isolate yourself even more by not giving full expression to your personality. In brief, you are not going to want to show other people who you really are. You will be inclined to withdraw.

    Again, all of this could have been avoided, and at the very least, Joyce feels The College should have taken some responsibility for its communication failings. Instead, The College authorities (professor, supervisor and program co-ordinator), as might be expected, shifted the blame to the student, suggesting various self-enhancement and self-esteem building strategies. College authorities also shifted responsibility from their academic bureaucracy to "the profession," with the professor closing our interview this way: "Our hands are tied. Academics is one thing, but placements–they're responsible to certification agencies, licensing authorities." This shifting of responsibility and blame from academic bureaucracy to profession and ultimately onto the student will be examined further in the next section. I shall conclude this section with a summary of Joyce's feelings about her fieldwork experiences.

In a word, Joyce feels betrayed. Her initial excitement about being placed with the youth detention facility soon gave way to dismay. She strongly believes that communication problems both hidden, and not-so-hidden, in the structure of the program were downloaded onto her. Her professional philosophy regarding interacting with the clients (playing card games, hanging out with them in the lounges and helping them to express themselves by respecting their vocabulary, their language, and listening to them) was given almost no room for expression and little credibility as the weight of the bureaucratic authority structure came down on her. Her "mistakes," what some observers call "teachable moments," were not seen by the authorities as learning opportunities, and she was not encouraged to learn from them (Smith 1986; Freire 1970-71). Joyce believes, and I concur, that her fieldwork and general program experience were mostly about institutional power and control over the suppliant student.

There was, from my sociological perspective, one bright spot in that Joyce's experiences did result in her developing a sociological explanation which in part replaced her initial personality-conflict view that the professor simply did not like her from the start. But, given all that occurred and the universal agreement of the supervisor, professor and co-ordinator that fieldwork at the detention centre is probably the toughest placement in the program, Joyce can be forgiven for at times wondering whether she was "set-up," whether they "wanted me to flunk out."

Beyond the obvious lesson she received in how-not-to-run a professional certification program, a lesson in education that does not work, Joyce felt that The College did not care about looking after one of their own. The con for her involved all of the above plus a good measure of missing loyalty. After all, she had been awarded an Associate of Arts Degree from The College had she not? Was she not one of them? Did they (the faculty and administrators) not accept her? The answers to these questions, as Joyce found out, were not to be found so much in individualized personality explanations, but rather, in the structure of the training institution itself and in its connections to the professions and businesses it serves.

Becoming a Professional and the Dictates of Bureaucracy: An Analysis of Schooling as Attitude Change

The key to understanding all of this case study material–the gate-keeping function of particular courses of study and field placements, the belief in an increasingly corporate and high-tech education, and the delivery of adult distance education programs to hinterland areas, is the interplay between the norms of professionalism and bureaucracy (Crane 1972). The dictates of bureaucracy are especially important as they complement those of corporate capitalist economics, the gold standard, and direct analysis beyond an overly simplistic technological determinism.

Many of The College's courses of study including child and youth studies, early childhood education, and law enforcement can be viewed as still in the process of professionalizing or becoming professions. The College instructors are acting as professionalizing agents by fulfilling their gatekeeping duties of "weeding out" students they deem unfit. Further, while most instructors are too busy teaching or have no desire to practice the professions they teach, they are helping fulfill *the* most important norm of professionalization–self-regulation. Acting for practitioners in each occupational group, The College instructors are part of the legitimated authority (often in part delegated and supported by government) which authorizes each profession "to set its own standards for entrance, to admit new members, to establish a code of conduct, to discipline members and [establish] claims to have a body of knowledge (achieved through education) which legitimizes its autonomy and distinctiveness" (Online Dictionary 2004).

The gatekeeping function of college instructors is perpetuated by the bureaucratic form of social organization at their workplace. All the norms of bureaucracy apply in explaining the case material cited above–The College's hierarchical structure is buttressed by an internal system of rules and regulations, (standards) as well as the impersonal detachment required of career-oriented workers in carrying out their official duties (Weber [1909]1955:125-131; Blau 1956). Both students and their instructors soon find out that academic and career success goes well beyond the body of knowledge connected to their occupational program. Both come to understand that school and work success in bureaucratic settings like The College "means that emotionality (subjectivity) has been to a significant degree schooled out of you" (Nelsen 1991:19). Further, "'Excessively' subjective people find it difficult to play [the] bureaucratic role for too long. In brief, some individuals resist attempts to forcibly control and standardize their behaviour" (p.19). Put another way, they resist both attitude change and training.

Understanding the difference between training and education is crucial to any analysis of professional socialization in today's schools. Among the several commentators describing this difference, David Noble's (2002:2; also see Nelsen 2007:104-113) description, part of his analysis of the commodification of school education, stands out:

> In essence, training involves the honing of a person's mind so that his or her mind can be used for the purposes of someone other than that person. Training thus typically entails a radical divorce between knowledge and the self. Here knowledge is usually defined as a set of skills or a body of information designed to be put to use, to become operational, only in a context determined by someone other than the trained person; in this context the assertion of self is not only counterproductive, it is subversive to the enterprise. Education is the exact opposite of training in that it entails not the disassociation

but the utter integration of knowledge and the self, in a word, self-knowledge. Here knowledge is defined by and, in turn, helps to define, the self. Knowledge and the knowledgeable person are basically inseparable. Education is a process that necessarily entails an interpersonal (not merely interactive) relationship between people–student and teacher (and student and student) that aims at individual and collective self-knowledge. (Whenever people recall their educational experiences they tend to remember above all not courses or subjects or the information imparted but people, people who changed their minds or their lives, people who made a difference in their developing sense of themselves. It is a sign of our current confusion about education that we must be reminded of this obvious fact: that the relationship between people is central to the educational experience.) Education is a process of becoming for all parties, based upon mutual recognition and validation and centering upon the formation and evolution of identity. The actual content of the educational experience is defined by this relationship between people and the chief determinant of quality education is the establishment and enrichment of this relationship.

Most of what The College does is not education but training, and student acceptance of this training focus is, in most cases, not a problem at the college level. After all, most students want a course of study that is "hands on" and leads to a well-paid job, or to experience "education that works." However, job-specific training is only part of the course of study at The College, for as several observers have argued, training and retraining is all about "attitude adjustment" (Swift and Peerla 1996:29-51).

Those students able to make the best adjustment model themselves after their instructors whose own schooling has made them adept at manipulating *potential* conflict in order to reinforce the complementarity of professional and academic hierarchies, thereby maintaining the present system (Schmidt 2000). By learning to switch reference groups at the right moment, College instructors, like other professionals, can play the horizontal authority of professional collegial relations against the vertical authority of bureaucracy. The result is often professional irresponsibility masquerading as responsibility and maintenance of the status quo promoted as social change. In other words, faculty who profit by and as a group do not want to change existing arrangements, and do not have to make any efforts in that direction. On the other hand, students who often are most exploited by the status quo are all but powerless to change it.

So, when the value of curriculum content, evaluation of teacher classroom performance, and the introduction of new technology that affects current pedagogy are the student issues, faculty can solidify their position within the academic hierarchy by calling on the canons of professionalism to question the students' competence as educational critics. When class attendance, formal examinations, and grading are of concern to students, faculty can shift responsibility from their professional selves to the rules and regulations of the academic bureaucracy and leave their professional status unthreatened. If instructors are well-schooled and moderately adept at

> playing this game of switching reference groups, they can, in both instances, force students to direct their animosities to realities (in the first instance, "the profession," and in the second case, the academic bureaucracy–"the organization") amorphous enough that the students' power to change academic structures is largely confined to their rhetoric. (Nelsen 1991:207)

In the end, most students, even those aware of and able to demystify this not-so-hidden curriculum, give in, turning their attention to completing requirements for their job credentials.

They become further addicted to authority and standardization. For them, form becomes content. They learn to look busy, to meet the requirements of shuffling paper and people rather than producing or providing much of substance, so they can hang on to their jobs. For them, like their College instructors, who are removed and remain at a discrete social distance from the social service clients and the everyday hassles of the professional practice they teach about, schooling never ends (Mayer and Nelsen 1986). For them, The College training is "education that works" because on the path to their diplomas and professional certificates they have learned and relearned the lesson of subordination. They have learned how to submit and to "cooperate," to take direction

> without worrying too much about whether or not the directions make sense to them. And the best part, from the prospective employer's point of view, is that they've learned to control their emotions–so that when they do complain about or chafe against the bureaucratic routine, they do so without upsetting it. (Nelsen 1991:205)

For those students who remain intent on upsetting (changing) it, their reward is simply to be dismissed from their program of study. Sometimes it is a failing grade in a particular course and often, as was the case with Joyce, it can be the result of perceived inadequacies in the student's fieldwork placement. These dismissed students failed to submit, to look professional by merging content with bureaucratically-acceptable form while maintaining proper social distance in their client interaction. Their failure to develop a new professional self, to don the school-prescribed "cloak of competence" means that they were unable to present a "normal case" to The College bureaucracy (Edgerton 1967). This threatened the status quo. Education that works did not work for these particular students; however, it may have changed their lives and not necessarily for the better.

Official explanations by The College authorities maintain existing arrangements by *Blaming the Victim* (Ryan 1971). Elsewhere in a critique of Sylvan learning, I have pointed out the shortcomings of a focus on individualized attitude change:

> The focal point is always upon changing individual attitudes and on other individualized change strategies, never upon changing the social organization and structure of the schools or the larger political economy which shapes them. In brief, the schools and the organized corporate system of which they are a part are exonerated, their needs served, while the responsibility for both problem students and student problems is placed exclusively on the shoulders of individuals [students] and their families...[Official] explanations pay scant attention to social circumstances...At [the College] the other side of blaming and the cure for victims is to be found in a kind of feel-good pop psychology which stresses the building of self-esteem as the remedial key to academic and other kinds of success. It is a remedy that, like victim blaming, focuses upon individual rather than social explanations of problems, encouraging individuals and sometimes groups [for example, students labelled "learning disabled" or "challenged"] to try harder in order that they might better learn to accept and make the best of their situation. (Nelsen 2002:117)

In short, this emphasis or focus is best understood as both a kind of reductionism and social control, useful in reinforcing the complementarity of professional and academic hierarchies which sustains professional schooling and the larger corporate system that shapes it.

Conclusion

The case study material reviewed here suggests that the warm-body syndrome at The College remains alive and well. Whether it is adult distance education or professionally-oriented certificate programs at The College headquarters, students are conned into compliance with professional norms supported by The College bureaucracy. As certificate supplicants, their schooling emphasizes attitude change. Success (graduation) means they are certified to join their college teachers and administrators in supporting and reproducing the status quo. Those students incapable of undergoing enough attitude and identity change to present a 'normal case' to the bureaucracy are punished for their deviance with expulsion. They move on to McJobs lower down the ladder of status, authority and pay. The College authorities rationalize their gate-keeping decisions by blaming the student victims. In this way, both failure and success are individualized, and The College's professionalized bureaucratic structure remains intact–a replica of and in service to prevailing socioeconomic arrangements.

In sum, the community college con is education that works and changes lives for the better only if the student can be bought, and taught to buy, into the system. Failure to comply means continued difference and deviance, an inability to normalize by undergoing a metamorphosis that emphasizes forced standardization and bureaucratization of the self. College teaching staff and administrators see this identity change as "professionalization." It is an ideological con job, and not education, that works. In a sentence, The College's training is a recipe for professionalized career advancement and fitting into the system, a recipe not for generating thoughtful change and perhaps even fundamental restructuring, but rather, for generational reproduction of current arrangements.

References

Blau, Peter M. 1956. *Bureaucracy in Modern Society.* New York: Random House.

Crane, Diana. 1972. *Invisible Colleges: Diffusion of Knowledge in Scientific Communities.* Chicago: The University of Chicago Press.

CYW Practices Manual. 2002-03. "The College."

Davis, Arthur K. 1978. "The Failure of American Import Sociology in Anglophone Canada." Pp. 212-230 in *Reading, Writing and Riches: Education and the Socio-Economic Order in North America,* edited by R.W. Nelsen and D.A. Nock. Kitchener-Toronto: Between the Lines.

Dunk, Thomas and Randle W. Nelsen. 1993. "After the Mill Closed: Retraining For What"? *Our Times* 12:30-34.

Edgerton, R.B. 1967. *The Cloak of Competence: Stigma in the Lives of the Mentally Retarded.* Berkeley: University of California Press.

Freire, Paulo. 1970-71. *Pedagogy of the Oppressed.* Translated by Myra Bergman Ramos. New York: Herder and Herder.

Mayer, Jan and Randle W. Nelsen. 1986. "Schooling Never Ends: A Study of Job Promotion Among Corporate Office Workers." *Human Affairs* 10:32-54.

Nelsen, Randle W. 1991. *Miseducating: Death of the Sensible.* Kingston, Ontario: Cedarcreek Publications.

_____. 1997. "Reading, Writing and Relationships Among the Electronic Zealots: Distance Education and the Traditional University." Pp. 184-210 in *Inside Canadian Universities: Another Day at the Plant,* edited by R.W. Nelsen. Kingston: Cedarcreek.

_____. 2002. *Schooling as Entertainment: Corporate Education Meets Popular Culture.* Kingston: Cedarcreek.

_____. 2007. *Fun & Games & Higher Education: The Lonely Crowd Revisited.* Toronto: Between the Lines.

Noble, David F. 2002. *Digital Diploma Mills: The Automation of Higher Education.* Toronto: Between the Lines.

Online Dictionary of the Social Sciences: A Resource for Students. 2004. Compiled by Gary Parkinson and Robert Drislane. Scarborough, ON: Thompson Nelson.

Oppenheimer, Todd. 2003. *The Flickering Mind: The False Promise of Technology in the Classroom and How Learning Can Be Saved.* New York: Random House.

Ryan, William. 1971. *Blaming the Victim.* New York: Pantheon.

Schmidt, Jeff. 2000. *Disciplined Minds: A Critical Look at Salaried Professionals and the Soul-Battering System That Shapes Their Lives.* Lanham, Maryland: Rowman and Littlefield Publishers.

Smith, Frank. 1986. *Insult to Intelligence: The Bureaucratic Invasion of Our Classrooms.* New York: Arbor House.

Swift, Jamie and David Peerla. 1996. "Attitude Adjustment: The Brave New World of Work and the Revolution of Falling Expectations." Pp. 29-51 in *The Training Trap: Ideology, Training, and the Labour Market*, edited by T. Dunk, S. McBride and R.W. Nelsen. Winnipeg/Halifax: Society for Socialist Studies/Fernwood Publishing.

Weber, Max. [1909] 1955. "Max Weber on Bureaucratization in 1909." Pp. 125-131 in *Max Weber and German Politics: A Study in Political Sociology*, J.P. Mayer. London: Faber and Faber.

Webster's Dictionary, Second Edition. 1996. Carol G. Braham, Project Editor. New York: Random House/Ballantine Books.

CHAPTER 12

The Future of Sociology as a Profession

Stephen E. Bosanac

Learning Objectives:

1. Consider the professionalization of sociology.

2. Think about how the education of sociologists affects their ability to communicate sociological knowledge.

3. Learn about the ideological climate that surrounds sociological knowledge building and shapes the future of sociology as a profession.

4. Consider how the credibility and respectability of a field is a socially constructed phenomenon.

5. Consider alternative approaches that might change the future work of sociologists

Acknowledgement

The following work is based on my presentation, "The Power of Learning/The Learning of Power: The Potential for the Demise of Sociology in the Current Pseudo-Scientific Academic Environment," given at the Society for Teaching and Learning in Higher Education (STLHE) Conference in June, 2004, at the University of Ottawa, Ottawa, Ontario. I would like to express my gratitude to each of those in attendance, and note the value of our interactions in motivating me to put pen to paper to produce a more refined version of this discussion. The surprisingly positive response I received indicated to me that the discussion that follows is both valuable and necessary.

Introduction

What is the tenor of sociological praxis today and what influence might this have over the future of sociology as a career? The goal of this chapter is to address these issues with an emphasis on academia, education, and the ideological climate shaping the work and professionalization of sociologists. In my attempt to examine these topics, I will pose two questions: Is the education and professionalization of sociologists detrimental to sociology? Is sociology adhering to the admittedly idealistic notion of being a helping humanistic field as established by Auguste Comte (1798-1857) when he (perhaps arguably) founded the discipline? Each of these questions represents a discourse that alone could fill a work of much greater depth and length than this one.

However, I believe that an examination of each of these questions will provide an interesting discussion of the history of the professionalization of sociology and the effect of this process on sociological discourse and work. Consequently, this work will be speculative, attempting to anticipate possible future directions for sociology. Nevertheless, I believe that by contextualizing contemporary sociology and its ideological underpinnings on a macro level I can shed some light on the direction of the field.

While examining each of these questions, I will consider two important issues: the abuse, overuse, and reproduction of sociology's jargon; and what I have labeled "pop-sociology." Pop-sociology is defined as a practical, concise, hands-on sociological praxis that features a strong emphasis on affecting public policy and opinion. I will consider whether pop-sociology has the potential to redress the problematic effects of the professionalization and hegemonic ideological underpinnings of sociology.

Just a Little Bit of History

Historically speaking, sociology as a profession is quite young, with its "official" origins in the early to mid-1800s. Many authors who are now known as early social theorists did not label themselves sociologists. Auguste Comte initially identified himself as a social physicist before coining the term "sociology" and eventually gaining notoriety within the discipline as the founder of the field. However, labeling Comte as the founder of sociology must be done carefully. His social physics, which he later renamed sociology because he believed that Adolphe Quetelet (1796-1874) stole the phrase, are strongly based in the work of Claude-Henri Saint-Simon (1760-1825) and Baron Charles de Montesquieu (1689-1755) among others. Comte appreciated the order provided by the scientific approach, but he did not—contrary to popular belief—privilege empirical knowledge over other types of knowledge. Rather, he believed that adhering to the tenets of a scientific praxis would provide a sound structure wherein sociology could develop a full body of knowledge for the benefit of humankind:

> He coined the word "sociology," a hybrid term compounded of Latin and Greek parts. It was to be patterned after the natural sciences, not only in its empirical methods and epistemological underpinnings, but also in the functions it would serve for mankind. (Coser 1977:4)

However, Comte's approach was problematic. He was what contemporary sociologists would describe as a post-positivist and came with all of the customary ideas that are associated with a post-positivist epistemological and ontological predisposition.

Emile Durkheim (1858-1917) asserted a similar philanthropic mission statement for sociology and considered himself a theologian before he became agnostic. He then described himself as a philosopher before being labeled by the French public as a leading social scientist. Karl Marx (1818-1883) spent the early part of his intellectual life studying law before moving into philosophy and committing to journalism as an occasional occupation while also receiving financial assistance from his wealthy intellectual collaborator Friedrich Engels (1820-1895). It was in this condition of quasi-employment and aristocratic sponsorship that Marx developed the social theory that was to make him famous after his death. This interest in journalism was shared by Herbert Spencer (1820-1903) who was first trained in mathematics and natural science. Originally, an historian and a philosopher, Georg Simmel's (1858-1918) interests eventually brought him to sociology. This phenomenon of early professionalization is evinced through an examination of many of the foundational sociological theorists (Coser 1977).

Where Do We Go from Here?

The process of professionalization for contemporary sociologists is not so free-flowing and circumstantial. In today's more technocratic, quantitatively demanding environment, sociologists have found themselves with two primary choices: professionalize or risk obscurity by forfeiting their status as an intellectual for that of a technician. Unfortunately, the process of professionalization can also reduce sociologists to technicians (Mills 1951). A technician lives off of the ideas of others as opposed to developing their own thoughts and insights. The technician is relegated to the position of administrator over, or processor of, ideas they had no hand in developing or implementing. Alienation is intimately associated with the psyche of the technician. An intellectual is (arguably) a creator and/or an implementer of ideas. However, the actual ability of the intellectual to create independent of any power structure must be considered on a continuum.

On one hand, sociologists may resist professionalization. On the other, they may (perhaps reasonably) give in to the pressure to conform with the quantitative and incremental approach to knowledge production that is so heavily favoured today (Vidich et al. 1981). Those who conform are generally considered more employable within mainstream occupations (Baritz 1960). Unfortunately, more researchers (not only sociologists) are choosing to submit to the increasingly intense professional, monetary, and managerial pressure to employ primarily quantitative approaches or approaches obscured by specialized jargon. These methodologies provide readers with an image of "knowledge beyond reproach."

This is achieved through a combination of scientific masking and obscurantism. Scientific masking is the idea that research can be presented in a manner that makes the work appear to have been conducted under the rigorous auspices of a quantitative praxis. This is achieved through the employment of quantitative methodologies (however inappropriate) and an "expert" language. Each of these is designed to appear strongly rooted in empirical principles while (incidentally) negating the unavoidable presence of the qualitative—or messy—aspects visible in any meaningful research on human beings.

It is important to note that the empirical is differentiated from the quantitative within sociological knowledge production. Empiricism is an orientation toward the collection of facts and observations for analysis. However, it does not specifically call for the negation of other types of observation and ways of knowing. Quantitative analysis specifically negates many, if not all, abstract forms of knowing. In empiricism, all forms of observation are open to analysis.

Obscurantism contributes to scientific masking. Obscurantism is defined as a presentational style aimed at the professionalization of knowledge and characterized by deliberate vagueness or complexity. Obscurantism is achieved in sociological works through the copious and purposeful application of jargon and conceptual abstractions to the presentation of research findings and/or theoretical queries:

> Whatever lofty claims they might make about their ideals (and there are few claims they do not make), academics share the same motives that animate the soul of every bureaucracy and closed guild...Every petty bureaucrat recognizes that power rests in large part on the ability to cloak his or her knowledge behind a veil of inflated and intimidating jargon. (Sykes 1988:109)

Jargon and difficult concepts have a place within any discipline. However, it is important to recognize when these tools are used as pedagogical enhancements and when they are unnecessarily employed to create an aura of expertise around both the author(s) and the work. Sociology appears to have its fair share of authors who utilize such an approach to professionalization: consider Talcott Parsons and his work on social structure, Stephen Edgell and his work on class, Thomas S. Kuhn and the twenty-one definitions of "paradigm" offered in his analysis of scientific revolutions, as well as many members of the Edinborough School and their work on the "New" Sociology of Science.

Because of scientific masking and obscurantism, straightforward analyses and/or more appropriate qualitative methodological approaches are often neglected. Qualitative analyses are on the rise within sociology and have been for a decade or more. However, these are often laden with jargon in order provide the work with an image of scientific validity. This generally leads to a greater level of acceptance and approval for the work among a broad audience (Wilson 1998; Ritzer 1998; Schwartz 1998). More direct and accessible approaches to sociological knowledge production would allow for allegedly non-scientific, but considerably more insightful, analyses (Mannheim 1936).

Is the Education and Professionalization of Sociologists Detrimental to Sociology?

Corporate positivism is a term I employ to identify both the overwhelming influence of corporations and globalization on knowledge production and education, and the associated emphasis on tangible and calculable data that (allegedly) only quantitative investigations can provide. The need for this emphasis is debatable as many authors state that quantitative investigation is generally done to the detriment of the character of the subject under scrutiny (Agger 1989; Mannheim 1936).

The use of the term "corporate" does not exclude other factors and their influence on knowledge production and education. However, it is intended to denote the powerful influence these institutions have on contemporary knowledge production (Nelsen 1997; Readings 1996). The rise of corporate positivism is accompanied by the demand of those entities controlling the distribution of financial resources for purely—or at least primarily—quantitative works. This environment of verificationism has led to increased demands for field validation for many professions. Sociological knowledge production is not removed from this phenomenon and the ideology that supports it (Baritz 1960).

Consequently, sociologists function in an ideological environment that tends to negate what is, perhaps, the most valuable part of a humanistic sociological praxis. The rich narrative that qualitative sociology can build around the nature of human social interactions is subjected to pseudoscientific analyses that often neglect the immeasurable human "essence" of a topic. Within corporate positivism, narration is criticized as too literary, too micro, and too "soft" methodologically. The image of science, which is generally associated with quantitative methodologies, is situated beyond this problem by the hegemonic ideology of corporate positivism. Nevertheless:

Science narrates. Yet its positivist version does everything possible to conceal its literary nature. Facts are just facts; science writers merely report the world; speculative reason falls victim to methodology. Science presents a chilly world in which inequality flourishes precisely to freeze it...Science constructs (Agger 1989: preface).

Both quantitative and qualitative methods socially construct knowledge. Quantitative methods do so covertly, while qualitative methods construct knowledge overtly. Because quantitative knowledge has been successful in hiding this aspect of its production, it has gained a position of authority under the current ideology that defines the social construction of knowledge as flawed.

Qualitative methods are also described as "messy" and therefore unattractive in comparison to quantitative approaches. Both of these ideas are disseminated through the education system and supported by the hierarchy of professional associations and publishing houses that set the path for the development of sociology (Ritzer 1998). Because of this, the full, rich and dynamic nature of knowledge that can be produced on the "messy" subject of human beings, and the processes that interconnect their existences, is often reduced to a relatively meaningless numerical index. It becomes "ideal" knowledge, so broadly and clinically applied to non-existent, ideal situations, that it can no longer be applied to "real" situations. Subject is subverted by method. Yet, the demand for this "ideal" knowledge remains high in an environment shaped by corporate positivism (Nelsen 2002).

Consequently, I argue that jargon and obscurantism have become necessary tools for the professionalization of contemporary sociologists. They are essential to scientific masking and provide the pseudoscientific image that is favoured by corporate positivism. The actual value of a body of knowledge can be secondary to the demand for this image. The education of sociologists works to provide these tools because universities exist within the context of the hegemonic ideology of corporate positivism (Readings 1996). Ideologies do evolve, but until one is shed in favour of another, institutions and individuals function under their influence. This influence may fluctuate on a continuum, but it still prevails to varying degrees.

The use of jargon and obscurantism as professionalizing tools is easily observed in many sociological texts and authors (including those previously mentioned). This is particularly true in regard to highly specialized sub-fields of the discipline. In fact, this specialization is yet another form of professionalization.

The macro level pressure on disciplines to validate their existence has filtered down. The acquisition of knowledge for its own sake is losing ground as a worthy endeavor. Centers of higher learning are now confronted with—and often encourage—a reductionist ideology that does not emphasize the development and exploration of intellectual thought. Instead, corporate positivism demands timely graduation rates and the development of practical and tangible job skills (Nelsen 1997).

Further, corporate positivism demands a labour force and a consumer base—technicians, not intellectuals. In this environment of verificationism, many academic institutions, departments, and students are now primarily concerned with field validation and justification. Each of these groups must work to justify their future value and utility. The easiest way to achieve this is through conforming to the pressure to sacrifice intellectual development and the production of "messy" knowledge in favour of a technical and quantitative approach.

Field validation is considerably less difficult for the natural sciences because they already regularly (if not exclusively) utilize quantitative methodologies in their research. Further, the subject matter of the natural sciences is usually conducive to quantitative analyses (even though it is often presented in a qualitative narrative as discussed earlier). Another important consideration is the relatively easy (although sometimes tedious) nature of gathering and providing quantitative data. "Proof" of the value and authority of the natural sciences is quickly compiled, and this serves to erode the position of the social sciences. Seidman (1991) explains, "a discourse that bears the stamp of scientific knowledge gives its normative concepts of identity and order an authority while discrediting the social agendas produced by other (scientific and non-scientific) discourses" (p.135). By staking a claim to absolute mathematical truth, the natural sciences are positioned as a powerful player in the current ideological environment. Unfortunately, power appears to be a finite commodity and is usually claimed at the expense of others.

For sociology and other humanities disciplines, the task of becoming "scientific" in the traditional sense is difficult because of the intangible nature of much sociological subject matter and knowledge production. Perhaps it is time to apply a new definition to the term "scientific," or thoroughly acknowledge that the literal and liberal application of this precept to all knowledge production is reductionistic and inappropriate. As Nettler (1970) notes, "The word 'science' derives from the Latin root meaning 'to know,' and for many moderns 'knowing' and 'sciencing' are coterminous" (p.86). This correlation is unnecessary, restrictive, and untenable.

The most effective and useful sociological knowledge is often provided by qualitative analyses. However, these approaches are labeled by corporate positivism as too abstract, unnecessarily complex, lacking scientific rigor, and too rooted in micro-level analyses to be widely applicable (Nettler 1970). Indeed, quantitative approaches are less complicated, less abstract, "rigorously scientific" and macro-level oriented. Nevertheless, these factors contribute to a type of knowledge production that (almost completely) lacks applicability because it represents the previously discussed "ideal" knowledge. Ideal knowledge is described as universal knowledge by advocates of quantitative methodologies, but in fact this knowledge is neither universally nor locally applicable. Measures of central tendency measure a center that rarely—if ever—exists. In other words, quantitative methodologies construct a generalized body of knowledge that is often not practically applicable (Bleier 1979).

It is difficult to do research and present data in a format that maintains the inherent meaningfulness of the subject under consideration. However, the knowledge that results from qualitative analyses is rich, fluid, and real. And, importantly, not all that we think and feel is directly knowable, and "much of it ought not to be so, at the peril of loss of its pleasure. Thus happiness defined and measured will appear as something other than happiness experienced" (Nettler 1970:29).

The education of sociologists encourages them to adhere to standard forms of measurement and method to the detriment of this type of knowledge. When traditional measurement is not possible, students are encouraged to develop an image of expertise around their work utilizing jargon and obscurantism.

Quantification is employed within the natural sciences in much the same manner as jargon is utilized within sociology:

> Figure is science's gestural work, carried out in the margins of the page as well as in its midst. Even prose can virtually become figural when enough technical jargon, acronym, and number are packed into it. Number is a crucial kind of figural work, enhancing the science aura directly. (Agger 1989:108)

Jargon and numbers are each metaphors for the subject matter under consideration. There have been several books published on the use, abuse, and inappropriate nature of statistical analyses. These texts describe numbers as mathematical jargon similar to linguistic jargon. For example, *How to Lie with Statistics* by Darrell Huff (1993) and *Innumeracy* by John Allen Paulos (2001) each describe the jargonistic, metaphorical, and intangible nature of quantitative methodologies that are positively reinforced on a regular basis in the education of sociologists.

Paulos also states his concern about a quasi-scientific world that is overly dependant on mathematics and science, but seems unconcerned with the scientific illiteracy of most of its members. Because academia and society each function within a culture adhering to a doctrine which holds that numbers do not lie, the less mathematical subjects in the humanities are devalued in favour of a pseudoscience that features more numerical representations. There exists, "an utter lack of respect for [sociology] by physical science colleagues" and society in general (Ponting 1998:9). This is demonstrated by the large amount of money, including research grants, fellowships, and scholarships, generally made available to the natural sciences as compared to the humanities.

The practice and defense of positivistic natural science is perhaps best viewed through Mannheim's concept of masking (1936). Through rhetoric and subjectivity, natural science attempts to shape the world and frame debate. This is not to imply that natural science is inherently a negative force. Natural science is simply working to guarantee its place in history and discourse. Nevertheless, this hegemonic position can only be attained by subordinating other perspectives: "Positivist social science postures a world it knows is incomplete in order to complete it" (Agger 1989:2). This has placed an enormous amount of pressure on sociology to develop a more socially acceptable—meaning scientific—praxis. This immediately puts sociology at a disadvantage by negating its best tool: sociology's insight into the unquantifiable (Agger 1989). The future of work for sociologists has surely been affected by the ideology that shapes the contemporary education process, and I believe this effect will come to be seen as somewhat negative.

Is Sociology Adhering to the Admittedly Idealistic Notion of Being a Helping Humanistic Field?

Sociology followed the lead of other respected professions and began to professionalize and diversify in order to ensure its academic and public future. Some authors state that professionalization in general has been occurring since pre-historic times. However, it is more prudent to locate the beginnings of academic professionalization on this continent in the mid- to late 1800s. This coincides with the timeline of the proliferation of urban institutions designed to promote cultural development and advanced education. It also coincides with the point in time when corporate positivism began to take root as the hegemonic ideology.

These urban institutions included libraries, academic societies, professional associations, and small informal mutual education collectives (Haskell 1984:84-106). Some of these evolved into many of the universities, trade unions, lobby groups, and professional associations of today. These institutions did exist prior to the mid-1800s. However, around the mid-1800s they became more commonplace and somewhat more accessible.

Professionalization and diversification lend to an image of expertise and viability in the public eye. However, this image is not necessarily linked to any concrete justification. Historically, the most effective example of this is the development of modern medicine. Years ago, medicine was practiced by community elders, spiritual leaders, and anyone that claimed to have the gift of healing. Sometimes this form of medicine was effective, sometimes it was not. Nevertheless, those recognized by society as medical professionals were highly respected and esteemed:

> The authority of the profession as gauged by the willingness of legislatures, philanthropists, physicians, and the general public to support and patronize medical institutions, was established long before the content of medical practice could justify it. (Haskell 1984:107)

Over time, the practice of surgery slowly evolved and became exclusive to barbers while the practice of general medicine eventually fell into the hands of apothecaries. Medical professionals lobbied their respective governments for laws and standards that would limit those who could practice medicine through credentialism. Haskell (1984) notes, "In our own time, this credibility is reinforced by law and by the dominant pro-scientific ideology" (p.107).

The American Medical Association (AMA) is a professional association that serves two primary purposes. First, it controls the production and dissemination of medical research. Second, it works as a lobby group or political action committee (PAC) with the maintenance of medicine's professional status as its primary objective. The success of the AMA's political agenda has pushed the professionalization of medicine to its zenith. The closed nature of medicine and the effectiveness of its professionalization process are easily demonstrated in the last three decades by the battle between chiropractic and traditional medicine and the public relations war medicine has waged against homeopathic/alternative forms of health care.

Diversification within sociology can be seen in the introduction of sub-fields. One such example would be feminist theory, which has only come into widespread acceptance in the last half of the twentieth century. Also relatively new to the field are sociologies of the family, the body, immigration and refugees, and criminology studies. One development of particular interest in the context of this discussion is the introduction of clinical sociology, which has yet to gain widespread acceptance (Hill 2000).

The choice of the term "clinical" is a topic that could fill another chapter. A discussion of that length is not appropriate here, so I will limit myself to a very brief analysis. I believe some sociologists looked to the most respected and esteemed field available—medicine—and determined that appropriating certain medical terms and placing them in a sociological context would give credibility to such an approach. However, I do not believe this process was quite so deliberate. Instead, I believe this field emerged from the ideology of corporate positivism that has saturated the sociological imagination (Mills 1959).

The epistemological and ontological ramifications of this ideology have clear effects on all levels of society and discourse (Kuhn 1996; Agger 1989; Haskell 1984). In its rigorous employment of appropriated medical terminology, clinical sociology is attempting to mimic the path medicine took to professionalization. If we are truly immersed in a climate of corporate positivism, then this may prove a wise choice. Consequently, clinical sociology's choice to emulate established scientific praxis might be somewhat premeditated in the sense that it is ideologically bound. Definitions and conceptualizations of professions and professionalization processes are intertwined with the idea of image building (Macdonald 1995:157-186). If current ideology demands a scientific image, then this is what "wannabe" (aspiring) professions will strive to project.

While diversification can lead to professionalization, it can also contribute to obscurantism. Within sociology, the clearest example of this is found in the development and implementation of the language of sociology. Sociological jargon has grown to such an extent that some professors find they spend much more time than would be preferable teaching students in introductory courses the specialized language of sociology (Nelsen 1999). Delaney et al. add that "Perhaps the most common source of disciplinary confusion is equating the sociological perspective with the language of sociology, whereby mastering sociologists' jargon is viewed as the ultimate goal of a sociology course" (Delaney et al. 1995:355).

Most disciplines and professions feature a specialized language. The development of jargon is an important and valuable sub-cultural and intellectual phenomenon. However, I believe sociology has gone too far in the development of its jargon and this is detrimental to the education of sociologists. As Agger points out, "Academic discourse increasingly suffocates thought" (Agger 1989:1). Sociological jargon can impede and prevent sociology students' effective and open access to sociological knowledge and its production. Many sociology students struggle to utilize sociological knowledge effectively or share it with the public in an accessible manner. This is contrary to sociology's original mission as a helping field. Introductory sociology textbooks can often be described as subordinating the entirety of the discipline to its vocabulary (Delaney et al. 1995:355).

Many sociologists appear to pride themselves on their multi-syllabic, obscure phraseology. Often, these sociologists view common language as too unsophisticated to accurately portray the depth of a subject. However, the relevance, usefulness, and comprehension of sociological jargon are rarely noted as areas of concern. Perhaps this is the area within sociology where a natural science tenet may be most effectively applied. Occam's Razor is the scientific maxim that the simplest and most direct explanation of a given phenomenon is likely the most accurate or "correct." This concept should be applied to the language of sociology.

This is not to imply that all sociological jargon is impractical. Some of this specialized language is useful, relevant, and expository. However, the overuse and unnecessary development of sociological jargon has contributed to a body of work that is difficult to access, lacks clarity, and obscures sociology's "real" contribution to academic discourse. Charles J. Sykes, in his book *Profscam: Professors and the Demise of Higher Education*, describes jargon as

> a direct product of the [academic] culture's Triple Imperative of Obscurantism. The slavish use of obscure jargon, convoluted syntax, and the symbols and trappings of mathematics are essential because: (1) They can make even the most trivial subject sound impressive and the most commonplace observation immeasurably profound, even if the subject is utterly insignificant. (2) They make it much easier to avoid having to say anything directly or even anything at all. And, most important, (3) It is easier than real thought or originality. (Sykes 1988:109)

There are now several different dictionaries of sociology, most exceeding 500 pages. Although a certain amount of material is recycled from one volume to the next, it is telling that so many different dictionaries exist, yet are diverse enough in their coverage of the specialized language of the field to remain viable. Within most disciplines there is more than one dictionary. However, the material featured in these dictionaries varies little from one volume to the next. A student will choose which dictionary to use based primarily on aesthetic preference. As a student of sociology, I have reviewed most of the dictionaries available in my field. I felt obligated to purchase five different volumes because each one represented a unique interpretation of what should be included and how these concepts should be defined.

This is significant because it demonstrates that not only has the language of sociology grown, it has diverged and does not share an internal universality. This lack of universality serves as an obstacle to establishing sociology as a fully viable, practical, professional and helping discipline. Instead, the language of sociology contributes to the reproduction of graduates, many of whom might be described as vocabulary rich and theory-free.

Nico Stehr views the concept of a universal sociological language as antiquated and condescending:

> That multiple discourse must give way to consensus is representative of a legacy of the seventeenth century. Such a legacy includes a distrust of common sense and natural languages and ultimately signals a quest for manipulative control. (Stehr 1982:52)

Criticizing the reductionist nature of universality is an easy task. However, this negates the crisis of accessibility that faces sociology (Horowitz 1971).

Sociological research is taking on an inappropriate character and losing touch with Comte's mission statement as it tries to accommodate the pressures of corporate positivism. The question is not one of choice between languages. Rather, it is how might sociology provide a more coherent and accessible body of work? A wider audience will later set the course for a universal sociological language regardless of the wishes of sociologists. If sociology can reduce the use of jargon and obscurantism, it will be able to produce a body of work that speaks to people as well as academics and high-level administrators (Wilson 1998).

Pop-Sociology

Pop-sociology can be conceptualized as a practical, concise, hands-on sociological praxis that features a strong emphasis on affecting public policy and opinion. I draw upon the prefix "pop" for two reasons. First, many sociologists seem uncomfortable with the idea of sociology becoming "popular." That the public might appropriate sociological knowledge for their own purposes makes many sociologists uncomfortable (Wilson 1998). The second—and less provocative reason—is that "pop" is the prefix generally applied to cultural artifacts that become widely accepted and utilized by the general public, i.e., pop-psychology, pop-culture, pop-music, and pop-art. However, in academic circles the prefix "pop" is often one of contempt.

Most of the obstacles hindering the popularization of sociology are related to miscommunication owing to the lack of a universal sociological language (Horowitz 1971). However, the need for a holistic approach to the communication of sociological knowledge does not require a reductionist "hack-and-slash" approach. Instead, it calls for the synthesis of terms, based on common sense, which would make sociological discourse accessible to a wide range of laypersons and professionals outside the field. This is the course of action sociology must take to avoid being assimilated or usurped by other disciplines.

Sociology needs to develop a meaningful connection with the public. This is vital because there are two primary methods of ensuring the survival of sociology in the current ideological state. On one hand, sociology can continue to try to prove that it is a scientific discipline through the concentrated use of quantitative data and analyses, jargon, and obscurantism. Alternatively, sociology can convince the public there is a necessary demand for sociological knowledge and that the discipline's contributions to policymaking effect positive social change. The latter is perhaps sociology's best hope for a strong future: "It is extremely important for sociology to demonstrate its utility to society if it's going to be viable in the long run" (Wilson 1998:435).

Some sociologists resist a directed effort at popularizing sociological knowledge on pragmatic grounds:

> They argue that it is good that sociological research draws very little attention from the media and policy makers because it both insulates the discipline from outside pressures to pursue certain research topics, particularly those that are topical, and protects the discipline from being sanctioned by the state if the research does not support a particular political agenda or ideology. (Wilson 1998:435-436)

This concern is fair, but it is also shortsighted and exclusionary. Moreover, it ignores the present climate of sociological knowledge production.

Professional and amateur sociologists alike already face sanctions by the ideology of corporate positivism and the power structures that support it. Sociological knowledge is shaped and directed by these structures. Corporate positivism covertly influences sociological research. In opening sociological knowledge to greater public scrutiny and analysis, we are certainly exchanging one form of influence for another. However, a communal/public ideology would influence sociological knowledge production overtly. This ideology would be less restrictive than the ideology that currently shapes sociology. A public-centered ideology would value methodologies not necessarily based on corporate positivism's focus on the quantifiable and the tangible. If nothing else, a public ideology would expose the inner workings of the field to the reader. This would allow for a thorough evaluation of the ideological underpinnings, motivations, and goals of the knowledge produced.

The obscurantism that has served to meet the ends of the ideology of corporate positivism has left sociology isolated and dependent. For instance:

> [T]he more sociology is ignored by the media and policy makers, the less attention it receives as an academic discipline and therefore the more removed it is from the decision-making arena, the fewer students it attracts, and the more difficulty it has in trying to obtain funding from private foundations and government agencies. (Wilson 1998:436)

In other words, an image of accessibility surrounding sociological knowledge production would attract the students and financial resources lost by denying corporate positivism (Wilson 1998). The introduction of a public ideology in combination with a concerted effort on the part of sociologists to make sociological work more accessible might also overcome the isolation and dependence Wilson discusses. Sociologists could more comfortably work on a greater variety of subjects, with a more diverse set of methodologies, and in a wider range of mediums (Schwartz 1998).

The technical language, the overuse of statistics, and the primary tenets of contemporary sociology contribute to the development of texts that do not allow for a smooth transition of materials into a format that is widely accessible and comprehensible (Ritzer 1998). This is primarily because less technical sociological writings are not considered as appealing to the exclusive journals and publishing houses that sociologists hope to impress. Consequently, these publishers shape a significant proportion of sociological knowledge production and presentation. They also construct normative values regarding what is considered "quality" writing. A jargon-free style that is not burdened by the overuse of technical terms and unnecessary statistics is described as mundane and superficial:

> But it is not merely stylistic matters that militate against sociologists writing for a general audience. Such writing tends to be demeaned, or at best merely tolerated, within...sociology; it is certainly not actively supported and rewarded.... Those who have achieved the greatest recognition in sociology are generally those who have been scrupulously faithful to the scientific model. (Ritzer 1998:449)

Sociology—the analysis of the structure of human social relationships as constituted by social interaction between humans and their cultural artifacts—is not conducive to a primarily quantitative methodological praxis. Sociological research can rarely maintain a significant level of meaning within the scope of predominantly quantitative analyses. When posing a question, i.e., "how do you feel about your work?" to a human respondent in a study on the sociology of work, the person will rarely respond, "A '3,' I feel like a '3.'" Rather, the answer they provide will be lengthy and rich with non-numerical and unquantifiable data. This phenomenon does not make the data any less real.

Amy Wharton's work in the edited volume *Working in the Service Society* (1996) is an excellent example of the inappropriateness of applying quantitative analyses to human attitudes and emotional responses. Wharton considers the work of her predecessor, Arlie R. Hochschild, as problematic when, in fact, it is *problematizing*. Hochschild qualitatively addressed the issue of emotional labour in a coherent and reasonable manner, and was innovative in his analysis of emotional work within sociological discourse (Hochschild 1983). Nevertheless, Wharton determined that while Hochschild's work did yield important insights into the subject, the research would be *most appropriately* completed through a quantitative project. Wharton then proceeded to apply a numerical scale to feelings and attitudes about emotional labour. She neither revealed this scale to her readers, nor did she effectively quantify the issues at hand. In the end, it is Wharton's work that is problematic.

Regardless, sociological research such as Wharton's often becomes authoritative because of its claims to scientific praxis. It is of little or no consequence that the object under consideration by Wharton is not amenable to these methods. The use of what are perceived to be empirical tools lends a kind of scientific aura, which then becomes an accepted claim of authority: "The science aura is the embellishment of the text with design, figure, and number, which in effect become texts themselves" (Agger 1989:70). Authority, too, becomes a text in this scenario:

> Positivism believes it can show the lawfulness of the world it pretends to portray without the aid of presuppositions, propositions, constructions. By doing so, it secretly hopes to complete a world it knows is incomplete; in the fashion of every ideology, it depicts a world without exit as a way of blocking the door. (Agger 1989:71)

By bringing this type of authority into sociology, sociologists buy into the scientific maxim of duality that implies opposition and brings the discourses of sociology and natural science into unnecessary conflict.

The work of sociologists is often beyond numerical description. Quantitative data are useful as literary tools within sociological writing to help increase a reader's understanding of the issues under investigation. These types of data are best described as adjectives—descriptors that elaborate and clarify the main point(s) of discussion. Nevertheless, in the dominant ideology of corporate positivism, the main points of sociology are subjected to, not supported by, quantitative data.

It is important to note that when sociologists formulate quantitative scales, they are not purely mathematical. For example, Likert scales are considered by some as efficient mathematical measures of attitude. But, these are not purely mathematical. In fact, they are transliterations of less "tangible" concepts that are not easily observed in the traditional sense. A socially constructed communication system of letters is replaced by an equally subjective system of numbers.

I am not trying to diminish the usefulness of positivism, empiricism, or quantitative methodologies for knowledge production in general. Nor do I oppose the appropriate application of these tenets to sociological praxis. Quantitative statistics and methodologies do have a place in sociology. However, it is a supplemental place, not a hegemonic one. For this there are three reasons: (1) human beings and their interactions are the primary materials for sociological research; (2) human beings and their interactions cannot be accurately, thoroughly, and objectively quantified; and (3) the analysis of human beings and their interactions loses a great deal in any attempted translation from the qualitative data that it is, to the quantitative data some researchers wish it to be.

Sociology is a worthy pursuit, requiring no infusion of the methodologies of the natural sciences to achieve value and purpose. However, my future work as a sociologist is being shaped and directed by a power structure that appears to divert my efforts from any meaningful connection with, or contribution to, public discourse: "Social scientists knowledge of the way the world works enables them to make better cause-and-effect connections than do other observers" (Wilson 1998:435). When sociological knowledge production is carried out at the most effective level, through predominantly qualitative methodologies with a supplemental blend of quantitative data, it has the unique ability to address human interactions. Consequently, sociology can contribute to public discourse and policy building in a manner that is notably different and arguably more pertinent than other disciplines.

Accessibility and obscurantism are important issues that prevent sociology from making this connection with the public. Qualitative methodologies have gained a level of acceptance in recent times. Nevertheless, the jargon-filled, pseudo-scientific approach to studying people is still prevalent in sociological knowledge production. While qualitative research does move towards a more effective balance, this movement alone is not enough to resolve sociology's accessibility issues. Qualitative studies are often filled with unnecessary jargon and overly complex conceptualizations that do little to illuminate a subject: "This climate, of course, creates protective camouflage—the ponderous sentence, the endless charts, the oblique jargon. How could anyone dare think us trivial now? We are appropriately impenetrable" (Schwartz 1998:443). The education and professionalization of sociologists offers some opportunities to study qualitative methodologies. Yet, it still reinforces the problematic linguistic practices that carry over into the careers of sociologists.

Pseudo-scientific sociology might provide legitimacy to the field in the ideology of corporate positivism, but this is a short-term solution. Pop-sociology might provide the timeliness, usefulness, and long-term public support that sociology needs. My call for pop-sociology does not require the transformation of sociology into a different or novel discipline. Sociology's area of study will remain the same, but it will focus on a new audience, an audience that is much larger, an audience that will allow sociological work to be more qualitative, an audience that will ensure the continuation of sociological discourse in terms that are more amenable to the study of people and their interactions.

The first step in finding this audience is to remove the cloak of linguistics that has made sociological work difficult to understand. Unnecessarily long sentences need to be broken into concise points and clarified. Necessary technical language should be operationally defined within the text without the use of tedious footnotes and endnotes that rarely shed light on a matter. Further, sociological work must be accessible in sources other than the requisite academic journals and textbooks. Currently, sociological writings appear to have difficulty entering the mainstream literary world (Schwartz 1998).

We live in a society of mass consumers who await the arrival of the "next big thing." A timely and concisely presented sociology might be welcome. Some will argue that I am catering to the "lowest common denominator." Why is this problematic? The phrase "lowest common denominator" signifies—negatively—a shared set of epistemological and ontological beliefs common among a large group of people. Why is this perceived negatively? I think of such a group as my target audience. I would like my work to reach, and benefit, the largest audience possible. Nevertheless, much of my education and professionalization as a sociologist has directed me away from this goal. In the current climate of edu-business (education as, and for, business), which is encouraged by corporate positivism, I have learned how to make myself "valuable" by following a pseudo-scientific praxis and producing knowledge that is difficult to access.

The proclaimed goal of positivistic, incremental knowledge production is the dissemination of new information that spurs discussion and debate and leads to further investigation. The practice of pop-sociology as I have described it meets this requirement. Sociological texts and research should be framed as purposeful and pertinent within the discipline *and* outside of the discipline. Pop-sociology is perhaps best viewed as a linguistic and epistemological form of affirmative action.

Conclusion

The influence of corporate positivism over and within the profession of sociology has been addressed here with emphasis on the education and professionalization of sociologists. The qualitative nature of sociology and the detrimental effect of inappropriate approaches to sociological knowledge production have been discussed regarding how they might contribute to these education and professionalization processes. The negative effects of jargon and obscurantism have been considered along with the future of sociology as a career. All of these issues have been put forth with the ultimate goal of revealing something about the future of work for sociologists.

Is the education and professionalization of sociologists detrimental to sociology? The time for conceiving of sociology as a "hard,"' positivistic science has come and gone, but contemporary sociology students are being deprived of an appropriate education and the tools necessary for developing an accessible and useful sociological body of work. We are learning qualitative methodologies to varying extents at most universities, but we are not learning how to make our knowledge accessible. A substantial portion of the education, and the education dollar of the sociology student, is directed toward ingraining an obscure and inaccessible linguistic and conceptual tradition and a methodological approach that is not always effective.

Is sociology adhering to its original, admittedly idealistic goal of being a helping humanistic field? I do not know for sure, but I am afraid that the commitment to humanitarian goals is less solid than it once was. My discussion herein has been less than optimistic, but I do have hope and I have identified a shift in the field regarding the use and acceptance of qualitative methodologies. As long as sociology can avoid the pitfalls of a postmodernism where nothing is relevant, I believe it can revitalize Comte's goal of improving people's lives and society as a whole.

Sociological discourse has moved away from its original cultural/helping mission to a mission of defending itself as a profession due to the pressures of corporate positivism. This has occurred to the detriment of the pertinence and usefulness of sociology, which further assures the dominant position of the institutions supported by the power structure of corporate positivism. Weber (2002) discusses this in his analysis of bureaucracy and rationalization. He asserts that once a bureaucratic or rational system is established, it is very difficult to overcome because as its assumed power and authority are legitimized, the system becomes hegemonic and it gains an almost subconscious influence over us.

In closing, if nothing else, this chapter poses at least one interesting question. If it is fair to say that the ideology of corporate positivism has pressured sociology into an inappropriate praxis, and if it is fair to say that sociology has made a strong attempt at functioning within this praxis, then, one must wonder; who is sociology's biggest enemy? Corporate positivism? Natural science? It could certainly be argued that perhaps, sociology is its own worst enemy.

References

Agger, Ben. 1989. *Reading Science: A Literary, Political, and Sociological Analysis.* Dix Hills: General Hall Inc.

Baritz, Loren. 1960. *The Servants of Power: A History of the Use of Social Science in American Industry.* New York: John Wiley & Sons Inc.

Bleier, Ruth. 1979. *Social and Political Bias in Science: An Examination of Animal Studies and their Generalizations to Human Behaviors and Evolution.* Madison: Women's Studies Research Center, University of Wisconsin-Madison.

Coser, Lewis A. 1977. *Masters of Sociological Thought: Ideas in Historical Context.* New York: Harcourt Brace Jovanovich Inc.

Delaney, Kevin, Rick Eckstein, and Rebecca Schoenike. 1995. "The Voice of Sociology: Obstacles to Teaching and Learning the Sociological Imagination." *Teaching Sociology* 23(4):353-363.

Haskell, Thomas L. 1984. *The Authority of Experts: Studies in History and Theory.* Bloomington: Indiana University Press.

Hill, Terry. November 21, 2000. Personal communication.

Hochschild, Arlie R. 1983. *The Managed Heart: Commercialization of Human Feeling. Berkeley.* California: University of California Press.

Horowitz, David. 1971. "Imperialism and Revolution." Pp. 283-307 in *Radical Sociology: An Introduction*, edited by David Horowitz. San Francisco: Canfield Press.

Huff, Darrell. 1993. *How to Lie with Statistics.* New York: W.W. Norton.

Kuhn, Thomas, S. 1996. *The Structure of Scientific Revolutions.* Chicago: The University of Chicago Press.

Macdonald, Keith M. 1995. *The Sociology of the Professions.* London: SAGE Publications.

Mannheim, Karl. 1936. *Ideology & Utopia: An Introduction to the Sociology of Knowledge.* San Diego: Harcourt Inc.

Mills, C. Wright. 1959. *The Sociological Imagination.* New York: Oxford University Press.

_____. 1951. *White Collar: The American Middle Classes.* New York: Oxford University Press.

Nelsen, Randle W. 2002. *Schooling as Entertainment: Corporate Education Meets Popular Culture.* Kingston: Cedarcreek Publications.

_____. 1999. Personal communication. October 25.

_____. 1997. *Inside Canadian Universities: Another Day at the Plant.* Kingston: Cedarcreek Publications.

Nettler, Gwynn. 1970. *Explanations.* New York: McGraw-Hill Book Company.

Paulos, John Allen. 2001. *Innumeracy.* New York: Hill & Wang.

Ponting, J. Rick. 1995. "Sociology: A Discipline in Jeopardy?" *Society* May:9-11.

Readings, Bill. 1996. *The University in Ruins.* Cambridge: Harvard University Press.

Ritzer, George. September 1998. "Writing to be Read: Changing the Culture and Reward Structure of American Sociology." *Contemporary Sociology* 27(5):446-453.

Schwartz, Pepper. 1998. "Stage Fright or Death Wish: Sociology and the Mass Media." *Contemporary Sociology* 27(5):439-445.

Seidman, Steven. Fall 1991. "The End of Sociological Theory: The Postmodern Hope." *Sociological Theory* 9(2):131-146.

Stehr, Nico. March 1982. "Sociological Languages." *Philosophy of the Social Sciences* 12(1):47-57.

Sykes, Charles, J. 1988. *Profscam: Professors and the Demise of Higher Education.* Washington D.C.: Regnery Gateway.

Vidich, Arthur J., Stanford M. Lyman, and Jeffrey C. Goldfarb. 1981. "Sociology and Society: Disciplinary Tensions and Professional Compromises." *Social Research* 48(2):322-361.

Watts, Sheldon J. 2003. *Disease and Medicine in World History.* New York: Routledge.

Weber, Max. 2002. *The Protestant Ethic and the Spirit of Capitalism.* Translated by Stephen Kalberg. Los Angeles: Roxbury Publishing Co.

Wharton, Amy S. 1996. "Service with a Smile: Understanding the Consequences of Emotional Labor." Pp. 91-114 in *Working in the Service Society*, edited by Cameron Lynne Macdonald and Carmen Sirianni. Philadelphia: Temple University Press.

Wilson, William Julius. 1998. "Engaging Publics in Social Dialogue through the Media." *Contemporary Sociology* 27(5):435-438.

INDEX

A
Power and Privilege 123, 124, 128
Abbott, A 58, 64, 71
Abele, F 221, 250
ACCESS! Report 235
Accountability 6
Accreditation 216, 217, 219, 220, 234, 237, 246, 247, 255
Affiliations 75, 77, 86, 90, 92, 94
Agger, B 281, 282, 284, 285, 286, 287, 291, 294
Agocs, C 122, 128
Alboim, N 229, 230, 246, 247, 250
American Medical Association (AMA) 286
Anderson, B 22, 49
Appleyard, R 249, 250
Arat-Koç, S 12, 17, 23, 41, 42, 46, 50, 51, 243, 250, 253
Armstrong, P 12, 14, 17, 19, 35, 36, 49, 111, 113
Arrow, K 233, 250
Ashley, J 101, 111, 113
Aylward, C 121, 128

B
Baccalaureate Model 106, 110
Backhouse, C 244, 245, 250
Baer, D 223, 250
Baker, M 228, 229, 250
Balakrishnan, T 220, 225, 253
Baldwin, J 92, 94
Bannerji, H 125, 128, 250
Barahona, F 193, 211
Barber, B 60, 61, 71
Baritz, L 280, 281, 295
Barley, S 94
Barndt, D 24, 49
Barriers 215, 216, 217, 219, 220, 227, 228, 232-237, 243, 247, 251, 253, 255
Basavarajappa, K 228, 251
Basran, G 227, 228, 237, 251
Baumgart, A 106, 113
Baxandall, R 28, 29, 37, 49
Beach, C 228, 231, 251
Becker, H 74-79, 82, 89, 94, 97
Bejian, D 74, 94
Bell, D 222, 251
Bell, J 196, 212
Benner, P 110, 113
Bingham, S 101, 106, 111, 113
Blachford, G 89, 94
Blaming the Victim 273, 275
Blankenship, R 79, 81, 94
Blau, P 69, 71, 79, 80, 81, 94, 270, 274
Blauner, R 91, 94
Bleier, R 283, 295
Blumer, H 76-78, 94
Boas, F 6
Bosanac, S 187
Bottoms, A 92, 94
Boyd, M 228, 229, 231, 251
Braithwaite, J 120, 128
Brandt Report 217, 251
Braverman, H 12, 16, 17, 21, 25, 26, 28, 29, 49, 63, 71
British Columbia Ministry of Advanced Education 212
Brouwer, A 220, 251
Brown, R 118, 119, 128
Bruner, J 74, 77, 94
Bullough, B 110, 113
Buon, T 201-204, 212
Bureaucracy 259, 260, 268-274
Burrage, M 60, 61, 69, 70, 71

C
Cairns, B 107, 113
Calliste, A 118, 119, 122, 128, 129, 243, 251
Canadian Air Transport Security Authority 212
Canadian Association of Schools of Nursing 187
Canadian Council on Social Development 118, 120, 125, 127, 129
Canadian Experience 228, 232, 233, 234, 237
Canadian Health Services Research Foundation 186
Canadian Immigration Act of 1869 221
Canadian immigration policy 217, 226, 241, 255
Canadian Information Centre for International Credentials 208, 209, 212
Canadian Labour Market 228, 230, 246, 253
Canadian Nurses Association (CNA) 105, 113, 177, 181, 182, 183, 186, 187
Canadian Race Relations Foundation 237, 251
Cantor, N 110, 113
Career 73-97
Carr-Saunders, A 55, 71
Castles, S 223, 251
Chitty, K 106, 113
Citizenship and Immigration Canada 210, 212
Clark, T 248, 251
Class Exploitation 247
Clement, W 80, 94, 222, 250, 251, 255
Cockburn, C 12, 23, 33, 34, 35, 49
College of Nurses of Ontario 113
Collin, A 94
Collins, E 119, 123, 129, 130,

132, 182, 183, 186, 187
Collins, H 12, 17, 23, 24, 33, 41, 45, 46, 47, 50
Committee on Citizenship and Immigration 219, 251
Commonwealth Centre for e-Governance 194, 212
Corporate Positivism 281, 282, 283, 285, 286, 288, 289, 290, 292, 293, 294
Corwin, R 103, 104, 113
Coser, L 279, 295
Cottle, M 197, 212
Credential Barriers 215, 216
Credentialism 189, 190, 191-216
Credentialism and Canada's Youth 193
Credentialism in Public Health Care 207
Credentialism Vs. Social Justice 191
Credentials 104, 106, 107, 108
Credibility 277, 286
Criminal Justice Professions 155-171
Crooks, J 131
CTV 186
Cult of Domesticity 169
Culture of Professions 73, 74, 76, 78, 80, 82, 84, 86, 88, 90, 92, 94, 96
Cumming, L 252
Cutbrush, G 190, 212

D
Dafoe, J 221, 252
Dalton, C 104, 113
Dalton, M 81, 95
Darroch, G 225, 252
Das Gupta, T 12, 20, 24, 27, 28, 41, 43, 44, 49, 122, 123, 129, 179, 182, 183, 186, 187
Davidoff, H 190, 212
Davis, A 263, 274
Davis, J 81, 95
Delaney, K 287, 295

Delgado, R 121, 129
Dennis, K 111, 113
Dingwall, R 67, 71
Disconnecting and Reconnecting 89
Discrimination 177, 179, 183-187, 220, 224, 225, 226, 227, 229, 230, 231, 233, 235, 237, 238, 239, 240, 243, 244, 245, 246, 249
Ditton, J 79, 82, 95
Diversity 54, 72, 182, 183, 185, 186
Domestic Work 16-19, 36-38, 41
Du Bois, W 248, 252
Dua, E 217, 252
Dubin on Health Care 114
Dubin, J 75, 95
Duclos, N 122, 129
Duffy, A 48, 49, 51, 68, 72
Dunk, T 263, 274, 275
Durkheim, E 21, 24, 29, 31, 32, 49, 54, 55, 61, 70, 71, 80, 95, 228, 252

E
Eastman 200, 212
Edgerton, R 272, 274
Education 216, 219, 222-225, 228-235, 237, 241-243, 249-253, 257, 260, 261, 263-265, 269-274, 277, 278, 281, 282, 284, 285, 287, 292-296
Education of Sociologists 277, 282, 284, 287
Education Quality Improvement Act 200, 201, 213
Edwards, R 12, 21, 26, 27, 29, 49
Eichler, M 101, 114
Entrepreneurship 230
Equity 2, 7, 177-187
Esland, G 61, 71
Esping-Anderson, G 222, 252
Essed, P 118, 127, 129
ethnicity 178

Ethnoracial Safety 117, 119, 120, 123, 126-128
Ethnoracial Safety as a Justice Concept of Balance 126
Etzioni, A 56, 71, 81, 95

F
Feagin, J 225, 252
Feminist Approach 67, 68 to Professionalization of Work 33
Feminization of Employment 38, 39
Fleischer, H 80, 95
Fleras, A 227, 234, 252
Florence Nightingale Pledge 102, 114
Flynn, K 122, 129
Foreign Credentials 209, 210, 212, 215, 217-220, 222, 224, 226, 228, 230-232, 234, 236-238, 240, 242, 244, 246, 248, 250-252, 254, 255, 256
Foreign Trained Professionals 216
Foster, L 215-257
Foucault, M 64-66, 71
Fox, A 80, 95
Fox, B 25, 49
Frankenberg, R 12, 41, 44, 45, 48, 50, 124, 129
Franz Boas and the Long Arm of the German University System 144
Freidson, E 3, 4, 62, 64, 67, 71, 100, 103, 112, 114
Freire, P 269, 274
Fudge, J 243, 252

G
Galabuzi 179, 186
Galabuzi, G 217, 252
Gender 2-51
Gender Roles 155-161, 166
Gender-Role Conflict 168
Gentlemen-Specialists 138, 148

German University System 135, 137, 139, 144, 145
Gerth, H 76, 95
Getting Connected 75, 83, 86, 87, 88
Giddens, A 30, 50, 79, 95
Giles, W 12, 23, 41, 42, 46, 50, 51
Glaser, B 78, 83, 95
Glass Ceiling 167, 168, 173, 175
Glass Wall 168
Globalization 215, 248, 249, 253
Goffman, E 77, 79, 95
Goldthorpe, J 59, 71
Goode, W 56, 57, 61, 70, 71
Government of Canada 106, 114, 203, 210, 213
Government of Ontario 200, 208, 213
Graham, S 71
Grandea, N 243, 252
Gray, D 95
Grow, S 101, 103, 114

H
Hage, J 222, 252
Hagey, R 117, 118, 119, 120, 121, 123, 124, 125, 126, 127, 128, 129, 130, 131, 132, 182, 183, 186, 187
Hall, H 6, 74, 88, 94, 95, 96
  Gentleman-Specialist of the Pre-Professional Era 137
Hamilton, P 80, 95
Harper Hospital 102, 114
Harvey, E 246, 252, 253
Haskell, T 285, 286, 295
Haug, M 62, 63, 71
Hedley, A 248, 253
Henry, F 124, 125, 130, 217, 253
Herberg, E 225, 229, 253
Heyl, B 84, 95
Hickson, D 56, 71
Hill, D 123, 130

Hill, T 286, 295
Hochschild A 15, 16, 22, 36, 37, 47, 50, 291, 295
Hohfeld, W 130
Holland, J 77, 95
Holnzer, B 95
Honderich, T 26, 50
Horowitz, D 288, 289, 295
Hospitals 178, 180-183, 185, 186
Hou, F 220, 225, 231, 253
Howlett 178, 186
Huff, D 284, 295
Hughes, E 58, 71, 74, 76, 78, 82, 83, 92, 94, 95, 101, 103, 112, 114, 180, 187
Human Capital Theory 224
Hunter, A 223, 253

I
Immigration and Refugee Protection Act 240
Infantalization 25, 44
Intersections of Race, Gender, and Work 12
Isajiw, W 225, 253, 254

J
Jackson, J 60, 71
Jacobs, M 24, 50, 51, 99, 101, 103, 104, 105, 107, 109, 111, 113, 114, 115, 123, 130, 179, 180, 182, 183, 187
Johnson, D 108, 114
Johnson, T 55, 56, 62, 63, 71
Jones, A 63, 72

K
Kalbach, W 231, 253
Kelefian, S 114
Kendall, D 191, 213
Keon, T 77, 95
Keung, N 234, 253
King, I 106, 108, 114
Kinney, C 103, 114
Knowledge Economy 223, 224, 242, 255

Krahn, H 26, 50, 228, 243, 247, 253
Kramer, M 114
Krause E 76, 78, 95
Kuhn, T 280, 286, 295

L
Labour Movement 189, 192, 198, 199
Lack of Accommodation 25, 44
Lankard, B 95
Larsen, J 106, 113
Larson, M 64, 72
Law Commission of Canada 118, 126, 130
Learning 259, 260, 264, 265, 267, 268, 269, 271, 273, 275
Leitch, S 66, 72
Lemert, E 76-78, 95
Lewis, P 71
Li, P 226, 251, 253
Licensing 109
Lipset, S 248, 251
Livingstone, D 213
Lore, N 74, 96
Lowe, G 13, 26, 50, 123, 130
Luxton, M 17, 50
Lyman, M 84, 96
Lynn, K 55, 72

M
Macdonald, K 54, 55, 62, 64, 72, 286, 295, 296
MacKay, R 117, 119, 121, 123-131
MacKenzie, I 120, 122, 131
Macklin, A 41, 42, 50, 243, 253
Mactavish, R 119, 131
Man, G 18, 19, 21, 26, 34, 47, 51
Mandell, N 68, 72
Mannheim, K 14, 50, 281, 284, 295
Marginalization 16, 21, 25, 39-43, 48, 217, 223, 249, 252

Marshall, K 118, 123, 131
Marshall, T 56, 72
Marx, K 12, 13, 21, 24, 26, 27, 30-33, 46, 50, 51, 61-64, 66, 72
Marxist approach 53, 59, 61, 63
Mass, M 103, 110, 114
Mata, F 254
Matza, D 77, 78, 85, 96
Maxim, P 230, 254
Mayer, B 126, 131
Mayer, J 272, 274, 275
Mayo, E 54, 55, 72
McDade, K 228, 231, 253
McDermott P 15, 40, 50
McFarlane, B 80, 96
McPherson, K 129, 131
McTair, R 131
Mead, G 57, 72
Meeks, D 127, 131
Meisenhelder, T 89, 96
Merchant, C 68, 72
Meritocracy 224, 231, 234, 250
Merton, R 58, 72
Milkman, R 17, 50
Mills, C 13, 47, 50, 59, 60, 61, 72, 76, 80, 95, 96, 279, 286, 295
Mischel, W 110, 113
Morehead, A 190, 213
Muff, J 111, 115
Multiculturalism 220, 226, 250, 251, 252
Mundinger, M 111, 115

N

Nabigon, H 126, 131
Nader, L 128, 131
Nakano Glenn, E 15, 20, 23, 38, 50
Nash, M 247, 254
National Commission on Terrorist Attacks Upon the United States 206, 213
National Right to Work Legal Defense Foundation Inc 198, 199, 213
Neal, R 42, 51
Nelsen, R 259, 261, 263-265, 267, 269-275, 281, 282, 287, 295
Neo-Colonialism 248
Neo-Weberian Approach 59
Nestle, S 131
Nettler, G 283, 284, 295
Neugebauer, R 24, 51
Neuman, P 114
Noble, D 270, 274
Nursing 99-132, 177-187

O

O'Day, R 126, 131
O'Reilly, D 121, 131
Occupational Sociology 82, 87
Occupations 1-5
Ontario Human Rights Code 119, 131
Ontario Human Rights Commission 119, 128, 131, 132, 187
Ontario Ministry of Health and Long Term Care 187, 208, 213
Ontario Ministry of Training, Colleges and Universities. 213
Ontario Nurses Association 129, 131
Open Society 228, 231
Oplatka, I 74, 96
Oppenheimer, T 264, 275
Orem, D 108, 114
Canadian Anthropology 134, 137, 151, 152
Ornstein, M 118, 131, 217, 220, 228, 243, 254

P

Parr, J 19, 51
Parsons, T 55-57, 61, 70, 72
Paulos, J 284, 295
Pavalko, R 72
Peerla, D 271, 275
Pendakur, K 232, 254
Pilette, P 111, 115
Pink Collar Professions 99
Pink Collar Work 101
PLAN 235-247, 250
Plummer, K 90, 91, 94, 96
Polyani, K 72
Ponting, J 284, 295
Pop-Sociology 278, 288, 293
Porter, J 80, 96, 224-254
Portes, A 230, 254
Post-Modernism 65, 70
Post-Structuralism 65
Prescott, P 111, 113
Presthus, R 80, 96
Preston, V 21, 51
Prior Learning Assessment Network (PLAN) 235
Professional Barriers in the CJS 164
Professional Practice 99, 100, 110, 111
Professional Training 260
Professionalism 259, 264, 267, 269, 271
Professionalization 1, 2, 3, 4, 5, 6, 7, 8, 9, 10, 133, 134, 136, 137, 138, 140, 142, 144, 146, 148, 150, 151, 152, 259, 260, 270, 274, 277, 278, 279, 280, 281, 282, 285, 286, 292, 293, 294
Professionalization of Anthropology 134, 136
Professionalization of Nursing 99, 104
Professionalization of Sociology 277, 278
Professions 1, 2, 3, 4, 5, 6, 7, 8, 9, 10, 53, 54, 55, 56, 57, 58, 59, 60, 61, 62, 63, 64, 65, 66, 67, 68, 69, 70, 71, 72
Prus, R 75, 84, 87, 96
PSW 181, 184
Pupo, N 12, 16, 17, 18, 22, 23, 36, 37, 38, 47, 49, 51

R

Race 2, 3, 4, 5, 7, 9, 10, 11, 12, 13, 14, 15, 16, 18, 19, 20, 21, 22, 23, 24, 25, 26, 27, 28, 29, 30, 31, 32, 34, 36, 38, 39, 40, 41, 42, 43, 44, 45, 46, 47, 48, 50, 51, 215, 217, 218, 220, 221, 224, 227, 228, 229, 231, 237, 238, 241, 244, 245, 247, 249, 251, 252, 255, 257
Racial Segmentation 125
Racialization 126
Racialization of Poverty 217, 232
Racialized Immigration 215, 226, 243
Racism 117, 119, 121-123, 125, 127-132, 180, 182-187, 217, 218, 220, 232, 233, 237, 241, 242, 245, 246, 250-256
Rajagopal, I 228, 231, 254
Ralston, H 228, 231, 254
Ramsden, I 126, 131
Readings, B 281, 282, 295
Reiter, E 12, 18, 39, 40, 51
Reitz, J 216, 217, 221, 223, 224, 226, 228, 232-234, 236, 254, 255
Reproductive Labour 15-22, 24, 36, 37, 40, 41, 43, 47, 48
Restitution 6
Restorative Justice 118, 120, 128, 130
Richmond, A 228, 245, 249, 255
Rinehart, J 12, 25, 26, 29, 32, 33, 51, 81, 88, 91, 96
Ritzer, G 83, 96, 222, 255, 281, 282, 290, 295
RN 180, 182
RNAO 105, 106, 109, 110, 111, 115
Rock, P 74, 77, 96
Romero, M 42, 51
Rosenfeld, R 80, 96
Ross, A 103, 115
Rossides, D 56, 60, 64, 68, 69, 70, 72
Roth, J 66, 67, 72
Ryan, W 273, 275

S

Saidulla, A 255
Saks, M 79, 96
Salaman, G 77, 78, 80, 82, 83, 95, 96, 97
Salomone, p 74, 94
Samuels, J 232, 237, 254, 255
Satzewich, V 218, 222, 230, 243, 250, 251, 255, 256
Schmidt, J 271, 275
Schooling as Attitude Change 269
Schwartz, P 281, 290, 292, 293, 296
Scott, M 79, 81, 84, 94, 96
Second Annual Law and Diversity Conference 232, 233, 236, 255
Seidman, S 283, 296
Self Identity 76
Semi-Professionalism 102
Sexual Harassment 157, 161-164, 171, 173, 175
Sexuality in Prisons 161
Shamai, S 229, 230, 255
Shareif, S 255
Sheehy, G 91, 96
Shields, J 217, 255
Silvera, M 243, 256
Silverman, D 74, 77-79, 81, 83, 96
Simmie, S 244, 256
Simmons, A 220, 229, 241-243, 256
Skilled Worker 241, 243
Skills Development Canada 196, 197, 213
Slocum, W 74, 80, 81, 96
Smith, A 220, 247, 256
Smith, D 101, 115
Smith, F 269, 275
Social Justice 182, 183, 185, 187, 189, 191
Social Justice in Nursing 120
Social Structure 75, 79, 90, 93, 95
Socioeconomic-Class Conflicts 247
Sociology 277-296
Sociology of Professions and Occupations 15
Sonnenfeld, J 75, 77, 96
Southern Association of Colleges and Schools 205, 213
Specialized Knowledge 100, 103, 105, 107-110
Spirit of Capitalism 59, 72
Squires, T 100, 115
Stallard, K 101, 115
Stasiulis, D 221, 243, 250, 252, 256
Statistics Canada 190, 194-196, 213, 214, 219, 223, 227-240, 256
Staying Connected 75, 87, 88
Stehr, N 288, 296
Stereotypes 156-159, 161, 163-167, 169, 171-173
Stinchcombe, A 81, 96
Strauss, A 76, 78, 82, 89, 90, 94-97
Structural Barriers 227, 234, 236, 237
Structural Functionalism 54, 61
Stryker, R 121, 132
Suryamani, E 103, 115
Swift, J 271, 275
Sykes, C 280, 287, 296
Symbolic interactionism 53, 57, 58

T

Targeting 24, 44
Tarnopolsky, W 120, 125, 132
Taylor, A 27, 51
Taylor, L 81, 97
Technology 178, 179, 182, 259, 264, 271, 275
Technology-Based Instruction

264
Tepperman, L 225, 256
Tokenism 25, 44, 167
Torstendahl, R 61, 69-71
Training 259-263, 267, 269-272, 274, 275
Transformative Justice 117, 118, 120-122, 124-128, 130, 132
Transnational 230, 254
Transparency 6
Travelbee, J 105, 115
Treasury Board of Canada Secretariat 203, 214
Trempe, R 256
Trovato, F 228, 231, 232, 255, 257
Turner, J 198, 199, 214
Turrittin, J 117, 119, 121, 123, 125, 127, 129, 130-132

U

United Nations Development Programme 204, 214
Unpaid-Work 101
Urbanski 207, 214

V

van Dijk, T 118, 124, 126, 132
Van Rijn, N 257
Vidich, A 280, 296
Viens, D 111, 115
Vosko 12, 18, 21, 27, 35, 38, 39, 41, 48, 51

W

Walker, J 123, 132
Walton, O 81, 97
Watson, T 54, 55-59, 65, 66, 72
Watts, S 296
Weber, M 12, 18, 21, 24, 29-31, 39, 50, 51, 59-61, 66, 67, 72, 77, 80, 97, 270, 275, 294, 296
West, W 88, 97
Westwood, S 12, 23, 41, 42, 43, 51
Wharton, A 291, 296
White House 207, 214
Whyte, W 81, 97
Williams, C 100, 115
Williams, R 34, 51
Willis, P 79, 84, 89, 97
Wilson, P 71
Wilson, W 281, 288, 289, 290, 292, 296
Witz, A 67, 68, 72
Woollacott, J 74, 97
Work 1-51, 177-187
World Bank Group 214
World Education Services 219, 257
Wuest, J 110, 112, 115

Y

Yancy, G 20, 51
Young, D 119, 120, 122, 132

Z

Zeytinoglu, I 243, 257
Zunker, V 97